KEY CONCEPTS IN SOCIOLOGY

Palgrave Key Concepts

Palgrave Key Concepts provide an accessible and comprehensive range of subject glossaries at undergraduate level. They are the ideal companion to a standard textbook, making them invaluable reading to students throughout their course of study and especially useful as a revision aid.

Key Concepts in Accounting and Finance
Key Concepts in Business Practice
Key Concepts in Cultural Studies
Key Concepts in Drama and Performance
Key Concepts in e-Commerce
Key Concepts in Human Resource Management
Key Concepts in Information and Communication Technology
Key Concepts in International Business
Key Concepts in Language and Linguistics (second edition)
Key Concepts in Law
Key Concepts in Management
Key Concepts in Marketing
Key Concepts in Operations Management
Key Concepts in Politics
Key Concepts in Psychology
Key Concepts in Strategic Management
Key Concepts in Tourism

Palgrave Key Concepts: Literature
General Editors: John Peck and Martin Coyle
Key Concepts in Contemporary Literature
Key Concepts in Medieval Literature
Key Concepts in Postcolonial Literature
Key Concepts in Renaissance Literature
Key Concepts in Victorian Literature
Literary Terms and Criticism (third edition)

Further titles are in preparation

www.palgravekeyconcepts.com

Palgrave Key Concepts
Series Standing Order
ISBN 1-4039-3210-7
(outside North America only)

You can receive future titles in this series as they are published by placing a standing order. Please consult your bookseller or, in the case of difficulty, write to us at the address below with your name and address and the title of the series and the ISBN quoted above.

Customer Services Department, Macmillan Distribution Ltd
Houndmills, Basingstoke, Hampshire RG21 6XS, England

Key Concepts in Sociology

Ken Roberts

First published 2009 by
PALGRAVE MACMILLAN
Houndmills, Basingstoke, Hampshire RG21 6XS and
175 Fifth Avenue, New York, N.Y. 10010
Companies and representatives throughout the world

PALGRAVE MACMILLAN is the global academic imprint of the
Palgrave Macmillan division of St. Martin's Press, LLC and of Palgrave
Macmillan Ltd.
Macmillan® is a registered trademark in the United States, United
Kingdom and other countries. Palgrave is a registered trademark in the
European Union and other countries.

ISBN-13: 978–0–230–21140–7
ISBN-10: 0–230–21140–2

This book is printed on paper suitable for recycling and made from
fully managed and sustained forest sources. Logging, pulping and
manufacturing processes are expected to conform to the
environmental regulations of the country of origin.

A catalogue record for this book is available from the British Library.

A catalog record for this book is available from the Library of Congress.

10   9   8   7   6   5   4   3   2   1
18   17   16   15   14   13   12   11   10   09

Printed and bound in China

Contents

Preface

My aim in this book has been to list all the words and names that students of sociology are very likely to encounter: names or words that are either never or rarely used outside sociology, or have particular meanings within the subject. A standard complaint of new students is that sociology is full of jargon. This book is the answer to this complaint; the jargon is explained in everyday language. The words and names are all likely to crop up in core sociology syllabuses. The book has not attempted to include all the specialist terms that are used in specialist sociological fields – the sociology of health, law, education and so on.

Entries are concise. They stick to key points about the meanings and uses of concepts and do not extend to detailed histories of their uses. Likewise the entries for names give the ideas for which the names are best known rather than comprehensive summaries of all their works.

Nearly all the entries are accompanied by key references to books or articles. With names I have usually listed works by the names themselves rather than commentaries. With concepts, I have opted for the books or articles in which the terms were first given their enduring meanings rather than recent publications that use the terms.

Most entries are cross-referenced to cognate names and concepts so that students, if they wish, can explore the wider terminology and key contributors on a particular topic.

In writing this book I have become aware that some topics in sociology have developed far more specialist terms than other, no less important, areas. There is an enormous specialist terminology associated with politics and government – different kinds of states, political systems, parties, ideologies and so on. Gender, a topic of greater interest to most current sociology students, has a much narrower specialist vocabulary, which may help to explain its popularity. Research methods are always part of the core curriculum in sociology, and quantitative methods contain far more specialist terms than qualitative research. However, no one is expected to read the book from cover to cover.

For students who want a quick introduction to the really key concepts and names in sociology, 20 names and 50 concepts are listed in a revision section towards the end of the book.

The book is designed as a student companion. It is not a textbook. It is a reference book in which words and names can be looked up as they are encountered. Please let me know if any word or name that you search for is not included.

Ken Roberts
University of Liverpool
k.Roberts@liverpool.ac.uk

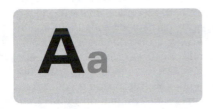

A priori/a posteriori

We say that something is known *a priori* if empirical (observation-based) evidence is unnecessary: something may be true by definition, or inferred logically from other known facts. We say that something is known to be true *a posteriori* if its validity is proven by observed evidence.

See also **Axiom; Kant, I.; Paradigm; Problematic.**

Accommodation

The process whereby culturally distinct groups adjust to each other's presence and may then co-exist indefinitely without either group losing its defining characteristics. Alternatively, accommodation may be a stage in acculturation which leads eventually to full assimilation of one group by the other.

See also **Acculturation; Assimilation; Migration.**

Acculturation

One of several terms which describe processes that are triggered by migration and other events that bring two cultures into contact. Acculturation is the process whereby one group acquires the culture of the other. During this process the group that is being acculturated loses its original identity. The end product of acculturation may be full assimilation. Note, however, that acculturation may be reciprocal, and the outcome may be a hybrid culture.

See also **Accommodation; Assimilation; Migration.**

Achievement/Achieved status, Ascription/ascribed status

Achievement and ascription are alternative ways in which individuals can be allocated to social roles. A position is ascribed when a person is allocated by criteria over which he or she has no control: for example, age, sex, race or family origins. Individuals can then be educated and otherwise socialised to fulfil their destinies. Achieved positions are entered on the basis of performance, in education, or in tests of occupational skills and knowledge, for example.

In practice there are usually elements of both ascription and achievement in operation. For example, jobs may require particular educational qualifications (which are achieved) but the likelihood of individuals gaining the qualifications may be related to their family origins (ascribed). Nevertheless, sociologists have always argued that, as societies modernise, ascription gives way to achievement. Hence the trends towards opening educational opportunities to all, outlawing labour market discrimination by race and sex, and nowadays combating ageism also.

See also **Social mobility; Sponsored (and contest) mobility.**

Action research

This is research where the investigator is involved in introducing changes in order to study the effects. The procedure is comparable to a scientific experiment except that in real social life it is very difficult to hold everything else constant, and there is always the danger of an observer effect, called a 'Hawthorne effect' in sociology.

See also **Experiment; Hawthorne effect.**

Action theory

The name for any approach in sociology that places the actor at the centre. The actor may be an individual or a collective actor (such as Protestants or the working class).

An action frame of reference (an alternative term for action theory) seeks explanations in terms of actors' goals and their knowledge and interpretations of their situations. Max Weber (1864–1920) is commonly regarded as sociology's founding advocate of this approach. His work was thus clearly distinguished from that of his contemporary, Emile Durkheim (1858–1917), who instructed sociologists to treat social facts as things and to seek explanations in terms of their relationships to other social facts. Symbolic interactionism is the leading example of an action theory.

Adopting an action frame of reference in sociology leaves open the question as to whether action creates social structure, or whether social structure is the source (via socialisation) of actors' frames of reference.

See also **Agency; Symbolic interactionism; Weber, M.**

A

Active citizen

An active citizen joins organisations as a member and to volunteer. Active citizens are the lifeblood of civil society.

One school of thought claims that active citizenship has declined. There has certainly been a steep decline in the memberships of the main political parties, trade unions and churches in many western countries. The debate is whether people are now active in different, newer organisations (concerned with the environment, for example), and whether they are participating in new ways (such as by email and in online communities).

> *See also* **Capital (social); Civil society; Communitarianism; Mobilisation; Social movements.**

> Etzioni, A. (1968), *The Active Society: A Theory of Social and Political Processes*, Free Press, New York.

Actor

The use of this term likens social life to a theatre where actors perform roles that are already scripted. This 'dramaturgical analogy' was prominent in the work of Erving Goffman (1922–1982). The analogy allows for actors to interpret and develop their roles in interaction with other players.

> *See also* **Agency; Goffman, E.; Role.**

Adolescence

A term coined by the American genetic psychologist, G. Stanley Hall (1844–1924), and applied to the life stage following puberty. Hall characterised the life stage as a period of personal crisis, emotional turbulence and rebelliousness. Subsequently the term has remained associated with the view that the psychological and social changes that occur during the teenage years have roots in biological changes.

Present-day sociologists are more likely to describe the life stage as 'youth' and to stress its social construction.

> *See also* **Mead, M.; Youth.**

> Hall, G.S. (1904), *Adolescence*, Appleton, New York.

Adorno, Theodor Weisengrund (1903–1969)

A member of the Frankfurt School who became best known as a co-author of *The Authoritarian Personality,* a survey-based research project which claimed to have discovered the psychological roots of support for authoritarian regimes (specifically fascist regimes).

However, most of Adorno's work was in aesthetics and musical theory. He believed that artistic forms, including musical forms, were products of class interests and struggle, and he was the Frankfurt School member who was responsible for stressing how the popular music produced by the capitalist culture industry stupefied the masses.

> *See also* **Authoritarian personality; Critical sociology/critical theory; Frankfurt School.**

> Adorno, T., Frenkel-Brunswick, E., Levinson, D. and Sanford, R. (1950, 1991), *The Authoritarian Personality,* Norton, New York.

A

Aesthetic labour

A term applied to jobs where the worker's appearance and personality are part of the service offered to customers. An alternative term is 'emotional labour'. Most such jobs are in consumer services – hotels, restaurants, private sector gyms, for example – where the staff are expected to use interpersonal skills to make consumers feel good, spend more and come again.

The term may also be applied to certain kinds of 'work' within the family.

See also **Domestic labour.**

Affect, affective

Affect is an alternative word for emotion. Affective behaviour is driven by emotion or is seeking emotional gratification.

Modern societies are believed to be different from earlier societies partly in the numerous areas of life that are affect-free and impersonal, with affectivity reserved for private life, especially life within families. Affectivity versus affective neutrality was one of the pattern variables identified by Talcott Parsons (1902–1979) to characterise and compare different cultures.

See also **Parsons, T.; Pattern variables.**

Affirmative action

See Positive discrimination.

Affluent society

A term that began to be applied to western societies from the 1950s onwards, when sustained economic growth was driving up living standards.

However, the term remains closely associated with the critique by John K. Galbraith (1908–2006), the distinguished American economist, who first drew attention (in the United States) to the contrast between private affluence and public squalor, and to a minority that was being left behind, excluded from all the benefits of economic growth. Many believe that his critique is as valid today as in the 1950s, and applies in more countries than ever.

Galbraith, J.K. (1958), *The Affluent Society*, Hamish Hamilton, London.

A

Affluent workers

This description was applied to manual workers in the 1950s (and subsequently) who were achieving year-on-year pay increases and enjoying progressively rising living standards.

There was a major debate in sociology in the 1950s and 1960s about the likely outcomes of this affluence. Supporters of an embourgeoisement thesis claimed that affluence would promote workers into the middle class, and that they would jettison their former working class identities, outlooks and political proclivities. The major intervention in the UK was a study of affluent workers in Luton which rejected the embourgeoisement thesis but claimed to have identified a new, privatised, instrumentally oriented section of the working class.

See also **Embourgeoisement.**

Goldthorpe, J.H., Lockwood, D., Bechhofer, F. and Platt, J. (1969), *The Affluent Worker in the Class Structure,* Cambridge University Press, Cambridge.

Ageism

A term coined by Robert Neil Butler (1927–), a US gerontologist; it refers to any stereotyping or discrimination on grounds of age. Ageism is slowly joining racism and sexism as an unacceptable form of discrimination. The victims of ageism may be old or young.

The 1967 Age Discrimination in Employment Act outlawed ageism in employment in the United States, but the Grey Panthers was formed in the early 1970s to campaign against and oppose all forms of discrimination against older persons. In Britain and the rest of the European Union age discrimination in employment, training and adult education was made illegal in 2006.

See also **Racism; Sexism.**

Butler, R.N. (1975, 2003), *Why Survive? Being Old in America,* Johns Hopkins University Press, Baltimore.

Agency

This is sociology's term for individuals' (alleged) ability to think, to reflect, to interpret, to exercise choice and to act accordingly.

A major division throughout sociology's history has been between those favouring explanations in terms of agency and those favouring explanations in terms of social structure. The division became so clear that in 1971 Alan Dawe wrote about 'the two sociologies'. Talcott Parsons (1902–1979) had previously attempted to reconcile these types of explanation. Subsequently Pierre Bourdieu (1930–2002) and Anthony Giddens (1938–) with his concept of structuration have made further attempts.

See also **Action theory; Bourdieu, P.; Giddens, A.; Parsons, T.; Structuration.**

Dawe, A. (1971), 'The two sociologies', in K. Thompson and J. Tunstall (eds), *Sociological Perspectives,* Penguin, Harmondsworth.

A

Alienation

The literal meaning is the removal of something from someone, but Marx gave the term a more specific meaning, namely, the separation of people from their true nature. The most natural, basic human activity, according to Marx, was to produce for one's own needs. Under capitalism workers were said to be alienated because they did not control their own labour power (they worked to employers' instructions), nor did they own the tools that they used or the things that they produced. Feelings of self-estrangement were said to arise from this condition.

In twentieth-century sociology the objective features of the Marxist concept were stripped away in empirical studies of alienation. The American social psychologist, Melvin Seeman (1918–), operationalised alienation as feelings of powerlessness, normlessness, meaninglessness, isolation and self-estrangement. Subsequently the sociologist Robert Blauner (1929–) used these definitions in his comparisons of alienation in different industries.

Anomie is an alternative (Durkheimian) concept that has been widely used in sociology in exploring maladies in the human condition.

See also **Anomie; Blauner, R.**

Blauner, R. (1964), *Alienation and Freedom*, University of Chicago Press, Chicago.
Seeman, M. (1959), 'On the meaning of alienation', *American Sociological Review*, 24, 783–91.

Althusser, Louis (1918–1990)

A French structural Marxist, and the intellectual leader in the French Communist Party in the 1960s and 1970s.

Althusser presented a Marxist alternative to the language-based structuralism that was becoming influential in France in the 1960s, but he was equally if not more engaged in re-asserting a non-Stalinist scientific (structural) Marxism in opposition to the humanistic versions of Marxism which were then becoming ascendant.

Althusser believed that there had been a clear epistemological break in Marx's thinking after 1845. He believed that the mature Marx was a structuralist, and following in these footsteps Althusser insisted that individuals were simply bearers of social relations. However, Althusser rejected economic reductionism, and he did not believe that major historical changes and outcomes were pre-determined. He argued that politics and ideology were conditions for the very existence of the (capitalist) economy, and that historical changes occurred through the interplay of economic, political and ideological forces.

Althusser is the inventor of some terms that have been assimilated into (Marxist) sociology: over-determination, and repressive and ideological state apparatuses.

See also **Ideological state apparatus; Ideology; Marx, K.; Over-determination.**

Althusser, L. (1971), *Lenin and Philosophy and Other Essays,* New Left Books, London.

A

Androcentrism

Male bias; neglect of female contributions and perspectives.

Feminist sociologists have drawn attention to the privileging of male perspectives and experiences in politics, business and everyday social life, and also within sociology where, it is claimed, women have been subjected to 'othering' – having themselves defined by more powerful others.

See also **Feminism; Smith, D.E.; Standpoint theory.**

Androgyny

A mixture of male and female characteristics; these may be physical, psychological or cultural. Androgyny is one (of many) alternatives to patriarchy that have been recommended by feminists.

Anomie

A term introduced into sociology by Emile Durkheim (1858–1917). Anomie literally means without norms, a situation of normlessness, where there are no rules. Durkheim believed that anomie could arise through the division of labour being pushed to an excessive extreme where individuals could not recognise their interdependence, and that it could also arise in times of rapid social change – economic booms as well as recessions.

Subsequent sociologists have added to the list of conditions that can produce anomie, most notably Robert Merton (1910–2003) who argued that in modern societies there is a disjuncture between goals that all people are encouraged to strive for and the legitimate means to achieve these goals (which cannot be used successfully by everyone). Merton argued that the inevitable outcome would be one of several kinds of deviance.

Anomie has competitor sociological concepts for diagnosing society's ills: alienation for example.

See also **Alienation; Durkheim, E.; Merton, R.K.; Strain theories.**

A

Anthropology

The study of humans: physical anthropology studies commonalities and variations in the biological characteristics of the species; social and cultural anthropology deals with the social and cultural dimensions. British practitioners describe their discipline as social anthropology, whereas cultural anthropology is the preferred label in North America.

Anthropology grew from the curiosity of explorers, traders and missionaries who, from the fifteenth century onwards, were making contact with non-Europeans. Their work became systematised in the discipline of anthropology in the nineteenth century, at exactly the same time that sociology was emerging. Sociologists studied their own societies. Social/

cultural anthropologists studied non-European, simpler, non-industrial societies.

By the early twentieth century armchair theorising based on reports from traders, colonial officials, missionaries and other travellers, and fieldwork based on interviews using interpreters, were being replaced by prolonged periods of observation during which investigators learnt their subjects' language and became participant observers within the societies that they were studying. Thus 'ethnography' became the characteristic research method of social and cultural anthropology.

At the time of social and cultural anthropology's emergence, a prevalent view was that the physical, psychological and social characteristics of different peoples were interdependent. Hence the development of social and cultural anthropology as branches of general anthropology. These alleged interdependences are now regarded as discredited. Furthermore, most of the simpler societies that anthropologists originally studied have become developing countries. Hence the distinction between sociology and social/cultural anthropology has collapsed except that anthropologists continue to work in the context of the bodies of knowledge and theory that anthropologists have built up, and claim special expertise in ethnography. Nowadays, however, social and cultural anthropologists are as likely to study modern as other societies.

See also **Ethnography; Participant observation.**

Apartheid

The regime of segregation by race which was implemented by South Africa's National Party from 1948 until 1994. Whites, Africans, coloureds and mixed races were separated into different kinds of employment, housing tracts, education, medical, recreation and other services. Apartheid was imposed by South Africa's whites, a minority of the population who held political and economic power. The regime made South Africa an international pariah, subject to economic and political sanctions and loss of sporting contacts. The main internal opposition to apartheid was from the African National Congress, led by Nelson Mandela (1918–), who spent 27 years in prison before being released. Mandela became South Africa's first post-apartheid elected president (1994–9).

A

Aristocracy

Originally a Greek concept, one of Aristotle's forms of government – by the best, in the interests of the entire community by the most virtuous citizens. The term was appropriated by the landed, titled, hereditary upper classes in pre-industrial Europe who shared (and sometimes contested) power with the monarchs.

See also **Estates; Feudalism.**

Ascription/Ascribed status

See Achievement/Achieved status.

Assimilation

This is the process whereby a typically migrant or conquered group is absorbed into a dominant culture. This may be the final stage in a sequence starting with contact, progressing through conflict and competition, and then accommodation, but full assimilation may or may not be the final outcome. The sequence may stall at any intermediate stage. This will depend on the character of the cultures concerned, and the context. Note also that a dominant culture is liable to change while assimilating an initially dissimilar population.

> *See also* **Accommodation; Acculturation; Migration.**

Asylum seekers

See Refugees.

Attitude

A psychological concept which is used extensively in sociology. An attitude is an enduring (but not necessarily totally rigid and unchangeable) tendency to perceive and/or act in a particular way towards particular persons and/or situations. Attitudes may contain cognitive (beliefs and ideas), affective (values and emotions) and behavioural (dispositions to act) dimensions.

An attitude is narrower than a personality trait. A personality may be generally sceptical. Irrespective of this, a person may be consistently sceptical towards, for example, the claims of a particular church, newspaper or political party.

Attitudes are normally measured using banks of questions which are called 'scales' because the findings enable individuals to be positioned somewhere along scales between extreme end points. The questions are usually statements with which individuals are invited to agree or disagree. Attitudes are said to be revealed if someone is consistently hostile or favourably disposed towards, for example, abortion, Europe or homosexuals.

Sociologists are interested in attitudes insofar as these personal dispositions are learnt and internalised, and characterise social groups, and therefore reflect the influence of societies and specific social milieux on the actors, and secondly insofar as attitudes explain why individuals and groups act in particular, characteristic ways in changing and possibly unpredictable and novel circumstances.

> *See also* **Personality.**

A

Authoritarian personality

A large-scale US research project following the Second World War claimed to identify a personality type that was pre-disposed to support authoritarian regimes (such as the German Nazis).

The authoritarian personality was said to be:

- extremely conformist
- submissive to authority
- rigid
- arrogant to inferiors
- prone to scapegoating (blaming ills upon vulnerable groups such as Jews and other minorities).

This personality type was said (incorporating Freudian theory) to be produced by childhood socialisation by authoritarian parents in rigid, hierarchical families. This theory, although much criticised, helped to make permissive parenting and progressive (child-centred) education fashionable in the 1950s and 1960s.

See also **Adorno, T. W.; Fascism; Fromm, E.; Marcuse, H.; Prejudice.**

Adorno, T., Frenkel-Brunswick, E., Levinson, D. and Sanford, R. (1950, 1991), *The Authoritarian Personality,* Norton, New York.

Authority

A sub-type of power, namely legitimate power, when people obey a command because they believe that they ought to do so.

Max Weber (1864–1920) famously identified three types and sources of authority:

- Tradition: when people obey because a commander has customary authority, or because a command accords with customary practice.
- Legal-rational: when people obey because a command complies with formal rules, and when the commander has been appointed through proper procedures, and is acting in accordance with the rules of his or her office (in an organisation, for example).
- Charismatic: when someone is obeyed on account of his or her extraordinary personal qualities.

See also **Charisma; Legitimacy; Power; Weber, M.**

A

Autopoiesis

See Luhmann, N.

Average

See Measures of central tendency.

Axiom, axiomatic

An axiom is a taken-for-granted assumption, which may be claimed as self-evidently true. These axioms are alternatively called domain assumptions.

All arguments (within and outside sociology) rest ultimately on axioms that cannot be proven. Examples include the existence of a real world outside our own minds, and that individuals' behaviour is capable of rational explanation.

See also **Ontology; Paradigm; Problematic.**

A

Barthes, Roland (1915–1980)

Barthes was a key figure in the promotion of semiotics (the study of signs) within the social sciences and cultural studies in the 1960s and 1970s.

Like Levi-Strauss, a fellow contemporary Frenchman, Barthes claimed to be adapting Saussure's arguments about language to the social and cultural sciences. However, whereas Levi-Strauss's adaptation sought universal underlying structures, Barthes' methodology was to distinguish what a sign literally stood for (denoted) from what it connoted (implied and suggested). Barthes' approach became highly influential in cultural and media studies. For example, designer labels were shown to 'connote' far more than they 'denoted'. Like Levi-Strauss, Barthes wrote extensively about myths and what they stood for. Also like Levi-Strauss, he delved behind surface appearances. However, Barthes' delving did not reveal stable underlying structures. In the world according to Barthes, everything is ideological: we can only perceive anything by decoding meanings (reading signs), but all coding schemes, all languages, are said to be repressive, imposing a particular set of meanings upon the reader, always misrepresenting reality and making the world in which we live appear natural and inevitable, and that life could not be conducted any other way.

See also **Post-structuralism; Saussure, F. de; Semiotics.**

Barthes, R. (1967), *Elements of Semiology,* Cape, London.

Barthes, R. (1972), *Mythologies,* Cape, London.

Base (and superstructure)

See Marx, K.

Baudrillard, Jean (1929–2007)

A French sociologist: one of the originators of the claim that we have entered a postmodern age, which Baudrillard characterised by turning Marxism on its head and arguing that culture and consumption had become the new bases.

Like members of the Frankfurt School half a century earlier, Baudrillard, originally a self-described Marxist, turned his attention to the media and popular culture to explain the failure of the working class to play its forecast revolutionary role. However, although he rejected the Marxist label, Baudrillard remained a fierce critic of capitalism – the new consumer capitalism.

Baudrillard's view was that the defining feature of the postmodern age is its saturation by outpourings of the mass media which turn populations into observers of endless spectacles. The media are said to regale us with an endless duplication of images. Images of images (simulacra) are produced. Reality thereby loses its earlier meaning. We are said to be witnessing the death of society as known hitherto. Baudrillard claimed that images have become the new reality, a condition that he termed hyper-reality. The costs are said to include a loss of stable meanings, relationships to the past are destroyed, and we are left rootless in a chaotic postmodern world. Baudrillard argued that people were no longer purchasing objects according to prior needs. Rather, advertising and media images create endless wants that are never satisfied.

Baudrillard was deeply pessimistic about the prospects for change. He believed that no effective resistance to the new postmodern condition could arise within that condition itself. The death of the social, in Baudrillard's writing, refers to the collapse of society into a sullen and resentful but inactive mass. In another characteristic over-statement, Baudrillard saw the death of the social as terminating the role of sociology.

See also **Consumption; Hyper-reality; Mass media; Postmodern; Simulacra.**

Baudrillard, J. (1988), *Selected Writings*, Polity Press, Cambridge.

Baudrillard, J. (1998), *The Consumer Society*, Sage, London.

Bauman, Zygmunt (1925–)

Born in Poland to non-practising Jewish parents; fled to Soviet-occupied territory in 1941; fought with the Soviet-controlled First Polish Army; after the war was part of the Corps for Domestic Security in Poland. Bauman became disenchanted with communism on intellectual grounds, following the discrimination he experienced after his father enquired about emigration to Israel (though Zygmunt Bauman was anti-Zionist), and more so during the purge of Jews in Poland in 1968. He joined Leeds University in 1971, retired in 1990, and entered the most prolific period in his academic career.

Bauman achieved international fame through his 1989 book which claimed that the Holocaust was a product of modern rationality (taken to a particular extreme) rather than a regression into pre-modern barbarism.

Although having previously used the term 'postmodern', Bauman has subsequently written numerous books about a new modernity; one which is 'liquid' as opposed to the 'solid' first modernity. The topics of these books include consumerism, the new poor, globalisation and individualisation.

See also **Holocaust.**

Bauman, Z. (1989), *Modernity and the Holocaust*, Cornell University Press, New York.

B

Bauman, Z. (2006), *Liquid Times: Living in an Age of Uncertainty*, Polity, Cambridge.

Beck, Ulrich (1944–)

A German sociologist, famous for his invented term, 'risk society'.

Beck argues that we have entered a new historical era which is characterised, above all else, by a new kind of risk. There were grave risks in pre-modern times – famine, floods, earthquakes. In modernity some of these risks were controlled by science and technology. At least, the risks could be calculated and insured against. The new risks are largely products of science and technology – nuclear disaster, ecological calamity. These risks affect everyone. No society and no class of people can protect themselves. The risks are uninsurable, and they are global. One consequence is that confidence in, and the authority of, science have been undermined.

Individualisation is another of Beck's concepts. It is said to be the outcome of the erosion of traditions, and also the erosion of modern structures and divisions, by class and gender for example. The undermining has been by globalisation and the welfare state, especially education which allocates life chances irrespective of class and gender.

See also **Individualisation.**

Beck, U. (1992), *Risk Society: Towards a New Modernity*, Sage, London.

Beck, U. (2000), *The Brave New World of Work*, Cambridge University Press, Cambridge.

Becker, Howard S. (1928–)

An American sociologist; one of the originators of the labelling theory of deviance, a product of the application of the symbolic interactionist perspective to this subject matter.

Becker was an accomplished jazz musician before and alongside being a professional sociologist. His writing extended over numerous topics including jazz musicians (of course), drug use, school teachers and teaching, occupational socialisation and student cultures.

See also **Labelling theory; Symbolic interactionism.**

Becker, H.S. (1963), *Outsiders: Studies in the Sociology of Deviance*, Free Press, Glencoe, Ill.

Behaviourism

A movement in psychology which advocates restricting research and basing theories exclusively on what can be observed, namely behaviour. This can include verbal behaviour, but in practice behaviourists usually prefer to work with a pure stimulus–response model.

B

Behaviourism was invented by the American psychologist Edward Lee Thorndike (1874–1949), but its best known advocates have been fellow Americans John B. Watson (1878–1958) and Burrhus Frederic Skinner (1904–1990), and the classical illustrations of the approach were by the Russian psychologist Ivan Pavlov (1849–1936) in his experiments with dogs. Behaviourist experiments are usually performed on non-humans, but the stimulus–response model remains popular in the treatment of psychological conditions, as in aversion therapy.

In sociology the influence of behaviourism has been minimal.

See also **Empiricism**.

Skinner, B.F. (1953), *The Science of Human Behaviour*, Macmillan, New York.

Bell-curve

See Normal distribution.

Benjamin, Walter (1892–1940)

A member of the Frankfurt School who developed a Marxist theory of aesthetics, and applied this theory in a critique of mass/popular culture under capitalism.

Benjamin has become fashionable in recent times due to the publication in 1999 of *The Arcades Project,* a record of observations and memories of nineteenth and early twentieth-century shopping arcades in Paris, Berlin, Naples and Moscow. Benjamin is now seen as a pioneer, ahead of his time, in studying cultures of consumption.

See also **Consumption; Frankfurt School**.

Benjamin, W. (1999), *The Arcades Project*, Harvard University Press, Cambridge, Mass.

Bentham, Jeremy (1748–1832)

See Utilitarianism.

B

Berger, Peter Ludwig (1929–)

Austrian-born, American sociologist, who has written mainly on the sociology of religion, but is best known throughout sociology as co-author (with Thomas Luckmann) of a 1967 book on *The Social Construction of Reality.*

This book made the phenomenological approach comprehensible to sociology students, and is still regarded as an important attempt to resolve sociology's structure–agency debate, in which Anthony Giddens subsequently engaged with his concept of structuration.

See also **Phenomenology; Social construction; Structuration.**

Berger, P.L. and Luckmann, T. (1967), *The Social Construction of Reality*, Allen Lane, London.

Bernstein, Basil (1924–1990)

A British sociologist of education, best known for his work on language and social class.

Bernstein contrasted elaborated and restricted linguistic codes. He argued that in their families working class children learnt to use only a restricted code whereas middle class children learnt both. The difference between these codes is not a matter of accent or width of vocabulary, but of syntax, how words are joined together to make meanings. In an elaborated code meanings are made explicit and are universal, comprehensible to all who know the language (English, French or whatever). Restricted code speech is particularistic and context bound, and meanings are implicit (often comprehensible only to someone who is part of the subculture). Bernstein believed that how we learn to talk governs how we think. He argued that since schooling is carried out in – and presumes competence in – an elaborated code, working class children are set at a culturally induced disadvantage.

In his later work Bernstein applied his concept of code to the organisation and transmission of knowledge in education, and to social control and the distribution of power in families, schools and the wider society.

Bernstein's work attracted considerable attention in British sociology in the 1960s and 1970s, but his long-term impact has been limited for several reasons:

- Most linguists have not accepted Bernstein's ideas on the relationships between speech, thinking and social class.
- The evidence from empirical research has never been wholly consistent with Bernstein's theories.
- Policy interventions based on Bernstein's ideas (language enrichment for working class pre-school children, for example) have not produced the expected results.

See also **Hidden curriculum; Linguistics.**

Bernstein, B. (1971–7), *Class, Codes and Control* (3 vols), Routledge, London.

Beveridge, William Henry (1879–1963)

See Beveridge Report.

Beveridge Report

This is the popular name for the 1942 report of a UK government enquiry

B

chaired by Sir William Henry Beveridge (1879–1963) which laid down principles (subsequently implemented) for the post-war development of a welfare state in Britain. The report identified five major evils which the government should address: idleness, ignorance, disease, squalor and want. All these evils were attacked strenuously by Britain's post-war Labour government.

The Beveridge Report advocated full employment policies, the creation of a National Health Service and the introduction of Family Allowances (child benefits). These, plus enhanced sickness and unemployment benefits, and retirement pensions, were to be funded by a contribution-based National Insurance scheme, with a National Assistance safety net.

The 'Beveridge principles' have had lasting effects, but over the years have encountered fierce criticism for the meagre level of benefits recommended (and introduced), and for consolidating a 'male breadwinner model' of normal family life.

See also **Poverty; Social policy; Welfare state.**

Beveridge, W. (1942), *Social Insurance and Allied Services*, HMSO, London.

Bias

Systematic error that leads to inaccurate, unreliable or invalid conclusions.

Bias plagues sociology; hence so much 'knowledge' is disputed. An interviewer can affect an interviewee's responses. Observers may unintentionally overlook some events while always noticing others. Bias can intrude into the design of questionnaires and interview schedules, and the interpretation of all evidence. Then there are sampling errors and bias introduced by non-response.

Efforts to eliminate bias assume that truth exists independently of any observer and method of measurement, which itself is debatable. Some sociologists argue that total objectivity and value freedom are unattainable, and that sociologists are best advised to be explicit and unapologetic about their biases.

See also **Axiom; Objectivity; Value freedom/neutrality.**

B

Biographisation

Said to be an outcome of the destandardisation of the life course. Personal biographies, constructed through choices made at successive life junctures, create the main threads in people's lives, and enable them to make sense of their pasts and their present circumstances, and to plan their futures. The 'self' becomes the most stable element in, and enables people to make sense of, their own lives. The contrast is with former modern life courses where standard careers were available in work organisations, accompanied by a standard family life cycle with marriage (for life) preceding parenthood and so on. It is claimed that people were formerly socialised after entering adult roles, whereas with biographisation they first imagine a path that can be followed, then test it against reality. Geographical mobility is another trend that is said to result in biographisation.

See also **Career; Individualisation; Life course; Postmodern; Reflexivity.**

Beck, U., Giddens, A. and Lash, S. (1994), *Reflexive Modernization: Politics, Tradition and Aesthetics in the Modern Social Order*, Polity, Cambridge.

Vinken, H. (2007), 'New life course dynamics? Career orientations, work values and future perceptions of Dutch youth', *Young*, 15, 9–30.

Biological reductionism

See Reductionism.

Birth cohort studies

These are follow-up studies of samples born in the same year. They are the ultimate panel studies. The same individuals can be tracked from birth to death. Indeed the studies can continue indefinitely if children of the original respondents are added to a panel.

In Britain four birth cohort studies are still in process: of people born in 1946, 1958, 1970 and 2000 (the Millennium Cohort). These studies and the data sets are all managed by the Centre for Longitudinal Studies at London's Institute of Education.

The data sets are among the crown jewels of UK social science. Collectively, they permit comparisons of what childhood was like, and similarly youth and other life stages, at different points in historical time. They also allow individuals' lives to be tracked, and the influence of their early experiences on the remainder of their lives can be investigated. Successive cross-sectional surveys cannot be equally illuminating. People may be able to recollect which schools they attended, but they are unlikely to be able to recall their attitudes and other mental states at earlier points in their lives.

See also **Cohort; Longitudinal study; Panel study.**

www.cls.ioe.ac.uk

B

Blauner, Robert (1929–)

An American sociologist, well known in the United States for his work on race relations, but best known internationally for his 1964 book, *Alienation and Freedom*.

Blauner operationalised the Marxist concept of alienation and studied the extent to which workers in four industries experienced powerlessness, meaninglessness, isolation and self-estrangement. He found that alienation was highest among assembly-line workers. The move from craft to 'Fordist' production appeared to have increased alienation. However, Blauner believed that fully automated technologies would enable workers to regain control and that alienation would subside.

These ideas have been criticised for their technological determinism, and for their failure to predict accurately how the next generation of technology would be used.

See also **Alienation; Fordism; Technology.**

Blauner, R. (1964), *Alienation and Freedom*, University of Chicago Press, Chicago.

Blumer, Herbert (1900–1987)

Blumer is famous in present-day sociology as the founder of 'symbolic interactionism'.

Blumer was originally a student of and successor to George Herbert Mead (1863–1931) at the University of Chicago (Blumer actually took over Mead's lectures upon the latter's death). Blumer took up and built on Mead's idea of the self as a social product, an outcome of interactions with others.

He was harshly critical of positivism. Blumer believed that the idea of science was being seriously misapplied, and he deplored the practice of reducing social reality to discrete 'variables'. Blumer wanted sociology to be a down-to-earth study of social life. He abhorred 'grand' abstract theory and was a fierce critic of his contemporary in American sociology, Talcott Parsons (1902–1979).

See also **Mead, G.H.; Symbolic interactionism.**

Blumer, H. (1969), *Symbolic Interactionism: A Perspective on Method*, Prentice Hall, Engelwood Cliffs, N.J.

Body

All action is embodied. The recent growth of sociological interest in the human body is in part a reaction to sociology's former (alleged) over-intellectualised view of social life, emphasising mind and neglecting body. The French sociologist Michel Foucault (1926–1984) has been a major inspiration of this recent 'body turn'.

Sociological attention to the body can be justified on several grounds:

- A society must maintain conditions conducive to bodily health and the reproduction of bodies. Hence sociology's attention to health, illness and disease, and sexuality.
- The body is (partly) a social product, regulated into a desired shape and appearance by cultural norms.
- We use our bodies to communicate, not just in speech, but with gestures, bodily posture, and the ways we adorn our bodies.
- The body's vulnerability makes violence and the threat of violence omnipresent features of our lives. We will act so as to avoid even moderate discomfort.

B

- We will be ingenuous in seeking ways to experience sensual pleasure, excitement, thrill.

See also **Dualism; Foucault, M.**

Shilling, C. (2003), *The Body and Social Theory*, Sage, London.

Booth, Charles James (1840–1916)

Booth was a Victorian businessman, a ship owner, but he was also an ardent social reformer and a pioneer of empirical social research. He was responsible for the first major social survey ever undertaken in Britain, *Life and Labour of the People of London,* which was published in 17 volumes between 1891 and 1903.

Booth's survey pre-dated sampling theory. In the 1890s it was believed that to obtain valid results it was necessary to conduct a census of an entire population. Accordingly, Booth had his research team visit every street in London to assess the living conditions of the residents and their ways of life. Booth's survey paid special attention to levels of income and poverty, a hot political issue in Britain at that time. His results indicated that around a third of the population of London was living beneath, on or little above a subsistence poverty line, and that the main causes of poverty were not individual failings (idleness, fecklessness) but unemployment, low wages and large families. In all these respects Booth's findings resembled those of his contemporary, Seebohm Rowntree (1871–1954), who conducted a survey to assess the extent of poverty in York in 1899.

The evidence from these early social surveys helped to pave the way for the development of a welfare state in Britain, specifically in the short term the old age pensions and unemployment insurance that were introduced by the 1906 Liberal government.

See also **Poverty; Rowntree, B.S.**

Simey, T.S. and Simey, M.B. (1960), *Charles Booth, Social Scientist,* Oxford University Press, London.

B

Bourdieu, Pierre (1930–2002)

A French sociologist, and from the 1970s onwards one of the most acclaimed sociologists in the world. Bourdieu's reputation rests on inventing concepts, and providing an explanation for how inequalities are maintained and reproduced over time.

Habitus is one of Bourdieu's key concepts. Habituses are the metaphorical dwellings in which we live, but they are not outside but within us, within our minds. They are formed during socialisation and comprise durable perceptions, understandings and predispositions to action. Bourdieu believed that members of different social classes develop different and distinctive habituses. These are accumulated products of class experience. A habitus can change, but only by building on existing predispositions. People are said to mix most easily and form social bonds with others who have similar habituses, that is, with members of the same class.

Capital is another key concept in Bourdieu's sociology. As well as economic capital, Bourdieu recognised cultural, social and symbolic capital. The use of the term capital is justified because each resource can be spent or invested in the hope that it will accumulate and yield a return. Bourdieu wrote extensively about cultural capital. This is composed of knowledge and tastes that are considered worthwhile. Who does the considering? Bourdieu argues that in any *field* (another key concept), classes and class factions with different types of cultural capital jockey for position. People are active agents in constructing their lives and futures but the normal outcome of the jockeying is that macro-structures are reproduced. How come? Because particular cultural judgments are endorsed by the holders of valuable economic and social capital (trusted relationships). In education for example, tastes and knowledge that are common in middle class milieux rather than those which are common in working class milieux are treated as indicators of educability (and ability also).

Needless to say, there are question marks against Bourdieu's claims:

* For English language sociologists, is Bourdieu using a novel set of concepts but saying nothing that we did not already know?
* Bourdieu's work is conceptually elegant and coherent, but only parts of it are backed by convincing evidence.
* The context in which Bourdieu developed his ideas was France in the 1950s and 1960s (though most of his work was translated into English only decades later). Do his ideas travel comfortably in time and space?

See also **Capital; Reflexivity**.

Bourdieu, P. (1984), *Distinction: A Social Critique of the Judgement of Taste*, Routledge, London.

Bourdieu, P. and Passeron, J.D. (1977), *Reproduction in Education, Culture and Society*, Sage, London.

Bourgeoisie

A French word, originally derived from *burgeis* (inhabitants of a town). The original bourgeoisie were citizens of towns who made their livings through trade and commerce, who formed guilds, associations and companies to conduct business and promote their interests. Karl Marx (1818–1883) adopted the term to describe the capitalist class, the new ruling class in nineteenth-century European countries (according to Marx), and the word has subsequently been incorporated into English and other languages.

It has become standard practice in sociology to separate the bourgeoisie proper from the petit bourgeoisie (owners of small businesses and the self-employed). The word may be used adjectivally (bourgeois), in which case it most likely refers to all groups that share bourgeois attitudes and lifestyles

B

(typically senior managers, civil servants, politicians, the self-employed and salaried professionals) as well as the bourgeoisie themselves.

See also **Capitalism; Class; Marx, K.**

Braverman, Harry (1920–1976)

Braverman was not a professional sociologist. He was an active (from the 1930s onwards) American communist, and spent 14 years as a factory metal worker. Then in 1974 he published a highly influential book which argued that twentieth-century trends under capitalism had been basically as Marx envisaged insofar as there had been a progressive degradation of labour.

Braverman argued that beneath successive fashions in management theory (such as the human relations movement), the underlying trend had been for capitalism to become forever more ruthless and systematic in controlling labour and extracting surplus value. This had involved progressively separating control from execution, so workers were progressively deskilled, starting on factory floors, then spreading into offices, then the professional grades and lower-level management.

Braverman's book inspired researchers to develop 'labour process theory' which, as the title suggests, focuses on the actual processes whereby goods are created.

See also **Human relations; Labour process theory; Scientific management.**

Braverman, H. (1974), *Labour and Monopoly Capital: The Degradation of Work in the Twentieth Century*, Monthly Review Press, New York.

Brazilianisation

A term used by the German sociologist Ulrich Beck (1944–) to describe the replacement of permanent, full-time skilled jobs by jobs that are deskilled, lower paid, temporary, fixed term or otherwise insecure, often part time or with flexible hours (at the employer's discretion).

See also **Working class.**

Beck, U. (2000), *The Brave New World of Work,* Cambridge University Press, Cambridge.

B

Bricolage

A term used by the French social anthropologist Claude Levi-Strauss (1908–) to describe the practice of creating new things out of whatever odd resources (objects or symbols) are at hand. An example is the Teddy Boy style which was created by young British males in the 1950s from items of Edwardian-style clothing.

See also **Levi-Strauss, C.**

British Crime Survey (BCS)

A victimisation survey, launched in 1982 and repeated bi-annually until 2000, and annually since then. The BCS is based on a representative sample of around 50,000 persons aged 16 and over.

This survey captures crime that is not reported to the police, and is accepted as offering more accurate indications of true rates of crime than the Criminal Statistics which are based on police and court records. The BCS identifies sections of the population that are most at risk of particular types of crime.

Information is also collected regularly on:

- attitudes towards crime, the police and the courts
- fear of crime
- measures taken to avoid crime.

http://www.homeoffice.gov.uk/rds/bcs1.html.

British Household Panel Survey (BHPS)

Launched in 1991 with a nationally representative sample of around 5500 households and 10,300 adult members, all of whom have been followed up at annual intervals.

The BHPS has built a unique (in Britain) data set because:

- It is a panel survey: the same individuals and households are interviewed repeatedly, thus generating longitudinal, biographical information.
- It is a survey of households thus enabling micro-social life to be investigated and related to macro-trends – in the economy and employment, for example.
- The successive annual surveys have gathered information on virtually every topic of interest to sociologists.

Since the mid-1990s the BHPS has been part of the European Household Panel Survey (EHPS) which produces harmonised data sets from similar household panel surveys, originally in 12 and now in 15 European Union countries.

These data sets are among the 'crown jewels' of British and European social science.

http://www.iser.essex.ac.uk/ulsc/bhps/

http://www.iser.essex.ac.uk/epag/dataset.php

B

Bureaucracy

Bureaucracy is one way, not the only way (custom and command by charismatic leaders are alternatives), in which large government and private sector organisations can be administered. In sociology, Max Weber (1864–1920) is the starting point on account of his systematic portrayal of the features of bureaucracy.

Weber believed that the spread of bureaucratically run organisations was an outcome of a wider spread of rationality (ends–means thinking and related behaviour) in modern society. His ideal type of bureaucracy listed a series of inter-related features:

- governed by written rules
- business conducted on the basis of written documents, all of which are filed
- work divided between offices, each run according to rules, and with circumscribed responsibilities
- strict hierarchy of offices and officials
- staff appointed on the basis of suitability, assessed impersonally, on salaries that are office-related, with long-term careers in prospect, and promotion according to seniority or merit
- strict division between official and personal life.

Weber believed that bureaucracies were unrivalled among large organisations in their efficiency and predictability.

This ideal type of bureaucracy is the base from which organisation theory has been developed. In the process, Weber's ideal type has been amended and qualified, but not dismantled. Subsequent researchers have identified inefficiencies that are now believed to be inherent in bureaucracies:

- Staff working 'to rule': that is, according to the letter, ignoring the intentions.
- An extreme division of labour can make jobs meaningless, leading to boredom and reduced effort.
- 'Departmentalism': staff developing stronger loyalties to their immediate colleagues than to the wider organisation.

Subsequent research has also shown that informal social relationships thrive within bureaucracies. These sometimes impede and sometimes facilitate official business.

We have also learnt that there are different kinds of bureaucracies, including differences that reflect the cultures of the countries where they are based.

See also **Ideal type; Organisations; Weber, M.**

Crozier, M. (1964), *The Bureaucratic Phenomenon,* Tavistock, London.

Merton, R.K. (1957), 'Bureaucratic structure and personality', in R.K. Merton, *Social Theory and Social Structure*, 2nd edn, Free Press, Glencoe, Ill.

Selznick, P. (1966), *TVA and the Grassroots*, Harper Torch Books, New York.

Business cycle

See Keynes, J.M.

Cambridge class scheme

A gradational class scheme, developed by sociologists at Cambridge University in the 1970s and continuously updated: it is an alternative to the Oxford (Goldthorpe) class scheme. The Cambridge scheme is based on different presumptions:

- The social hierarchy is singular; it is counterproductive to separate class from status.
- The hierarchy is gradational with no clear breaks/divisions.

The Cambridge scheme is based on extensive research into who people associate with as social equals (based on choices of friends and marrying couples). This data distributes occupations along a continuous scale which, its supporters demonstrate, gives better predictions of matters that class is supposed to predict (children's education and voting intentions, for example) than the alternative class schemes.

See also **Class.**

Prandy, K. (1990), 'The revised Cambridge Scale of Occupations', *Sociology,* 24, 629–55.

Capital

In sociology this term is applied to any assets that can be invested with a view to accumulation (capital growth) and profit.

The capital concept has been taken from economics. In economics capital is wealth that is invested. Marxists treat individuals who make their livelihoods from their capital as a separate capitalist class. We should note that capital is different (in terms of how it is used) from wealth that is held in consumer goods (houses, motor cars etc), or which is deposited in a bank and which earns interest (which is different from profit).

Pierre Bourdieu (1931–2002) argues that other assets can be used in the same way as economic capital:

- Cultural capital: tastes and knowledge, some of which are certified by educational qualifications.
- Social capital: trusted social relationships; people one can turn to for assistance in finding a job, for example.

- Symbolic capital: anything that attracts respect (status), but to do this it must normally indicate possession of some other type of capital.

Bourdieu illustrates how any one type of capital can be converted into another. In his work all types of capital are used to make distinctions, to claim exclusivity, to close positions to outsiders.

Robert Putnam (1941–), an American political scientist, takes a somewhat different view of the role of social capital. He distinguishes bonding capital (between members of a particular group) from bridging capital (relationships which cross group boundaries), but believes that each type of capital stimulates the other. For Putnam, social capital is a collective rather than an individual asset. Where social capital is high, individuals tend to be healthier and happier, educational attainments are higher and crime rates are lower than where social capital is weaker.

See also **Bourdieu, P.; Putnam, R.**

Capitalism

An economic system with the following features:

- private ownership of economic assets
- businesses run for profit
- transactions through markets (including labour markets) with the price mechanism balancing demand and supply.

All market economies are regulated to some extent (variously by governments, trade unions, professional associations and employers associations). It is possible to contrast highly regulated capitalist economies (as in most of the pre-2004 European Union) and weakly regulated (neo-liberal) market economies (as in the United States, UK, and most of the states that joined the European Union in 2004). Also, all countries have public sectors, albeit of various sizes. In western countries governments raise (through taxes) and spend around 40 per cent of the national product (GDP). There are no pure capitalist economies (except on paper, as ideal types). Economies are called capitalist when this is the dominant form of economic organisation as opposed to when capitalism occupies niches within basically publicly owned and state-managed economies (as in Poland and Hungary before 1989).

In the twentieth century capitalism had rivals. In most of the undeveloped third world economic life was still ruled by custom. There was also a second developed world of state socialism (communism). By the early twenty-first century the third world was developing, communism had ended in the Soviet Union and east-central Europe, and the capitalist economy was expanding in China. Only Cuba and North Korea remained apart from the global capitalist economy.

A main global difference today is between capitalist countries where the state retains ownership and/or control of key economic assets, most likely energy stocks and distribution (as in Middle East states, China, Russia,

Azerbaijan, Kazakhstan and Turkmenistan, and gas and cotton in Uzbek-istan), and, on the other hand, places where regulation is weak and the role of capitalism is wider and stronger.

Capitalist

An owner of capital, not just wealth itself, but wealth that is invested with the aim of making profit (rather than just earning interest). In rich countries many people own small amounts of capital (usually held in pension funds, insurance policies and suchlike). True capitalists' life chances (their oppor-tunities in life in the broadest sense) depend primarily on how they deploy their wealth rather than on selling their labour.

A capitalist may personally run the business that he or she owns. Sole or dominant share-owners sometimes run large companies (the Glazer family at Manchester United, and Rupert Murdoch's media businesses, for exam-ple). However, it is now more common for control to be impersonal. Wealthy persons may spread their investments across shares in many companies. Alternatively and more likely, they may use financial intermediaries (invest-ment trusts and banks) which nowadays operate globally. Large trans-national companies also operate globally but personal wealth can be, and often is, spread globally across separate businesses, all of which operate mainly in specific countries. Wherever capitalists are personally based, their wealth is likely to be channelled through major global financial centres such as London, New York and Tokyo. Thus capitalists have become a truly global class. Their wealth flows through financial institutions, then to countries and companies where it will gain the best returns. Businesses and countries compete for investment. Neither workers (through trade unions) nor governments (through trans-national political institutions such as the Euro-pean Union and the United Nations) can mobilise power to match global capital.

See also **Class; Trans-national corporations.**

Career

Any sequence of statuses or roles where each movement is enforced or enabled by the actor's previous position.

The concept is usually associated with occupational careers, but in soci-ology the term is used to analyse biographies in all spheres of life – careers as parents, lovers, drug users, football fans and so on. Career paths can be pre-structured (by the rules of career progress in an organisation, for exam-ple), or built by the agency of actors who may plan future steps. Subjective careers may be constructed retrospectively to give meaning to an actor's current position.

The career concept was introduced into sociology by Everett Hughes (1897–1983), a member of the Chicago School, and was then used widely by symbolic interactionists in the 1960s and subsequently. Sociologists value

C

the career concept for its ability to inject a biographical dimension into analyses of social life.

See also **Biographisation**.

Becker, H.S., Geer, B., Hughes, E. and Strauss, A. (1961), *Boys in White: Student Culture in Medical School,* University of Chicago Press, Chicago.

Case study

A detailed examination of a single case that is undertaken in order to clarify more widespread events or social patterns.

A case may be selected because it is believed to be typical or exceptional. The case may be a single actor, a small group, an organisation or a country. The aim is always to gain insights into processes, meanings and motivations which then enable us to better understand or explain more widespread instances, or to develop hypotheses which can then be interrogated in larger scale enquiries.

Caste

A form of social stratification in which positions are ascribed by birth and govern a person's entire way of life – type of occupation, place of residence, who can be married, who can be a friend. The purest form of caste stratification existed (and continues to be influential) in Hindu India, where castes are believed to possess different degrees of religious purity. The lowest caste, the outcastes, are known and regarded as 'untouchables'.

There is an unresolved debate in sociology about whether caste is peculiar to Hindu India, or whether this is one example of a larger number of cases where strata are entered at birth (usually on the basis of race or ethnicity) and are endogamous (members must inter-marry), or whether caste is just a variant of stratification into economy-based classes.

See also **Stratification**.

Cox, O.C. (1959), *Caste, Class and Race*, Monthly Review Press, New York.

C

Castells, Manuel (1942–)

A Spanish sociologist, originally a Marxist, who has repeatedly revised his thinking in response to trends in the economy and society. In the 1970s Castells argued that crucial class struggles were no longer occurring at sites of production but through new social movements which addressed issues of collective consumption in cities. More recently Castells has examined the implications of the information age for capitalist businesses and their resisters.

In the 1970s Castells' response to the failure of the working class to become a revolutionary force was to argue that proletarian resistance was being channelled into new social movements in cities which sought improved housing, better schools, the protection of parks and open spaces and the like – all matters of collective consumption.

In the 1990s, along with many other sociologists, Castells decided that we had entered a new information age as a result of developments in computing and communications. The outcome, according to Castells, is a 'network society'. The economy is transformed. Castells argues that businesses can survive only by becoming part of flexible networks. Power is now located in information and diffused through networks rather than concentrated in organisations. These trends are said to be resisted by another new generation of social movements, themselves using new information technologies and therefore different in character from older social movements such as trade unions and political parties. Resistance itself is fragmented. Feminist, anti-globalisation, environmentalist, nationalist and religious fundamentalist movements are all given as examples.

> See also **Information economy/information society; Network; Social movements.**

> Castells, M. (1977), *The Urban Question: A Marxist Approach*, Edward Arnold, London.

> Castells, M. (2000), *The Rise of the Network Society*, Blackwell, Oxford.

Catharsis

In psychology catharsis means release of pent-up tensions, emotions or anxieties. In sociology the term has a similar meaning, referring, for example, to how potentially dangerous feelings may be channelled into sport or expressed by identification with screen stars or events.

Cause, causal explanation

A cause usually occurs before or alongside and leads to an effect. However, in sociology a complication is that we may behave in a particular way in order to achieve an outcome, in which case the result may be regarded as the cause of the preceding behaviour. Another complication is that causation may be reciprocal: a top sports team may owe its position to having the best players, and its top position may be why it attracts the leading stars. A further set of complications is that there can be different kinds of causal relations:

- A cause may be *necessary*; without it the effect cannot occur.
- The cause may be *sufficient* in itself to result in an effect, or it may do so only in the presence of other causal factors.
- A cause may be the *sole* cause or just one among many instigators of a particular outcome.

A common aim in sociological enquiries (as in all sciences) is to separate

C

causal from spurious relationships (when two factors occur together because each is caused by the same third factor).

A point to remember is that causal relationships can never be observed (in any science). Causation is always attributed theoretically, as the best possible explanation of the available evidence.

Celebrity

Created by the media saturated world in which we now live. The status of a celebrity may arise from achievements in sport, the arts, entertainment, business or even politics, but celebrities' images achieve wider recognition, and thereafter they attract attention (and are used by advertisers) simply through being celebrities.

Rojek, C. (2001), *Celebrity*, Reaktion Books, London.

Census

A census is a survey of an entire population (as opposed to a sample). The best-known censuses are government-sponsored population censuses, but there are also censuses of industrial output, housing and employees, among others.

The first ever population census was conducted in the United States in 1790. The second was in Britain in 1801. Since 1841 British censuses have been conducted every ten years (except in 1941). Participation is compulsory in government-sponsored general population censuses (but even this never results in 100 per cent coverage).

Census data is extremely useful in sociology:

- Benchmarks are created against which to measure the accuracy of sampling.
- There is now a long time series (back to 1801 in Britain).
- Because everyone is (intended to be) included, it is possible to learn about small sub-populations (ethnic groups for example) that are rarely represented adequately in sample surveys.

C

Change

See Social change.

Charisma

Originally a religious term meaning 'gift of grace'; imported into sociology by Max Weber (1864–1920) as one of three sources of authority, the others being traditional and legal-rational. Charisma refers to outstanding personal qualities that inspire followers or disciples. A charismatic person is always a leader – in religion, politics, business or community life. Charisma is liable to disrupt ongoing stable ways of doing things.

A charismatic leader may arise within or outside existing organisations. In either case, following the death of the charismatic individual, his or her authority must be 'routinised' into traditional or legal-rational authority, otherwise his or her influence gradually fades away.

See also Authority; Routinisation; Weber, M.

Chicago School

The United States's first sociology department opened at the University of Chicago in 1892, and in 1895 the department launched the world's first sociology journal, the *American Journal of Sociology*. Until the Second World War, the Chicago department dominated US sociology. The term 'Chicago School' refers to the sociologists who worked at the department during that period, and to the types of sociology that they pioneered.

These were, first, detailed empirical studies using participant observation, ethnography and case study methods. The output of the school included classic studies of boy gangs, hobos and taxi dance halls. Second, a theory of city growth, said to be driven by ecological processes – competition for space which led to growth in concentric circles and the formation of neighbourhoods, each with its own distinctive subculture and residents with specific biographies, and employed in particular types of occupations. Third, the development of social psychology through the work of George Herbert Mead (1863–1931) and Herbert Blumer (1900–1987), which in the 1950s blossomed into the symbolic interactionist approach in sociology.

All these kinds of work have subsequently spread throughout sociology worldwide, but before 1940 they were very different from the type of 'grand theory' from which European sociology was born, and also from the problem-focused fieldwork-based studies (into poverty and unemployment, for example) that were being undertaken in Britain and elsewhere.

See also **Blumer, H.; Mead, G.H.; Symbolic interactionism; Urbanism; Wirth, L.**

Bulmer, M. (1984), *The Chicago School of Sociology*, University of Chicago Press, Chicago.

C

Chomsky, Avron Noam (1928–)

An American linguistic theoretician, best known in linguistics for his claim that language competence is innate, but at least equally world famous as a radical political activist, initially against the war in Vietnam.

Chomsky claims that language competence is innate, and that the proofs are:

- the ease with which young children learn language
- the existence of the same 'deep structures' beneath the syntaxes of all languages.

These ideas gained attention in sociology in the 1960s alongside a broader recognition of the importance of language in social life, and particularly through the work of linguistic structuralists such as Claude Levi-Strauss (1908–).

> See also **Language; Levi-Strauss, C.; Linguistics; Socio-linguistics; Structuralism.**

> Chomsky, N. (1957), *Syntactic Structures*, Mouton, The Hague.

Church

Can be defined as any body of people and institutions that cohere around a set of religious beliefs. However, in sociology there is a narrower definition which separates churches from sects (and kindred movements). This defines churches as highly organised and well established, with priests who are set apart from laity, and with beliefs that are regarded (within and outside the church) as orthodox. It is said that churches (so defined) tend to be conservative in their religious and also in their socio-political outlooks, that churches tend to support the political status quo, and therefore that churches tend to appeal to the more conservative and privileged sections of a society.

A problem with this church–sect typology is that it was developed, originally by Ernst Troeltsch (1865–1923) in studying Christianity, and is less easily applied to other religions.

> See also **Religion; Sect.**

> Troeltsch, E. (1912, 1956), *The Social Teachings of the Christian Churches*, Allen and Unwin, London.

Churning

This term describes an effect of some government measures intended to reduce unemployment. People are said to be churned when they experience a training scheme and are then returned to unemployment, or when an endless stream of the unemployed spend short spells in temporary (maybe subsidised) jobs.

The effects of churning are to reduce the numbers of long-term unemployed (unemployment is fractured into shorter episodes), to spread the experience of unemployment among a larger number of people than would otherwise be the case, and (possibly) to maintain the work motivation and habits of the unemployed.

> See also **NEET; Unemployment.**

Citizenship

This term is derived from the status of citizens in the city-states of ancient

Greece. A citizen is entitled to the full set of rights from, and is subject to a full set of responsibilities to, the government of the territory.

In ancient Greece and throughout pre-modern times, most residents in most states were not citizens. In the modern era citizenship has been extended, typically to all residents, and rights of citizenship have been expanded. The British sociologist Thomas H. Marshall (1873–1982) described how citizenship had been extended from civic rights (the protection of the law and freedoms such as freedom of expression), to political rights (to vote and to organise politically), and latterly to social rights (to a basic income and welfare services such as education, healthcare and housing). This expansion of citizenship was believed to have extinguished demands for revolutionary change.

Subsequently it has been noted:

- By feminists, that women have still not been accorded full citizenship rights in that access to some rights (as in the case of children) is via a male head of household.
- Citizenship can be rolled back as well as expanded.
- Immigrants (who have become more numerous in western Europe) do not always have full citizen rights.

See also **Government; State.**

Marshall, T.H. (1963), *Sociology at the Crossroads*, Heinemann, London.

City

A major urban settlement. Unless a city is also a state, the title of city is bestowed by the national government.

In most countries the size of a settlement is the deciding factor but this is not the case in the UK where the title is bestowed by the monarch advised by government ministers. In Britain possession of a cathedral was once considered necessary for city status, but this was always just a convention and is no longer considered crucial. Competitions for city status are now held on occasions such as major royal anniversaries.

In practice, all over the world, cities are characterised by a combination of their size and the range of activities that they accommodate – economic, political, educational, religious and cultural – through which they dominate their surrounding territories.

See also **Sassen, S.; Urbanism.**

C

Civil society

This originally meant simply a state of civility, where citizens treated one another with respect. This was said to be a hallmark of civilisation. Subsequently, in the nineteenth century, civil society referred to the intermediate realm between the state and the family. Nowadays it refers to this realm minus the economy. So civil society is of composed of voluntary associations – churches, charities, sports and arts associations, community groups, trade unions, professional bodies, political parties and interest groups of various types. Civil society is the realm of the active citizen, where full citizen rights are exercised.

Civil society is considered important because it acts as a buffer between the state on the one side and private life on the other. Totalitarian governments destroy civil society, after which the state is liable to invade private life. Western-type democracy depends on the existence of a sphere in which people can form and join political parties and pressure groups of various kinds. The development of civil societies has been among the criteria against which the European Union has judged whether ex-communist countries qualify for membership.

We must note, however, that maintaining the space in which civil society develops, the creation and then protection of rights of citizenship, and even a general state of civility (the original meaning of civil society), all depend ultimately on effective government and the rule of law.

See also **Active citizen; Citizenship; Democracy; Totalitarianism; Voluntary associations.**

Civilising process

See Elias, N.

Clash of civilisations

A thesis associated with Samuel P. Huntington (1927–), an American political scientist; developed as a reply to claims of an 'end of history' following the end of communism. Huntington argues that cultural-religious divisions that pre-date the Cold War will be the principal global divisions and lines of conflict in the future.

The civilisations named by Huntington are:

- Western
- Orthodox
- Latin American
- Islam
- Sub-Saharan Africa
- Hindu, Buddhist, Sinic (Chinese) and Japanese which are likely to coalesce into a single bloc.

Lone countries (such as Israel) are recognised, as are some torn countries (such as Turkey).

Wars in the former Yugoslavia and Chechnya, and clashes between India and Pakistan are presented as examples of new conflicts. However, Huntington contends that the major and bloody clashes will be between the Christian west and Islam because both religions seek converts, and the west is intent on exporting and if necessary imposing its ways in Muslim countries.

See also **End of history**.

Huntington, S.P. (1996), *The Clash of Civilizations and the Remaking of World Order*, Simon and Schuster, New York.

Class

Sociologists are agreed that:

- Class is the main form of stratification (socially structured inequality) in modern societies.
- Classes have an economic base.
- People's class positions depend on how they make their livings.

The way people earn their livelihoods, their normal occupations, is considered highly significant on account of the large amounts of time that people spend at work, preparing for it, looking for it and recovering from it, plus the implications of their types of employment for virtually all other aspects of their lives. Classes have economic foundations, but they are likely to develop social and cultural dimensions. People are more likely to associate with others from the same class than across class lines in their workplaces, in the labour market, in their neighbourhoods and in their leisure activities. It is likely that their similar experiences at work and in the labour market will generate common outlooks and distinctive types of class awareness, and thereafter classes may become political actors. All the above may happen; and the circumstances in which all these processes of class formation take effect are among the issues addressed in class research.

There are juxtaposed views in sociology on exactly how classes are formed and, related to this, the main class divisions. Marxists argue that classes are defined by their relationships to the means of production, so the main classes are owners (bourgeoisie) and workers (proletariat), but additional groups are recognised; those occupying ambiguous or even contradictory class locations (managers who perform functions of capital yet are salary earners, for example), and the existence of class factions is acknowledged. The best-known Marxist class schemes have been developed by the American sociologist, Erik Olin Wright (1947–).

Weberian sociologists argue that classes arise in markets, specifically in labour markets, that a major class division is between those hiring and those selling labour power, but that there are also class divisions among the latter based on the kinds of labour power that they can offer (their experience, qualifications and skills). The class scheme developed by the British sociologist John H. Goldthorpe (1935–) has Marxist and Weberian features insofar as occupations are placed in classes on the basis of their typical market and work situations.

Marxist and Weberian sociologists conceptualise classes relationally, that is, in terms of their relationships to one another – employing and being employed, managing and being managed, for example. Functionalist sociologists conceptualise class inequalities gradationally. Occupations and people are said to be ranked according to their functional importance. The

C

UK Registrar General's class scheme, which was first used to analyse the 1911 census and which initially placed occupations into one of five classes according to their social standing, and after 1981 (by when six classes were recognised) by skill levels, is an example of a gradational scheme. A more recently developed gradational scheme, based on more thorough research than the Registrar General's class scheme ever benefited from, is the Cambridge Scheme which situates occupations along an unbroken continuum on the basis of who people interact with as close associates (who they marry and who they choose as friends). Different class schemes were compared in the survey-based study of *Social Class in Modern Britain* (Marshall et al, 1988).

Fortunately, whatever class scheme is adopted, it is possible to distinguish a middle class and a working class, and these are the labels that people are most likely to use if invited to name the classes to which they belong.

> *See also* **Cambridge class scheme; Functionalism; Goldthorpe, J.H.; Marxism; Middle class; Service class; Social mobility; Status; Stratification; Working class; Wright, E.O.**

> Crompton, R. (1998), *Class and Stratification: An Introduction to Current Debates*, Polity, Cambridge.

> Marshall, G., Rose, D., Newby, H. and Vogler, C. (1988), *Social Class in Modern Britain,* Hutchinson, London.

> Roberts, K. 92001), *Class in Modern Britain,* Palgrave, Basingstoke.

> Savage, M. (2000), *Class Analysis and Social Transformation,* Open University Press, Buckingham.

Closure

See Social closure.

Cluster analysis

A set of statistical techniques (there are several) for identifying patterns in multivariate data. Cluster analysis identifies variables that vary conjointly, which may justify treating them all as indicating a single underlying phenomenon.

Market researchers may find that the same people who purchase football team strips also attend football matches, purchase football videos and subscriptions to TV sport channels, indicating that the people concerned are football fans.

> *See also* **Factor analysis.**

Codes, coding

These terms have two quite different meanings in sociology.

Coding is an operation in research whereby evidence is transformed into a limited number of categories. In quantitative survey research these categories are represented by digits and recorded on electronic files for computer processing. Self-completion questionnaires may be respondent-coded, as when the appropriate male/female box is ticked. In face-to-face interviews the interviewer may tick the correct box. Other responses (typically to open-ended questions) may need to be office coded. This applies when people are asked a set of questions about their jobs, and all this information needs to be coded into a limited number of occupational groups (or classes). It also applies when people are asked their views on any topic, and answers are subsequently read and coded into, for example, positive and negative, then according to the reasons given.

Qualitative evidence (tape-recordings of open-ended interviews, press reports and films) can also be coded – according to the 'themes' that are present, or the 'frames' that are used to structure perceptions and interpretations. Computer software (for example, NVivo) is available to assist in the coding of this kind of evidence.

The term 'code' is used differently in semiotics, the study of signs. Actors are said to encode the meanings that they wish to convey into sets of words, gestures, dress and the like. The reader of these signs must then decode the meanings. Actors will therefore understand each other only if they are using the same coding schemes.

See also **Barthes, R.; Bernstein, B.; Interviews; Questionnaires; Semiotics; Surveys**.

Coercion

See Power.

Cognitive dissonance

A concept and theory of the American social psychologist Leon Festinger (1919–1989). The theory explains why people hold on to beliefs despite mounting evidence that the beliefs are wrong. Why do believers retain their faith when repeated forecasts of the end of the world fail to come true? What about Marxists whose forecasts of a proletarian revolution are repeatedly confounded?

Festinger argued that we have a deep-seated psychological need for consistency, and it can be far easier psychologically to explain away contrary evidence than to revise ideas in which we have invested heavily, psychologically and socially. Alongside like-minded companions, it is relatively easy to discount hard evidence.

Festinger, L., Riecken, H.W. and Schachter, S. (1956), *When Prophecy Fails*, University of Minnesota Press, Minneapolis.

C

Cohabitation

When a male and female live together in a sexual relationship without being legally married.

Cohabitation has risen sharply in Britain and in many other western countries since the 1960s. In Britain today marriage is usually preceded by cohabitation. However, cohabitation may be, but is not necessarily followed by marriage; couples may treat cohabitation as an alternative to a married relationship.

See also **Family; Marriage.**

Cohesion

A type of solidarity in a society, neighbourhood, workplace or any other group that is based on shared norms and values, and group identification, as in Emile Durkheim's (1858–1917) mechanical solidarity. A cohesive group will 'pull together'.

See also **Durkheim, E.; Solidarity.**

Cohort

People with a common time-specific experience, usually born in a certain week or year, but maybe graduating from university in the same year.

Cohort studies follow up samples who were born at the same time or who left school at the same time, for instance. Cohort analysis divides samples according to when they had a particular experience such as birth or leaving school. Cohorts may be defined narrowly (born in a particular week) or more widely (born in a particular decade).

Colonialism

Imperialism, the political rule of one country by another, has a long history. Colonialism refers to the particular kind of imperialism practised by European countries throughout the rest of the world from the fifteenth century onwards, which became fully developed in the nineteenth and twentieth centuries.

The European powers always established protected trading relationships with their colonies. However, there were differences in the extent to which local rulers, religions and customs were allowed to remain in place, and in the extent to which colonies were settled by immigrants from the colonising countries. During the colonial era the development of these empires was regarded, in the imperial countries, as a 'civilising mission', and was accompanied by the development and spread of racist theories and ideologies.

Colonialism retreated when most former colonies gained independence in the second half of the twentieth century. This was the result of the rise of nationalist movements in the colonies and the exhaustion of the European powers after the Second World War. However, there are continuing debates:

- about the extent to which neo-colonialism has survived (weaker countries, despite their formal independence, remaining subordinate to western counties)
- about the enduring impact of the colonial era on the economies of the colonised countries, and the destruction or subjugation of their own political, religious and social customs and practices, and on the psychology of the populations.

See also **Dependency theory; Development; Subaltern studies; World system theory.**

Commodification

Originally a Marxist term but now used more widely to refer to the transformation of goods and services into commodities that can be bought and sold, and therefore produced and marketed for profit. Under capitalism commodification is a continuing trend which has spread from the foods we eat and the clothes we wear to entertainment, conversation (by telephone) and company (dating agencies, various contact clubs).

Commodity fetishism

Fetishism has many meanings: attributing religious properties to ordinary objects, and sexual attraction to inanimate objects, for example. However, commodity fetishism is a Marxist concept which means conferring naturalness on objects that are produced by people. Even more specifically, it means mistaking the exchange value of objects (how much money they cost) for their real value – their use value, and the value of the labour required to produce them.

Communism

The doctrines and associated political and economic practices of the Bolsheviks who seized power in Russia in 1917, spread their system throughout the Soviet Union (which replaced the former Czarist Empire), then into the countries of eastern and central Europe that were liberated from German occupation by Soviet forces in 1945. The communist regimes in eastern and central Europe were overthrown in 1989, and the Soviet Union and its communist system ended in 1991. The sole regimes claiming to be communist which survived into the twenty-first century were in China, Cuba and North Korea.

Communist doctrine claims to be derived from the writings of Friedrich Engels (1820–1895) and Karl Marx (1818–1883), which were interpreted by Vladimir Lenin (1870–1924), the leader of the victorious Russian Bolsheviks,

C

his successor Joseph Stalin (1879–1953), then subsequent Soviet leaders. The defining features of communist systems were:

- Rule by communist parties to which no organised opposition was permitted. The communist parties claimed to be run according to 'democratic centralism' and to be exercising a 'dictatorship of the proletariat'.
- State ownership and control of all significant economic assets, and central economic planning, resulting in a 'command economy'.

See also **Engels, F.; Marx, K.; Socialism; Stalinism.**

Pipes, R.E. (2002), *Communism: A History of the Intellectual and Political Movement*, Phoenix Press, London.

Communitarianism

A US-based movement, inspired largely by the ideas of the American sociologist Amitai Etzioni (1929–), which seeks to re-invigorate social bonds.

The movement is suspicious of state collectivism and welfare which are believed to undermine genuine communities where the care of members is based on shared values, and where rights are balanced by responsibilities. These ideas are promoted in the United States by the Communitarian Network. In Europe similar ideas are promoted by the Social Capital Foundation.

See also **Active citizen; Capital (social); Civil society.**

Etzioni, A. (1968), *The Active Society: A Theory of Social and Political Processes*, Free Press, New York.

www.communitariannetwork.org

www.socialcapital-foundation.org

Community

A group that is wider than an extended family, but whose members are bound by kin-type relationships, among whom there is a sense of belonging, and a shared identity.

The term is applied most frequently to territory-based 'neighbourhood communities'. Studies of neighbourhood communities were inspired by the Chicago School, and community studies became popular in sociology between the 1920s and 1960s. The German sociologist Ferdinand Toennies (1855–1936) contrasted *Gemeinschaft* and *Gesellschaft* (translated as community and association), and saw urbanisation as undermining the former. Subsequent sociologists demonstrated the survival of communities within urban areas.

Sociologists have accepted that communities can have bases other than neighbourhoods: hence studies of occupational, religious, gay and lesbian communities, and so forth.

The term community has positive connotations, and is often used (outside sociology) to mobilise support for the creation of a European community, even a world community, among others. It is applied liberally to activities such as community work, community care and community development. The value of the concept is constantly threatened by over-use. Community remains a valuable concept in sociology only by insisting on more precise and restricted use.

See also **Chicago School; Toennies, F.**

Delanty, G. (2003), *Community,* Routledge, London.

Comparative method

This involves the systematic comparison of two or more cases – of individuals, groups, practices, beliefs, institutions, whole societies.

All sociology is explicitly or implicitly comparative. This is not a particular methodology in sociology (one among many). The issue (a matter for perpetual debate) in sociology is how to use comparisons. A classical use of the comparative method in sociology is Emile Durkheim's (1858–1917) study of suicide rates. His aim was to identify factors which varied alongside suicide rates, and thereby verify or falsify, or induce hypotheses (explanations). Debate still rages as to whether this method is appropriate in sociology given that usually we are unable to experiment, the number of cases that can be compared is fairly small, especially when we are comparing whole societies, and in any case social action is not caused in exactly the same way as stimulus–response relationships in the natural sciences.

See also **Durkheim, E.; Positivism.**

Smelsner, N.J. (2003), 'On comparative analysis, interdisciplinarity and internationalisation in sociology', *International Sociology*, 18, 643–57.

Comprador class/elite

Comprador is a Spanish word, which refers to a local overlord who is appointed by an empire to rule a colony. In sociology a comprador class or elite are members of a national business class who derive their positions and status from connections with foreign governments, businesses or other organisations, and who use their influence to encourage local economic developments that benefit other nations rather than their own.

See also **Colonialism; Dependency theory; Post-colonial theory.**

Comte, Auguste (1798–1857)

The French social theorist who invented the word 'sociology' (earlier on he had called the new discipline 'social physics'), and the 'law of three stages'.

Comte believed that human thought developed through three stages: the theological (where events were explained as the work of a wind spirit, a fire spirit etc.), through the metaphysical (explanations in terms of natural law and the will of God), to the ultimate scientific or positive stage (explanations in terms of laws of cause and effect). He believed that societies evolved in a corresponding way from the primitive, through an intermediate stage, to the positive, and he also believed that he himself lived in an age in which the era of positivism was dawning. The term 'positive' was used to indicate that scientific thought was progressive, capable of improving things. Comte expected his sociology to become a social movement, the religion of the positive age. Sociologists would guide their societies into this era. He divided sociology into the study of social dynamics (where the aim is to discover laws of development) and social statics (the study of the anatomy of society).

Comte may have been wrong on most specifics but his vision for sociology proved enduring: his conviction that applying scientific (positivist) methods would enable sociology to improve people's lives, and his division of the subject matter of sociology into what would subsequently be called social change and social structure.

See also **Evolution; Positivism; Science.**

Andreski, S. (ed.) (1974), *The Essential Comte*, Croom Helm, London.

Thompson, K. (1976), *Auguste Comte: The Foundations of Sociology*, Nelson, London.

Conditioning

A form of learning in which a subject is trained to respond to a stimulus in a particular way.

The classic demonstration was by the Russian psychologist Ivan Pavlov (1849–1936), who trained dogs to salivate on the ringing of a bell by conditioning them to associate the sound of a bell with being given food. Behaviourists have applied the stimulus–response model in the study of human behaviour.

Conditioning does occur in social life, but most human learning and socialisation, and the causation of most social behaviour, are far more complex.

See also **Behaviourism; Socialisation.**

C

Conflict theory

The label applied to and adopted by certain opponents of functionalism in the 1950s and 1960s. Rather than starting from a presumption of shared norms, social integration and cohesion (which then need to be explained), conflict theorists insist that societies can be better understood by starting from a presumption that different groups have different (often conflicting) interests, and that relationships between groups usually involve power and control, efforts to exclude and struggles to overcome. The original self-styled conflict theorists in sociology drew inspiration from the works of Karl Marx (1818–1883) and Max Weber (1864–1920).

Conflict theory is an approach, a perspective, and in itself does not explain which interests or groups dominate at any time. These issues remain open for investigation and debate. So conflict theory has never amounted to a coherent body of knowledge. As the influence of functionalism in sociology faded, conflict theory fragmented, and the juxtapositioning of conflict and functionalist perspectives became blurred with the recognition that there were many ways in which conflict could be functional.

See also **Consensus**.

Coser, L. (1956), *The Functions of Social Conflict*, Free Press, New York.

Conjugal

An adjective that refers to the roles and relationships between married persons. There is still uncertainty as to whether the term should also be applied to cohabitees.

See also **Cohabitation; Family; Marriage**.

Conscience collective

See Durkheim, E.

Consensus, Consensus theory

Consensus means agreement; consensus theory maintains that a society is based on a consensus over norms and values. This view is associated with functionalism, and particularly with the functionalism of Talcott Parsons (1902–1979). The opposing school of thought in sociology is conflict theory.

Conflict theorists argue that apparent consensus is usually the result of a dominant group imposing its views on others. However, all will agree that any society requires a minimal consensus over language and other symbols because members need to communicate with each other.

See also **Conflict theory; Functionalism; Parsons, T.**

Conspicuous consumption

See Positional goods.

Consumption

The opposite of production (where value is created): when goods or services are consumed their value is depleted.

C

Since the 1970s consumption has commanded increased attention in sociology. This attention is associated with claims that as the economy and therefore both production and consumption have expanded, consumption has assumed a stronger role in personal identity formation and maintenance, group formation, government policies and political party alignments.

Consumer culture refers to the meanings (usually generated or amplified by commercial marketing) that are associated with the consumption of particular goods and services, and the places where they are consumed.

Consumerism/consumerist may mean equating personal happiness and fulfilment with consumption, or government policies which favour consumption or address consumer interests.

Consumer movements and organisations seek to protect or advance the rights of consumers.

Miles, S. (1998), *Consumerism – As a Way of Life,* Sage, London.

Content analysis

The analysis of 'texts' which may be documents, interview transcripts, films, TV programmes and so on.

Texts can be scanned for the use of specific words, topics, themes, discourses or frames (forms of argument and presentation), and stylistic features. The outcomes of such scans may be amenable to numerical analysis (for example, the frequency with which particular words or themes occur). Nowadays various computer software packages are available to assist all these processes.

The outcomes of content analysis may be generated systematically, but it is never possible to claim to have achieved *the* authoritative, objective results because meanings can sometimes be conveyed by absences, or by the contexts in which words, topics and other features occur, and outcomes are always governed by what an analyst searches for.

See also **Texts.**

Krippendorf, K. (2004), *Content Analysis: An Introduction to its Methodology,* Sage, Thousand Oaks.

Contest mobility

See Sponsored mobility.

Contingent, contingency theory

In philosophy something is contingent if it may be true, but is not necessarily true.

In all the social and natural sciences a contingency table is simply a cross-tabulation of two or more variables showing that the value of x is contingent (dependent) on the value of y.

C

In sociology contingency theory is a theory of organisations and management which claims that there is no one best way, but that this depends on the tasks to be undertaken or the technology, or the environment, or whatever.

Contra-culture

See Counter-culture.

Control group

Used in the natural and the human sciences. A change is introduced into an experimental group while a control group is not subject to the intervention (though a placebo may be administered). If further changes are observed in the experimental group but not in the control group, this strengthens confidence that the intervention was responsible for any other changes in the experimental group.

In sociology it is rarely possible to experiment (or to use placebos), but experimental and control groups can sometimes be simulated by the careful selection and matching of cases then investigating the effects, for example, of a set of changes that are introduced into just one set of schools, or of new methods of payment for some groups of employees.

See also **Action research; Experiment.**

Conurbation

A term coined by Patrick Geddes (1854–1932) to describe the outcome when two or more urban areas expand and fuse together.

See also **Urbanism.**

Geddes, P. (1915), *Cities in Evolution*, Williams and Norgate, London.

Convenience sampling

Members of such a sample are selected because they are easily accessible (convenient) for a researcher.

One student might interview fellow students. One member might interview other members of a particular football club. Convenience samples can never be treated as if they were representative of wider populations, but they are often used in the pilot stage of a project. Alternatively, such samples can be used to generate insights or hypotheses to be explored in subsequent fieldwork.

See also **Sampling.**

Convergence thesis

This thesis, which enjoyed considerable support in the 1950s and 1960s, claimed that all industrial societies would grow increasingly alike.

The argument was that whatever a country's traditional practices and culture, and whether its route into the industrial age was via capitalism and the market or communist planning, powerful organisational and technological imperatives would lead to the societies growing more and more alike. Running a steel mill, for example, was said to require much the same mix of skills and much the same management practices, whether the mill had been built and was being run by private capitalists or state planners. At the time of this thesis's popularity (between the 1950s and 1970s), governments in western countries were playing a larger role in the (Keynesian) management of the economies, while communist countries were at least talking about the introduction of market mechanisms into their planned systems.

A parallel 'end of ideology' thesis claimed that throughout the world, and within western countries where fascist, socialist and liberal ideologies had once confronted each other, broad agreement was being reached about 'ends' and the remaining disputes were mere technical issues to do with 'means' (for example, how to maximise economic growth).

Capitalist and communist countries have converged, but through a collapse of the communist systems rather than a gradual drawing together. The successor to the convergence thesis is an 'end of history' thesis which claims that the capitalist market economy and western-type democracy are destined to triumph all over the world.

> *See also* **End of ideology; Industrialisation: Managerial revolution; Technocracy.**
>
> Galbraith, J.K. (1967), *The New Industrial State*, Penguin, Harmondsworth.
>
> Kerr, C., Dunlop, J.T., Harbison, F.H. and Myers, C.A. (1962), *Industrialism and Industrial Man,* Heinemann, London.

C

Conversation analysis

Pioneered by Harvey Sacks (1935–1975), originally grew out of ethnomethodology, but now an independent method which has become widely used in sociology.

Conversations are important, core features of social life. Moreover, conversations can be recorded then made available to different analysts. The analysis of conversations has proved highly revealing. It reveals the techniques people use to maintain orderliness in their conversations (and relationships), how conversations are opened, how turn-taking is governed, how topics are chosen (and avoided), the operation of power relationships, and how conversations are closed. The specific rules of conversation that operate in and distinguish different settings – such as courtrooms, university seminars, office workplaces – have been identified.

See also **Ethnomethodology; Garfinkel, H.**

Sacks, H. (1992), *Lectures on Conversation* (2 vols), Blackwell, Oxford.

Cooley, Charles Horton (1864–1929)

Cooley is best known today for his phrase 'the looking glass self'.

Cooley did not regard himself as a sociologist but saw himself as working at the crossroads between history, philosophy and psychology. Nevertheless, he has since been claimed by sociology as a first generation American sociologist. Another term coined by Cooley that has been absorbed into mainstream sociology is 'primary group'. However, it is the notion of the 'looking glass self', the idea that our images of ourselves, our personalities, are maintained through the real and imagined judgements of others, which was adopted and built-on by George Herbert Mead (1863–1931) and others in the Chicago School (Cooley himself worked at the University of Michigan) that has made the greatest lasting impact.

See also **Mead, G.H.**

Cooley, C.H. (1909), *Social Organization*, Scribner, New York.

Corporate crime

See White-collar crime.

Corporations

See Organisations.

Corporatism

Over the centuries this term (or alternatively corporativism) has been applied to different political systems, but they have shared three features:

- Individual interests have to be represented by organisations (corporations) which are recognised by the state.
- Governments rule in partnership with these corporations.
- The outcome is that an entire society can be run as if it were a single corporation.

In the late nineteenth and early twentieth centuries the Roman Catholic Church advocated corporatism as an alternative to class-based party politics. Later on the term was applied to Europe's fascist regimes. Subsequently it has been applied to Japan, Singapore and other Asian countries, and most recently to Putin's Russia. However, in western Europe the term is now associated with the partnership arrangements that were established in the 1960s and 1970s between governments, trade unions and employers'

C

organisations. Through these arrangements consensus was sought on levels of pay increases, welfare entitlements (the social wage) and much else. The partner organisations were expected to impose or 'sell' these agreements to their members. Such arrangements were strongest in West Germany, Austria, the Netherlands and the Scandinavian countries. Corporatist arrangements have since been weakened by the decline in trade union membership and power, globalisation (especially the globalisation of capital), and by governments adopting neo-liberal (free market) economic policies. However, the politics of the European Union are emphatically corporatist, seeking consensus between national governments and the so-called 'social partners' (trade unions, employers and other interest groups).

Sociologists today find it useful to distinguish different kinds of corporatism. They recognise that the balance of power between the partners can vary. The dominant feature may be state control of trade unions and businesses, or one of the latter groups controlling the state.

Advocates of corporatism have argued consistently that these arrangements are the most effective way of running a capitalist, market economy, and best serve the interests of all sections of a population. Critics see corporatism as incompatible with civil liberties, democracy and all truly radical agendas.

See also **Fascism**.

Crouch, C. (1990), *Corporatism and Accountability: Organised Interests in British Public Life*, Clarendon Press, Oxford.

Corporeal

This means simply 'relating to the body', usually the human body.

See also **Body**.

Correlation

These are measurements (there are several) of the extent to which the values of two variables (such as parental social class and children's educational achievements) increase or decrease together. A correlation may be strong or weak, and positive or negative (from +1 to −1).

A correlation may, but does not necessarily, indicate a causal relationship. The relationship may be spurious: both of the measured variables may be responding to a common third factor.

Cosmopolitan

Derived from the Greek word *cosmos* (the universe).

Cosmopolitanism is the idea (political philosophy) that humanity belongs to a single moral community. A country or city is described as cosmopolitan if people of different ethnicities, nationalities and cultures live in close proximity without conflict. A cosmopolitan individual is an otherwise rootless world citizen who disavows political borders.

Counter-culture

Alternatively described as contra-culture: standing in direct opposition to the dominant culture of a society.

The term counter-culture was applied to the student cultures of the 1960s that rejected capitalism and conventional family life, and championed sexual freedom and recreational drug use. The Green movements may be regarded as contemporary examples of counter-cultures.

Roszak, T. (1970), *The Making of a Counter-Culture*, Faber, London.

Creative industries

This term and its derivatives – creative economy, creative workers, creative class – are hotly contested. Creative industries are those which exploit intellectual property rights – computer software, the arts, films, TV content, computer games, fashion design, advertising and so on. These industries are said to depend on the individual creativity of their key personnel who comprise the 'creative class'. The economic fortunes of cities, regions and countries are said to depend nowadays on their ability to attract and hold creative workers, who will bring creative industries with them.

It is counter-argued that all industries depend on creativity and employ creative staff (and have always done so), and that jobs in the so-called creative industries are not all especially creative (cleaners and security guards for example).

'Cultural industries' refers to an overlapping but different and larger set of industries.

See also **Cultural industries.**

Florida, R.L. (2002), *The Rise of the Creative Class: And How it's Transforming Work, Leisure, Community and Everyday Life*, Basic Books, New York.

C

Credentialism

The allocation of persons to positions on the basis of their educational qualifications.

There is a heated debate in sociology and other social sciences about whether this trend is a fair and meritocratic process which strengthens a society by appointing the most suitable individuals, or whether it too often results in the appointment of the technically unsuitable and distorts education.

See also **Achievement/achieved status; Human capital; Social mobility; Sponsored (and contest) mobility.**

Collins, R. (1979), *The Credential Society*, Academic Press, New York.

Dore, R. (1976), *The Diploma Disease*, Allen and Unwin, London.

Crime

Crimes are acts which break the law.

Sociologists have noted that laws create crimes, and the larger the set of acts that are criminalised, the more crime will occur. Whether a particular act is a crime varies by time and place. Until 2007 smoking in public places in England and Wales was not unlawful. Behaviour regarded as admirable enterprise in market economies was illegal under communism.

Sociologists have found that laws are most likely to be obeyed when they accord with people's views about what is right and what is wrong. Crime must be distinguished from deviance – a wider category of acts which include breaking the rules of any organisation or the norms that prevail in particular subcultures. Sections of the public may feel that certain crimes are not truly wrong – certain motoring offences, and tax evasion, for example. Certain crimes may actually earn approval and status in particular subcultures – carrying and even using a weapon in certain youth subcultures, for example. On the other hand, behaviour considered immoral by sections of the population may be perfectly legal, as when company directors pay themselves huge salaries and bonuses while the businesses are failing and employees are being made redundant. Hence the questions that sociologists address include who makes the law and in whose interests.

See also Deviance.

Criminal Statistics

In England and Wales these have been compiled from police and court records since 1837, and so have the advantage of being a long time series.

Until the British Crime Survey was launched in 1982, the Criminal Statistics were our main source of evidence about crime rates and trends. It was always known that much crime was unreported and undetected and therefore unpunished. The British Crime Survey (which asks a nationally representative sample about their experiences as victims) is now regarded as our most valid source of evidence on crime rates and trends.

However, the Criminal Statistics are still our main source of nationwide evidence about who commits criminal offences, though there are known to be differences between offenders who are caught and punished on the one hand, and on the other, those whose crimes go undetected. There have been surveys inviting respondents to self-report their own criminal acts anonymously, but it is believed that people are far less likely to answer these questions truthfully than when faced with most survey questions.

See also British Crime Survey.

Criminology

The study of crime. Sociology is just one of many disciplines in this field. Its main companions are psychology and law. Needless to say, sociology focuses on the social aspects of crime – its distribution (who commits different types of crime and who are the victims), the social contexts that produce or are conducive to crime, and crime as a social activity (as when crimes are committed in groups, or when there is an ongoing relationship between a victim and an offender).

Sociologists are interested in who makes laws (and therefore creates crimes), and whose interests the law serves.

Sociologists also study the interplay between criminal behaviour and the police, court and penal systems. They have noted that chances of detection and arrest depend on the type of crime and the character of the offender. Sociologists have noted how law enforcement may amplify crime – by publicising exciting and heroic role models (such as mods and rockers) for others to emulate, and how the public labelling of offenders may push those concerned deeper into deviant subcultures.

See also **Deviance; Labelling theory; Penology.**

www.britsoccrim.org

Critical realism

A school in philosophy which maintains that objective, mind-independent knowledge of external reality is possible, but perceptions always need to be treated critically since there will be distortions created by our own internal mental processes.

In sociology this has been the orthodox 'default' position, except among relativists and (some) phenomenologists. However, in Britain in the 1970s the 'critical realist' label was claimed simultaneously by a variant of Marxism and the then fashionable structuralism. Both claim that events that we perceive are governed by structures which exert causal powers.

A non-Marxist view of the character of these underlying structures is therefore possible: the operation of the human mind, revealed by language, according to French structuralists.

Marxist critical realists treat relationships of production as the underlying structures. The laws of the natural sciences are treated as analogous underlying structures. Sociological explanation must therefore be via identifying the structures that govern particular events, a process called 'retroduction'. A problem is how to rescue this methodology from circularity: structures are inferred from perceived behaviour and are then used to explain the behaviour. Critical realists say that the test is 'practical adequacy'.

See also **Althusser, L.; Relativism; Structuralism.**

Bhasker, R. (1975, 1997), *A Realist Theory of Science*, Verso, London.

Critical sociology/critical theory

A sceptical stance towards evidence and arguments is standard in all social sciences. However, the Frankfurt School gave 'critical' a more precise meaning which, in sociology, it has retained.

The Frankfurt School's critical sociology involved uncovering hidden assumptions, plus self-criticism. They rejected the instrumental (means–ends) rationality that they associated with capitalism. Operating unquestioningly within this rationality was rejected as uncritical. The Frankfurt School sought an alternative. They saw themselves as the true heirs to the spirit of the enlightenment. Their critical sociology was intended to be uniquely enlightening and emancipatory, enabling people collectively to take charge of their lives, circumstances and destinies.

Jurgen Habermas is the leading current exponent of the Frankfurt School's critical sociology.

Within American sociology, critical sociology has a more specific meaning: critical of professionalised, policy-serving, mainstream sociology.

See also **Frankfurt School; Habermas, J.**

Burawoy, M. (2005), 'For public sociology', *American Sociological Review*, 70, 4–28.

Connerton, B. (ed.) (1976), *Critical Sociology*, Penguin, Harmondsworth.

Held, D. (1980), *Introduction to Critical Theory*, Hutchinson, London.

Cult

See Sect.

Cultural anthropology

See Anthropology.

Cultural capital

See Capital.

Cultural deprivation

This term couples a factual proposition – that an individual or group lacks cultural (non-material) assets such as language skills, attitudes, values, motivations, knowledge, tastes – and a value judgement: that this absence is a deprivation, that is, damaging to those concerned. The question then arises as to who makes the value judgement. Is it those who are allegedly deprived or other parties?

In the 1950s and 1960s 'cultural deprivation' became a much debated explanation of the educational failure of children from working class and some ethnic minority backgrounds. Critics of the cultural deprivation thesis counter-argued that working class and ethnic minority children had cultures which were simply different from mainstream, dominant, middle class culture, and that these different cultures were not deficient in an objective, absolute sense. 'No child can be deprived of its own culture.' This counter-argument proceeded to allege that the failure of working class and minority children was due to the schools' failure to build squarely upon these children's own cultural assets.

See also Deprivation; Hidden curriculum; Relative deprivation.

Keddie, N. (ed.) (1973), *Tinker, Tailor: The Myth of Cultural Deprivation*, Penguin, Harmondsworth.

Cultural industries

The term always refers to the mass media (all of them), and also (usually) to the performing arts, galleries and museums, heritage, advertising and design. Sometimes sport, tourism and hospitality are included. Different writers draw different boundaries. It is difficult to identify a common element which does not occur elsewhere. It is sometimes claimed that the cultural industries have a distinctive core activity in the production of meanings – products whose significance is primarily symbolic – but this could be said to apply to some manufacturing industries also. The cultural industries, wherever the boundaries are drawn, are always somewhat broader than 'creative industries', but narrower than the 'leisure industries' and much narrower than the entire service sector of the economy.

The cultural industries have gained a high profile in contemporary sociology on account of their (alleged) elevated importance in the economy, and in contemporary social life and culture more generally. Some sociologists argue that the cultural industries (specifically the mass media) are the prime source of a postmodern condition.

The term 'culture industry' was originally used in the 1940s by the Frankfurt School social scientists Theodor Adorno (1903–1969) and Max Horkheimer (1895–1973) to describe the United States's new capitalist mass media industries which they found just as oppressive, albeit in a rather different way, as the Nazi regime in Germany from which they had fled. Nowadays most writers prefer to use the plural 'cultural industries'.

See also **Adorno, T. W.; Baudrillard, J.; Creative industries; Frankfurt School; Horkheimer, M.; Lyotard, J-F.**

Hesmondhalgh, D. (2007), *The Cultural Industries,* 2nd edition, Sage, London.

Cultural lag

A term invented by the American sociologist William F. Ogburn (1886–1959), who believed that many social conflicts indicated that cultural phenomena (laws, attitudes, norms) were lagging behind technology-driven changes.

> Ogburn, W.F. (1964), *On Culture and Social Change: Selected Papers*, Chicago University Press, Chicago.

Cultural studies

Simultaneously a specialism within sociology and an independent interdisciplinary field of study. Cultural studies was founded by (in the sense of being inspired by the work of) Richard Hoggart (1918–) and Raymond Williams (1921–1988). Cultural studies examines cultural production (in the cultural industries), the consumption of cultural products, and more generally the cultural (non-material) dimensions of social life, most notably the everyday lives of ordinary people and their lived experiences of class, gender, race and so on.

Cultural studies has flourished alongside the expansion of the cultural industries, but its appeal to students probably owes far more to its being less quantitative than other human sciences (including sociology) and leaving more scope for imagination and interpretation.

> *See also* **Cultural industries**.

> Hoggart, R. (1957), *The Uses of Literacy,* Chatto and Windus, London.

> Williams, R. (1963), *Culture and Society*, *1780–1950,* Penguin, Harmondsworth.

Culture

'...that complex whole which includes knowledge, belief and morals, law, custom and any other capabilities and habits acquired by man as a member of society.' This definition, penned by Edward Tylor (1832–1917), an early English social/cultural anthropologist, has been cited in sociology textbooks up to and including the present day.

The definition given by Tylor covers everything that we learn as members of our societies (as opposed to behaviour that is governed by biology). However, present-day sociologists are likely to restrict the definition of culture to the non-material aspects of social life, thus, for example, distinguishing a school building and textbooks themselves from the knowledge and beliefs which determine how these artefacts are used.

In sociology 'culture' never refers exclusively to the arts. Sociologists are interested in high culture, low culture, middlebrow culture, mass culture and all other cultures, and do not presume that any are better or higher than others.

> Tylor, E.B. (1871, 1958), *Primitive Culture*, Harper, New York.

Culture industry/industries

See Cultural industries.

Culture of poverty

This term draws attention to how material deprivation can breed a culture (values, attitudes, view of the world) that becomes a further barrier to escape and locks people into deprived conditions.

Research has shown that long-term unemployment typically leads to people giving up hope of finding work. They become resigned and fatalistic. This culture may be passed through families to children and young people, and amplified in neighbourhoods and peer groups. Poverty of aspiration then becomes part of a subculture, possibly a dependency subculture in which people become reconciled to life on state welfare.

The analysis can appear to blame the poor for their poverty and the unemployed for their joblessness. The orthodox policy response to an alleged culture of poverty is to try to break the culture, or at least prevent its transmission down the generations. Sociologists always point out that unless structural sources of unemployment and poverty are removed, attacking the culture will achieve no more than 'churning' the disadvantaged: those who escape from deprivation will be replaced by others who sink.

See also **Churning; Culture; Cycle of deprivation/disadvantage/poverty; Poverty; Subculture.**

Lewis, O. (1961), *The Children of Sanchez,* Random House, New York.

Custom

An established way of thinking and acting that members of a group, community or society are expected to observe.

Cybernetics

A term coined by Norbert Wiener (1894–1964). It is the study of communication and control systems, especially feedback loops which enable systems to remain in balance internally and with their environments alongside internal and external changes. In sociology cybernetics has been used in systems theories.

See also **Luhmann, N.; Social system.**

McClelland, K.A. and Fararo, T.J., (eds) (2006), *Purpose, Meaning and Action: Control Systems Theories in Sociology*, Palgrave Macmillan, New York.

Wiener, N. (1949), *Cybernetics: Or Control and Communication in Man and Machine*, MIT Press, Cambridge, Mass.

C

Cyberspace

This term originates in science fiction but now refers to the space in which electronic data is exchanged in networked systems. The term is used synonymously with the Internet and the World Wide Web.

Cycle of deprivation/disadvantage/poverty

This term describes the transmission of disadvantages from generation to generation via family, neighbourhood and peer group cultures.

There is massive evidence that parents who are poor and/or unemployed are unable, or at any rate fail, to equip their children with the motivations and learning experiences that augur well for success at school and in later life. Parents and children who view social ascent as unlikely are liable to learn not to try or even to hope.

Sociologists do not dispute these general tendencies but point out that:

- At all social levels there is a tendency for individuals to remain close to their social origins, and 'stickiness' is no greater at the base than at other social levels. Many children from deprived backgrounds do succeed and move up.
- Focusing upon and trying to break the inter-generational transmission of disadvantages deflects attention from structural sources of disadvantage: for example, the ways in which poverty and unemployment are outcomes of the normal operations of the economy and the labour market.
- In the absence of structural change, more disadvantaged children can ascend only if more advantaged children descend. In other words, cycles of advantage would also need to be broken. Proposals to break the inter-generational transmission of advantages are likely to arouse significant social and political resistance.

See also **Culture of poverty; Poverty; Poverty trap; Social exclusion; Social mobility; Underclass.**

C

Dahrendorf, Ralf (1929–)

German-British sociologist who argued that functionalism and conflict theory could be bed-fellows, and who revised Marxism by claiming that the main lines of class conflict formed not around ownership but around authority and control.

Dahrendorf was German-born but became a British citizen (and a life peer) in 1988. He was at the London School of Economics in the 1950s and again in the 1980s (as Director). In the intervening years he built a successful career in German politics, becoming a member of the German government and a European Commissioner.

Dahrendorf's reputation in sociology is still based mainly on his 1959 book. This argued that the sociological analysis of stratification needed functionalism (to explain the inevitability of inequality) and conflict theory (to account for change). The book also attempted a revision of classical Marxism by arguing that the main class conflicts arose not between owners and employees but between those with and without authority and control, the order-givers and the order-takers.

See also **Class**; **Conflict theory**.

Dahrendorf, R. (1959), *Class and Class Conflict in an Industrial Society*, Routledge, London.

Darwinism

See Social Darwinism.

Decentring

Anything can be decentred, that is, pushed from the centre of a search for truth, explanation or interpretation. However, in practice decentring is a concept used by structuralists and post-structuralists, and the object of their decentring is the thinking and acting individual.

For structuralists, decentring means identifying another location where truth might be discovered. The alternative might be a language system, the unconscious, or a culture. Post-structuralists insist that there is no secure centre on which we can focus.

Decentring (the process, not the word) is a standard practice in sociology insofar as its focus is on roles, institutions, structures and systems rather than individual actors.

See also **Derrida, J.**

Deconstruction

This is a post-structuralist technique, a riposte to structuralism. The claim is that there can be no single, correct reading of any text. All texts are said to be ambivalent, meaning that they can be 'deconstructed' in various ways by different readers, each deconstruction having an equal claim to validity. If societies are to be treated as texts, the implication is that sociology is misconceived insofar as it seeks correct descriptions and explanations.

See also **Derrida, J.; Post-structuralism.**

Definition of the situation

See Thomas, W. I.

De-industrialisation

See Post-industrialism.

Delinquency

This term is often is used for crimes committed by juveniles, and it can include deviant acts that are not technically criminal.

See also **Crime; Deviance.**

Democracy

D

This means rule by the people, but note that in the ancient Greek city-states where the term originated, 'the people' did not include women or slaves. Nowadays when democracy is claimed, 'the people' means all adult citizens (so non-nationals may be excluded, along with convicted criminals and the mentally insane). Unlike in the ancient city-states, the modern version is always representative democracy, and in western democracies the representation is by political parties.

The extent to which a society is truly democratic is normally judged (in the west) by whether all people are able to vote, and whether political parties are able to organise, disseminate their policies and campaign for election on equal terms. Some writers believe that this kind of political system is the one best suited to economically advanced societies with educated populations. They explain the spread of democracy in these terms, and predict it spreading worldwide.

See also **End of history; Lipset, S.M.; Politics.**

Arblaster, A. (1987), *Democracy*, Open University Press, Milton Keynes.

Demography

This is the study of populations and their composition (age, sex, marital status, ethnicity). The key statistics in demography are rates of fertility, mortality, marriage and migration.

Demonisation

An extreme set of labels applied to certain deviant acts and their perpetrators. The acts are considered especially abhorrent, awful, and the perpetrators are considered depraved, different from normal humans. Their presence, or even rumours of their presence, provokes public fear and panic. Examples include child murderers and paedophiles – categories of offenders who are at risk of serious violence from other prison inmates.

See also **Labelling theory; Moral panic.**

Denomination

See Sect.

Dependency culture

See Culture of poverty.

Dependency theory

Claims that the economic backwardness of some countries is not the result of their own failings but is a direct result of their exploitation by developed countries. Richer countries are said to have enslaved weaker countries' people, taken their raw materials, and required them to produce for the west rather than their own needs. In other words, the countries have been deliberately underdeveloped.

Critics point out that some originally poorer countries have now developed, and argue that the failure of others to do so must be at least partly due to their own characteristics.

See also **Colonialism; Development; World system theory.**

Frank, A.G. (1969), *Capitalism and Underdevelopment in Latin America*, Monthly Review Press, New York.

D

Deprivation

Not possessing something that one would like to have. The something may be food, housing, education, fashion clothing, emotional care ... anything. The concept is broader than poverty. A person can be multiply deprived. Like poverty, deprivation can be absolute or relative, but because the concept of deprivation itself incorporates a feeling of being deprived (of something one would like to have) there is always a subjective dimension.

The classic study of deprivation was by Samuel A. Stouffer (1900–1960) and colleagues, of the US soldier during the Second World War. This study found that feelings of deprivation depended on the individuals or groups (reference groups) with which comparisons were made, and because people tended to make comparisons with others close to themselves, there was only a weak relationship between objective inequalities and relative (to a reference group) deprivation, and therefore feelings of being deprived.

See also **Cultural deprivation; Poverty; Reference group; Relative deprivation.**

Stouffer, S., Suchman, E.A., DeVinney, L.C., Star, S.A. and Williams, R.M. Jr (1949), *The American Soldier, Vol. 1, Adjustment During Army Life,* Princeton University Press, Princeton, N.J.

Derrida, Jaques (1930–2004)

Derrida was an Algeria-born French philosopher who devised the idea of 'deconstruction' and inspired post-structural/postmodern trends throughout the humanities and social sciences, including sociology.

Derrida accepted Saussure's proposition that the meaning of any sign resides in the context, the surrounding 'text'. He believed that all evidence – all of which could be reduced or likened to speech or writing – could be treated as texts, and that no meaning could be discovered outside any text itself. However, contrary to the structuralists, he denied that language could be a carrier of unambiguous truth, or that texts could be given one correct, unambiguous, authoritative interpretation. Derrida argued that texts had to be 'deconstructed', which meant revealing the various ways in which they could be interpreted.

Derrida's ideas, if accepted, have enormous implications. They imply that the entire enlightenment/modernist project – which is said to have embarked on a search for final, ultimate truth – must be abandoned, that we must recognise that there can only be fictions, and that our thinking should advance into a postmodern era where we embrace rather than try to erase ambiguity and paradox.

Derrida has been most influential in literary criticism. In sociology his impact was to undermine the structuralist project which, he believed, was attempting unwarranted closure to what should be an open-ended search for meanings. He wanted to restore openness to language and thereby to thinking in all disciplines. Postmodern, post-structural sociology therefore abandons the search for *the* correct descriptions, explanations and theories.

D

It opens the door to various standpoint sociologies and recognition that there can be many equally plausible interpretations (all fictions, or with equal claims to truth) of any situation.

See also **Barthes, R.; Deconstruction; Post-structuralism; Postmodern; Texts.**

Derrida, J. (1978), *Writing and Difference,* Routledge, London.

Derrida, J. (1981), *Positions,* Athlone Press, London.

Deschooling

See Illich, I.

Development

Development studies, to which the sociology of development contributes, emerged after the Second World War. Countries were categorised into first world (capitalist, western), second world (communist) and third world. It was assumed that economic growth in the third world would lead to the countries becoming more like one of the more advanced types. Today the second world has disappeared. There is just one set of developed countries. Development studies now investigate how to trigger the economic growth that will transform underdeveloped countries.

The word 'development' is used in other contexts such as child development, and there has been a presumption in development studies that social change is analogous to human maturation. Since the 1960s this assumption has encountered fierce criticism. First, there is the assumption that all societies will follow the same evolutionary path. Second, it is argued that some countries became developed at the expense of others that remained undeveloped, and that the undeveloped countries are kept in this position through neo-colonial dependency relationships.

This means that the very concept of development has become controversial.

See also **Colonialism; Dependency theory; Evolution; Modernisation; Social change.**

Apter, D.E. (1987), *Rethinking Development: Modernization, Dependency and Postmodern Politics*, Sage, Newbury Park, Calif.

Deviance

Norm violation; departure from socially prescribed normality.

Deviance is broader than crime. The criminal law is just one set of rules. The use of foul language and heavy drinking may not be illegal but may still deviate from what is expected and required, and lead to sanctions (expressions of anger, maybe even ostracism) from families and peer groups, and dismissal from work organisations.

D

Both the law and other social norms vary by time and place. In recent decades there have been remarkable changes in some countries in attitudes towards cohabitation, homosexuality and smoking in public places.

It is of interest that sociology's main theories of crime are in fact applications of broader theories of deviance. A large part of the explanation for this is probably that laws are most likely to be obeyed when they accord with and are reinforced by the norms of a population. Deviance in general (crime is just one example) is usually explained in sociology in terms of the norms of particular subcultures differing from the norms of the groups that make the rules, and 'strain' that is created by a disjuncture between goals that all are encouraged to strive for and the legitimate means that are available. Other crossovers from deviance theory into criminology concern the effects of publicly labelling offenders as deviants, a societal reaction that may lead to deviance amplification, and the functionalist view that deviance is a necessary part of social life because a society where social control was 100 per cent effective would prevent welcome innovations, and in any case, infractions and the punishment of offenders are useful in enabling support for rules to be re-affirmed throughout a population.

See also **Crime; Criminology; Labelling theory; Strain theories.**

Dialectics, dialectical materialism

A two-sided interplay.

G.W.F. Hegel (1770–1831) believed that thought (and societies) developed through an idea (a thesis) being opposed (by an antithesis), which led to a synthesis, which became the new thesis, and the cycle was repeated.

Karl Marx (1818–1883), one of the young Hegelians, and his collaborator, Friedrich Engels (1820–1885), invented dialectical materialism by replacing Hegel's ideas with classes that possessed antagonistic interests due to their contradictory relationships to the means of production.

See also **Hegel, G.W.F.; Marx, K.**

D

Diaspora

A people who have been dispersed but who retain their original identity. The classic example is the Jews who became scattered around the world after their expulsion from Palestine in the fourth century BC.

As migration has become more common in modern times, many more diasporas have been created, and modern communications have simultaneously made it easier for dispersed people to retain contact with each other and with their homelands where they may continue to play an important political role.

See also **Migration.**

Digitisation/digitalisation

The process whereby data, text, sound and images are reproduced as digits (usually 0 and 1) while being scanned or otherwise input into computers, and can then be stored and transferred instantly all around the world by cable or wireless (using satellite links).

Every year more and more of humanity's information is digitised. This has already happened to nearly all recorded music, to over half a million films, and over 5 per cent of all text that has ever been written. The sheer quantity of information that can be stored in digital form, then accessed by anyone anywhere in the world who is online, has inspired talk of a knowledge economy, an information society and a digital age.

See also **Information economy/society; Knowledge economy/society.**

Dilthey, Wilhelm (1833–1911)

See Hermeneutics.

Discourse

A term associated with the French philosopher and sociologist Michel Foucault (1926–1984). A discourse is a way of talking and thinking: not any specific instances of speech or thought, but the discursive frameworks within which these are formulated.

Foucault argued that the discourses that are available in a society govern what can be thought and said. In this sense, he regarded discourses as the bedrock of social reality. Foucault also claimed that it is within discourses that we create objects including types of people and social roles. For example, it is only within a particular medical discourse that it becomes possible to conceive of, and for anyone to become, a patient. Sociological discourse enables us to identify objects such a social structures and social classes.

Even if discourses are not (regarded as) a bedrock, they clearly exist before individuals learn to talk and think. Discourses must thereby play a role in shaping our thoughts and related actions, and are therefore of interest to sociologists irrespective of whether all Foucault's claims are accepted.

See also **Foucault, M.**

D

Discrimination

This is a ubiquitous social process which becomes controversial, and therefore likely to be the subject of sociological enquiry, when there is dissensus over whether particular forms of discrimination are reasonable and justifiable, and especially when discrimination persists despite having been made illegal.

We discriminate throughout our daily lives. We do so when we decide whom we will befriend, whom we will date and consider as a live-in partner. Depending on the situation, we may discriminate on the basis of age, gender, religion, place of residence, lifestyle or whatever. The grounds on which we discriminate usually mean that we are discriminating for and against not just particular persons but entire categories of people. Most instances of discrimination are uncontroversial, though sociology often tries to make a problem out of what is ordinarily taken as perfectly normal, rational behaviour. For example, is it reasonable to discriminate on the basis of educational qualifications when awarding university places and in the labour market? Some types of discrimination have been made illegal in Britain and in many other countries. These include most acts of discrimination on the grounds of race, religion, age, gender and sexual orientation. There is invariably some controversy over what is acceptable and what should be outlawed. For example, despite strong protests, in 2007 faith organisations in Britain that wished to continue to do so lost their right to refuse to consider gay and lesbian couples as potential adopters.

Most sociological research into discrimination has sought to explain how and why, despite having been made illegal, discrimination (in the labour market, for example) continues against women and racial/ethnic minority groups. This research has distinguished a variety of ways in which discrimination can occur:

- The perpetrators may believe that they are acting rationally and justifiably.
- Alternatively they may be prejudiced, meaning that they pre-judge certain groups as unsuitable on irrational grounds. There is evidence that a particular personality type (the authoritarian personality) is especially prone to seek scapegoats for all problems and develop prejudices against groups other than their own.
- Institutionalised discrimination occurs when an individual is not personally prejudiced, but acts in discriminatory ways through conformity with the norms in an organisation or group to which he or she belongs. For example, it has been argued that a 'canteen culture' in police forces is institutionally racist, and that pre-judging young ethnic minority males as actual or potential offenders is accepted by individual officers as just normal practice. In 1999 the Macpherson Report of the inquiry into the murder in South London of Stephen Lawrence, a black teenage male, and the failure of the police to secure a conviction, accused the police of institutional racism, a charge subsequently accepted by many police authorities.
- Structural discrimination, or indirect discrimination, occurs, for example, when one group is less likely than others to possess a quality needed for equal treatment. For example, working class young people are less likely than middle class young people to be admitted to universities because of the former's inferior educational credentials. Giving preference to long-standing residents among applicants for social

housing is indirect discrimination against ethnic groups that are recent immigrants. In all such cases, the crucial issue becomes whether the ground on which discrimination occurs can be justified.

See also **Authoritarian personality; Positive discrimination; Prejudice; Scapegoat.**

Macpherson, S.W. (1999), *The Stephen Lawrence Inquiry*, HMSO, London.

Disenchantment

A term introduced into sociology by Max Weber (1864–1920). Disenchantment is a consequence of the rationalisation of the economy, government and social life. Mysteries disappear, everything can be explained rationally, controlled and organised, so life becomes routine, boring.

According to George Ritzer (1940–), rationalisation has now spread from work and politics into consumption, a process that he calls McDonaldization. A reaction to this has been a demand for spectacular displays and really enchanting films and TV series. So these are produced, rationally, which means that they soon become boring and routine, whereupon something even more outrageous must be offered, and so the cycle goes on.

See also **Rationalisation; Ritzer, G.; Weber, M.**

Ritzer, G. (1999), *Enchanting a Disenchanted World: Revolutionizing the Means of Consumption*, Pine Forge Press, Thousand Oaks, Calif.

Disorganised capitalism

A term used to describe the new capitalism that followed the organised, corporatist capitalism that existed in most western countries from the 1940s–1970s. Organised capitalism was regulated jointly by employer federations, trade unions and governments. Disorganisation is attributed to globalisation (national governments lose control), the adoption of neo-liberal economic policies, de-industrialisation which has involved the decline of the industries where the workforces were most thoroughly unionised, and the growth of employment in service sectors where establishments tend to be smaller. As 'social compacts' between labour and capital have been abandoned, state welfare protection has weakened.

See also **Capitalism; Corporatism; Neo-liberalism.**

Lash, S. and Urry, J. (1987), *The End of Organised Capitalism*, Polity Press, Cambridge.

D

Displaced persons

See Refugees.

Division of labour

This refers to the splitting of tasks into specialised roles that can be performed by different individuals. The division of labour is most easily illustrated in the economy, in workplaces, but sociologists extend the phrase into other domains such as the family, where there is usually a division of labour between husbands and wives (and, where they are present in a household, children and grandparents). Adam Smith (1723–1790) explained and approved of the advantages that can accrue through specialisation with individuals becoming highly proficient at the tasks on which they are able to concentrate, but he recognised that an extreme division of labour could lead to workers becoming bored, inattentive and disaffected.

Emile Durkheim (1858–1917), the sociologist, largely agreed with Adam Smith but had more to say. He believed that the division of labour undermined mechanical solidarity but could generate an alternative form of organic solidarity. However, he also believed that the division of labour could take pathological forms, namely, when it was 'forced' or when it became anomic.

See also **Anomie; Durkheim, E.; Scientific management; Smith, A.**

Divorce

The legal termination of a marriage where both partners are still alive and are free to remarry.

Divorce has become more common than in the past in most western countries. In Britain it is now estimated that 40 per cent of first marriages will be terminated while both partners are still alive. Alongside becoming more common, divorce has become more acceptable socially (lone parenthood is no longer a stigma), and also more affordable due to increased female employment rates. Divorce has risen alongside trends towards later marriage and pre-marital cohabitation. This indicates that marriage is now a more carefully considered decision than in the past. Yet more marriages fail. The explanation probably lies in rising expectations of conjugal relationships (partners expect love and companionship), and the financial feasibility of terminating a relationship. In other words, rising divorce rates may not indicate a decline in the quality of family life but partners becoming less willing to tolerate and more able to terminate relationships that are no longer experienced as fulfilling.

See also **Family; Marriage; Pure relationship.**

Domain assumption

See Axiom.

D

Domestic labour/Domestic division of labour

Domestic labour can have three entirely different meanings.

First, it can refer to employment and self-employment where work is done at home. Industrialisation relocated most paid work from homes to mines, factories and offices, but in recent times information technology (particularly the laptop computer and the Internet) have led to increased use of the home as a workplace. In order to distinguish this from other kinds of domestic labour, the alternative term 'home-based work' is often used.

Second, domestic labour can be paid work in someone else's home. This is also increasing after declining in the earlier stages of industrialism. There are more people earning livings as domestic cleaners, gardeners and nannies. This is a symptom of widening economic inequalities.

The third and most common meaning of domestic labour in sociology is unpaid housework (which may or may not be defined to include childcare and so-called emotional labour). The term 'domestic division of labour' always refers to unpaid housework. Sociologists are interested in the amounts of time spent on housework and childcare, and whose time is spent on these activities. Perhaps surprisingly, there has been no overall decline despite the spread of labour-saving domestic technology (washing machines, microwave ovens, dish washers etc). Rather, it appears that expected and actual standards of home and childcare have risen. Sociologists are equally if not more interested in the division of housework between males and females. Men are doing more than in the past, but women still do much more than men. Over the life course this is typically counter-balanced by men spending more time in paid employment. Fair deal? Not according to feminists who point out that this division of labour confines women to the private sphere and leaves them financially dependent on male partners.

Domination

See Power.

Dramaturgy

See Actor; Goffman, E.

Dual-career family

One of the terms coined in the 1960s and 1970s in response to rising rates of employment among married women. In the ideal typical dual-career family, the husband and wife have equal labour market careers and housework is also shared equally. An alternative term is 'symmetrical family'. Conjugal relationships in such families are supposedly between equal 'colleagues' or 'companions' rather than a traditional male breadwinner (whose primary role in the family is instrumental – earning its living) and a housewife (whose primary domestic roles are socio-emotional).

Even today, 40 years after the term dual-career family was first used, sociologists emphasise how rare genuine dual-career families are. Women are still far more likely than men to interrupt their labour market careers and work part time. Men in full-time jobs still tend to work longer hours and earn more than women with full-time jobs. Women with full-time jobs still do much more housework than their male partners and have much longer total work-weeks.

See also **Family; Symmetrical family**.

Rapoport, R. and Rapoport, R.N. (1971), *Dual Career Families,* Penguin, Harmondsworth.

Dual labour market

In practice there is not a single labour market. There is segmentation into different kinds of jobs and different kinds of workers (with different kinds and levels of qualifications, skills and experience). There is further segmentation into different local labour markets, and into different firms' internal labour markets. Dual labour market theory draws attention to a particularly stark division – between primary and secondary labour markets, jobs and workers.

In the primary sector jobs are typically full-time, permanent, skilled and well paid. In the secondary sector they are typically low skilled, low paid, often temporary and part time. Like jobs, workers become divided and the division between primary and secondary workers is likely to coincide with divisions by gender, ethnicity, age and place of residence.

It is claimed that recent and current trends in the economy (new technology, globalisation, deregulation) are widening this divide. Employers recruit, train and endeavour to retain primary workforces from whom they require functional flexibility which is supplied by continuous up-skilling, re-skilling and retraining. With secondary workforces numerical flexibility is sought, and pay levels and other terms and conditions are the lowest possible in prevailing labour market conditions. This divide is said to create separate strata of workers, localities, countries and world regions.

See also **Labour markets; Post-Fordism; Segmentation**.

Piore, M.J. and Sabel, C.F. (1984), *The Second Industrial Divide: Possibilities for Prosperity,* Basic Books, New York.

Dualism

Dualism states that there are irreducible differences between classes of phenomena.

One dualism that is relevant in sociology, and which is adopted by most sociologists, is the distinction between statements of fact and judgements of value.

D

Another famous (in philosophy) dualism is between mind and body, the mental and the material. Mind is a theoretical construct, a concept, that refers to mental faculties and processes – our thoughts, unconscious processes, and self-consciousness. René Descartes (1596–1650), the French philosopher, is regarded as the founding father of mind–body dualism. He based his philosophy on a principle of 'radical doubt' and concluded that the only certainty was, 'I think therefore I am', later extended to 'I am a mind'.

Sociology rarely engages in debates about mind–body dualism, but in practice sociology has always focused on the mind – on individuals' internal mental states, and relationships between people and groups have been conceptualised and researched as relationships between minds. A critical response in current sociology is to urge greater attention to the body.

See also **Body**.

Durkheim, Emile (1858–1917)

Durkheim is universally recognised as *a* founding father of modern sociology. He actually saw himself as *the* founding father. Auguste Comte (1798–1857) had invented the word 'sociology', but Durkheim was a professor of sociology and believed that he was setting the discipline on secure foundations. He wrote a set of methodological rules for sociologists to follow, as well as writing classic texts on the division of labour, suicide and religion.

In *The Rules of Sociological Method* Durkheim insisted that sociology should 'treat social facts as things'. Social facts were deemed to have an independent existence, external to individuals, and to have the power to regulate the conduct of individuals. Examples of Durkheimian social facts include crime rates and migration rates. Each social fact was to be explained by another social fact rather than by reducing social phenomena to individual behaviour and motivations.

Durkheim is regarded as a champion of positivism. He believed that sociological evidence should be collected by observation, and that analysis should proceed by identifying relationships between different sets of social facts.

In *Suicide* Durkheim illustrated his 'rules'. He explained variations in suicide rates by showing that these variations were related to other social facts. Suicide rates were found to be higher among Protestants than among Catholics and Jews, and higher among divorced people than among married people. What was the common denominator? Durkheim suggested that it was how tightly people were knit into social groups (religious or familial). However, he recognised another kind of altruistic suicide which could result from excessive integration, when individuals sacrificed their lives for the good of the social whole.

In *The Division of Labour in Society* Durkheim contrasted the ways in which social order was maintained in societies where the division of labour

D

was rudimentary and in societies where it was complex. The former type of societies were said to be bound together by 'mechanical solidarity': a powerful *conscience collective* (which translates into English simultaneously as collective consciousness and collective conscience) was outraged when rules were infringed, and society took revenge and exacted retributive justice. As the division of labour became more complex, the *conscience collective* was said to weaken (though it never disappeared completely) and people were bound together by 'organic solidarity' – their very interdependence became a moral force. Here the law operated on restitutive principles: individuals who offended were required simply to make good the damage done. Durkheim identified pathological forms of the division of labour. One was 'anomic', where relationships between roles were unclear and people could not see how they depended on each other. Another was the forced division of labour where people were forced into roles for which they were unsuited. Durkheim regarded these states of affairs as abnormal.

In *The Elementary Forms of Religious Life* Durkheim selected the totemic practices and beliefs of Australian aboriginals as religion's most elementary, simple form He proceeded to argue that the definitive feature of religious rites and objects was their sacredness – they were set apart from profane life, and were to be worshipped. Durkheim believed that totems (the core, elementary feature of all religions) actually represented a society itself, and that through collective worship individuals were submitting to their societies, strengthening solidarity, and maintaining order that could withstand all threats (from famine, war, earthquakes etc.).

As a result of his work on religion and the division of labour, Durkheim is regarded as a key source of functionalist perspectives in sociology as well as a champion of positivist methodology.

See also Anomie; Division of labour.

Durkheim, E. (1893, 1938), *The Division of Labour in Society*, Free Press, Glencoe.

Durkheim, E. (1895, 1938), *The Rules of Sociological Method*, Free Press, Glencoe.

Durkheim, E. (1897,1970), *Suicide: A Study in Sociology*, Routledge, London.

Durkheim, E. (1912, 1956), *The Elementary Forms of Religious Life*, Allen and Unwin, London.

D

Dysfunction

A term coined in functionalist sociology to classify activities that are socially harmful. However, functionalists have been ingenuous in identifying positive functions of crime, poverty, unemployment and the like. Meanwhile, conflict theorists and other opponents of functionalism always ask, 'Functional or dysfunctional for whom?'

See also Functionalism.

Dystopia

The opposite of utopia.

See Utopia.

D

Ee

Ecological fallacy

A term invented by the American sociologist William S. Robinson. The fallacy is the assumption that what applies at one level of aggregation will also apply at other levels. For instance, Britain is wealthier than Bangladesh, but it does not follow that every neighbourhood in Britain will be wealthier than every neighbourhood in Bangladesh, still less that every single Briton will be wealthier than every single Bangladeshi.

Robinson, W.S. (1950), 'Ecological correlations and the behaviour of individuals', *American Sociological Review*, 15, 351–7.

Ecology

This term was first used in the 1860s by the German biologist, Ernst Haekel (1834–1919), who at that time was studying plant life. Ecology explains the relative abundance and distribution of organisms within a territory in terms of interdependencies and competition for environmental resources. Haekel's contemporary, Charles Darwin (1809–1882) did not use the term, but employed exactly the same thinking in his theory of natural selection and the development of different species. Note that from the outset it was realised that certain plants and certain species were interdependent. So ecology became the study of how organisms interact and adapt to each other within their environments, thus producing a 'web of life'.

An ecological perspective was originally imported into sociology by the Chicago School between the world wars to explain the territorial distribution of different groups within cities and patterns of city growth. Their explanation was in terms of competition for space. The weakest groups (recent immigrant groups in Chicago at that time) became concentrated in unattractive inner-city zones of transition (where residential dwellings were being replaced by industry) while stronger groups enjoyed more space and generally better environmental conditions on the city outskirts.

Ecology has returned to sociology's agenda since the 1970s due to a heightened awareness of the interdependencies between human activities and the natural environment.

See also **Chicago School**.

Economic life/Economy

For lay people the economy is where they go to work and the sources of their incomes – the wages or salaries, rent or profits that they earn. Transfer payments from governments are funded by taxing other people's incomes. Sociologists define the economy in basically the same way except in insisting that work need not be paid work, and income need not be in money – it may be in goods, services or just gratitude. Productive economic activity creates value (objects and services that people value). Consumption is the obverse economic activity wherein value is depleted. Sociologists tend to say that they study 'economic life' rather than the economy, thereby distinguishing their broader perspective from that of economists.

Sociologists are interested in all kinds of productive activity. As well as work in the official economy there are black/grey/second economies, legal and illegal, where business is untaxed and unrecorded for official (government) purposes. Then there are various informal economies where work is unpaid (in cash). People work voluntarily for charities, trade unions, political parties, churches, sports clubs and so on. They also work for kin and neighbours (maybe in exchange for reciprocal favours), and we work for ourselves in our households when we prepare food, launder clothes, paint and decorate our houses. Sociologists are often sceptical about official statistics that record rates of economic growth. If instead of painting my own house I pay a neighbour to do the job, and if the neighbour declares the income for tax purposes, the economy will appear to have grown, but this will be without additional work being accomplished or value being created. To an unmeasured (and probably immeasurable) extent, the economic growth of the last century has been a statistical delusion resulting from a trend towards paying other people to do things that we once did for ourselves.

Sociologists are interested in the total picture and composition of economic life in their own societies. We know that government statistics grossly understate the total amount of work that is undertaken and value that is created. Sociologists are also interested in how economic systems have differed over time and between societies. Distinctions are made between subsistence economies (where most production is for households' own needs), command economies (where all or most economic activity is planned and controlled by the government) and market economies. Sociologists compare different social relationships within which work is done: waged or salaried labour for an employer, or for oneself or as a member of a workers' cooperative, serfdom (where peasants were tied to their land – in practice an owner's land – by law and custom), and slavery, for example.

A further set of interests concerns the relationships between the economy and society: how, on the one hand, particular social and cultural conditions foster particular forms of economic behaviour – modernisation, industrialisation, growth. Then, on the other hand, we are interested in how individuals' particular economic roles, specifically their occupations, affect the rest of their lives.

E

The economy is the concern of a specialist social science, economics, but it is also and has always been a core interest in sociology. Sociology and economics differ in sociology having the wider lens (taking account of more kinds of value-creating work), and also in their approaches to the official (narrower) economy. Economists work with mathematical models. One is of utility-maximising economic man from which predictions and deductions can be made about how particular actors will behave in given situations. Another set of models deals with the macro-economy and enables economists to predict, for example, all the ramifications of a rise or fall in interest rates. If sociologists start with theories these are more likely to be related concepts and ideas rather than mathematical models, but their preferred starting point is more likely to be examining how people actually behave.

See also **Capitalism; Employment; Work.**

Education

This is socialisation which takes place in specialised institutions (schools, colleges, universities). Education can be distinguished from training, where people are taught specific skills in order to perform particular tasks. In education the value of the skills and knowledge that are imparted is more open-ended and diffuse.

The creation of specialised educational institutions in modern societies is just one instance of a broader historical process of social differentiation. Another example is the way economic activity has been allocated to workplaces which are separate from people's homes.

Sociologists have identified, and concentrated their attention on, two key processes in education. First, socialisation – the transmission of (some of) a society's culture. Some skills and knowledge are taught to all children (typically the national language and history, and basic mathematics). Other parts are taught to particular groups depending on their social origins or other ascribed statuses (whether they are male or female, for example), or depending on their intended social destinations. In addition to what is formally taught, sociologists recognise that schools and classrooms as social organisations are important socialising milieux where children learn to behave as members of groups that are wider than their families, kin and neighbours.

Second, in all modern societies education plays an important part in role allocation, specifically allocation to occupational roles. Entry to more and more types of jobs has become dependent on possessing educational credentials (qualifications). Hence sociologists' interest in which social groups (social classes, sexes and ethnic groups) have access to different kinds of education, and which groups are the most likely to succeed when all are formally offered equal opportunities.

See also **Credentialism; Hidden curriculum; Socialisation; Sponsored (and contest) mobility.**

Efficacy

The ability to produce a given effect. Self-efficacy is the belief by a person that he or she has the capability to execute a course of action and achieve a desired outcome.

Social psychologists have shown that self-efficacy is related to being willing to take on a challenging task, to expend effort and to persist, and to a belief that one can control and shape one's own life.

Elaborated code

See Bernstein, B.

Elective affinity

See Weber, M.

Elias, Norbert (1897–1990)

A sociologist of German-Jewish origin, who left Germany when Hitler came to power, and taught at Leicester University from 1954–62. Elias's major work, *The Civilizing Process*, attracted little attention when first published (in German) in 1939, but after his formal retirement Elias remained an active sociologist, and by the time that an English translation was published in 1978 he had become something of a cult figure with enthusiastic bands of followers, mainly in Britain, the Netherlands and Germany. Elias discovered 'the civilising process' and invented figurational sociology.

Elias's supporters argue that *The Civilizing Process* places its author alongside the recognised founding fathers of sociology such as Marx, Durkheim and Weber (whose ideas Elias was able to incorporate and supersede). The core argument in the book is that over time western societies have become more civilised in that external controls over individuals have been replaced by internal controls of emotions and actions. Critics query whether external controls really have been relaxed, and point to the absence of any satisfactory explanation of the alleged historical master process.

Figurational sociology starts with an individual or group or a form of behaviour, then maps the surrounding, constantly changing, figuration of which it is a part. Figurational sociologists claim that this is entirely different from, and superior to, taking the individual, the social structure, or a whole society as the basic unit for analysis. Critics wonder whether the Elias way really is different from the orthodox sociological practice of setting any norm, actor, group or institution in its total social context.

Elias, N. (1939, 1978), *The Civilizing Process*, Blackwell, Oxford.

E

Elites

Elites are groups that head organisations and institutions. So we can speak of business elites, the political elite, academic elites and so on.

Elite theories were developed in the first half of the twentieth century as an alternative to class analysis by a number of European social scientists who argued that, albeit for somewhat different reasons, elite domination was inevitable. At that time these theories acted as both an explanation and justification for the rise of fascist regimes in several European countries (Italy, Germany, Austria, Spain and Portugal). Gaetano Mosca (1858–1941), an Italian political scientist, argued that rulers' superior organisation always gave them an advantage over disorganised masses. Wilfredo Pareto (1848–1923), another Italian, argued that circulation into and out of elites was necessary and inevitable. Incumbent elites had either to absorb talent from below or face overthrow, but rule by elites was inevitable. Robert Michels (1876–1936), a German, authored the iron law of oligarchy – 'Who says organisation says oligarchy'. He argued that even left-wing democratic political parties inevitably succumbed to oligarchy. This was due to incumbent leaders acquiring organisational knowledge and skills that made it far easier for them to secure democratic confirmation in office than for challengers from the rank-and-file to mobilise support. Michels also claimed that over time left-wing political parties tended to be de-radicalised as their leaders' lifestyles and their experiences consorting with other elites resulted in their embourgeoisement.

Despite their historical associations with authoritarian regimes, these arguments have been tacitly accepted in sociology. Since the Second World War, interest has centred on whether different elites countervail against each other (the orthodox view of how market economies and Western democracies work) or whether, as C. Wright Mills (1916–1962) claimed had happened in the United States by the 1950s, different elites merge to form a single power elite or ruling class.

See also; **Democracy; Michels, R.; Mills, C.W.; Pareto, W.; Stratification.**

Michels, R. (1962), *Political Parties*, Free Press, New York.

Mills, C.W. (1956), *The Power Elite,* Simon and Schuster, New York.

Mosca, G. (1939), *The Ruling Class*; McGraw-Hill, New York.

Pareto, W. (1973), *The Mind and Society: A Treatise on General Sociology*, Dover, New York.

Emancipatory sociology

Originally, emancipation meant the collective freeing of a slave population. Today the label is claimed by sociologists who regard themselves as intellectual powerhouses of comparable projects. Sub-types of feminist theory, queer theory and post-colonial theory claim to promote identities and worldviews that will emancipate the oppressed.

Auguste Comte (1798–1857), who invented the term sociology, believed that once people understood the laws of social statics and dynamics they would be able to take charge and become masters of their lives. Karl Marx (1818–1883) believed that his theory would empower the proletariat in destroying capitalism and creating a classless society in which alienation would be vanquished and control would be handed to the masses. Sociological research into social problems has always been inspired by the conviction that understanding and explanation will lead to control and social improvement. In nurturing such aspirations sociology can be regarded as part of a longer-running enlightenment project with its belief in reason's capacity to change the world for the better.

During the twentieth century many sociologists came to realise that none of this was actually happening. Instead of liberating the masses, mainstream sociology (and other social and natural sciences) were criticised for having become servants of power. Thus the emancipatory label was claimed by sociologists who thereby distinguished themselves from (allegedly) conservative colleagues. The founding father from whom emancipation sociologists have drawn most inspiration is, of course, Karl Marx, but in formulating their brand of critical theory the Frankfurt School realised that Marxism needed to be developed (radically). Today, the German sociologist Jurgen Habermas (1929–) sees himself as working in a direct line of descent, but it is the sociologies of and for the oppressed of the earth (women, gays, post-colonial people) that speak loudest about emancipation.

They now have a new opposition from two rather different streams of postmodernist thought. The first sees the embrace of the global market economy and consumer capitalism as so suffocating that no effective resistance is possible. The second argues that the entire modernist or enlightenment project has run its course, manifestly failed, and that the only rational response is to abandon faith in reason.

See also **Critical sociology/Critical theory; Enlightenment; Feminism; Habermas, J.; Post-colonial theory; Queer theory; Standpoint theory.**

Embourgeoisement

Middle class aspirations, lifestyles and identities spreading downwards into the working class.

The embourgeoisement thesis was at the centre of a major debate in British sociology in the 1950s and 1960s. Several trends were said to be responsible. Foremost was affluence which enabled workers to become home owners, to take overseas holidays and purchase consumer goods such as televisions, motor cars and washing machines. Embourgeoisement was also believed to be aided by the changing character of working class jobs: increasingly in service sectors rather than manufacturing and extractive industries, while automation was removing the physical effort that had been a prime value in masculine workplace and neighbourhood cultures Supporters of the embourgeoisement thesis included Ferdynand Zweig

(1896–1988). Opponents such as John H. Goldthorpe (1935–) and his colleagues claimed that an affluent worker was just an affluent worker, not necessarily a middle class worker.

> See also **Affluent worker.**

Goldthorpe, J.H., Lockwood, D., Bechhofer, F. and Platt, J. (1969), *The Affluent Worker in the Class Structure,* Cambridge University Press, Cambridge.

Zweig, F. (1961), *The Worker in an Affluent Society*, Heinemann, London.

Emigration

See Migration.

Emotion

See Affect.

Emotional labour

See Aesthetic labour.

Empathy

Feeling, thinking and experiencing what others are feeling, thinking and experiencing. The concept is similar to sympathy, but in empathy accuracy is all-important; sincerity in sympathy.

In sociology, empathy, taking on the role of another, is regarded as a crucial social process, a skill that is required to participate in the everyday life of any society. Empathy is also a research method that is used in interpretive sociology.

> See also **Hermeneutics; *Verstehen*.**

E

Empirical, empiricism

An empirical statement is based on sensory evidence, usually sight or hearing in sociology. Empiricism is a doctrine which insists that the only true knowledge is based on sensory experience. This was the view of the enlightenment philosophers David Hume (1711–1776) and John Locke (1632–1704).

In present-day sociology these labels are sometimes applied as terms of approval and sometimes indicate disapproval. Someone who states that his of her own evidence is empirical is likely to be expecting approval for avoiding untested claims. However, when applied to the work of others the intention may be to criticise the research for its atheoretical character – mere head counting and number crunching. Yet in principle there is no incompatability between doing empirical research, even being an empiricist, and formulating and testing theories, and all enquiries that are not purely theoretical are at least quasi-empirical.

Most sociological research which is described as empirical should really be classed as quasi-empirical. Researchers may directly observe what people do and say in natural situations but they are more likely to rely on people's reports (in interviews and questionnaires) on how they behave and what they believe. If the concept of empirical is stretched sufficiently (to include evidence from books and articles which report other people's findings) then all the evidence dealt with in sociology becomes empirical: there is no non-empirical evidence.

See also **Positivism.**

Employment

A social relationship within which work can be organised. An employer hires labour power (which is sold as a commodity) for a stipulated period of time (hours of work) or to accomplish specified tasks. This is different from serfdom, which is a lifelong relationship, and slavery, where the slave (not just his or her labour power) is the property of the owner and the slave's entire life is at the owner's disposal.

In all modern societies a great deal of work continues to be undertaken outside employment. Nevertheless, employment has become the central way (in the economy and in people's everyday lives) in which work is organised. Employment has two features that make it efficient, effective and acceptable. First, it is flexible: an employee can quit or be dismissed at the end of a contract, or for failing to fulfil contracted duties, or due to redundancy (the labour no longer being required). Second, there is the personal freedom which allows employees to change jobs, and to live their own lives once their work is done.

See also **Economy; Labour markets; Work.**

E

Enculturation

This term is synonymous with socialisation, and the latter term is normally used in sociology. Enculturation is part of the vocabulary of cultural anthropology and refers to individuals acquiring the patterns of thought and behaviour that are prescribed by a culture.

See also **Socialisation.**

End of history

This thesis was an early response to the collapse of communism between 1989 and 1991. There appeared to be no alternatives to the global, capitalist market economy and multi-party democracy, which therefore seemed destined to spread throughout the world without encountering serious opposition. Thus Francis Fukuyama (1952–), an American philosopher and political economist, predicted 'the end of history' (albeit while expressing major caveats).

This thesis was soon wilting due to:

- an apparent 'clash of civilisations' (primarily Islam versus the west)
- China, Russia and some central Asian states developing managed versions of the market economy and democracy
- environmental issues provoking a search for alternative ways of living.

See also **Clash of civilisations; End of ideology.**

Fukuyama, F. (1992), *The End of History and the Last Man,* Penguin, London.

End of ideology

This phrase was coined by Daniel Bell (1919–), an American sociologist, commenting on trends in politics and economic affairs in western countries following the Second World War.

Before 1939 there had been fierce ideological battles between defenders of capitalism, socialists and fascists. Many employers had been anti-union: the trade unions were seen as part of a movement that was seeking to destroy the employer class. By the 1950s an era of relative tranquillity seemed to have dawned. Employers were accepting trade unions in collective bargaining arrangements. Governments, employers and trade unions were collaborating in tripartite macro-economic management. The 'right' was accepting a role for the state in macro-economic management and in the provision of welfare services. Meanwhile the 'left' was accepting the permanence of 'mixed' economies (part capitalist and part state-owned and controlled). In Britain the 1950s and 1960s are recalled, and were experienced at the time, as an age of consensus politics.

Has the end of ideology thesis stood the test of time? There have been renewed ideological disputes between a neo-liberal new right and defenders of the old consensus. On the other hand, communist systems have collapsed, inspiring an 'end of history' thesis. However, some predict a future 'clash of civilisations' (Christian, Islamic etc.).

See also **Clash of civilisations; Convergence thesis; End of history; Industrialisation.**

Bell, D. (1960), *The End of Ideology*, Collins, New York.

Endogamy/exogamy

Endogamy means marriage within a group. The opposite, exogamy, is marriage outside a group. The group may be a family lineage, a class, a religion, or an ethnic or any other group. Endogamous or exogamous practices

E

may simply be statistically the most common, preferred, or prescribed by custom, religion or law.

See also **Family**; **Marriage**.

Engels, Friedrich (1820–1895)

Engels was a co-founder of the body of theory and social movement known as Marxism.

Engels was from a wealthy family of German textile manufacturers, whose business took him to Manchester. By that time he was already a socialist. During the early 1840s he published a critique of the capitalist market economy and was working on his major book, *The Condition of the Working Class in England*. This work brought him to the attention of Karl Marx (1818–1883). Thereafter they collaborated and jointly created Marxism.

Throughout his adult life, Engels was active in international socialist movements through which he disseminated and popularised Marxism. It could be due to Engels' success as a disseminator that the body of theory and related socio-political movements have subsequently been known as Marxism rather than Engelism or Marxism-Engelism. Engels was a collaborator and financial supporter of Marx, but Engels' independent contributions to Marxism (as a body of theory and as a social movement) should not be underestimated. Apart from his major book on the condition of the English working class, which was based mainly on evidence gathered in Manchester and Salford, Engels wrote the first Marxist account of the family and gender relations, he coined the terms historical materialism and dialectical materialism, and made Marxism into a uni-linear theory of evolution.

See also **Marx**; **Marxism**.

Engels, F. (1845/1958), *The Condition of the Working Class in England*, Blackwell, Oxford.

Enlarged family

See Extended family.

Enlightenment

This term describes the period of intense intellectual activity in Europe from the seventeenth century to the early nineteenth century. It was characterised by a willingness to challenge all traditions (including religion) and an espousal of rational enquiry (hence the alternative title, the Age of Reason) as a basis for ordering human affairs.

The main centres of the enlightenment were France and Scotland. In France the major enlightenment figures were René Descartes (1596–1650), Voltaire (1694–1788), Montesquieu (1689–1755), Denis Diderot (1713–1784) and Jean-Jacques Rousseau (1712–1788). The latter coined the phrase,

E

'Liberty, Equality, Fraternity', the aspiration of the French Revolution (1789–99) and which still strikes chords in French national culture. The ideas of the French enlightenment philosophers were not *the* cause of the French Revolution – anger on the streets of Paris played the major role – but the philosophers had done much to undermine legitimacy and confidence amongst those in power under the *ancien regime*.

The Scottish enlightenment did not lead to a revolution. Rather, it was associated temporally with economic progress and major achievements in literature, architecture and engineering. Its leading philosophers were Adam Smith (1723–1790) (still acclaimed today as the founder of free market economics), David Hume (1711–1776), William Robertson (1721–1793), Adam Ferguson (1723–1816) and John Millar (1735–1801).

There is no dispute that the achievements of enlightenment philosophy (not least freeing reason from tradition and religious dogma) were linked to the development of sociology in nineteenth-century Europe. However, the nature of this link is currently controversial. One view, subscribed to by the Frankfurt School and currently enjoying wider popularity, is that the creation and subsequent development of sociology can be regarded as part of an enlightenment (or modernist) project which aspired to use human reason to improve the human condition and emancipate humanity by making people masters rather than subjects of the conditions in which they lived. Postmodernists claim that this project has run its course and has manifestly failed, and that this realisation propels us into a postmodern age. An alternative view is that sociology developed primarily as a response to the political upheavals in France in the revolution (1789–1799), then throughout Europe in the nineteenth century, and to the changes associated with industrialisation and urbanisation; that sociology derived its mission from the fact that these transformations were not rationally planned but were driven (so it appeared) by hidden forces which sociology sought to identify; and that doing this required a scientific approach in which reason operated on evidence rather than ideas alone.

See also **Smith, A.**

Entrepreneur

In economics an entrepreneur is an actor who brings together the other factors of production (land, labour and capital), produces and markets a good or service, thereby takes risks, and expects or hopes to make a profit. Such an entrepreneur can be a person, a large company (and its owners), or an investment fund (and its investors). Sociological interest in these entrepreneurs has been primarily about how to locate the petit bourgeoisie and the very wealthy in the class structure.

The term entrepreneur has its origins in economics, but it can also be applied to moral entrepreneurs (who campaign against pornography, for example), social entrepreneurs who create businesses under public or cooperative ownership, political entrepreneurs who found new political parties or pressure groups, and community entrepreneurs who mobilise local groups for or against the presence of CCTV cameras, and for or against new road building, for example. How social movements are initially brought into existence is a still neglected topic in sociology.

See also **Social movements.**

Environment

Environment means surroundings. In sociology it has usually meant all that is not hereditary.

However, during recent decades, as the world has become aware of natural environmental limits to growth, the depletion of the natural resources on which our lifestyles are based, and the threat of climate change and other such catastrophes, more attention has been paid to the relationship between human societies and the global natural environment. It has always been accepted that the natural environment influences human activities, and that the latter make an environmental impact. A (natural) environmental sociology has been slow to develop, probably because this is already the core interest of another discipline, geography.

See also **Ecology.**

Episteme

See Foucault, M.

Epistemology

The study of knowledge, a branch of philosophy. The core issue in epistemology is what it is possible to know to be true. Historically in philosophy the big debate has been between rationalists (who say that truth claims need to be grounded in reason) and empiricists (for whom true statements must be based on observation).

Whether we realise this or not, all sociological arguments rest upon an epistemological position, our domain assumptions or axioms.

See also **Axiom; Ontology.**

E

Esping-Andersen, Gosta (1947–)

A Danish sociologist who invented a subsequently widely used classification of welfare states according to:

- degree of de-commodification, that is, the extent to which welfare services are withdrawn from the market and publicly funded
- whether benefits are provided universally (to all in a social category, such as everyone who is retired from employment) as opposed to means-tested.

Three welfare regimes were thereby distinguished:

- Social democratic: highly de-commodified and universal benefits (the best examples are the Scandinavian countries).
- Conservative-corporatist: high de-commodification but benefits are not universal – they depend on type of occupation and contributions paid (France and Germany are examples).
- Liberal: highly commodified with means-tested benefits for the needy (as in the United States).

A fourth type of regime, where welfare is left primarily to the family, may be added (southern European countries being examples).

Using this typology, the UK was once close to the social democratic type, but has moved in a liberal direction.

See also **Social policy; Welfare state.**

Esping-Andersen, G. (1990), *The Three Worlds of Welfare Capitalism,* Princeton University Press, New Jersey.

Essence, essentialism

An essence is the essential property or characteristic that lies behind specific appearances and enables us to recognise a family, a woman, a social class, a democracy and so on. Once we have identified essences, it is said that we can define things correctly and classify correctly phenomena that we encounter.

There are probably no essentialists in present-day sociology. Social classes or families, for example, are treated as social constructs rather then springing from essences. Definitions are not treated as essentially right or wrong but as proposals or agreements to use words in particular ways, which turn out to be more or less useful.

See also **Social construction.**

Estates

A system of social stratification that existed in pre-modern Europe and Russia. There were similar systems in China and Japan. Estates were defined by law and were created politically.

The main estates in Europe were clergy, nobility and commoners. The latter could be divided into peasants and city dwellers. Each estate had its own political representation (or none), was subject to its own laws and had its own courts. There were ranks within estates, and each had a prescribed way of life which could include detailed rules of etiquette. Mobility was possible (the clergy was an open estate – Roman Catholic clergy were not allowed to marry), but estates were less open than modern classes.

See also **Feudalism; Stratification.**

Esteem

See Status.

Ethics

A branch of philosophy which seeks principles whereby we can determine how people ought to behave and more generally what ought to be. Societies, churches, professions and other groups may have their own ethics, which may or may not be written down and enforced by prescribed sanctions.

Sociologists study the ethics of their subjects, though except where there are written ethical codes, ethical principles usually have to be inferred from the more specific values and moral rules that people are aware of and observe.

The conventional view in sociology throughout the twentieth century and subsequently has been that the discipline deals with questions of fact and does not seek to make value judgements. However, it has been acknowledged that this does not make sociology completely value free because decisions about what to study and how evidence is interpreted are likely to be influenced by sociologists' own values. Nowadays most universities and professional associations in sociology (including the British Sociological Association) have ethical codes that members are expected or required to observe in their teaching and research.

See also **Morals; Value freedom/neutrality; Values.**

Ethnic

Ethnic groups see themselves, and may be seen by others, as distinctive in sharing a common history (real or imagined) plus other cultural commonalities, usually some combination of religion, language, dress and food preferences.

Sociologists today usually prefer to describe groups as ethnic (purely cultural formations) rather than races (which has biological connotations). Ethnicity, since it is learnt, is more fluid. New ethnicities are always being formed. Recent examples include Blacks, Latinos in the United States, and the various hyphenated ethnicities such as Irish-Americans. In contrast, the Jews are an ancient ethnic group. Ethnicity can also be multi-layered. For example, someone can be English, British and European. Which ethnicities are foregrounded in people's identities and social interaction can change over time, and according to the situation. Someone from Britain, France or Germany may well feel most European when in the United States. Unlike nations, ethnic groups do not necessarily achieve or even aspire to statehood.

A current debate in sociology concerns whether ethnicity is declining or rising in importance. Is globalisation creating a worldwide melting pot and

E

will an outcome be an undivided humanity? Or will more frequent and more intense interaction increase sensitivity to ethnic differences? A further debate is whether ethnicity is becoming the new racism. It may be illegal and socially unacceptable to discriminate on racial grounds, but what about dislike of ethnic cultures (which can be changed), and ethnic identities over which individuals may have some choice? Some ethnic cultures condone or require circumcision and restricted forms of dress. Are these legitimate grounds for criticism, objections to immigration and negative discrimination?

See also **Discrimination; Nation; Race.**

Bulmer, M. and Solomos, J. (eds) (1999), *Ethnic and Racial Studies Today*, Routledge, London.

Song, M. (2003), *Choosing Ethnic Identity*, Polity Press, Cambridge.

Ethnocentrism

This means more than just seeing things from the perspective of one's own group (which is probably inevitable). Ethnocentrism also means making judgements about others by applying a group's own standards, regarding one's own culture as superior, and therefore mistrusting people from other cultures. All of these are regarded as cardinal sins when practising sociology, though in other circles they may well be regarded as virtues.

For over 50 years researchers have investigated whether ethnocentrism is associated with a particular personality type (the authoritarian personality). Rather less attention has been paid to whether some cultures are less ethnocentric than others and, if so, why.

See also **Authoritarian personality; Xenophobia.**

Ethnography

Detailed first-hand study, often by participant observation, of a subculture, a group or even a small society. The researcher aims to immerse himself or herself in the lives of the people being studied. This has been the basic research method in social anthropology, but it is also used widely in sociology; in community studies and studies of youth subcultures, for example.

See also **Anthropology; Participant observation.**

Ethnomethodology

This approach to sociology was founded in the 1960s by the American sociologist, Harold Garfinkel (1917–). The word 'ethnomethodology' is meant to be construed literally. It means the study of the methods that people, ordinary members of society, use to decide and agree upon what is happening around them, what is 'actually the case', and thereby succeed in living their daily lives.

E

Ethnomethodology claims to apply the definition of sociology's subject matter offered by phenomenology. Here the bedrock of all social life is said to reside within people's minds, in their 'natural attitudes', their ordinary everyday outlooks on things. Phenomenology notes that orderly life is possible only if people can agree on 'what is actually the case'. How can sociology explore how this agreement is achieved?

Ethnomethodologists have developed two distinctive research methods. One is to disrupt ordinary life. For example, Garfinkel asked his students to go home and act as if they were lodgers. Another experiment was to engage strangers in conversation then ask repeatedly, 'What do you mean?' The victims in these experiments typically became angry, annoyed and distressed to find that assumptions they had taken for granted were not shared, and thereby (it is claimed) revealed what was ordinarily just taken for granted.

The second method pioneered by ethnomethodology, specifically by Harvey Sacks (1935–1975), is conversation analysis. Conversations are usually tape-recorded and transcribed which enables analysts to pore over them endlessly. Ethnomethodologists are interested not in the content of conversations but rather the 'rules' whereby conversations are kept orderly: how people 'take turns' to speak, how they indicate when a turn is ending and when a conversation is complete. In the process of conversation analysis, ethnomethdologists have re-discovered a basic sociological premise – meaning depends on context. The meaning of a word or phrase depends on its place in a conversation. In ethnomethodology this 'situatedness' is called 'indexality'.

Ethnomethodology always was and remains a small and somewhat esoteric movement in sociology, though one of its methods, conversation analysis, has been absorbed into the mainstream. Critics accuse ethnomethodologists of investigating trivia and ignoring the big issues of class, exploitation and so on. Ethnomethodologists reply that they are filling the core that is absent from other sociological accounts. They claim to be addressing a big central sociological problem – the problem of order, how it is established and how it is maintained. Ethnomethodologists claim that mainstream sociology, despite its pretensions, takes order for granted and fails to see how ordinary members of society, in the course of their ordinary everyday lives, are involved in the maintenance of order.

Ethnomethodology can be turned onto sociology itself and, indeed, onto any scientific discipline. A contention of phenomenology is that a scientific outlook is just one instance of a 'natural attitude'. So ethnomethodologists are interested in how sociologists (and physicists, medical doctors etc.) agree on what is actually the case and establish rules of enquiry, debate and for resolving disputes.

See also **Garfinkel, H.; Phenomenology.**

Garfinkel, H. (1967), *Studies in Ethnomethodology*, Prentice Hall, Engelwood Cliffs, N.J.

Sharrock, W. and Anderson, R. (1986), *The Ethnomethodologists*, Tavistock, London.

E

Ethology

Studies of animal behaviour where the findings are meant to be extrapolated to humans. When similarities are noted between human and animal behaviour, the inference is that the behaviour is instinctive.

There has been, and there still is a large popular audience for ethology, but most sociologists take the view that we can learn little about human society from this kind of research or from socio-biology (a kindred type of enquiry).

See also **Socio-biology**.

Eugenics

This term was invented by Francis Galton (1822–1911), and eugenics became an influential social movement in the first half of the twentieth century. It sought to improve the human race by selective breeding. Financial support was advocated to encourage intelligent adults to have children. The fertility of the mentally and physically defective was to be controlled by compulsory sterilisation or their confinement in sex-segregated institutions.

These practices, which were used by, but not only by, the Nazi regime in Germany, became unacceptable after the Second World War. The term eugenics is now tainted. However, some eugenic practices have become acceptable and increasingly common. For example, genetic testing in the womb makes it possible to abort foetuses with physical defects. Sperm donors can be selected on the basis of physical and mental fitness. In some parts of the world (China and India) abortion is used (unofficially) to enable parents to have a child of the sex that they prefer (the outcome is an excess of male births).

See also **Social Darwinism**.

Galton, F. (1869, 1892), *Hereditary Genius*, Macmillan, London.

European Household Panel Survey

See British Household Panel Survey.

Event history analysis

A way of analysing life history data in which the primary unit for examination is not the individual or a group of individuals but a type of event such as marrying, divorcing, leaving full-time education, becoming unemployed.

Advances in data storage and computer software have facilitated the development and use of this technique. Once a type of event has been isolated, investigators can ask about its antecedents and sequels, and how these differ between social groups, societies, by life-stage and over historical time.

Evolution, evolutionary theory

Evolution means simply that something developed out of something else rather than being created ready-made. This was a contentious idea in the nineteenth century when it was applied to plants and animals. The Christian churches had taught that God created the different species separately. The evolutionists won that argument, though creationists and intelligent design theorists are currently fighting a rearguard action, with some success in the 'court' of public opinion in the United States. By the end of the nineteenth century Charles Darwin's (1809–1882) explanation of evolution was generally accepted: species evolved by becoming better adapted to their environments through a struggle for life in which the fittest survived.

During its birth sociology was influenced profoundly by these evolutionary theories. All the major sociological theories of that time were theories of evolution. European societies were changing dramatically, and this process could be likened to the evolution of plant and animal organisms. The evolutionary theories of the nineteenth century incorporated what now appear to be naïve if not foolish assumptions:

- Industrial societies had evolved from feudal societies, which was true, but exactly how? There had been no process of natural selection.
- Nevertheless, it was assumed that the latest products of societal evolution were the best, the highest, the most advanced, and that evolutionary change could be equated with progress.
- It was assumed that all societies would travel along the same evolutionary path, though in the world of nature evolution has created a vast variety of species.
- It was assumed that a society's evolutionary path could be projected into the future.

Functionalist sociologists including Talcott Parsons (1902–1979) have continued to argue that there is a single evolutionary path, which is towards ever greater structural and functional differentiation, and that this trend does leave societies better adapted to their environments. However, most sociologists have abandoned the idea of a single path of change, along with attempting to predict the future. Twentieth-century sociology predicted neither the world wars nor the collapse of communism.

Today sociologists are more likely to study specific changes – economic development in less developed countries, and the transition from communism in eastern Europe, for example. Laws of evolution are no longer sought: they have been replaced by the softer notion of path dependence, meaning that a society's current condition has evolved from and remains influenced in some ways and to some extent by its condition in the past.

See also Path dependence; Progress; Social change.

E

Exchange theory

Proposes that social conduct is based on giving and receiving, governed by a universal norm of reciprocity, and that individuals give and receive in order to maximise their personal gratifications (as in economic exchange). Exchange is said to be the most elementary social relationship on which larger social formations are built.

Exchange theory enjoyed a wave of popularity in American sociology in the 1960s, then encountered criticisms. There remain different views in sociology on whether the theory is able to handle the criticisms:

- How can the theory explain altruism? Exchange theorists argue that altruism is rewarded by gratitude and goodwill which can be drawn on in the future.
- Much behaviour is governed by tradition and custom, or is just routine: people do not normally calculate the benefits of their actions. Exchange theorists argue that tradition, custom and the like simply institutionalise exchange terms and conditions that all parties have found, and continue to find, beneficial.
- Exchange theory may work when there are just two persons, but can it handle larger networks? Supporters say that networks are created and maintained because for all participants the personal gratifications exceed the personal costs of their contributions.
- Can the theory explain power and inequality? Exchange theorists say that power accrues to whichever party gains least in the short term from a two-way relationship. For example, the costs to an employee of dismissal are likely to outweigh the costs to the employer if an employee quits (and can be easily replaced). Inequalities are said to benefit in the long run those who accumulate power.

Rational choice theory, which also borrows from economic thought, is an alternative to, and is currently more popular in sociology than, exchange theory.

See also **Rational choice theory; Reciprocity.**

Blau, P.M. (1964), *Exchange and Power in Social Life*, Wiley, New York.

Homans, G.C. (1961), *Social Behaviour: Its Elementary Forms*, Harcourt Brace, New York.

E

Existentialism

The existentialist project is the systematic investigation of the nature of human existence which, in most existentialist accounts, seems to be pervaded by loneliness, despair and death coupled with feelings of moral responsibility and inescapable choices. The 'stars' of existentialism are Soren Kierkegaard (1813–1855), Friedrich Nietzsche (1844–1900), Martin Heidegger (1889–1976), Jean-Paul Sartre (1905–1980) and Maurice Merleau-Ponty (1908–1961).

Existential sociology combines the above concerns with a theoretical grounding in phenomenology. It studies people in natural settings and, unusual in sociology, incorporates human feelings into its accounts.

Up to now almost all of the small number of existential sociologists have been based in the United States

Kotarba, J.A. and Johnson, J.M. (eds) (2002), *Postmodern Existential Sociology*, Altamira Press, Lanham, Md.

Exogamy

See Endogamy.

Experiment

Experiments are associated with scientific laboratories where a change is introduced to an organism or substance and the effects are observed. When the subjects are humans (as in medical research), control groups (where no change is made or to whom placebos are administered) may be used to check for any changes that are independently occurring among the subject populations and for experimenter effects (called Hawthorne effects in sociology).

For ethical and practical reasons, sociologists' ability to experiment is limited except in small group research where laboratories can be used, but a problem with such experiments is that the experimental conditions are unlikely to resemble real life, and context can be an important influence on social behaviour.

However, it is sometimes possible to simulate experiments. For example, the effects of different teaching methods may be observed in otherwise similar schools. Alternatively, in quantitative research with large numbers of cases, experimental techniques can be simulated through multivariate analysis.

See also **Action research; Hawthorne effect; Multivariate analysis.**

Extended family

All socially recognised kin (relatives) as well as the nuclear family of sexually relating adults and their dependent children. Extended families include grandparents, aunts, uncles, cousins, nieces and nephews and anyone else who is recognised as a relative. Members of an extended family may or may not live together. When a household includes other (non-nuclear) kin, the family is called 'enlarged'. In some societies the boundaries of extended families have merged into larger kinship groups.

Membership of the extended family (who is socially recognised) varies from society to society and time to time, and can also vary between families in a society at a particular time. The conventional view in sociology is that extended families become weaker when societies modernise, which requires geographical and social mobility, and some former functions of the extended family such as childcare and care of the elderly are transferred to

E

other institutions. However, all the relevant studies have found that extended families remain important in modern times. For example, young couples often depend considerably on support from relatives when establishing their own households and bringing up their own children. The change over time seems to be that extended family relationships have become optional, activated according to convenience, need and interpersonality congeniality. Thus it may be more accurate to speak of the modern extended family as 'modified' rather than 'weakened'.

See also **Family**; **Kinship**.

Therborn, G. (2004), *Between Sex and Power: Family in the World, 1900–2000*, Routledge, London.

E

Factor analysis

A family of statistical techniques for reducing an initially large number of variables to a smaller number of variables that are called factors. Factor analysis starts with a correlation matrix in which all of the separate variables are correlated with one another. Factor analysis then seeks the minimum number of factors that will account adequately for the correlations in the matrix. The investigator then inspects the items that load onto each factor, and on this basis gives the factor a name.

Factor analysis is used most frequently with attitude variables. If it is discovered that attitudes towards capital punishment, sexual morality and strikes in industry all correlate positively, the underlying factor might be labelled social authoritarianism.

See also **Cluster analysis; Correlation.**

False consciousness

A Marxist concept which describe a situation where workers fail to perceive their real interests (as identified by Marxists). Marxists offer a variety of explanations for the failure of the working class to develop the kind of revolutionary consciousness that Marx predicted.

Non-Marxist sociologists are usually critical of the implied dismissal of workers' actual views. Most sociologists claim knowledge superior to everyday common sense. However, non-Marxists have been more likely to treat existing forms of consciousness as phenomena to be described accurately and explained rather than criticised and changed.

See also **Gramsci, A.; Hegemony; Ideology; Lukacs, G.; Marx, K.; Marxism.**

Family

Family sociology has produced a vast vocabulary. The nuclear family comprises a sexually relating couple and their dependent children (birth children, adopted children and step-children). An extended family includes all other kin who are socially recognised as family. In modern societies the nuclear family is the normal residential unit. If other relatives are present the family household is described as enlarged. When two or more nuclear families live together the family household is called conjoined.

The nuclear family is claimed to be the sole universal social institution. Whether it is the sole such institution can be debated, but there is no dispute that the nuclear family has been found in all known human societies. Attempts to obliterate the nuclear family in communal living arrangements have proved unsuccessful. Either the nuclear family has re-asserted itself, as in all the Israeli kibbutzim, or the communities have broken up within a generation. None of this is in dispute, but there are persistent debates about the significance of the nuclear family's universal presence. Functionalists say that this is proof that only the family can perform certain essential social functions – regulating sexual conduct, procreating and socialising young children, and acting as a unit of consumption through which all members of a society can share in that society's resources. Critics of the nuclear family point to costs. Personal freedom is restricted. Feminists claim that women are exploited, oppressed and abused. However, none of these charges undermine the functionalist case.

A major debate in modern societies is about whether the family is in decline (which would be catastrophic for the entire societies if the functionalists are correct). The evidence of decline is higher rates of divorce and separation, more births outside marriage and more children being reared by lone parents. The counter argument is that the family is changing and adapting to new circumstances, including the aspirations of its members for a higher quality of family life than people accepted in the past. Conjugal partners separate and circulate more rapidly than in the past, but this is not the same as a flight from family life itself. Also, a wider variety of family forms are now considered acceptable – lone parents as well as two parents, and gay and lesbian as well as heterosexual child-rearing couples.

See also **Dual-career family**; **Extended family**; **Kinship**; **Marriage**; **Pure relationship**; **Symmetrical family**.

Therborn, G. (2004), *Between Sex and Power: Family in the World, 1900–2000*, Routledge, London.

Fascism

This term describes the authoritarian, totalitarian, anti-communist political movements and the states that they created in certain European countries after the First World War.

Since the Second World War the term fascism has often been used loosely to refer to any right-wing, authoritarian politicians, parties, policies and governments, but in political sociology fascism has a more precise meaning. The term was first used by the Italian political party led by Benito Mussolini and the corporatist state that it created in Italy between 1922 and 1943. It was adopted by Germany's Nazi (National Socialist) Party led by Adolf Hitler that ruled Germany from 1933–45, and by the movements and governments led by Franco in Spain (1936–75) and by Salazar in Portugal (1932–68).

Defining fascism (except by referring to examples, as above) has always been difficult because (probably on account of their anti-intellectualism) the movements themselves did not produce coherent political ideologies. However, the features that linked the above fascist regimes were:

- rule by a single party with a nationalist ideology
- distrust in democracy
- faith in a charismatic party leader
- hatred of communism
- fusion of state apparatuses: no separation of powers or rule of law.

The state was regarded as the sole representative of the society: other associations including trade unions were either incorporated or suppressed. Racism and the use of physical violence and terror against opponents are probably best treated as associated with specific fascist regimes rather than defining features of fascism.

Sociology's problem has been how to explain the rise then the fading away of fascism in Europe. There have been many hypotheses about fascism's rise:

- sexual repression
- response to crises, the crises having different sources in different countries: loss of territory, war reparations which were believed to be unfair, hyper-inflation, political fragmentation (splintering of political parties)
- fear of rising working class power on the part of the capitalist class, the petit bourgeoisie and the middle classes more generally.

Sociologists collectively have also remained unsure of whether to treat fascism as an extreme example, or as entirely different in kind, to the corporatist political regimes that developed in West European countries after the Second World War. There is similar confusion in sociology about the causes of the rise and fall of communism, the other Goliath of the twentieth century.

See also **Corporatism**.

Kallis, A.A. (ed.) (2003), *The Fascism Reader*, Routledge, London.

Paxton, R.O. (2005), *The Anatomy of Fascism*, Penguin, London.

F

Fashion

Sought-after and acceptable styles that change periodically, maybe each decade or even each year, but less frequently than fads. Fashion has been created alongside the growth of the mass marketing and advertising of consumer goods, and the role that clothing, hairstyles and furniture play in modern social identities. Creative self-expression and commercial manipulation are interwoven in fashion, and in how what is fashionable changes.

See also **Consumption**.

Fecundity

The ability to have children.

See also **Fertility**.

Feminine/Femininity

Characteristics that are associated with women, which are likely to include dress, speech, behaviour in public, types of jobs and family roles. Masculine and masculinity are the corresponding terms for men.

The big debate is between essentialists who believe that these character-istics express men's and women's biological natures, and social construc-tionists (who include virtually all sociologists, certainly female sociologists) who insist that masculine and feminine roles and notions of masculinity and femininity are cultural, inscribed into males' and females' personalities and bodies by socialisation rather than by biology. As evidence, social construc-tionists cite inter-cultural variations in what is considered masculine and feminine.

Feminists argue that femininity has been constructed within patriarchal societies and serves men's interests rather than the interests of women themselves.

See also **Essence; Feminism; Gender; Other(s); Patriarchy**.

Beauvoir, S. de (1972, 1997), *The Second Sex,* Vintage, London.

Freidan, B. (1965, 1997), *The Feminine Mystique*, Norton, New York.

Mac an Ghaill, M. and Haywood, C. (2006), *Gender, Culture and Society: Contemporary Femininities and Masculinities*, Palgrave Macmillan, Basingstoke.

Segal, L. (2007), *Slow Motion: Changing Masculinities, Changing Men*, Palgrave Macmillan, Basingstoke.

Feminism

F

A body of theory and a social movement dedicated to ending the (alleged) oppression of women and their subordination to men.

There is general agreement that modern feminist thought started with Mary Wollstonecraft (1759–1797). There was a feminist movement (now known as first-wave feminism) in the late nineteenth and early twentieth centuries whose principal aims were political and legal equality, and careers for single women. Second-wave feminism dates from the 1960s and has been concerned to achieve equality in education, employment, family life and inter-personal relationships, and to claim for women control over their own bodies and fertility. Feminist thought has subsequently splintered into a series of feminisms, among which the most important in sociology have been:

- Liberal feminism: seeking equal rights guaranteed by law (equal pay, for example).
- Marxist feminism: regards the oppression of women as a sub-set of the more general oppression of the working class.
- Radical feminism: whose opponents are men and patriarchy.

There are also black, lesbian, eco and a variety of additional feminisms.

In sociology feminism has challenged the discipline's mainstream/ malestream theories, research methods and knowledge. Sociological research is said to be too empiricist and rationalist and insufficiently affective (all allegedly masculine traits). Sociological theory is criticised for being written by men about society as experienced by men. Sociological knowledge is criticised for foregrounding men's lives and leaving women invisible.

Second-wave feminism is still alive but amid claims that we have now entered a post-feminist age in which the latest cohorts of young women are less concerned to mobilise in search of more freedoms and equalities than to use the freedoms that they now possess.

See also **Standpoint theory**.

Kemp, S. and Squires, J. (eds) (1997), *Feminisms*, Oxford University Press, Oxford.

Wollstonecraft, M.A. (1792, 2004), *A Vindication of the Rights of Women*, Penguin, Harmondsworth.

Fertility/Fertility rate

The number of children who are born. The fertility rate of a population is normally expressed as the average number of births per woman, or births per year per 1000 population. An age-specific fertility rate is the number of births per year per thousand women in a specific age group.

See also **Demography; Fecundity**.

Feudalism

Basically a political system that existed in most of Europe between 1000 and 1400 AD, for longer in eastern Europe, and until the late nineteenth century in Russia. The core relationship was between a lord and a vassal. The vassal pledged service to the lord. The service would always include military service. In exchange the vassal was granted the use of land (a fief). Lord–vassal relationships were reproduced at successive levels. A monarch was at the top. Serfs (peasants who worked for a lord) were at the base.

This regime evolved into the estate system of stratification that existed in Europe until the modern era.

At the time when evolutionary theories were influential in sociology, feudalism was generally regarded as a political regime, an associated

F

economic system where land was the basic resource, and corresponding social arrangements, which occurred as a stage in the development of all societies, and comparable systems did exist in China, Japan and in much of Latin America. However, alongside dispensing with unilinear evolutionary theories, the tendency in sociology has been to stress the specificities of European feudalism.

See also **Estates**.

Bloch, M. (1961), *Feudalism* (2 vols), Routledge, London.

Fieldwork

This is how sociologists describe going out into society to collect information, whatever the research method. Fieldwork-based investigation is thereby distinguished from library/documentary research, the secondary analysis of existing data sets, and armchair theorising.

Figurational sociology

See Elias, N.

Focus group

These are focused discussion groups, usually lasting around an hour, with 6–10 participants, who are usually selected for their similar backgrounds, interests, lifestyles or attitudes. A leader (the investigator) focuses the discussion. The aim is to stimulate discussion among group members thereby allowing points of agreement and disagreement to be identified clearly. It is normal to pay participants for their time and to reimburse expenses. The events are normally tape-recorded and, if transcribed in full, may be subjected to formal content analysis.

Focus groups were pioneered by market researchers, then began to be used regularly by political parties, and are now also widely used by sociologists, usually alongside other methods of investigation. Focus groups may precede larger-scale fieldwork, enabling investigators to decide exactly which questions to include in interview schedules and questionnaires. They may also be used following quantitative surveys to clarify the meanings of recorded answers to set questions.

F

Folk society

One of the terms used in sociology to describe pre-modern, agrarian societies. The folk concept stresses the characteristics of the lives of ordinary people, their cultures and their ways of life.

In a folk society culture is transmitted orally, by the folk to the folk.

People's everyday lives are dominated by family and kin relationships, and by religious beliefs and rituals. Life changes little, if at all, from generation to generation.

See also **Traditional societies**.

Redfield, R. (1930), *Tepozlan, a Mexican Village: A Study of Folk Life*, Chicago University Press, Chicago.

Forces of production

See Marx, K.

Fordism

This refers to the type of assembly line production pioneered by Henry Ford (1863–1947), and (in sociology) to the accompanying political and social arrangements.

Between 1908 and 1914 Henry Ford applied the principles of scientific management to the production of motor cars. By the end of the 1920s over 15 million Model-T Fords had been sold, the company had become spectacularly profitable, and its employees were the highest paid workers in the world (in exchange for a greatly intensified work regime). Its apparent success led to Ford's methods being copied by other motor companies and other manufacturing industries in all industrial societies, including the Soviet Union.

The concept of Fordism was introduced into the social sciences by the Italian Marxist Antonio Gramsci (1891–1937), who treated Fordism as a total economic, political and social regime rather just a production strategy.

Fordism is now believed to have enjoyed its heyday between the Second World War and the 1970s when western capitalist countries expanded their economies and workers enjoyed full employment and progressively rising standards of living.

The key features of Fordism are:

- Assembly-line methods.
- Standardised products.
- Large semi-skilled, but well-paid workforces, with relatively secure jobs since successful Fordist firms were able to survive recessions.
- Mass markets.
- Protected national markets.
- Keynesian macro-economic management to maintain full employment and high levels of consumer demand.
- Strong welfare states to help maintain high levels of consumer demand and to spread the benefits of prosperity.
- Workers incorporated into industry via trade unions and collective bargaining. Before the Second World War the Ford Motor Company (and many other employers, especially in the United States) were

F

anti-union, but trade unions were subsequently accepted as (junior) partners in the management of industry.
- Tripartite macro-economic planning by governments, employers associations and trade unions.

The Fordist era is believed to have ended in the 1970s due to a combination of globalisation, new technologies, and the economic and political crises that had by then developed within the Fordist regime itself.

See also **Keynes, J.M.; Post-Fordism; Regulation theory; Scientific management.**

Gramsci, A. (1971), *Selections from Prison Notebooks*, New Left Books, London.

Formal sociology

Separates form from content and deals exclusively with the former, 'the geometry of social life'. Georg Simmel (1858–1918), the German sociologist, is regarded as the pioneer of this kind of sociology.

Examples of forms include dyads, triads, small groups, large organisations, status passages, conflict, competition, alliances and role sets. Law-like proportions can be developed 'geometrically', by pure logic: the larger a group, the higher the proportion of members who will be passive; the greater the conflict of expectations among members of a role set, the greater the likelihood of an actor experiencing role strain. However, the truth of all such propositions is contingent. The experience of role strain will also depend on whether an actor identifies with or distances himself or herself from the role in question. Formal propositions hold only while all other things remain equal, and a feature of social life is that content and context tend to be all-important and do not remain equal. Hence the preference of most sociologists for retaining content (and context) in their investigations.

See also **Simmel, G.**

F

Foucault, Michel (1926–1984)

A French philosopher and sociologist who specialised on the history of thought from early modern times up to the present day. Foucault's impact in sociology (which has been considerable) arises from his claim that, far from liberating us, modern rationality and science envelop us in unprecedented intricate and pervasive controls.

Foucault argued that every historical period has been characterised by particular unconscious structures for thought, which he called *epistemes*. Within epitsemes discourses are constructed. Discourses are rule-governed ways of thinking and speaking. All Foucault's work emphasised the power of discourses. He claimed that particular objects, including social roles and types of people (patient and homosexual, for example), could only be created (as thoughts, then enacted) within particular discourses.

Foucault described present-day societies as carceral (administered) societies. He argued that knowledge is power, and that scientific discourses have subjected people to increasingly detailed and insidious surveillance and control. Foucault's main books are about clinics, prisons, asylums and sexuality – all claimed as examples of how scientific knowledge has led to the creation of professional and administrative functionaries who claim the authority and expertise to discipline people into normality. However, Foucault was not arguing that one group (the experts) dominates others. In Foucault's view of the world, power is everywhere – it resides in discourses that regulate everyone. Present-day discourses are said to make us acquiescent and passive, cooperating in our own subordination.

For sociology these are challenging allegations, to which a standard (though not universal) riposte has been that the claims are products of the discourses that Foucault has developed or adopted, and that the real world is entirely (or somewhat) different.

See also **Discourse; Surveillance.**

Foucault, M. (1963, 1973), *The Birth of the Clinic,* Tavistock, London.

Foucault, M. (1975, 1977), *Discipline and Punish: The Birth of the Prison,* Tavistock, London.

Foucault, M. (1976, 1980), *The History of Sexuality*, Random House, New York.

Frame analysis

Invented by Erving Goffman (1922–1982); it is the study of how people understand situations, events and activities. The basic idea is that we react not to events themselves but according to how we 'frame' the events: whether a speech act is understood as a joke or an attack on our integrity, and whether smoking is seen as a health or civil liberties issue, for example. We understand or misunderstand each other according to whether or not our frames are aligned.

Frame analysis has been used extensively in media research: how events are presented as news, for example. The method has also been used in research on political and social movements, and by these movements themselves: their success is seen to hinge on persuading the public to adopt a preferred frame.

Frame analysis has also been developed as a procedure in the formal content analysis of texts. These can be analysed according to the frequency with which particular words are used, the frequency with which particular themes or discourses occur, or the frames within which themes and words are used.

See also **Content analysis; Discourse.**

Goffman, E. (1974), *Frame Analysis*, Penguin, Harmondsworth.

F

Frankfurt School

The name given to the sociologists who worked at the Institute of Social Research, which opened in Frankfurt in 1923. The Chicago School is sociology's only other example of a group with a single base pioneering a distinctive body of theory and method. The Frankfurt School developed Marxist theory in novel ways, and claimed to be practising a distinctive type of critical sociology.

The best-known pre-1939 members of the Frankfurt School are Theordor Adorno, Walter Benjamin, Eric Fromm, Max Horkheimer and Herbert Marcuse. Most were Jews, and they and their institute relocated from Germany to New York after the Nazis assumed power in Germany in 1933. The institute and some of its original members returned to Frankfurt in 1949. The institute formally closed in 1969 but its influence continues, most notably in the work of Jurgen Habermas (1929–).

The Frankfurt School responded to the changing world in which its members lived and worked – the rise of fascism, the creation of the USSR as the world's first communist society, and the spread of affluence in the west. The school's members all believed that Marxism needed to be developed to analyse developments that Marx himself had not foreseen. They rejected economic determinism. They were critical of capitalism, but no less so of Soviet-type socialism. Their main contributions to Marxist thought were through the incorporation of Freudian psychoanalytic theory, and stressing the role of 'the culture industry' in dowsing the revolutionary potential of the working class.

See also **Adorno, T.W.; Benjamin, W.; Critical sociology/critical theory; Fromm, E.; Habermas, J.; Horkheimer, M.; Marcuse, H.; Marxism.**

Bottomore, T. (1984), *The Frankfurt School*, Tavistock, London.

Freud, Sigmund (1856–1939)

A German-Austrian; trained in medicine; specialised in neurology; became interested in psychology, hypnosis and 'talk therapy'; and invented psychoanalysis which is both a therapy and a theory of personality.

For sociology, it is mainly the theory of personality that makes Freud and psychoanalysis significant. Freud argued that humans are less rational than many of his contemporaries assumed. A part of the mind which he called the 'id' was said to be the home of powerful instinctive urges, called 'libido', always liable to break out and take charge of behaviour.

Freud stressed the importance of early childhood experience in personality development. He argued that children internalised the views of figures (usually a mother or father) with whom they had developed strong emotional bonds. These internalised views became a 'super-ego' which could regulate behaviour by bestowing praise or inflicting feelings of guilt or shame upon the 'ego', the conscious, rational part of the mind. The ego had to mediate between and somehow reconcile the demands of the id and super-ego, and according to Freud this balance became increasingly fragile as the development of civilisation demanded stronger control over human

F

instincts which simply had to find acceptable expression as otherwise the outcome would be personal discontent (including psychological illness) and/or social breakdown.

Sociologists of various theoretical persuasions have drawn upon Freud to enrich their social theories by exploring how social and personality systems are entwined. Functionalists such as Talcott Parsons (1902–1979), and Marxists such as Herbert Marcuse (1898–1979), have incorporated (usually selected) elements of Freudian theory.

See also **Lacan, J.; Marcuse, H.; Mead, G.H.**

Freud, S. (1930), *Civilization and its Discontents*, Hogarth Press, London.

Friendship

People today are often uncertain as to who or what is a friend. Hence the fuzziness in sociological definitions. Yet friendship has been a recognised social relationship in all societies. The meaning of friendship has varied according to historical time, from place to place, and from group to group within societies, and present-day societies are no exception. Friends are variously said to be cooperative, mutually supportive and affectionate, and to enjoy each other's company, to be knowledgeable about each other and useful to one another. But exactly how useful to each other should friends be? Maybe this conflicts with the norms of universalism which are expected to prevail in economic life in modern societies, Are friends chosen or just given? Can family members be friends? Friendships vary from the fleeting to lifelong. They also vary in intensity: soulmate to Internet friend. At what point does an acquaintance become a friend?

Friendship is a seriously under-researched topic. We have mere titbits of information about friendship in present-day societies:

- Friends (social capital) are important sources of job information when seeking employment.
- They may be important in careers in politics and other professions and work organisations.
- But note that people often feel uneasy about using friendships in the above contexts: they realise that this may incur criticism.
- People are most interested in making friends with others who they regard as 'good looking'.
- Friendships tend to form within age, class, gender, ethnic and geographical boundaries.
- The middle classes are better than the working class at forming and maintaining circles of friends.
- Women are better than men at maintaining close same-sex friendships: men may be inhibited by homophobia.
- Friendships are especially important in the youth life-stage.

It is unclear whether friendships are currently becoming more or less important, wider and thicker, or narrower and thinner. Weaker family bonds,

F

more job insecurity, and pressure and competitiveness at work could be strengthening the role of friendships as a form of 'social glue'. Alternatively, these trends could be making it more difficult for people to form and maintain friendships. We know that many people have few close friends. A quarter of all Americans say that they have no close confidantes.

See also **Capital (social)**.

Allan, G. (1996), *Kinship and Friendship in Modern Britain*, Oxford University Press, Oxford.

Pahl, R. (2000), *On Friendship*, Polity, Cambridge.

Fromm, Eric (1900–1980)

A radical social psychologist; member of the Frankfurt School. Fromm argued that under capitalism people failed to develop the psychological resources that were needed to cope with freedom. Rather, they tended to develop a psychological need to be led by authoritarian figures. His solution was 'spontaneous love': the spread of affirmative, positive, cooperative relationships among equals.

See also **Adorno, T. W.; Authoritarian personality; Frankfurt School; Marcuse, H.**

Fromm, E. (1955), *The Sane Society*, Holt Rinehart, New York.

Functionalism

May alternatively be called structural-functionalism. This theory contends that the principal task of sociology is to identify the functions that any group, institution or practice performs for the larger system of which it is a part.

Functionalism was anticipated by nineteenth-century sociologists who likened societies to biological organisms (for example, Herbert Spencer, 1820–1903), and in Emile Durkheim's (1858–1917) work on mechanical and organic solidarity. However, explicit functionalist explanations, and functionalism as a full-blown theory, were first advocated by British social anthropologists Bronislaw Malinowski (1884–1942) and Alfred Radcliffe-Brown (1881–1955). They argued that instead of seeking origins and elementary forms of the family and other institutions, researchers should enquire about the functions that these institutions performed in the ongoing social systems. A tribe might believe that performing a rain-making ceremony increased the likelihood of rainfall, but the real function of the practice, and the reason why it endured, might well be revealed as bolstering social solidarity during times of crisis. Functionalist thought was incorporated centrally into Talcott Parsons' (1902–1979) theory of social systems and then became the most influential theory in American sociology in the mid-twentieth century.

Strong versions of functionalism claim that to identify its function is to explain something, to which there are a number of powerful objections:

- A function is an effect and an effect cannot be a cause unless one postulates that in society there are organs akin to the brain and the central nervous system in the human body, or that a process of natural selection eliminates all but the most functional practices.
- Functionalism presumes consensus, equilibrium and integration. It overlooks the possibility of basic conflicts in society. The theory is therefore socially and politically conservative.
- The theory allows insufficient scope for human agency.
- By ignoring conflict and human agency, functionalism renders itself incapable of developing convincing explanations of social change.

Despite these weaknesses, functionalism had a mid-twentieth-century appeal because it appeared capable of revealing things of which we (in sociology and outside) were unaware, especially by distinguishing between manifest and latent functions (the official or everyday explanations of things as opposed to their real consequences). For example, it could be argued that crime was functional insofar as the punishment of offenders allowed law-abiding citizens to affirm their values, and that poverty performed certain functions such as enabling the better-off to feel good and fortunate, and creating jobs in poverty alleviation. Most famously, or infamously, it was argued that stratification was functional, a necessary feature of all societies, because it motivated people with rare but crucial talents to fill important roles and perform to their maximum ability.

There are softer versions of functionalism (nowadays called neo-functionalism), developed by, among others, Jeffrey Alexander in the United States and Nicos Mouzelis in Britain, which do not purport to offer explanations, but simply point out that there are functional requirements that have to be met if any society is to endure, and that it can therefore be both interesting and useful to ask which functions, if any, particular practices, groups and institutions perform, which are dysfunctional, and which are functionally neutral. However, the objections to strong functionalism also apply to the softer varieties.

Sociologists have to continue to engage with functionalism if only because functional explanations have always been and remain popular in politics and in everyday life. Educational policies are justified in terms of the needs of the economy and society. It is said that top business people and financiers need to be handsomely rewarded for their efforts from which the entire society benefits. Thus, in sociology, functionalism is born again every autumn in order to be ritually and publicly slaughtered for the benefit of each new cohort of students.

F

See also **Merton, R.K.; Parsons, T.; Social system**.

Alexander, J. (ed.) (1985), *Neo-Functionalism*, Sage, London.

Davis, K. and Moore, W.E. (1945), 'Some principles of stratification', *American Sociological Review*, 10, 242–9.

Mouzelis, N.P. (1995), *Sociological Theory: What Went Wrong?* Routledge, London.

Gg

Gadamer, Hans-Georg (1900–2002)

See Hermeneutics.

Game theory

The games are mathematical constructs which explore how two or more parties behave given the objectives of each, the resources and strategies that are available to them, and their knowledge of what others are doing and thinking. The game can be zero-sum (where one side can win only at the expense of the other) or non-zero-sum. Players can compete, they can all cooperate, or some can form alliances against others. The game may be cards, a war, negotiations between trade unions and employers, a competition between political parties, or anything else where parties with different objectives interact.

Games may be played by computer or by real people in quasi-laboratory situations. A well-known game is the prisoners' dilemma. This illustrates a general finding from the relevant research: real people tend to act selfishly and try to maximise their own outcomes even when there is a mathematically preferable option which would mean conceding some ground to another party, or just taking full account of the other party's likely actions. However, laboratories are not real life where customs and rules may guide the players to the best outcomes. A purpose of playing games is to enable the players to learn to act effectively in real life situations.

Sociology has made little use of game theory though it bears resemblances to exchange theory and rational choice theory.

See also **Exchange theory; Rational choice theory; Zero-sum.**

Von Neumann, J. and Morgenstern, O. (1944), *Theory of Games and Economic Behaviour,* Princeton University Press, Princeton, N.J.

Garfinkel, Harold (1917–)

The American sociologist who founded ethnomethodology in the 1960s.

Ethnomethodology means literally the study of members' methods, the members being ordinary members of society. It studies what is omitted in other kinds of sociology, namely, how people manage to live their everyday lives, how they decide 'what has happened', 'what is really going on' in any situation, and how all this is grounded in common taken-for-granted assumptions. Ethnomethodology aims to uncover these assumptions. In working out how this could be done, Garfinkel believed that he was applying the insights of phenomenology.

See also **Ethnomethodology**; **Phenomenology.**

Garfinkel, H. (1967), *Studies in Ethnomethodology*, Prentice Hall, Engelwood Cliffs, N.J.

Gated communities

These are physically gated and guarded residential developments. Residents within the enclaves may have their own schools, health services, power and water supplies, sanitation and recreation facilities.

The original gated communities were constructed for wealthy foreigners who were living or holidaying in poor countries, but since the 1990s they have spread throughout Latin America, into North America and into Europe. They are regarded as symptoms of wide inequalities, fear of crime, and the desire and ability of the well-to-do to insulate their lives from the surrounding societies.

See also **Urbanism.**

Low, S.M. (2003), *Behind the Gates: Life, Security and the Pursuit of Happiness in Fortress America*, Routledge, New York.

Gatekeeper

Used metaphorically in sociology: gatekeepers control access to information, goods or services.

In conducting sociological research, whoever grants or refuses access to databases, and gives or withholds permission for members or staff to be interviewed, is an important gatekeeper. In the rest of life, editors are gate-keepers between journalists' output and what is actually printed or broad-cast. Other gatekeepers decide which hotel guests are allocated upgraded rooms, and which travellers obtain upgraded seats on airplanes.

G

Gay and lesbian movements

These movements share the common aim of social acceptance.

Their beginnings can be traced to the 1860s, but the modern movements are usually dated from a Gay Rights march in Philadelphia in 1965. Subsequently Gay Liberation movements spread throughout the world. Today a wide variety of groups have fierce arguments about philosophies, theories and tactics. Their activities include street marches, lobbying, 'outing', support groups, community events, magazines, films, businesses and academic research.

See also **Queer theory; Sexuality**.

Miller, N. (2006), *Out of the Past: Gay and Lesbian History from 1869 to the Present*, Alyson Books, New York.

Gaze

This term was first used in film criticism in the 1970s and has subsequently been adopted by sociology. A gaze is a way of looking, a viewpoint, that can be objectified in cultural products. The original argument (in film criticism) was that mainstream cinema objectified a male view (gaze) of women. Subsequently a tourist gaze has been identified, which is said to lead to places and cultures being managed so as to fit the gaze.

See also **Frame analysis**.

Urry, J. (1990), *The Tourist Gaze*, Sage, London.

Gemeinschaft

See Toennies, F.

Gender

Since the 1970s sociology has followed Anne Oakley's suggestion. The term 'sex' is used to refer to biological differences between males and females. 'Gender' is used to refer to everything that is socially constructed and culturally transmitted. Masculine and feminine are characteristics of men and women respectively, Exactly which of these characteristics are explicable in terms of biology, and which are gendered, is a battleground of ideas in the social and natural sciences, and in society. Sociologists are the party that stresses the extent to which differences are due to gendering rather than biology.

See also **Feminine; Sex; Sexuality**.

Oakley, A. (1972), *Sex, Gender and Society*, Temple Smith, London.

G

Generalised other

See Mead, G.H.; Significant other.

Generation

People who experience specific historical conditions and events when at a critical age in the life course (usually taken to be childhood, youth or young adulthood), when these conditions and events leave a lasting imprint on the lives and outlooks of the generation in question, and distinguish them from older and younger generations. A generation may extend over a decade, two decades, or longer until there is a further generation-defining event or change in historical conditions.

Examples of generations are the baby boomers who were born in western countries between 1945 and the 1960s, and who were the first cohorts to grow up in post-scarcity conditions; the generations who experienced high levels of unemployment during their early labour market careers in the 1920s/30s, and in some European countries since the 1970s; and the post-communist generation in present-day eastern Europe.

It has proved relatively easy to identify events and conditions which form generations at the time, but the imprint of these events and conditions is inevitably blurred by the generation's subsequent experiences, and by divisions by social class, gender, ethnicity and so on.

See also **Cohort**.

Mannheim, K. (1952), 'The problem of generations', in *Essays on the Sociology of Knowledge,* Routledge, London.

Gentrification

A term coined by Ruth Glass, the British sociologist. It refers to the middle or upper classes moving into formerly run-down areas.

Such a trend has been identified in western countries since the 1950s, and is associated with young professionals, typically singles and childless couples, taking advantage of relatively low property prices in run-down inner-city districts (which then become fashionable and expensive), and choosing to live close to their employment and preferred places of entertainment.

See also **Urbanism**.

Glass, R. (ed.) (1964), *London: Aspects of Change*, MacGibbon and Kee, London.

Geodemographics

G

Groups people according to where they live. This is not a new practice. People can be grouped into rural, urban and suburban, and according to the specific towns, cities, regions and countries where they live. However, modern geodemographics groups people into smaller units based on their neighbourhoods or even their postcodes. This procedure assumes (correctly) that like tends to live alongside like in terms of occupation, life stage and lifestyle. Its supporters claim that geodemographics identifies more meaningful groups than the standard categories used in sociology – social class, gender and age – even when these are used in combination to separate people into specific age/gender/class 'cells'.

Geodemographics has been adopted throughout much of the market research industry. Our postcodes therefore affect who tries to sell us different goods and services, and our credit ratings. People can discover (on the Internet) their own geodemographic categories, and those of other people whom they know. They may decide where to live partly on this basis, and identify one another using market researchers' labels, which in Britain include 'industrial grit', 'cultural leadership' and 'golden empty nesters'.

However, since most of us change addresses several times during our lives, these geodemographic identities seem unlikely to be as stable or to become as deeply rooted as those associated with ethnicity, gender and social class.

See also **Class; Lifestyle; Urbanism.**

Burrows, R. and Gane, N. (2006), 'Geodemographics, software and class', *Sociology,* 40, 793–812.

Gerontology

The study of the elderly and ageing in later life.

Gerontology used to be dominated by health and welfare issues. Today the agenda has widened. This is due in part to the ageing of the populations in modern societies. Sociologists now investigate the social construction of age, and the politics of ageing. There is a movement to make ageism as reprehensible as sexism and racism, and to add age to the list of discriminations that are outlawed. Other current issues include how to provide sufficient financial support for the growing number of older people, how to meet their health and welfare needs, and whether older people should and can be encouraged to work longer and retire later. There is also a growth of interest in older people as voters and as consumers.

See also **Demography; Life course.**

Gilleard, C. and Higgs, P. (2005), *Contexts of Ageing: Class, Cohort and Community,* Polity, Cambridge.

Gesellschaft

See Toennies, F.

G

Ghetto

A term originally applied in the Middle Ages to the parts of European towns and cities where Jews were required to live. During the twentieth century the term was applied to any area inhabited (wholly or mainly) by a particular ethnic or religious group – Black ghettoes in US cities, for example. With this extension to any ethnic or religious group, there has been interest in identifying a common ghetto mentality.

See also **Urbanism.**

Wirth, L. (1928), *The Ghetto*, University of Chicago Press, Chicago.

Giddens, Anthony (1938–)

One of Britain's most prolific sociologists; certainly British sociology's most renowned contemporary public intellectual.

Giddens' early work was a reassessment of sociology's founding fathers and their interpreters. One outcome from this early work was the concept 'structuration'.

Subsequently Giddens turned his attention to the character of present-day societies and to the predicaments of individuals in a runaway, globalising world in which we are increasingly dependent on institutions which we need to trust, where tradition offers no guidance, where we are forced to choose in situations of risk and uncertainty, where reflexivity becomes increasingly important, as does intimacy as people seek personal security in 'pure relationships'.

In his latest stage (but not necessarily the last) Giddens has become a public intellectual through his writing on the 'Third Way', a rationale for Britain's New Labour governments. The Third Way is said to be simultaneously a modernised version of social democracy and beyond the old left–right dimension of politics in addressing challenges posed by globalisation, new technologies and environmental sustainability.

See also **Pure relationship**; **Reflexivity**; **Structuration**.

Giddens, A. (1973, 1981), *The Class Structure of the Advanced Societies*, Hutchinson, London.

Giddens, A. (1984), *The Constitution of Society*, Polity Press, Cambridge.

Giddens, A. (1993), *The Transformation of Intimacy: Love, Sexuality and Eroticism in Modern Societies*, Polity Press, Cambridge.

Giddens, A. (1998), *The Third Way: The Renewal of Social Democracy*, Polity Press, Cambridge.

Global cities

See Sassen, S.

G

Global village

A term originally made popular by the Canadian scholar, Marshall McLuhan (1911–1980), who was referring to how electronic communications were restoring to western civilisation some features of oral (village) cultures. The entire world was said to be acquiring village-like characteristics.

Nowadays the term 'global village' has been appropriated for the communities created by the World Wide Web.

See also **Globalisation**.

McLuhan, M. and Fiore, Q. (1967), *The Medium is the Message*, Penguin, Harmondsworth.

Globalisation

This refers to the spread of interdependencies between countries. These trends are not new – trade, empires and world religions have long histories. However, during the twentieth century globalisation is believed to have accelerated.

There are several dimensions to globalisation:

- Economic: more and freer trade in goods and services, and movements of capital, promoted by bodies such as the European Union and the World Trade Organization, and more business conducted by trans-national companies.
- Political: increasing collaboration between governments through the United Nations, NATO and the EU, for example.
- Human: more people travelling for economic reasons, for asylum and as tourists, in all these cases because people are better able to afford to do so than in the past.
- Cultural: electronic satellite and cable communications by telephone, TV and the Internet enable fashions, music and sport to be followed and adopted simultaneously in all parts of the world.

The hot issues in globalisation theory are:

- whether all societies and cultures are becoming more similar, or whether they are accentuating their distinctive features thus producing myriad instances of glocalisation
- whether globalisation is a cloak and euphemism for imperialism by richer countries, or whether the trend is making the world more multi-centred.

See also **Dependency theory; Time–space distanciation; World system theory.**

Held, D. and McGrew, A. (eds) (2003), *The Global Transformations Reader*, Polity, Cambridge.

Lechner, A.J. and Boli, J. (eds) (2000), *The Globalization Reader*, Blackwell, Oxford.

Scholtz, J.A. (2005), *Globalization: A Critical Introduction*, Palgrave Macmillan, Basingstoke.

G

Goffman, Erving (1922–1982)

Goffman was a hugely influential American sociologist in the 1960s and 1970s when he became famous for introducing the dramaturgical perspective. Goffman was a maverick who broke all the normal rules. His fieldwork methods and sources were never reported fully. He was also highly productive – 11 books between 1959 and 1981 – and throughout his career he had a knack of generating concepts and insights that everyone else had missed.

Goffman's first book, *The Presentation of Self in Everyday Life* (1959), was loosely based on fieldwork in Scotland's Shetland Isles. In this book Goffman introduced his dramaturgical perspective. Society was metaphorically likened to a theatre. Actors came onstage to play roles. They behaved differently depending on whether they were front stage (visible to the public) or backstage. Goffman appears to have been influenced by his observations in hotels and restaurants. In this book we were also introduced to role identification and role distance. In *Asylums* (1961) we learnt about total institutions and how inmates became institutionalised. In *Stigma* (1964) we learnt about how individuals handle spoiled identities when in public. All Goffman's books are good reads.

Unfortunately, but true to character, Goffman never wrote a textbook from which we might all learn how to practise his brand of sociology with equal effect.

See also **Frame analysis; Stigma; Total institution.**

Goffman, E. (1959), *The Presentation of Self in Everyday Life,* Doubleday Anchor, New York.

Goffman, E. (1961), *Asylums,* Penguin Harmondsworth.

Goldthorpe, John H. (1935–)

A British sociologist. In the 1960s Goldthorpe co-directed *The Affluent Worker* study which rejected the embourgeoisement thesis and claimed to discover a new privatised, instrumentally oriented section of the working class.

Subsequently Goldthorpe launched a major study of social mobility in Britain, which was followed by a series of comparative international studies. At the start of this research Goldthorpe developed the Goldthorpe Class Scheme, which has subsequently become widely used by sociologists in Britain and beyond. In 1998 a version of this class scheme was adopted as the UK official classification, and in 2007 another slightly amended version was adopted by the European Union for collating standardised data from across the continent.

See also **Affluent workers; Class; Embourgeoisement; Service class; Social mobility.**

Goldthorpe, J.H., Lockwood, D., Bechhofer, F. and Platt, J. (1969), *The Affluent Worker in the Class Structure,* Cambridge University Press, Cambridge.

Goldthorpe, J.H., Llewellyn, C. and Payne, C. (1980, 1987), *Social Mobility and Class Structure in Britain,* Clarendon Press, Oxford.

G

Gorz, Andre (1923–2007)

French philosopher, though Austrian-born as Gerhard Hirsch; first used Andre Gorz as a pseudonym when writing for *Les Temps Modernes.*

Gorz's work which captured attention in sociology addressed the transformation of work and working time. He argued that the advanced capitalist societies were in the grip of a system that was fast abolishing work as we had known it, but the problem was not the destruction of work itself so much as the capitalist system's efforts to perpetuate the idea of work (in a paid employment relationship) as a source of rights, most importantly the right to an income. Gorz looked forward to a post-capitalist age in which the productivity gains won by capitalism would be used to enhance individual well-being and the quality of social life instead of allowing a system-induced job shortage to intensify competition and social divisions. In Gorz's ideal future, work would be reclaimed for its real value and would once more become a useful and fulfilling activity.

See also **Economy; Leisure; Unemployment; Work.**

Gorz, A. (1999), *Reclaiming Work: Beyond the Wage-Based Society*, Polity Press, Cambridge.

Government

The ultimate power in a territory. When there is such a power we can say that a state exists. Its institutions are likely to include a parliament or congress, maybe a monarch, and a civil service. The power of a government is most likely to be consolidated by a system of law, courts and judicial punishments, plus a police force and the threat and sometimes the use of military force.

Power may be delegated from a state to regional and local governments.

The term government is sometimes used metaphorically to refer to the government (management and administration) of businesses, trade unions, churches and other bodies.

Up until now, supra-national/world government is just an aspiration (of some people). Supra-national institutions can perform government functions only insofar as states agree to pool their power.

See also **Authority; Politics; Power; State.**

G

Gramsci, Antonio (1891–1937)

Secretary of the Italian Communist Party from 1924–6 when he was imprisoned by the Italian fascist government. While in prison he wrote his famous 'notebooks' in which he criticised vulgar economic determinism and advocated a more humanistic type of Marxism.

Gramsci is the source of the concept of hegemony. He argued that under capitalism ideological control was just as important, if not more important, than coercive control. Hegemony is a condition where the interests of the dominant class are accepted as everyone's interests; thus consent to domination is secured. The institutions that allegedly establish and maintain hegemony include education, the mass media, churches and the family.

Gramsci also broadened the concept of Fordism to encompass the political and social arrangements that accompanied and stabilised Fordist production.

See also **Fordism; Hegemony; Ideology; Marxism.**

Gramsci, A. (1971), *Selections from Prison Notebooks*, New Left Books, London.

Grand narratives

A term first used by the French postmodern theorist Jean-Francois Lyotard (1924–1998). Grand narratives, as defined by Lyotard, are stories (told by positivists and Marxists, for example) about the development of science (and knowledge more generally) bringing humanity closer and closer to the truth.

Lyotard claimed that by the late twentieth century knowledge had come to be valued purely for instrumental reasons rather than for its own sake, and that this would undermine all claims to have the right answers in the eyes not only of intellectuals such as himself but the general public also.

See also **Lyotard, J-F.**

Grand theory

A term used by the American sociologist C. Wright Mills (1916–1962) to lampoon over-ambitious, over-generalised theories which were insufficiently grounded in evidence, and which were too abstract to be useful to anyone. The main target of Mills' criticisms was his contemporary American sociologist, Talcott Parsons (1902–1979).

See also **Mills, C.W.**

Grounded theory

A phrase coined by the American sociologists Barney Glaser and Anselm Strauss, who believed that sociology had become less successful in developing new theories than in testing existing ones. They also wished to skirt the two pitfalls for sociology identified by C. Wright Mills (1916–1962) – grand theory on the one side, and extreme atheoretical empiricism on the other.

Grounded theory was to be discovered via qualitative research. 'Sensitising concepts' were to be formulated on the basis of initial observations, then developed into theories through the 'constant comparison' of critical cases. Glaser and Strauss's book is still among the few attempts to set out systematic methods for conducting qualitative fieldwork.

See also **Qualitative analysis, qualitative research.**

Glaser, B. and Strauss, A. (1968), *The Discovery of Grounded Theory,* Weidenfeld and Nicolson, London.

G

Group

A set of social relationships within a boundary which separates members from non-members, though members may range from core to marginal/peripheral. Groups are thereby distinguishable from other social categories such as women and authors. Groups may be large or small, primary (based on face-to-face interaction) or secondary (where relationships are relatively formal). Large groups are likely to be called organisations or associations. Groups are likely to confer identities on their members, and to have stable patterns of interaction among the members.

In sociology there was a flurry of interest in small groups in the 1940s and 1950s. This was partly due to a wave of interest in formal sociology, and partly to claims by exponents of human relations to be able to identify styles of group management that would maximise both effectiveness (in performing set tasks) and morale.

See also **Formal sociology; Human relations.**

G

Habermas, Jurgen (1929–)

A German social theorist who has built upon the critical sociology of the Frankfurt School. Habermas treats the modernist 'enlightenment project' not as a failure but as unfinished business which may still be brought to a conclusion wherein people achieve freedom through reason, thereby becoming masters rather than victims of their circumstances.

Habermas argues that emancipatory knowledge is achieved only though free and open dialogue, which takes place in an 'ideal speech situation' which exists in an ideal typical 'public sphere'. He rejects the view that truth can be established through a scientific method or by adopting an objective vantage point. The only truth, according to Habermas, and this applies to issues of morality as well as matters of fact, is agreement that is reached in open and free communication, which is described as 'communicative reason' and is engaged in for its own sake. The associated behaviour is called 'communicative action' wherein people are interested in one another for their own sakes. Dialogue and action that arise simply because people wish to associate and communicate with one another (as in a family) are said to be the basic kinds of human speech, thought and action. These arise in and create an intersubjective 'lifeworld'. Here Habermas departs radically from orthodox Marxist thought which has always treated work (and the associated forms of thought and knowledge) as the basic human activity.

According to Habermas, an unintended outcome of lifeworld interaction is the creation of a system of institutions wherein action is governed by instrumental reason. Here, people and other objects are treated as means, and speech and communication are geared to achieving ends. Habermas argues that 'the system' can become, and under capitalism has become, decoupled from the lifeworld in which it has its origins and roots. Not only this, the system may colonise – and has in fact, extensively 'colonised' – the lifeworld, thereby undermining the conditions for the maintenance of the system. The symptoms are said to include meaninglessness, anxiety, deviance and conflict (collectively known as a 'legitimation crisis'). However, the colonisation of the lifeworld can be countered by new social movements. These may be for sex equality, against nuclear power or whatever, but their importance lies in creating space, enlarging a public sphere, for genuine communicative reason and action. In this way, Habermas envisages, the system may be brought under control and emancipation accomplished.

See also **Critical sociology/Critical theory; Emancipatory sociology; Enlightenment; Frankfurt School; Social movements.**

Habermas, J. (1976), *Legitimation Crisis,* Heinemann, London.

Habermas, J. (1984, 1988), *The Theory of Communicative Action* (2 vols), Polity, Cambridge.

Habitus

See Bourdieu, P.

Hall, Stuart (1932–)

Born in Jamaica, moved to England in 1951, Head of the Centre for Contemporary Cultural Studies at Birmingham University 1968–79, and Head of Sociology at the Open University 1979–1997.

Stuart Hall is one of British sociology's genuine public intellectuals who has engaged in a career-long search for alternatives to left-wing orthodoxies. He was centrally involved in the launch of the *New Left Review* following the Soviet invasion of Hungary in 1956, and in the quest for renewal on the left following Margaret Thatcher's election victories in the 1980s. Hall's work is noteworthy for the addition of a strong cultural dimension to orthodox Marxist class analysis. In his work on the media he has insisted that the meanings of texts must always be sought in the cultural backgrounds of the encoders and decoders.

See also **Cultural studies**.

Hall, S. (1992), *Modernity and its Futures,* Polity Press, Cambridge.

Hall, S., Critcher, C., Jefferson, T., Clarke, J. and Roberts, B. (1978), *Policing the Crisis: Mugging, the State, and Law and Order,* Macmillan, London.

Hall, S. and Jacques, M. (1989), *New Times*, Lawrence and Wishart, London.

Halo effect

A finding of social psychology, first noted by Edward L Thorndike (1874–1949), that people who create favourable first impressions (that they are attractive, clever or pleasant) tend thereafter to be judged in uniformly positive terms. This is a process that occurs in social life, and it is a potential pitfall in social research where an interviewer's or observer's first impressions can govern how subsequent evidence is interpreted.

Halsey, A.H. (Chelly) (1923–)

British sociologist; pioneer of research into education and social mobility.

See also **Social mobility**.

Halsey, A.H., Heath, A.F. and Ridge, J.M. (1980), *Origins and Destinations: Family, Class and Education in Modern Britain,* Clarendon Press, Oxford.

Hawthorne effect

This occurs when the findings recorded are due to the research process itself. Hawthorne effects are experimenter, interviewer or observer effects.

The name derives from the initial discovery of such effects during what was really a poorly designed 1920s study of work groups at the Hawthorne plant, near Chicago, of the Western Electric Company. The research found that output increased when conditions of work (illumination, break times) were experimentally deteriorated as well as when they were improved. This was (controversially) attributed to improvements in group morale, due to the investigators displaying an interest in the employees' tasks, attitudes and feelings. Remarkably, this interpretation of accidentally generated evidence gave rise to the influential human relations movement in industrial management.

See also **Human relations.**

Health

Health means the absence of illness and disability (temporary or permanent), which in turn can be defined as bodily and mental states that are deemed undesirable. Some definitions extend the health concept 'upwards', incorporating what is otherwise called well-being.

Researchers distinguish between a person's state of health (which can vary from day to day) and health status which refers to the person's normal health condition. There is a consensus that health status can be assessed satisfactorily by simply asking people to self-rate their normal health (sometimes compared with other people of the same age and sex). This is far less complicated than asking multiple questions about their health histories.

The sociology of health is one of the largest and most buoyant sub-fields in sociology. It studies the social distribution and inter-societal variations in rates of illness and disability, and the organisation and operation of health-care. This has led to criticism of the bio-medical model of health insofar as improvements in living conditions have been shown to be responsible for a greater part of the decline in mortality rates over time than improvements in medical services.

See also **Medical model; Well-being.**

Bury, M. and Gabe, J. (eds) (2004), *The Sociology of Health and Illness: A Reader,* Routledge, London.

Taylor, S. and Field, D. (eds) (2007), *Sociology of Health and Health Care*, Blackwell, Oxford.

Hegel, Georg Wilhelm Friedrich (1770–1831)

A German philosopher, a colossus of nineteenth-century European philosophy, who believed that history was driven by the unfolding of humanity's potential. Hegel was an idealist who believed that thought – a collective mind or spirit – was the driving force behind history, and that ideas determined social and political forms.

According to Hegel, thought did not develop smoothly but through a dialectical process whereby an idea (a thesis) would be attacked as inadequate by an antithesis, leading to a synthesis, which became the new thesis. He believed that this process would continue until humanity had gained full knowledge and understanding, ultimate truth, a condition of freedom, which would be the end of history.

Hegel appears to have convinced himself that historical development was reaching maturity in the Prussia of his day whereas the Young Hegelians (who included Karl Marx) disagreed, and looked forward to further progress.

See also **Dialectics; Idealism.**

Singer, P. (1983), *Hegel,* Oxford University Press, Oxford.

Hegemony

This means domination by ideology to such an extent that no alternative to the present is believed to be possible or can even be imagined. The concept was developed by Antonio Gramsci (1891–1937), the Italian communist leader, while in prison in the 1920s and 1930s.

Hegemony is secured by presenting the interests of the dominant class as common interests, thus eliminating the possibility of dissent and conflict. This is achieved through the mass media, education, religion, the family and even through trade unions.

Gramsci argued that under capitalism hegemony could never be complete. Workers were said to possess a dual consciousness composed partly of hegemonic ideas of the dominant capitalist class, and partly from workers' own experiences of exploitation. A condition for a successful proletarian revolution was said to be workers establishing their own ideological supremacy.

The concept of hegemony as developed by Gramsci has played a key role in shifting western Marxist thought away from economic determinism towards acknowledging the (at least partial) independence of ideological and political processes.

See also **Althusser, L.; False consciousness; Gramsci, A.; Hall, S.; Marxism.**

Gramsci, A. (1971), *Selections from Prison Notebooks*, New Left Books, London.

H

Hermeneutics

Originally this was a method of interpreting texts, specifically Biblical texts. In sociology it is a theory and method of interpreting meaningful human action.

According to Wilhelm Dilthey (1833–1911), a nineteenth-century German historian and philosopher, this was the method that had to be used in what he called the cultural sciences. Ever since then interpretive (or hermeneutic) sociology has been juxtaposed with positivist sociology.

The core problem in hermeneutics (as in the days when the Bible was the subject matter) is how to decide whose and which interpretation is valid. Dilthey's recommended method was *Verstehen* (understanding). The analyst was to place himself or herself in the situation of the subject, whose actions would then be comprehensible by virtue of sharing a common humanity. Another more sophisticated solution, adopted by Max Weber (1864–1920), was to try to grasp the worldview of the subject(s) through the use of ideal types.

Contemporary sociologists who accept that interpretation and understanding must play a part in explanation are most likely to agree with Hans-Georg Gadamer, a twentieth-century German philosopher (1900–2002), who argued that interpretations must always remain tentative and subject to revision.

See also **Methodological individualism; Phenomenology; Symbolic interactionism; Weber, M.**

Dilthey, W. (edited by H.P. Rickman) (1976), *W. Dilthey, Selected Writings,* Cambridge University Press, Cambridge.

Gadamer, H. (1960, 1975), *Truth and Method,* Sheed and Ward, London.

Heteronormativity

The view or assumption that heterosexuality is normal or natural, and should be accorded primacy over other sexualities.

See also **Queer theory.**

Hidden curriculum

All education institutions have an official curriculum. Sociologists have also identified a hidden curriculum, unavoidably present in all education institutions. The hidden curriculum is constructed from:

- The organisation of school life: this, among other things, usually teaches pupils to respect authority figures and to compete with each other.
- Role models in reading, history, science and geography books.
- Teachers' attitudes and behaviour.
- Pupil cultures.
- Staffing: the types of people who are in authority positions.

It has been variously argued that a hidden curriculum in schools perpetuates women's disadvantages and the subordination of ethnic minorities, and accustoms pupils to their future positions in the class structure. These claims are easily and plausibly asserted, but so far research has produced little sound evidence of hidden curriculum effects.

See also **Bourdieu, P.; Capital; Education; Social mobility.**

Bowles, S. and Gintis, H. (1976), *Schooling in Capitalist America,* Routledge, London.

Willis, P. (1977), *Learning to Labour*, Saxon House, Farnborough.

H

Historicism

A term that will forever be associated with Karl Popper's (1902–1994) denunciation. Popper identified two historicist arguments:

- Historical eras are unique, and each must be understood in its own terms, which leaves no place for scientific generalisations.
- From the study of history we can derive laws of history which enable us to predict the future (as in Marxism).

Popper contended:

- Scientific laws take the form of 'if–then, under given conditions' propositions, and attempts to identify general laws of history from past trends, and extend these trends into the future, are basically misconceived.
- Therefore, the uniqueness of historical eras is no obstacle to the application of scientific methods.

See also **Popper, K.R.**

Popper, K.R. (1957), *The Poverty of Historicism*, Routledge, London.

Holism

In sociology holism is the opposite of individualism. Holism contends that social entities such as groups and institutions must be treated as wholes with a character that is distinct from, and should not be broken down into, individual conduct. The clearest exposition of the holist viewpoint is Emile Durkheim's (1858–1917) insistence that we treat social facts as things in themselves.

See also **Durkheim, E.; Methodological individualism; Reductionism; Reification.**

Holocaust

The systematic slaughter of up to 6 million Jews by Hitler and the German Nazis (and their collaborators) during the Second World War.
  Sociology's problem is how to explain the Holocaust:

- Hitler's charismatic powers combined with his peculiar ideas?
- Specificities of German history and culture, and social, political and economic conditions in Germany between the wars?
- A particular personality type (the authoritarian personality) that was unusually widespread in inter-war Germany?
- A throwback to pre-modern barbarity?

More disturbing for us today:

- Zygmunt Baumann (1925–) argues that the Holocaust was an

extension, to an extreme extent and in a particular form, of the kind of rationality that is dominant in all modern societies.

- Stanley Milgram (1933–1984), an American social psychologist, conducted experiments which suggest that many of us will commit horrific acts if instructed to do so by an authority figure.

See also **Authoritarian personality; Charisma; Fascism; Rationality.**

Bauman, Z. (1989), *Modernity and the Holocaust*, Cornell University Press, New York.

Milgram, S. (1974, 2005), *Obedience to Authority: An Experimental View*, Pinter and Martin, London.

Homeostasis

A process that regulates a system so as to maintain its equilibrium within itself and with its environment. Homeostatic mechanisms can be built into machines. They can be identified in living organisms. The idea that there are analogous processes in societies is among the controversial propositions of functionalism and (social) systems theory.

See also **Functionalism; Luhmann, N.; Social system.**

Homosexuality

See Sexuality.

Horkheimer, Max (1895–1973)

The Frankfurt School's main exponent of critical theory.

See also **Critical sociology/critical theory; Frankfurt School.**

Horkheimer, M. (1972), *Critical Theory: Selected Essays*, Herder, New York.

Human capital

A concept that is central in the work of economists who have examined education, most notably the US economist Gary S. Becker (1930–). Human capital comprises the productive skills and knowledge that are embodied in the worker.

Boosting human capital is said to make workers more productive, more valuable to employers, therefore increasing firms' productivity and enabling workers to earn higher wages and salaries, and expanding a country's economy. Investing in human capital is claimed to yield a better return than any other kind of investment, and human capital is said to have become the key factor of production in today's knowledge economy. Individuals can invest in their own human capital, and countries can boost the value of their

H

collective human capital through the investment of public funds in appropriate education and training.

This entire way of thinking has been embraced by some, and harshly criticised by other sociologists. The objections are:

- It distorts education, which should aim to develop all human potential regardless of its economic value.
- Correlations between levels of education and earnings are misinterpreted. The benefits to individuals are largely a result of positional competition, and 'credentialism' which leads to the appointment of qualified incompetents. Richer countries spend more on education because they are richer; education is not the cause.
- Wage and salary differentials reflect power rather than productivity and value created.

See also **Capital; Credentialism; Knowledge economy.**

Becker, G. S. (1964, 1993), *Human Capital: A Theoretical and Empirical Analysis with Special Reference to Education*, University of Chicago Press, Chicago.

Human relations

The human relations movement in management thought and practice began in the United States and became influential worldwide between the 1930s and the 1960s. As the title suggests, the importance of good human relations in the workplace is stressed.

The movement arose from a series of studies in the 1920s and 1930s at the Hawthorne branch (near Chicago) of the Western Electric Company. The studies were into workers' responses to changes in their jobs such as the length of breaks and the strength of lighting where they worked. However, the researchers concluded that the results that they were recording were actually responses to the research process itself. Subsequently this type of researcher effect has been known as the Hawthorne effect. The researchers concluded that changes in productivity and in the workers' opinions were due to the fact that someone (the research team) was taking an interest in their jobs and views.

Roethlisberger and Dickson (1939) wrote an account of the Hawthorne experiments. Later Elton Mayo (1949) gave the findings an unambiguous human relations interpretation. It was argued that employees need to feel that their work is valued and that their opinions count. Supervisors need to foster group morale, and ensure that workers' personal and social needs are met. It was argued that employees need to feel involved and allowed to participate in decision making. Exponents of human relations argue that a happy worker is a productive worker. The human relations movement rejected (and for a time replaced) the formerly fashionable approach of scientific management.

Since the 1960s human relations has been marginalised in management thought and practice. The main criticisms have been:

- The presence and role of trade unions are ignored.
- The movement exaggerates social expectations at the expense of employees' financial motivations.
- The extent to which good human relations can be practised is limited by technology, market forces, and the basic realities of the employer–employee relationship.

See also **Braverman, H.; Hawthorne effect; Human resource management; Labour process theory; Scientific management; Self-actualisation.**

Mayo, E. (1949), *The Social Problems of an Industrial Civilization*, Routledge, London.

Roethlisberger, F. and Dickson, W. (1939), *Management and the Worker*, Harvard University Press, Cambridge, Mass.

Rose, M. (1988), *Industrial Behaviour*, Penguin Harmondsworth.

Human resource management

Formerly called personnel management. Personnel departments used to handle hiring and firing, absences, employees' tax and National Insurance contributions, and industrial relations. These remain among the functions of human resource departments, but there has been a change in philosophy as well as name. Human resource management (HRM) starts with an organisation's customers or clients, then asks what skills and what numbers of employees are required to satisfy the demands of the market. Recruitment and, more important, employee training, can then be organised accordingly.

There is a controversial management ideology behind HRM. It is claimed, or hoped, that employees will be empowered and enabled to pursue personal career development, thus harmonising workforce and organisational goals. Sociologists are mostly sceptical as to whether this is possible when firms are at the mercy of wider market forces, and while there are basic differences in the interests of employers and workers, and sometimes between different groups of workers as well.

See also **Human relations; Industrial relations; Trade unions.**

Legge, K. (2004), *Human Resource Management: Rhetorics and Realities*, Palgrave Macmillan, Basingstoke.

H

Humanism

Developed as an alternative to religious belief; insists on placing human needs, well-being, fulfilment, dignity and worth ahead of all else, whether the else be God or nature. This position has been incorporated within:

- Humanistic Marxism: this is said to be the Marxism of the young Marx, who was concerned about alienation, and appeared to take the condition of humanity rather than the social/class structure as his prime concern.

- Humanistic psychology: stresses human potential for growth and self-actualisation.
- Humanistic sociology: this seeks to place sociology at the service of humanity, recognises human subjectivity and creativity, insists that human intention and activity can play determining roles in life, and thus sides with 'agency' in any structure–agency debates.

In recent times the main challenge to humanist perspectives has come not from religion but from structuralist and post-structuralist attempts to decentre the human subject.

See also **Decentring; Post-structuralism; Structuralism.**

Husserl, Edmund (1859–1938)

The German philosopher who founded phenomenology.

Husserl's central contention was that all that we can possibly know is what we perceive rather than the world out there as it actually is. This view had been expounded earlier by Immanuel Kant (1724–1804) who distinguished phenomena (what we perceive) from nuomena (things as they really are that we can never apprehend directly). According to Husserl, this meant that true knowledge had to be about our lived-in worlds (*Lebenswelt*), our inner mental states.

These ideas were imported into sociology by one of Husserl's students, Alfred Schutz (1899–1959).

See also **Kant, I.; Phenomenology; Schutz, A.**

Husserl, E. (1970), *The Crisis of the European Sciences and Transcendental Phenomenology,* Northwestern University Press, Evanston, Ill.

Hyper-reality

One of the concepts coined by Jean Baudrillard (1929–2007), the French social theorist. Hyper-reality is when a media representation is treated as if it were reality. Baudrillard claims that in our media saturated, postmodern world, the distinction between reality and media representations has broken down completely.

See also **Baudrillard, J.; Simulacra.**

H

Hypothesis

A proposition which can be, and needs to be, tested by obtaining or consulting the relevant evidence. Also, according to Karl Popper (1902–1994), the proposition must be falsifiable.

See also **Popper, K.R.**

Ideal speech situation

See Habermas, J.

Ideal type

This concept was introduced into sociology by Max Weber (1864–1920), who borrowed it from economics. An ideal type is an idealised representation of something. Idealised here means logically pure rather than ethical, average or modal. Model is an alternative term.

Ideal types are products of the imagination of an investigator who selects what are considered to be important features of a situation or process, then relates them to one another in a logical way. Examples from economics include utility-maximising economic man and perfect competition. Weber's own ideal types included traditional authority and the Protestant ethic. The value of ideal types is that they highlight in an extreme form processes or tendencies that are present, and thereby assist in understanding and explaining what is happening, in the real world.

See also **Models; Weber, M.**

Idealism

In everyday life an idealist is someone with pure and probably unrealisable aspirations. In philosophy and sociology an idealist believes that ideas are the source of actions. The opposite is materialism (ideas reflect material conditions/actions).

Georg Hegel (1770–1831) is usually regarded as the arch-idealist, and the mature Karl Marx (1818–1883) as the classic materialist. In present-day sociology symbolic interactionists are close to the idealist position, while most other theoretical positions combine elements of idealism and materialism, or agency and structure.

See also **Agency; Hegel, G.F.W.; Symbolic interactionism.**

Identity

This refers to an individual's sense of self, and also to how the person is identified by others. Ever since the time of Charles Horton Cooley

(1864–1929) and George Herbert Mead (1863–1931), sociologists have treated these as interdependent.

Identity and self have gained renewed prominence in sociology in recent times. It is accepted that to some extent identities have always been situation specific. So whether I feel that I am, and whether others treat me as, a father, a sociologist or a football fan depends on the situation. However, it is believed that in earlier, simpler societies, where people interacted with the same others in their neighbourhoods, workplaces and at play, identities would be integrated and stable, whereas in the modern world, where we interact with entirely different sets of others in different places, identities become more compartmentalised and fragmented. This can create a disjuncture between a surface me (how I appear at present) and my sense of the real underlying me. Some sociologists argue that in late- or post-modern societies life has become so fluid and fragmented that we are liable to lose any sense of who we really are, that identities are now subject to constant revision, and can even be changed and chosen deliberately, then advertised to others by wearing the appropriate clothing or having cosmetic surgery, for example.

See also **Cooley, T.H.; Goffman, E.; Mead, G.H.; Role; Self.**

Ideographic

An approach that focuses on the particular – a person, a situation, an event, a country – and seeks to understand through intensive study. The opposite approach is nomothetic. This examines a large number of cases and seeks generalisations (laws, for example), which are then said to explain the particular.

In Germany in the latter part of the nineteenth century there was an intense debate – the context in which Max Weber (1864–1920) lived and worked – about which of these approaches was best suited for the study of history and social life.

Ideological state apparatus

This term was coined by Louis Althusser (1918–1990), the French structural Marxist, to refer to certain institutions which help to maintain the conditions for the reproduction of capitalist relations of production. State apparatus here does not refer only to government departments but to any institution which is supported by the state or which transmits the state's ideology. These institutions, in Althusser's view, included the family, schools, the media, and even political parties and trade unions.

Althusser also identified 'repressive state apparatuses' (the army, police, courts and prisons) which functioned with the ultimate sanction of force. These institutions were regarded as a necessary fallback, but Althusser believed they needed to be complemented by ideological apparatuses and that, in the long term, the ruling (capitalist) class would be unable to maintain its position if it lost its ideological hegemony.

See also **Althusser, L.; Gramsci, A.; Hall, S.; Hegemony.**

Ideology

In sociology this term has a general and a more specific (Marxist) meaning. The general meaning is any coherent set of ideas that justifies a situation, action, event or set of policies. Thus we can speak of the ideologies of churches, political parties, the Green movement, feminism and so on.

Marxists have given the term a more specific meaning. Here ideas are ideological if they are untrue and justify exploitative economic, political and social practices. The Italian Marxist Antonio Gramsci (1891–1937) used the term hegemony to describe a situation where the ruling class's ideology came to be accepted as factually true, with no alternative imaginable. Subsequent Marxists, including the French theorist Louis Althusser (1918–1990), have stressed the importance of ideology in securing the compliance and acquiescence of subordinate groups. However, critics, using survey evidence, have queried the importance of dominant (or any consensual) ideas in maintaining a capitalist system.

See also **Althusser, L.; Gramsci, A.; Hall, S.; Hegemony; Ideological state apparatus; Marx, K.**

Abercrombie, N., Hill, S. and Turner, B.S. (1980), *The Dominant Ideology Thesis*, Allen and Unwin, London.

Illich, Ivan (1926–2002)

Vienna-born to Croatian-Jewish parents, one-time Roman Catholic priest and Vice-Rector of the Catholic University of Puerto Rico, where Illich became disillusioned with the Vatican's support for modern development in the Third World. He believed that visitors, including missionaries, should behave as respectful guests. Subsequently based in Mexico, Illich resigned as a priest in the late 1960s and embarked on a savage critique of modern life.

Illich believed that modern life made people far too dependent on institutions, experts and professionals, and that this resulted in a loss of useful knowledge and skills that had been nurtured and treasured throughout human history. In his best-known book, *Deschooling Society,* Illich argued that people are best educated outside schools, in informal learning webs and peer matching networks. In *Medical Nemesis* he argued that people enjoy best health when they retain the ability to care for themselves, their families, friends and neighbours, and do not treat doctors and hospitals as first resorts in times of illness. Illich was a passionate advocate of simpler, more convivial, and ultimately more satisfying alternatives to twentieth-century modernity.

Illich, I. (1972), *Deschooling Society*, Calder and Boyars, London.

Illich, I. (1975), *Medical Nemesis*, Calder and Boyars, London.

Illness

See Health.

Immigration

See Migration.

Immiseration

A Marxist term which refers to the (expected) condition of the working class under capitalism with wages held down to subsistence levels, and threatened by unemployment.

See also **Marx, K.**

Imperialism

See Colonialism.

Indigenous group

Alternatively called 'native people'. An indigenous group is an ethnic group whose origins are in the territory that it inhabits, which has also been settled by migrants (maybe colonisers). The term is normally used when the indigenous people have become a minority in their own homeland.

See also **Migration.**

Individualisation

A term introduced to international sociology by German sociologists, most notably Ulrich Beck (1944–). Individualisation is treated by Beck as part of a broader set of changes associated with the transformation of western (and other) societies into risk societies. Globalisation, new technologies, serious imbalances between human behaviour and the natural environment, the decline of employment in older manufacturing and extractive industries and the expansion of service sector employment are all implicated, but in Beck's account the development of welfare states (an enduring feature of modern societies in Beck's view) and the weakening of families, neighbourhood and religious communities have made the greatest contributions to individualisation. Beck sees individualisation as the outcome of releasing individuals from former structural constraints, enabling, and indeed obliging, them to gain control over their own biographies.

However, there is a weaker version of the individualisation thesis that decouples some of the processes that Beck packages together. This defines individualisation simply as a trend towards each individual having a unique biography. The causes of individualisation then remain open for investigation, as does whether former predictors of individuals' life chances have become weaker, or whether they remain in place but operate in ways that are less likely than in the past to make individuals aware of what they share in common with any wider social categories.

All versions regard a heightened awareness of the self, and acceptance of personal responsibility for one's current position and future, as necessary aspects of individualisation.

See also **Beck, U.; Biographisation; Career**.

Beck, U. (1992), *Risk Society: Towards a New Modernity*, Sage, London.

Roberts, K., Clark, S.C. and Wallace, C. (1994), 'Flexibility and individualisation: a comparison of transitions into employment in England and Germany', *Sociology*, 28, 31–54.

Individualism

In sociology individualism is the opposite of holism. Individualism means explaining social phenomena in terms of the intentions and behaviour of individual actors. Interpretive sociology is always individualistic in its explanations. Methodological individualism is a softened version of individualism. Nowadays in sociology the individualism–holism debate is normally presented as structure versus agency, with most sociologists seeking somehow to combine these approaches.

Outside sociology's own discourses, but as a phenomenon that sociologists study, individualism is a set of doctrines that stress the rights and responsibilities of individuals rather than collectivities in religious life, politics and economic life.

See also **Hermeneutics; Holism; Methodological individualism; Rational choice theory**.

Industrial relations

Alternatively called labour relations or (more occasionally) workplace relations. In sociology industrial relations is the sub-discipline that studies relationships between employers and workers, and more specifically in practice, between employers and trade unions.

This sub-discipline addresses the legal framework within which industrial relations are played out, then deals with the trade unions in which workers are organised, together with national and workplace bargaining. This subject has always been one of the arenas in which sociology's big theories have confronted one another: functionalism (the so-called unitary, one big happy family, view of industrial relations), then Marxist and Weberian (pluralist, recognising divisions among workers) perspectives.

See also **Human resource management; Labour process theory; Strikes; Trade unions.**

Ackers, P. and Wilkinson, A. (2003), *Understanding Work and Employment: Industrial Relations in Transition*, Oxford University Press, Oxford.

Industrialisation

Between approximately 1760 and 1850 England became the world's first industrial nation and the extent and tempo of the changes led to their description as 'the industrial revolution'. This general process of change became known as 'industrialisation', leading to the creation of 'industrial society'.

In England there was no revolution akin to the French Revolution (1789–99). Industrialisation in England was evolutionary, but the immensity and speed of the changes led to the process being experienced as revolutionary. The main changes involved in industrialisation in England were:

- Movement of labour from agriculture into manufacturing industries. This required a parallel agricultural revolution in order to feed an expanding total population with a reduced agricultural workforce.
- The use of inanimate power, first water power then steam power, in the manufacture of textiles, iron and steel, and in coal extraction and transport.
- Rapid technological developments – new machines, some made possible only by the availability of inanimate power – for use in textiles, coal mining, and in metal production and manufacturing.
- The spread of a factory system, which led to a greatly increased division of labour, and increased employer control over workers.
- Urbanisation.

There were other associated changes – population growth, the expansion of education, the development of new welfare services, and demands for political change – all alongside an expansion of economic output and consumption.

The industrial revolution in England was soon followed by the industrialisation of, and broadly similar changes in, other west European countries and the United States.

The search for an explanation of these changes, and a better understanding of the emergent social order, inspired the birth of sociology, and major controversies in the discipline have always been about the answers offered by the so-called founding fathers – Comte, Marx, Spencer, Durkheim, Weber and others.

The extent to which all industrial societies share many other features in common, and hence the value of the concept of 'industrial society', have been queried as more and more countries have industrialised (under communism, and in the Far East and Latin America, for example). Another continuing controversy is whether the common features shared by the original industrial societies were consequences of industrialisation itself or its capitalist character.

See also **Convergence thesis; Post-industrialism.**

Thompson, E.P. (1968), *The Making of the English Working Class,* Penguin, Harmondsworth.

Inequality

See Stratification.

Information economy/Information society

It is not the type or even the sheer quantity of information that is now at our fingertips that is said to make the crucial difference (though the quantity is of some importance) so much as how information is stored and communicated (in computers and via the Internet) that is allegedly transforming our social relationships.

New information technologies make place less important than it was in the past. Employees in an organisation based in one place can just as easily communicate with employees in an entirely different organisation (and on a different continent) as with their colleagues down the corridor. Thus it has become easier, and often highly convenient, for groups based in different organisations to work jointly on a task. People can work from home or in other locations that are miles apart from their organisations' offices. Communication networks and computers are said to have become the new basis for production. Former boundaries – between organisations and between countries – are said to be breaking down. People now work in networks with no fixed centres and through which power is diffused.

Outside our work roles we can act similarly, establishing and maintaining relationships at a distance. We can become part of virtual communities. We can create virtual identities for ourselves – a variety of them. This means that in social interaction identities are constantly being remade rather than taken as given from our pasts.

Manuel Castells (1942–), the Spanish sociologist, detects an emergent network society made possible by the globalisation of communications.

Many sociologists are deeply sceptical. Because something may happen does not mean that it necessarily will happen. Up to now, few employees of organisations work solely or mainly from home. They feel that they need to 'go in' in order to feel part of real work groups. Trans-national companies congregate in global cities partly because only face-to-face interaction enables people to create trust relationships. This also applies in non-work life. Rather than changing the character of our personal networks of friends, communications technology (the Internet and the telephone) may simply add another dimension to relationships with other bases.

See also **Castells, M.; Creative industries; Cultural industries; Knowledge economy/Knowledge society; Network; Post-industrialism; Time–space distanciation.**

Castells, M. (2000), *The Rise of the Network Society*, Blackwell, Oxford.

Information technology

An information technology is any non-human means of storing, processing and transmitting information. In this sense, a book is an item of information technology. However, when anyone mentions information technology today, they are sure to be referring to the electronic, digitised information and communication technologies associated with the computer and the Internet which have joined and enhanced earlier wireless, television, telephone, cable and satellite technologies.

Sociologists are aware that these new technologies are now affecting all areas of people's lives. There can be few occupations that have not been affected in some way. Most people in richer countries now have plenty of new technology in their homes. Many of our leisure activities are affected in some way. The effects are so generalised that an issue for sociology is whether we are entering a new information age and living in new kinds of information societies. However, an older debate has been revived: technological determinism versus the view that the specific technologies that are developed and the uses to which they are put are governed by pre-existing social, economic and political relationships.

See also **Information economy/Information society; Technological determinism.**

Institution

See Social institution.

Institutionalisation

This term has two meanings in sociology.

First, it is the process whereby social institutions are created and changed as initially novel patterns of behaviour become settled, routine, and enforced by some combination of group/public opinion, custom (eventually), organisational rules and law.

The second meaning is the effects on individuals of long periods of confinement within total institutions.

See also **Social institution; Total institution.**

Instrumentalism

This refers to a type of rational outlook and behaviour where actions are selected solely to achieve desired ends. In ideal typical instrumental action, behaviour is not influenced by tradition or chosen for affect (expression of emotional feelings).

It has been claimed that this kind of rationality becomes increasingly widespread as societies modernise. So approaches to work become basically instrumental (a source of income), we view membership of trade unions and professional associations as means to private ends, and decide to support political parties in a similar way, with no emotive, solidaristic attachment.

An alleged result is that people feel an increasing need for outlets for their emotions which have to be sought in leisure activities and in private life, sometimes exclusively within the family. However, another debate in sociology is about whether the family is any longer a secure haven for expressiveness in an otherwise cold, impersonal, rational world.

See also **Affect; Pure relationship; Rationality.**

Intellectuals

These are well educated, and work in intellectual occupations, nowadays most likely in the cultural, knowledge and creative industries. Sociology's main interest is in the social role of intellectuals.

In the mid-twentieth century there was a debate in sociology about whether it was possible for intellectuals to contribute impartially, objectively, on matters of public interest. This debate was resolved by agreeing that, on social issues, impartiality, value neutrality, was not possible, and that intellectuals either viewed things from a specifically professional viewpoint, or aligned themselves with wider movements.

Intellectuals may be a recognised social group, an intelligentsia, with a recognised role in cultural and political affairs. Intelligentsia strata were formed in Russia after the 1860s and then in other European countries, but survived to (almost) the end of the twentieth century only in communist countries.

Elsewhere any specialised extra-professional role has been played by public intellectuals who address the 'general public' rather than just advise non-academic organisations or groups. In practice, today, addressing a general public means that public intellectuals are in the mass media, using their professional status and communication skills to gain a platform from which to participate and make expert contributions in wider public and political debates.

Sociology, like other disciplines, has produced public intellectuals, but an aspiration of some sociologists has always been that sociology itself should be a public sociology, addressing issues of interest to a wider public and commanding public attention. However, in practice in the twenty-first century there is concern that the public space that could be occupied by sociology and other public intellectuals is now taken by media presenters, and, to some extent, by the staff of the 'think tanks' that are associated with political parties.

See also **Creative industries.**

Burawoy, M. (2005), 'For public sociology', *American Sociological Review*, 70, 4–28.

Intelligence

See IQ.

Interaction(ism)

See Symbolic interactionism.

Interpretive sociology

See Hermeneutics.

Interviews

The interview is a standard way in which sociologists gather information about their subjects. Interviews can be face to face or (increasingly common) by telephone. Telephone interviewing is cheaper, and the absence of non-verbal interaction is compensated by a reduced risk of interviewer effects. When teams of interviewers are used there are ways of checking for interviewer effects: are there differences in their results that are otherwise inexplicable? Face-to-face interviews can last longer than telephone interviews unless the telephone interview is pre-arranged and the subject knows the likely timescale. Otherwise it is easier to replace a telephone receiver than to break off a face-to-face encounter.

The self-completion questionnaire is the main alternative to the interview. Response rates are usually much lower with questionnaires, whether delivered by post or email (but there are ways of checking whether non-response is affecting the representativeness of a sample). Interviewers have the advantage of being able to probe and prompt for answers to open-ended questions, and in asking follow-ups depending on initial answers. Interaction with the interviewer may produce more revealing answers than a self-completion questionnaire, but sometimes, with sensitive topics, respondents may be more forthcoming in a wholly anonymous situation, and questionnaires eliminate the possibility of interviewer effects which can be checked for but, if found, cannot be eliminated.

Somewhat different interviewing techniques are required depending on whether respondents are simply members of the public, or from a particular group (a profession, for example), or whether they are key or expert informants.

Interviews may or may not be tape-recorded (always with the permission of the respondent). Tape-recording allows the interviewer to remain engaged with the respondent, to reproduce verbatim quotations, and if fully transcribed, recorded interviews can be subjected to formal content analysis. However, full transcription is expensive and time consuming, and recording an interview may inhibit the subject. The alternative is for an interviewer to take detailed notes and to write up each interview with as little time delay as possible.

It is increasingly common for answers to fully structured (closed) questions (where there is a pre-set list of possible answers) to be input electronically on a laptop during an interview itself, but this is impossible when questions are open ended, and being able to ask such questions is one of the advantages of interviewing.

Professional ethics require sociologists to explain the purposes of a research project to their respondents, and what will happen to the information collected, to guarantee individual anonymity, to explain that participation is voluntary, and that a respondent is able to decline to answer particular questions and to terminate an interview at any time.

See also **Codes, coding; Questionnaires; Response rates; Surveys.**

IQ

IQ stands for intelligence quotient, which is calculated from the results of intelligence tests. The first intelligence test was constructed by the French psychologists Alfred Binet (1857–1911) and Theodore Simon (1872–1961) at the beginning of the twentieth century. From answers to blocks of questions, average scores for children of different ages were calculated. On this basis each individual could be given a mental age, which was divided by that individual's chronological age to produce the intelligence quotient. The procedure is technically different with present-day IQ tests, but 100 remains the average score; 140 and above is described as genius.

There has been persistent controversy about what these tests measure. They predict academic performance, future occupational status and earnings, but what is the predictor, IQ? Is it a 'thing' in the brain? Or is IQ just a mathematical construct? Or, as sociologists have always tended to argue, is it a social construct which enables some people to be labelled intelligent?

Sociologists have always been interested in how intelligence is produced, and equally in the uses of IQ tests. Binet and Simon developed their test to assist in identifying schoolchildren who could benefit from remedial education, but before long IQ tests were also being used to select pupils for academic programmes, and to select job applicants. Users tended to act on the belief that intelligence was a 'thing' and that this 'thing' was largely inherited. Relevant research, with special attention (which continues to this day) to identical twins who have been reared apart, has suggested that the greater part of the variance in IQ scores is due to hereditary processes. By the mid-twentieth century supporters of IQ tests were envisaging an age when societies would be led by elites of the brightest (genuine meritocracies). MENSA was established: an international society with membership restricted to the top 2 per cent according to their intelligence test scores.

Males and females have always scored similarly on IQ tests, but there have been substantial differences between the mean scores of children from different social class backgrounds and different 'racial' groups. Blacks in North America and Africa have lower mean scores than North American whites, who in turn have lower mean scores than some Asian populations in North America. There is continuing controversy as to what this information means, and how it should be used.

Towards the end of the twentieth century, confidence that IQ tests measure inherited ability was shattered by the discovery of the Flynn effect, named after the New Zealand political scientist James R. Flynn. He pointed out that that in developed countries average scores on identical tests had been improving by approximately three points per decade. Flynn has attributed this improvement to more stimulating environments. It had already been shown that performances on IQ tests could be improved by coaching.

Sociologists collectively have always leant heavily towards the social construction and environmentalist wings in debates about what IQ tests measure, and have pointed out that, whatever these tests measure, other attributes also play important roles in success in education, the labour market and politics. Sociologists have been especially critical of uses of IQ tests that serve to perpetuate existing social class and ethnic inequalities.

See also **Meritocracy; Murray, C.**

Fraser, S. (1995), *The Bell Curve Wars: Race, Intelligence and the Future of America*, Basic Books, New York.

Gould, S.J. (1983), *The Mismeasurement of Man*, Penguin, Harmondsworth.

Herrnstein, R.J. and Murray, C. (1994), *The Bell Curve: Intelligence and Class Structure in American Life*, Simon and Schuster, New York.

Young, M. (1958), *The Rise of the Meritocracy*, Thames and Hudson, London.

Iron law of oligarchy

See Michels, R.

Jameson, Fredric (1934–)

American literary critic and cultural theorist: relevant in sociology on account of his fierce critique of postmodern thought and postmodernist thinkers such as Jean Baudrillard (1929–2007) and Jean-Francois Lyotard (1924–1998).

Jameson defends an orthodox, classical Marxist position, resisting relativism and arguing that the production and consumption of art and culture are always grounded in the prevailing economic realities. He believes that postmodern thought is 'the cultural logic of late-capitalism' which has thoroughly colonised the cultural sphere. Postmodern thought is said to stem from the conditions of intellectual labour imposed by multinational, corporate capitalism.

See also **Baudrillard, J.; Lyotard, J-F.; Postmodern.**

Jameson, F. (1991), *Postmodernism, or, The Cultural Logic of Late Capitalism*, Verso, London.

Justice

Philosophers debate the meaning of justice. They generally agree that justice means applying rules impartially, then disagree over how to decide whether a society's distribution of resources is just, and likewise on what amounts to just treatment (punishment) for people who break the law and other rules.

Sociology's interest is in what ordinary people believe to be just, and the research evidence shows that people's values vary between cultures, as therefore do people's ideas on whether particular practices and outcomes are just. In sociology, it is consistency with people's values that matters, and which is considered necessary for a society's patterns and practices to be experienced as justifiable, and therefore fair and legitimate. There is no social order that can be identified as objectively and absolutely just, independently of the cultural context and the values that this prescribes.

See also **Values.**

Kant, Immanuel (1724–1804)

Revered German philosopher who is relevant in sociology for his rejection of empiricism, his insistence that all our knowledge about 'things out there' is really phenomenal, and his categorisation of how things can be known.

Kant argued that the human mind must play a role in organising our knowledge. He argued that we can never know about 'things as they really are' (which he called nuomena), but only about phenomena (things as they seem to us). So Kantian philosophy is the foundation of phenomenology.

However, Kant distinguished three different ways in which can know that statements are true:

- They may be true by definition (tautological).
- They can be known to be true as a result of observation and experiment.
- They can be proven *a priori*, simply by thinking. For example, we can work out the properties of triangles and squares by pure thought.

*See also **A priori**; **Empiricism**; **Ontology**; **Phenomenology**.*

Keynes, John Maynard (1883–1946)

The English economist who revised orthodox economic thinking and gave his name to the Keynesian economic policies which are generally considered responsible for the full employment and steady economic growth experienced in western countries during the '30 glorious years' that followed the Second World War.

Orthodox economic thinking had insisted that governments should balance their own budgets, and use interest rates to preserve the exchange value of national currencies. Levels of employment, investment and growth were to be left to market forces. Keynes argued that governments could and should manage aggregate demand in an economy so as to smooth out booms and recessions, maintain full employment and achieve steady economic growth. This could be done by lowering taxes and increasing government spending (even if this left a budget deficit) when unemployment and recession threatened, and reversing these policies during economic upturns.

Keynesian economic management retains supporters but from the 1970s onwards these ideas were challenged by monetarist and neo-liberal economists.

*See also **Fordism**; **Monetarism**; **Neo-liberalism**.*

Keynes, J.M. (1936), *The General Theory of Employment, Interest and Money*, Macmillan, London.

Kinship

Family are kin, but kinship can extend beyond a family. Kinship was, and sometimes still is, extremely important in the societies studied by social and cultural anthropologists. In these societies an individual's entire life can be spent with kin and regulated by rules of kinship. Membership of a kin group may be by descent (lineage) or by marriage (affinity).

Kinship systems, where they still exist, are governed by intricate rules and customs. These deal with inheritance, which may be patrilineal (father to son) or matrilineal (mother's brother to sister's son, that is, uncle to nephew). Other rules govern residence: patrilocal (wife joins husband's family), matrilocal (husband moves), or neolocal (marrying couple create independent household). There are rules governing marriage. An incest taboo (no marriages between close relatives) appears to be universal. Thereafter a person may be required to marry within a kin group (endogamy) or outside (exogamy), and in the latter case there will be rules prescribing with which other groups marriage is acceptable or prescribed. Marriages may be monogamous or polygamous (polygyny allows men to have more than one wife, while polyandry allows wives to have more than one husband).

These rules, and the kinship systems that they held together, have disappeared from modern societies. In many senses, kinship has been replaced by the family on one side, and ethnic groups and nations on the other. Practising old rules by favouring relatives, for example, is now likely to be condemned as nepotism.

See also **Extended family; Family**.

Knowledge economy/Knowledge society

The use of these terms implies that we have entered or are on the threshold of an age in which knowledge will be the key factor of production in a 'weightless economy'; that a country's economic strength now depends less on its material resources and financial capital than the quality of its workforce; and that the best investment that any country can make is in the education of its people, making them innovative and creative. Some claim that intelligence now needs to be treated as a collective rather than just an individual asset.

It is claimed that a growing proportion of employment is in knowledge industries, and that a growing proportion of workers are becoming knowledge workers, processing information in a quest for innovative solutions to problems. These workers can be found in all industries, but maybe especially in computer software, the media, other entertainment industries, education, training and research. Knowledgeable workers are said to be

K

knowledgeable consumers, technologically literate, seeking uses of free time that will exercise and develop their intellectual powers.

These claims are very difficult to substantiate. Critics ask how many workers are required to be truly creative as opposed to just processing information in routine ways. In any case, surely the abilities to design new products and to find improved ways of working have been important throughout the industrial age.

Another claim is that the knowledge society will accord the highest status, and will be run by, the most knowledgeable people, namely highly educated professionals. Maybe, but in the 1950s and 1960s some sociologists were forecasting rule by 'technocrats', and claims of a 'managerial revolution' predate the Second World War.

See also **Creative industries; Information economy/Information society; Managerial revolution; Post-industrialism; Technocracy.**

Bell, D. (1974), *The Coming of Post-Industrial Society,* Basic Books, New York.

Leadbetter, C. (1999), *Living on Thin Air: The New Economy,* Viking, London.

Kuhn, Thomas Samuel (1922–1996)

A US historian of science who claimed that scientific knowledge did not develop in a smooth, linear fashion but through relatively tranquil periods of normal science punctuated by scientific revolutions.

Kuhn was a historian, not a philosopher of science, who asked what scientists actually did in their day-to-day work lives. The claim which made Kuhn world famous was that scientists were not forever critical, developing new insights and testing novel ideas. Kuhn claimed that for most of the time scientists worked uncritically within accepted paradigms – definitions of the problems to be investigated and the methods to be used. However, points were reached when the knowledge accumulated by normal scientific research became so overwhelmingly incompatible with the prevailing paradigm that the stage was set for a revolutionary upheaval, such as had been instigated by Isaac Newton (1643–1727), Charles Darwin (1809–1882) and Albert Einstein (1879–1955), following which the scientific community would settle into another period of normal science. So major breakthroughs were not the outcome of scientists constantly playing with big new ideas but were forced by their much more mundane, unglamorous work as accumulators of evidence through normal scientific activity.

K

Ever since their publication, Kuhn's arguments have inspired debates about:

- Was he right about how scientific knowledge develops? (The jury is still out.)
- What are the implications for sociology and other social sciences? (We are still unsure.)

See also **Positivism; Science.**

Kuhn, T. (1962), *The Structure of Scientific Revolutions,* Chicago University Press, Chicago.

Labelling theory

This theory was formulated in the 1960s as part of a 'new criminology', at a time when symbolic interactionism was becoming influential in sociology. The theory is not only about deviance, but this was the original, and is still the most vivid illustration.

The theory notes, first, that deviance (and criminal) are labels applied to particular acts rather than inherent in any acts themselves. Second, there are obvious senses in which a person becomes a criminal by simply breaking the law, but the label of criminal is applied to the person only following detection and conviction, from which there are likely to be consequences. These may well include social ostracism which drives the person into a deviant subculture, which leads to secondary deviance and a general process of deviance amplification. The classic illustration is Howard S. Becker's (1928–) study of the process of becoming a marijuana user.

Labelling occurs in all areas of social life, and recognising the significance of labelling always adds to our understanding. Mental illness and football hooligan are labels. So is extremist (religious or political). There were no homosexuals (though the acts were well known) before the term was first used in the 1860s.

See also **Deviance; Symbolic interactionism.**

Becker, H.S. (1963), *Outsiders: Studies in the Sociology of Deviance*, Free Press, Glencoe, Ill.

Labour

See Employment; Work.

Labour markets

A labour market exists when the sellers of labour power (workers) and the purchasers (employers) establish contractual relationships on the basis of price (wage or salary, and any other benefits). The contract enables the relationship to be terminated by either party. Labour markets make labour power a commodity that is bought and sold, like other commodities.

Labour markets do not exist where there is a command economy, that is, where terms and conditions of employment are fixed by the state, and where labour is directed and allocated to employers by state planners. Nor are there labour markets when labour is bound to a master by law or custom (as under serfdom and slavery).

Labour markets differ from most other markets in a number of ways:

- Labour markets are often regulated by collective bargaining between trade unions, professional associations and employers, and by state regulations which stipulate minimum wages, maximum working hours, and very likely other terms and conditions as well.
- Pay relativities between occupations tend to become traditional and fluctuations are marginal, however great the imbalances between demand and supply.
- Labour mobility is sluggish because workers become reluctant to change occupations and move geographically, which usually means leaving family, friends and places towards which attachments have developed.
- All parties operate with imperfect labour market knowledge, and useful, detailed labour market information is often obtained through informal channels.
- Labour power is not a uniform commodity. Workers not only offer different kinds and levels of skills and qualifications. They are also divided by gender, age and ethnicity, which may influence their perceived suitability and the jobs for which the workers consider themselves suited.

These are the reasons why sociology has probably contributed more than economics to our understanding of how labour markets work.

See also **Dual labour market; Employment.**

Fevre, R. (1992), *The Sociology of Labour Markets*, Harvester Wheatsheaf, Hemel Hempstead.

Labour process theory

A neo-Marxist body of work, inspired by Harry Braverman's (1920–1976) book *Labour and Monopoly Capital* which argued that beneath changes in management theories there had been a progressive separation of control and execution, deskilling and systematically extracting surplus value.

Labour process theory is not so much a theory as a body of work within a critical Marxist perspective that explores behind other theories and ideologies to examine the labour process, focusing on how managements (try to) control labour, and how workers resist.

See also Braverman, H.; Human relations; Human resource management; Scientific management.

Braverman, H. (1974), *Labour and Monopoly Capital: The Degradation of Work in the Twentieth Century*, Monthly Review Press, New York.

www.hrm.strath.ac.uk/ILPC

Labour theory of value

See Marx, K.

Lacan, Jacques (1901–1981)

A French psychoanalyst – a practitioner as well as a writer and theoriser – who re-interpreted Freud in the light of modern (Saussurian) linguistics.

Lacan's key idea was that the unconscious could be likened to, and treated as, a language, and that in childhood the acquisition of language and the development of a sense of self are closely interwoven. Lacan's combination of Freud and Saussure was influential in the development of structuralist thought in the social sciences in France in the 1950s and 1960s. He believed that our self-awareness (our sense of who we are) was a product of unconscious 'discourses' that the self could not control nor readily bring to consciousness.

> *See also* **Freud, S.; Saussure, F. de; Structuralism.**
>
> Lacan, J. (1989), *Ecrits: A Selection*, Routledge, London.
>
> Lacan, J. (1995), *Lacan's Four Fundamental Concepts of Psychoanalysis*, State University of New York Press, New York.

Laissez-faire economics

See Neo-liberalism.

Language

Language is believed to distinguish humans from all other species. We compose thoughts in language. Language shapes how we perceive the world, and what we are able to know. We build and maintain social relationships through language. Hence the importance that some sociologists attach to the analysis of conversations. French structuralists such as Claude Levi-Strauss (1908–) have argued that in identifying the structure of language we are revealing the foundations on which all thoughts, social relationships and practices are based.

This is why some sociologists regard the study of language not as a specialism but as central to all sociology.

> *See also* **Conversation analysis; Levi-Strauss, C.; Linguistics; Socio-linguistics; Structuralism.**

Latent function

See Functionalism; Merton, R.K.

Law

For laws in science (and sociology) *see* Positivism; Science.

Law (here) comprises the rules made by the legislative branch of government (Parliament in the UK), and how these laws are enforced (or not enforced).

There are different types of law (criminal, civil and constitutional). Law plays an important role in social life. It regulates citizens' relationships with one another and defines their responsibilities to the state. Law also confers rights – freedom within the law, vis-à-vis other citizens and from otherwise arbitrary state power.

Sociology is interested in how laws are made by governments and by courts (where laws are interpreted and developed into case law). We are interested in how courts and other law enforcement agencies operate, the roles of specialist personnel, and how offenders are dealt with. In total, the task of sociology is to understand the ways and senses in which law is made by a society and how, in turn, the law governs (or otherwise affects) society in general.

> *See also* **Criminology; Deviance; Government; Penology; Socio-legal studies; State.**

> Banakar, R. and Travers, M. (eds) (2002), *An Introduction to Law and Social Theory*, Hart, Oxford.

Legitimacy

In everyday life, legitimate means lawful. Sociology gives the term a broader meaning: any act that is authorised (in the eyes of the actor and others).

Following Max Weber (1864–1920), sociologists continue to classify sources of legitimacy as:

- Traditional: where an act is considered legitimate because it is customary.
- Legal-rational: where the rules of an organisation or the law are being applied impartially by someone authorised to act under these rules.
- Charismatic: where legitimacy is conferred by the exceptional, inspirational qualities of an actor.

> *See also* **Authority; Weber, M.**

Legitimation crisis

See Habermas, J.

Leisure

Leisure is time unaccounted for by the various kinds of work that people do (education, paid work, housework, childcare and self-maintenance). Leisure activities are whatever people do in their leisure time.

Leisure, as we know it today, is a product of industrialism and the modernisation of life:

- The separation of paid work from the rest of life as a result of its location in factories and offices, and its temporal separation by fixed work-time schedules.
- The rationalisation of work, which means that opportunities to do things purely for fun, amusement, for their own sake, become concentrated within leisure time.

Sociology is interested in how the distribution and uses of leisure are related to social roles associated with age, gender and occupation; the experiences – the satisfactions and frustrations – that people gain from their leisure; and the wider social consequences of their uses of leisure.

Sociological interest in leisure has grown alongside the growth of leisure time and spending; as cities, regions and countries have increasingly looked to the leisure industries to regenerate their economies; and as the contributions (positive and negative) of leisure to physical and mental health and well-being have been recognised.

See also **Consumption; Geodemographics; Lifestyle.**

Roberts, K. (2006), *Leisure in Contemporary Society*, 2nd edition, CABI, Wallingford.

Lesbianism

See Sexuality.

Levi-Strauss, Claude (1908–)

Levi-Strauss was the leading figure in structuralism (a France-based intellectual movement) in the 1960s and 1970s. He sought, largely through an examination of myths, to identify basic and universal categories of human thought, and therefore of social organisation.

One of Levi-Strauss's major claims is that we think in binaries such as up and down, hot and cold, sweet and sour, raw and cooked. Using examples from a range of cultures as evidence, he purported to show that certain binaries recur cross-culturally. The task of the social scientist in examining a particular set of beliefs and related practices is to reveal the specific binaries that are in operation.

Another of Levi-Strauss's major claims is that so-called primitive and so-called advanced people think in basically the same ways, and that allegedly primitive societies and cultures are really no simpler, no less complex, than the people and cultures that are regarded as civilised.

The main criticisms of Levi-Strauss's brand of structuralism are, first, its ahistoricism, its dismissal of all the specific characteristics of societies as

L

superficial. Second, critics claim that the propositions are untestable – that in practice it is always possible to detect a number of binaries, and non-binary structures as well, in any set of beliefs and practices. Third, by stressing the power of underlying structures, the theory is accused of underplaying the role of human agency in social life. Finally, post-structuralists argue that structuralism fails to grasp the genuine implications of Saussurian linguistics for the social and cultural sciences.

See also **Language; Myth; Post-structuralism; Structuralism.**

Levi-Strauss, C. (1969), *Totemism,* Penguin, Harmondsworth.

Levi-Strauss, C. (1972), *The Savage Mind,* Weidenfeld and Nicolson, London.

Life chances

The chances of gaining in life all the things that people value including, literally, life(time) itself.

In practice in sociology, following Max Weber (1864–1920), life chances mean chances of achieving upward social mobility and avoiding downward mobility. This is probably a reasonable proxy since occupational class predicts how long people will live, their health and their wealth.

See also **Social mobility.**

Life course, life cycle

These concepts bring a biographical perspective into sociology. The life course is composed of successive identifiable life stages – childhood, youth, adulthood and senior citizenship, for example – with major status passages marked by 'life events' such as leaving full-time education, marriage and retirement.

In sociology the process of moving from life stage to life stage is not treated as driven purely by biology. Sociology is interested in how the life course is socially constructed. The length of life stages varies by time and place. In recent years in many modern societies, youth has been extended as a result of young people remaining longer in education, and marrying and becoming parents at later ages than formerly.

Nowadays life course is generally preferred to the term life cycle. The latter pictures successive generations experiencing the same journeys through life, and is less receptive than life course to the possibility of changes. However, the life course or cycle still begins with birth and ends with death.

Sociology is interested in how the life course is socially constructed, differences between societies and changes over time. We are interested in how the life course differs between ethnic groups, social classes, and males and females. A further interest lies in identifying 'critical ages' when 'critical events' typically have lifelong implications. For example, educational attainments in childhood influence one's adult occupation and earnings, which predict one's likely prosperity and risks of impoverishment in later life.

L

See also **Biographisation; Career; Cohort; Generation; Individualisation.**

Pilcher, J. (1995), *Age and Generation in Modern Britain*, Oxford University Press, Oxford.

Lifestyle

Until quite recently, throughout history, all over the world and in all societies, people had a way of life that was prescribed, customary or just inevitable given the constraints of how they earned their livings, their incomes and their family circumstances. Lifestyle implies a larger element of choice which is possible in consumer societies where people have money that can be spent on non-essentials. By virtue of the kinds of dwellings that they choose to purchase or rent, the districts where they choose to live, the cars that they drive, the places where they holiday or visit to eat, drink and for entertainment, the clothing that they wear and the music that they listen to, people can align themselves and become publicly associated with specific lifestyle groups. The underlying idea is that there are bundles of tastes, purchases and activities which cluster together, confer identities, and allow those concerned to be identified as a particular kind of person.

Nowadays market researchers routinely identify lifestyle groups whose members can be expected to purchase particular products, whereas others are highly unlikely to purchase ocean cruisers, crates of fine wines or whatever.

Some sociologists now argue that the identities that lifestyles confer are displacing and reducing the significance of longer-standing social markers such as social class and gender. Yet there are clear impediments to lifestyles (however useful for marketing purposes) playing these roles.

There is a tendency for the same people to be active in, and to purchase, a very wide range of leisure goods and services. This is partly an income effect. It is also partly due to a leisure multiplier which works by one activity and one set of leisure relationships introducing those concerned to additional interests and activities. There are people who are particularly interested in sport, and it is sensible for firms that are trying to sell sports goods and services to target these people, but sport will not necessarily dominate their entire lifestyles.

Lifestyles are age and life stage related. Some are lived only on holiday, at weekends or on nights out. Are such lifestyles sufficiently stable to offer similar identities to social class, gender and ethnicity?

See also **Consumption; Geodemographics; Leisure.**

Veal, A.J. (1993), 'The concept of lifestyle: a review', *Leisure Studies*, 12, 233–52.

Lifeworld (*Lebenswelt*)

See Habermas, J.

L

Likert scales

A method of measuring attitudes developed by the American psychologist, Rensis Likert (1903–1981). Individuals are asked to rate statements, usually on 5-point scales ranging from strongly agree to strongly disagree. All the statements purport to tap the same attitude (towards sex, drugs, religion, inequality etc). Statements where the answers correlate with each other are retained. Others are discarded. Individuals' answers to the retained statements are then aggregated, thus enabling the attitude to be measured on a multi-point scale.

See also **Attitude.**

Liminality

A concept invented by the French ethnographer Arnold Van Gennep (1873–1957), then refined by the Scottish anthropologist Victor Turner (1920–1983).

Van Gennep's liminality was a state of mind experienced during life-stage transition rituals, when those involved were between statuses. The concept was subsequently extended to cover experiences during other rituals, and indeed any state where a person was in between (immigrating and settling, for example).

A state of liminality is said to be characterised by ambiguity, indeterminacy and openness. Individuals are said to be disoriented. Normal social divisions (by social class, for example) among participants who share a liminal state are said to dissolve. Normal limits to thought and self-understanding are purportedly relaxed. Mass events – sports events and rock concerts for example – are said to create liminal experiences.

Van Gennep, A. (1909, 1960), *The Rites of Passage,* University of Chicago Press, Chicago.

Turner, V. (1967), *The Forest of Symbols: Aspects of Ndembu Ritual,* Cornell University Press, Ithaca, New York.

L

Linguistics

The study of language and languages, which seeks their rules of grammar, and identifies features that are universal and those that are specific to particular languages.

See also **Chomsky, N.; Language; Saussure, F. de.; Socio-linguistics.**

Lipset, Seymour Martin (1922–2006)

An American political sociologist, best known for his pioneering work on the social conditions for the development and stabilisation of western-type democracy. In addition, Lipset published major works on democracy in trade unions, social mobility, and on why, unlike in Europe, socialism had made so little headway in the United States.

See also **Democracy; Politics.**

Lipset, S.M. (1960), *Political Man: The Social Bases of Politics*, Doubleday, New York.

Lipset, S.M. and Marks, G. (2000), *It Didn't Happen Here: Why Socialism Failed in the United States,* Norton, New York.

Liquid modernity

See Bauman, Z.

Lombroso, Cesare (1836–1909)

An Italian, often regarded as the founder of modern criminology. Lombroso believed that serious criminals were born, not made; that they were human degenerates, throwbacks; and that they could be recognised by physiological characteristics such as large jaws and low sloping foreheads. Alongside these views, Lombroso was an advocate of the humane treatment and, where possible, the rehabilitation of criminals.

Lombroso's ideas are long discredited, but he lived at a time when biological explanations of human behaviour were fashionable and respected in mainstream scientific circles, when phrenology was developing as a mainstream science, and when the eugenics movement was emerging. Also, despite the sidelining of Lombroso's ideas, biological explanations of criminality have never disappeared from criminology.

See also **Criminology; Eugenics; Socio-biology.**

Gibson, M. (2002), *Born to Crime: Cesare Lombroso and the Origins of Biological Criminology*, Praeger, Westport.

Longitudinal study

This gathers information from the same group, or about the same institution or the same situation, at successive points in time. The panel study is an example where the same individuals are interviewed on successive occasions, potentially extending from childhood to retirement.

The main advantage of longitudinal over cross-sectional research is the enhanced possibility of identifying cause–effect links in the development of individuals' lives and attitudes. The disadvantages of longitudinal study are the expense, the time that must elapse before results are available, and the possibility of a Hawthorne (observer) effect as a result of the researchers' repeated interventions.

A quasi-longitudinal study relies on people recalling their education, labour market and marital histories, for example. Here there are risks of memory lapses, but the main limitation is that people cannot be relied on to recall accurately their subjective states (opinions and attitudes) at earlier points in their lives.

See also **Birth cohort studies; British Household Panel Survey; Panel study.**

Looking glass self

See Cooley, C.H.

Luhmann, Niklas (1927–1998)

A German sociologist who developed a rival to Talcott Parsons' systems theory.

Luhmann treated societies as systems which owe their character primarily to being systems (like mechanical systems, biological systems etc.) rather than to being social. A society, according to Luhmann, is a system of communication which occurs through and between people, but strictly speaking humans (as bio-psychological systems) are part of a society's environment rather than internal to it. Luhmann argued that capacities for self-organisation and reproduction (processes called autopoiesis) are features of all systems, which all selectively filter information from their environments according to their own needs.

Communication is global and therefore, according to Luhmann, the social system is global, but contains sub-systems (states, economies, education systems etc.) each of which works according to its own code. Major problems (conflicts and contradictions) are said to arise not within systems (which have self-correcting mechanisms) but in the relationships between systems and their various environments.

Like Parsons, Luhmann has been criticised for the abstract character of his theory. Also like Parsons, he has attracted many disciples, mainly outside the English-speaking world.

See also **Parsons, T.; Social system.**

Luhmann, N. (1997), *Social Systems*, Stanford University Press, Stanford, Calif.

Lukacs, Gyorgy (1885–1971)

A Hungarian Marxist, best known for his justification of an existing set of beliefs among Marxists:

- The working class has a unique insight into historical truth.
- Actual workers may be unable to perceive this truth.
- The job of the Marxist theorist is therefore to think for the working class.
- The job of a theoretically informed political vanguard is to act on behalf of the working class.

Lukacs argued that truth could not be established through orthodox scientific methods but could only be discovered and demonstrated through historical praxis (theoretically informed action). He argued that the working class could be blinded to its own objective interests and role by its inability to perceive its position in the social totality (by virtue of its limited experience and perspectives), and through reification (treating as independent and unalterable things such as the market and private property which are actually artificially created).

Lukacs also developed a Marxist theory of aesthetics, arguing that there is a connection between literary and other artistic forms on the one hand and, on the other, the class relationships within which they are created and used.

See also **False consciousness; Gramsci, A.; Marxism; Praxis; Reification**.

Lukacs, G. (1923, 1971), *History and Class Consciousness,* Merlin Press, London.

Lumpenproletariat

Literally the proletariat of rags. This was one of the terms used by Karl Marx (1818–1883) to describe the strata beneath the employed working class. Another of his terms was 'reserve army of labour'.

Marx had a jaundiced opinion of the *Lumpenproletariat*. He typified its members as a mixture of thieves, swindlers, vagabonds, beggars and suchlike: unlikely comrades in a revolutionary movement.

See also **Marx, K.; Social exclusion; Underclass**.

Lyotard, Jean-Francois (1924–1998)

A French sociologist; one of the original exponents of the idea that we have entered a postmodern age. However, unlike philosophers such as Jacques Derrida (1930–2004), Lyotard believed that the relevant changes in modes of thought were driven by changes in society, and most fundamentally by changes in the economy.

Lyotard argued that changes in economic production, especially those associated with the rise and use of computers, have transformed knowledge into something that is valued, above all else, as a productive force which can be treated as a commodity and bought and sold. The development of knowledge is thus driven by a quest for 'performativity', meaning practical, economic efficiency.

Lyotard contended that during the modern era certain 'grand narratives' (such as positivism and Marxism) had given meaning to economic progress – a sense of where the world was heading. He argued that these narratives, always myths, were losing their hold. They were simply unable to encompass the diversity and fragmentation of contemporary (postmodern) society. Aesthetic and ethical commentaries were judged to have been sidelined as the business of experts. Older solidarities were therefore dissolving.

According to Lyotard, we are now witnessing the empty triumph of rationalism.

See also **Grand narratives; Postmodern.**

Lyotard, J-F. (1984), *The Postmodern Condition: A Report on Knowledge*, Manchester University Press, Manchester.

L

Macpherson Report

The official report into the Metropolitan Police's investigation into the murder of a black teenager, Stephen Lawrence, who was fatally stabbed in a unprovoked attack in April 1993. Nobody has been convicted of this murder.

The report accused the police of incompetence and institutional racism. It made 70 recommendations including improved police attitudes towards ethnic minorities, and the recruitment of more black and Asian police officers.

See also **Discrimination; Race; Scarman Report.**

Macpherson, S.W. (1999), *The Stephen Lawrence Inquiry*, HMSO, London.

Macro-sociology

The study of large-scale social phenomena – whole societies, historical change and inter-societal relationships.

The opposite is micro-sociology, the study of small-scale phenomena such as school classrooms, small work groups and interaction within families. Meso-sociology (a rarely used term) refers to the study of intermediate-scale phenomena such as political parties, churches, businesses and other formal organisations.

Magic

Attempts to activate the spiritual or supernatural through ritual. The ability to do this may (according to people's beliefs) be confined to magicians. Magic may occur within or outside larger religions, but is distinct from religious beliefs and practices in that magic seeks to achieve specific and material ends.

In modern societies magic has been pushed into the realm of entertainment, but in pre-modern times, in some societies, people lived in fear of witchcraft and sorcery (the use of magic for socially disapproved ends), while shamans offered medical services by mobilising supernatural or spiritual forces.

See also **Myth; Religion; Rituals.**

Malthus, Thomas Robert (1766–1834)

English clergyman and political economist who published a famous essay on population in 1798. Malthus argued that populations tend to expand geometrically whereas food production grows only arithmetically. Hence there will be constant pressure on resources, and unless checked by moral restraint (sexual chastity and the postponement of marriage), population growth will be checked by disease, starvation and war.

These views led to economics being christened 'the dismal science' by the Victorian historian Thomas Carlyle (1795–1881).

See also **Demography**.

Malthus, T.R. (1798, 1986), *An Essay on the Principle of Population*, Pickering, London.

Management

To paraphrase Marxists, management is a function of capital. Managers control other employees and coordinate the work of organisations.

Management positions were originally created as businesses and state departments grew too large to be commanded by a single person or even a small group. Managers became even more essential in businesses when share capital was divided among numerous distant owners.

In all industrial societies, the number of management positions has grown steadily (since the nineteenth century in the oldest industrial countries). In large organisations there are now numerous management levels – junior, middle and senior. Management theory (starting with scientific management) has a huge literature, and business and management have become popular specialisms in higher education.

In all sociological class schemes, managers are located towards the top, alongside professionals who perform expert labour in off-management line positions. However, there is considerable interchange of roles between professionals and managers, with accountants, scientists, lawyers and other professionals often moving into mainline management, and there has been a trend towards the professionalisation of management itself.

One of sociology's most challenging and heated debates since the 1920s has been about an alleged managerial revolution, leaving managers as the real controllers of businesses, a new ruling class.

See also **Bureaucracy; Managerial revolution; Organisations; Professions; Service class; Technocracy.**

Parker, M. (2002), *Against Management: Organization in the Age of Managerialism*, Polity, Cambridge.

Watson, T. and Harris, P. (1999), *The Emergent Manager*, Sage, London.

M

Managerial revolution

This is the earliest version of a claim, subsequently repeated under different labels, that power is drifting out of the hands of the formal owners of businesses and elected politicians, and is being appropriated by experts because only they have the knowledge required to run large complex organisations and to apply advances in scientific and technological knowledge.

During the first half of the twentieth century there was much discussion about the trend towards dispersed ownership of joint stock companies. It was argued that large numbers of dispersed shareholders lacked the coordination and the knowledge to run their companies. James Burnham (1905–1987), an American political theorist, argued that expert managers were replacing owners and believed that this was happening most rapidly under fascism and communism in inter-war European countries.

Subsequent research demonstrated that in most large companies a controlling block of shares was held by a single dominant owner or a small group of key shareholders.

See also **Knowledge economy/Knowledge society; Technocracy.**

Berle, A. and Means, G. (1932), *The Modern Corporation and Private Property*, Harcourt Brace, New York.

Burnham, J. (1943), *The Managerial Revolution*, Putnam, London.

Manifest function

See Functionalism; Merton, R.K.

Maoism

Mao Tse-Tung (Mao Zedong) (1893–1976) was the leader of a faction of the Chinese communists from the 1920s, through to their victory in 1949, and then the leader of the communists in government until his death in 1976. Maoism comprises Mao Tse-Tung's ideas and the practices of the Chinese communists under his leadership.

Mao's ideas were at odds with the Soviet Union's Marxism-Leninism, mainly in claiming a revolutionary role for the peasantry. Mao also became renowned for his major campaigns – the Hundred Flowers Movement and the Great Leap Forward in the 1950s, and the Cultural Revolution (1966–) which sought to bypass Communist Party officials and directly mobilise the masses. With these campaigns Maoism became a source of hope for western Marxists who hoped that this was a viable alternative to bureaucratic, Soviet-style state socialism. Mao's *Little Red Book* of sayings sold well throughout the world.

In China, Mao's leadership style left him vulnerable (after his death) to accusations of fostering a cult of personality (the same ground on which Stalin was denounced by his successors in the Soviet Union). Even so, Mao

M

is still a revered figure in China despite his policies having been rejected in favour of the 'capitalist road' that Mao detested.

See also **Communism; Marxism.**

Spence, J.D. (1999), *Mao,* Weidenfeld and Nicolson, London.

Marcuse, Herbert (1898–1979)

A member of the Frankfurt School who insisted that authentic existence was impossible in a capitalist society which created artificial needs, spread false consciousness, gave people an 'illusory freedom' and smothered them with a 'repressive tolerance'.

Marcuse incorporated Freudian ideas into his own thinking. He argued that sexual repression made people susceptible to repression by employers and governments, and that sexual liberation could lead to other kinds of liberation. This made Marcuse a cult figure in the student movements of the 1960s.

Marcuse abandoned hope of the working class becoming a revolutionary force, but was optimistic about the potential of an alliance between radical intellectuals such as himself and various outcaste groups (ethnic minorities, for example).

See also **Critical sociology/critical theory; Frankfurt School; Freud, S.**

Marcuse, H. (1955, 1991), *Eros and Civilization: A Philosophical Inquiry into Freud*, Beacon Press, Boston.

Marcuse, H. (1964), *One Dimensional Man: Studies in the Ideology of Advanced Industrial Society*, Routledge, London.

Margin, marginalisation

These terms have the same meaning in sociology as in everyday life: on the edge, the last in line. Marginalisation is the process whereby persons or groups are pushed to the edge (of society).

Indicators of marginalisation are minimal (if any) participation in employment, politics and mainstream social life. This may be due to discrimination on the basis of race, religion, ethnicity, criminality or lifestyle. Alternatively or in addition, marginalisation may be the outcome of cultural deficits of those concerned (lack of knowledge of the society's language, for example). A marginal position may be regarded as the last stage before social exclusion.

In economics the term marginal is used to refer to the marginal cost of producing one extra unit, or the marginal revenue that will accrue from one extra sale.

See also **Social exclusion.**

M

Markets

These are places where buyers and sellers of a good, service, capital or labour interact freely, where all actors are seeking to maximise utility (to gain as much value as possible from their transactions), and prices are fixed by the balance between demand and supply. A market may be a physical place, but nowadays it is often a virtual location.

Free markets actually need a strong state, which can keep markets free of violence, theft, extortion and similar problems, and which can enforce contracts.

A problem with all markets is that they tend to generate over-supply (of goods in shops, and labour for hire). In this sense markets are wasteful. State planning is an alternative (command economy) way of allocating resources and output, but nowadays it is believed that markets have the over-riding advantages of efficiency (maximising output from given inputs) and responding to purchasers' wants.

See also **Capitalism; Labour market.**

Marriage

The sanctioning of a permanent union between sexually relating partners, which legitimises their children.

In pre-modern societies, where family and kin were involved in most areas of people's lives, there were usually detailed rules stipulating who could and who could not marry whom, and other members of the partners' families were usually involved in the choice of mates. In modern societies individuals typically have an open choice of partners, and it is not only permitted but expected that romantic love will be decisive.

See also **Cohabitation; Family; Kinship.**

Marx, Karl (1818–1883)

A German philosopher; one of the Young Hegelians who became a political activist and revolutionary; lived as an independent scholar and journalist from the early 1840s; based in London from 1849; collaborated with and was supported by Friedrich Engels (1820–1895).

In his early writing Marx developed a fierce critique of the human condition under capitalism, said to be characterised by 'alienation', a condition in which people were estranged from their selves and were not in control of their own lives. Contrary to Hegel (1770–1831), the leading intellectual figure in Berlin at the time, Marx decided that further revolutionary change would be needed for humanity to experience genuine freedom.

In his later work Marx developed a dialectical materialist theory of history. He is said to have 'stood Hegel on his head'. Hegel had believed that ideas were the determining force in historical change. Marx disagreed. He argued that work was the basic human activity (necessary for life), and that the economy was the primary influence on social and political life. Marx noted that in order to work, to produce, people had to enter into relationships

M

with one another (relationships of production). In societies where it was possible to produce a surplus (more than necessary for a population to subsist) it was possible for a class of owners to dominate and exploit by extracting the 'surplus value' from workers. Marx argued that conflict between classes with antagonistic interests was the motor that drove history forward.

He believed that societies had developed through distinct historical stages, rather than in a smooth progression. The main stages were said to be primitive communism, slavery, feudalism, then capitalism. The details of the relationship between the dominant and subordinate classes were said to depend, in the final analysis, on the character of the prevailing forces of production (technology and other materials). Points were said to be reached when the forces of production were developed to a level that could not be fully exploited within the prevailing relationships of production. Thus a revolutionary situation arose and the time was ripe for a formerly subordinate class, or a faction of it, to take control of the forces of production, recast the relationships of production, and become the new socially, politically and ideologically dominant class.

Marx believed that such a point was fast approaching in the latest capitalist stage. The system, according to Marx, was riven by contradictions and prone to recurrent crises. The population was expected to polarise into two great classes, bourgeoisie and proletariat, and the latter, inspired by the theory that intellectuals such as Marx were supplying, would seize control of the forces of production and usher in a classless society, which would be the end of history. It would be a society where the forces of production were under collective control, where alienation would be replaced by freedom, and all human needs would be satisfied.

The Communist Manifesto, written by Marx and Engels in 1848, a year of political turmoil throughout Europe, was intended to inspire the revolutionaries and provide a purpose. Throughout the rest of his life, much of which was devoted to writing the three-volume *Capital,* Marx hoped to be part of a successful revolutionary movement. In this he was disappointed, but his ideas lived on, inspiring millions on account of the promise of 'bread and freedom' and the assurance that history was on the side of revolutionary change. However, contrary to Marx's expectation, the capitalist system remains stronger than ever.

See also **Alienation; Class; Engels, F.; Marxism.**

Marx, K. (edited by D. Sayer) (1989), *Readings from Karl Marx*, Routledge, London.

Marx, K. (edited by T.B. Bottomore and M. Rubel) (1979), *Selected Writings on Sociology and Social Philosophy,* Penguin, Harmondsworth.

Marx, K. and Engels, F. (1848, 1985), *The Communist Manifesto*, Penguin, London.

McClellan, D. (1975), *Marx,* Fontana/Collins, London.

Reiss, E. (1996), *Marx: A Clear Guide,* Pluto Press, London.

M

Marxism

This becomes a huge topic – impossibly huge if all work that has used Marx as a starting point is included, especially as the rest of theoretical sociology may be regarded as an attempt to develop an alternative theoretical scheme with equal explanatory power and an equally inspiring vision. However, if we confine attention to authors who accept the label Marxist, or at least neo-Marxist, their contributions can be condensed under three headings.

Marxism-Leninism

Contrary to what Marx expected, the first Marxist party to seize power was the Russian Bolsheviks in 1917. According to Marx's own analysis, revolution should have occurred in the most advanced capitalist countries, not a society where the economy was still mainly agrarian and where most people were peasants. Prior to and following their seizure of power, the Russian Bolsheviks developed a distinctive body of doctrine known as Marxism-Leninism (Lenin, 1870–1924, was the leader of the Russian Bolsheviks). This purported to explain how the Communist Party was the voice of the true interests of the working class, and why true democracy required all members to accept central party decisions (a doctrine known as democratic centralism). Marxism-Leninism regarded Russia, and other countries that became communist, as moving through a socialist stage towards a golden age of communism. During the socialist stage the persistence of inequalities and social strata was acknowledged, but these were said to be qualitatively different from the antagonistic classes that capitalism bred. Marxism-Leninism also explained how capitalism had stalled revolutions at home by exploiting colonies (which enabled the home working classes to be lifted out of immiseration) and why global revolution was likely to be sparked by colonised peoples.

There were bitter disputes among leading Bolsheviks, most notably between Stalin (who succeeded Lenin) and Leon Trotsky (1879–1940) in the late 1920s. Subsequently Marxists who supported the original aims and tactics of the Russian Bolsheviks, but who believed that the Soviet system had taken a false turn, were generally described as Trotskyists. Later on the Soviet Union and its satellites produced numerous dissidents who challenged all the propositions of Marxism-Leninism.

M

The true Marx

Western Marxists have been able to engage in more open debates about the correct reading of Marx. The major controversy has been about the extent to which Marx was really an economic determinist. This issue has been regarded by many as depending on whether Marx changed his mind in the late 1840s. In his earlier writing it is agreed that Marx was not an economic determinist, and the correct reading of his later work is seen as depending on whether the reader decides that Marx had shifted his position.

Classes under twentieth and twenty-first-century capitalism

Western Marxists have needed to explain why, contrary to Marx's forecast, the working classes in the most advanced capitalist societies have never become a revolutionary force. False consciousness, affluence, the impact of the cultural industries, and repressive socialisation in the bourgeois family have been among the favoured explanations.

Also, again contrary to Marx's forecast, the capitalist societies have not polarised into two great juxtaposed classes, bourgeoisie and proletariat. Rather the middle classes have expanded. Marxists have need to identify the class positions of the middle classes, which has usually meant identifying 'contradictory' class locations, such as those of managers who are salaried yet perform functions of capital.

See also **Alienation; Althusser, L.; Class; Engels, F.; Frankfurt School; Marx, K.; Lacan, J.; Wright, E.O.**

Gamble, A., Marsh, D. and Tant, T. (1999), *Marxism and Social Science*, Macmillan, Basingstoke.

Joseph, J. (2006), *Marxism and Social Theory,* Palgrave Macmillan, Basingstoke.

Masculine/Masculinity

See Feminine/Femininity.

Mass culture/Mass society

The coming of the mass media between the 1890s and 1930s led to a debate in the social sciences about the likely spread of mass culture and the creation of a mass society.

Media audiences were clearly unlike crowds and congregations. Media communication was one-way. There was no interaction among atomised audiences. It was feared that the mass would be vulnerable to skilled propagandists (Hitler's success in Germany reinforced these fears), and that high culture and other cultures would be compressed into a 'lowest common denominator'.

These fears proved unfounded.

- The 'hypodermic model' which envisaged audiences absorbing media output uncritically proved mistaken. The media were plural. People read, watched and listened selectively. A 'uses and gratifications' model was therefore adopted by media researchers.
- Researchers discovered a two-step flow of communications: media messages were filtered and interpreted through primary groups.

Thus the terms mass culture and mass society (but not mass media) slipped out of sociology's vocabulary.

See also **Frankfurt School; Mass media.**

Giner, S. (1976), *Mass Society*, Martin Robertson, London.

Kornhauser, W. (1960), *The Politics of Mass Society*, Routledge, London.

Swingewood, A. (1977), *The Myth of Mass Culture*, Humanities Press International, New Jersey.

Mass media

The mass media (often shortened to media) are so called because they reach a mass that is beyond the immediate reach of sight and sound. Printed and even handwritten books might therefore be included, but the media usually referred to are the mass circulation newspapers that date from the 1890s, and which were joined before the Second World War by films, recorded music, radio and television. The Internet (since the 1990s) is the latest addition.

Early fears that the media would create a mass culture and mass society proved wrong. Even so, sociologists recognise that the media are extremely important in all present-day societies.

Most of our news and entertainment come from the media. People may not believe everything that they hear and see, and it has proved difficult to identify any short-term direct effects of sex and violence in films and television, or media effects on voters' political partisanship during election campaigns. Even so, there are likely to be long-term 'drip–drip' effects that are difficult to measure. So sociologists are interested in how media content is influenced by production processes, in who owns and controls the media (increasingly international multi-media conglomerates), and in the shift in Europe from mainly public service to mainly commercial radio and television, and how this might make a difference.

Another reason for sociology's interest is that their growth has increased the media's importance in the economy, as a source of jobs, especially since the media are among the 'creative industries' and provide high proportions of high-quality jobs.

See also **Baudrillard, J.; Creative industries; Cultural industries; Mass culture/Mass society.**

Hesmondhalgh, D. (2007), *The Cultural Industries,* second edition, Sage, London.

M

Materialism

In sociology and philosophy materialism is the opposite of idealism. A materialist believes that people's ideas (including values and political dispositions) arise ultimately from their material circumstances and that ideas are not a primary cause. Karl Marx (1818–1883) is generally regarded as sociology's arch-materialist and his teacher Georg Hegel (1770–1831) as the arch-idealist.

In present-day sociology these sides are represented by theoretical positions developed from materialist and idealist foundations: agency (idealism) versus structure (materialism), and structuralism (materialism) versus, for example, symbolic interactionism (idealism).

In sociology these terms do *not* refer to people's values: inspired by high ideals (idealism) versus wanting more and more possessions and bodily comforts (materialism).

See also **Idealism; Marx, K.; Marxism.**

Matriarchy

See Kinship.

McDonaldization

See Ritzer, G.

Mead, George Herbert (1863–1931)

Mead is the member of the Chicago School who is now regarded as the father of 'symbolic interactionism' (though Mead himself did not use this term) as a result of arguing that the self (our sense of who we are) is a product of social interaction.

Mead regarded himself as working at the crossroads between philosophy and psychology rather than a sociologist. He described his work as social behaviorism (to distinguish it from 'behaviorism'). He argued that language, the ability to communicate using symbols (which stand for something else, language being the prime example), set humans apart from other animals and enabled them to transcend biology. Mead built on Charles Horton Cooley's (1864–1929) notion of the 'looking glass self'. He argued that the self is a product of social interaction. Due to our mastery of language, we are said to be able to take on the role of others and to imagine how they see ourselves. Mead argued that the outlooks of 'significant others' became internalised in individuals' minds as a 'generalised other', thus enabling people to engage in internal conversations between an 'I' (myself as I really am) and a 'Me' (as I imagine others see me).

Mead's student, Herbert Blumer (1900–1987), took over these ideas and described his sociological work as 'symbolic interactionism'.

See also: **Blumer, H.; Chicago School; Cooley, C.H.; Identity; Self; Symbolic interactionism.**

Mead, G.H. (1934), *Mind, Self and Society*, Chicago University Press, Chicago.

Mead, Margaret (1901–1978)

American social and cultural anthropologist who became famous following the 1928 publication of *Coming of Age in Samoa*.

In Samoa Mead found that adolescence was nothing like the stormy life stage that was being debated in the United States. In this and later work she also claimed to show that gender roles and sexual mores owed much more to culture than to biology. Mead became a friendly critic of American/western societies by viewing their own 'quaint' beliefs and practices from her external, anthropological perspective.

See also **Adolescence; Gender; Youth.**

Mead, M. (1928, 1961), *Coming of Age in Samoa,* Penguin, Harmondsworth.

Mead, M. (1935, 1963), *Sex and Temperament in Three Primitive Societies*, Morrow, New York.

Mean

See Measures of central tendency.

Means of production

See Marx, K.

Measures of central tendency

Sociologists and other statisticians can use alternative measures of central tendency (to identify the typical case among a population):

- The *mode* is the most common value. So if most people have zero stock exchange investments, zero is the mode. If some people have investments, the average will necessarily be higher than the mode.
- The *average* or *mean* is the sum of all values divided by the number of cases.
- The *median* is the middle instance when all cases are arranged in an ascending order of values. The median will be lower than the average when the latter is skewed upwards by a small number of outlying cases (as in income distribution, for instance).

Measures of dispersion

Sociologists (and others who use statistics) have alternative ways of measuring how widely cases are spread around a central tendency:

- The *range* is the difference between the largest and the smallest values.
- The *variance* is the average of squared deviations from the mean.
- The *standard deviation* is the square root of the variance.

M

Variance and standard deviation figures do not map onto anything in real life but are simply standardised ways of measuring which enable the dispersion around a central tendency in different populations to be compared.

Mechanical solidarity

See Durkheim, E.

Media

See Mass media.

Median

See Measures of central tendency.

Medical model, Medicalisation

The term medical model was first used by the Scottish psychiatrist Ronald David Laing (1927–1989). When the term is used by sociologists this is invariably in criticism, and nowadays the model is acknowledged by all concerned to be a parody of current medical thought and practice.

The target of criticism is treating social phenomena (usually social problems) as if they were akin to the illnesses and injuries dealt with by medical doctors. In this model illnesses and injuries are diagnosed, isolated, then treated. Sociologists have serious objections to importing this thinking into the analysis and treatment of social phenomena such as crime, poverty and domestic violence, and even into issues claimed by medicine such as obesity, the care of the elderly and mental illnesses (Laing's original target).

Medicalisation refers to the application of the medical model, plus placing medical professions in overall charge of programmes, especially in fields such as social work and community care.

Sociology's objections to the medical model are:

- Social constructionist: the conditions being addressed are not akin to 'germs' but are socially created labels.
- The conditions cannot be treated in isolation because they arise as parts of a social system that needs to be examined in its entirety.

See also **Health**.

Laing, R.D. (1971), *The Politics of the Family and Other Essays*, Tavistock, London.

Meritocracy

This term sprang to prominence through a book authored by the British sociologist, Michael Young (1915–2002). His book is a critique of trends in education and society in post-1945 Britain.

Meritocracy means rule by the meritorious. This should result from promoting only people who merit promotion, and measuring merit objectively and impartially. Young believed that Britain was becoming *apparently* meritocratic as a result of the 1944 Education Act and other educational reforms, and was alarmed by what seemed an uncritical acceptance of the desirability of meritocracy across the political spectrum.

Young highlighted the problems:

- Exactly what is merit?
- Do IQ tests measure merit?
- Can merit be measured independently of socially transmitted advantages and disadvantages?
- A meritocracy, if achieved, would strip the lower strata of talent.
- Those who succeed would feel that this was purely on their own merits.

Young envisaged a time when people who were consigned to mundane jobs on grounds of their limited abilities and merit would have a statutory right to have their IQ retested at given intervals.

See also **Credentialism; IQ; Social mobility.**

Young, M. (1958), *The Rise of the Meritocracy*, Thames and Hudson, London.

Merton, Robert King (1910–2003)

Merton's specialist topic was the sociology of science and technology, but he is best known for his contributions to functional analysis, and even more so for the huge number of concepts that he either coined or adopted and worked into mainstream sociology.

Merton studied under Talcott Parsons (1902–1979) but did not adopt the entire Parsonian body of theory; rather he worked on functional analysis to try to make it more useful in sociology. Merton insisted that sociology should identify dysfunctions and eufunctions (functionally neutral) as well as functions themselves. He advocated 'middle range theory' which would eventually link the findings of empirical research to 'grand theories' (such as Parsons'). Merton applied Durkheim's (1858–1917) concept of anomie to the analysis of crime in the United States, and is the source of an impressive list of concepts that have entered mainstream sociology. These include manifest and latent functions, unanticipated consequences, self-fulfilling prophecy and opportunity structure.

See also **Functionalism; Parsons, T.**

Merton, R.K. (1957), *Social Theory and Social Structure,* Free Press, Glencoe, Ill.

M

Metaphysics

Any theory about the fundamental nature of reality, the universe as a whole.

Rationalists have believed that such a theory can be developed and will constitute the highest possible level of knowledge. Empiricists, who believe that true knowledge is based on observation, are liable to dismiss metaphysics as pure speculation. Critics of empiricism say that what we observe depends on untested assumptions (metaphysics) about what is out there.

See also **Ontology.**

Meta-theory

A theory about another theory or theories.

There are plenty of meta-theories in sociology. Most sociological theory (as it is generally known) is strictly meta-theory. Functionalism is a meta-theory about functionalist accounts of particular societies and groups. Symbolic interactionism is a meta-theory about symbolic interactionist accounts of behaviour in classrooms, courtrooms and other environments.

Meta-theories can be built by examining other 'smaller' theories. Metaphysics is the ultimate level of meta-theory. However, it can be argued that before we undertake any research or theory building, we must make 'domain assumptions' and work from 'axioms', that is, truths that are just assumed or taken to be self-evident, about the character of social life.

See also **Axiom; Ontology; Metaphysics.**

Methodological individualism

This method claims that adequate sociological accounts must be intelligible at the level of the individual actor, and must refer to the actor's motives, reasons and interpretations of his or her circumstances. The opposing view of how sociology should proceed is represented by Emile Durkheim (1858–1917): 'treat social facts as things'. Methodological individualism insists that 'things' such as capitalism and social classes need to be divisible into (maybe idealised) individuals who see the world in particular ways, and have particular motives and other attributes.

See also **Agency; Durkheim, E.; Holism; Ideal type; Individualism; Rational choice theory; Weber, M.**

M

Methodology

Literally means the study of methods, but this is not how the term 'methodology' is normally used in sociology.

Methodology may refer to the techniques used in an investigation (sampling, interviews etc.), but these are more likely to be described as research methods. Methodology can then refer to the theoretical underpinnings of these methods. So a methodology might, for example, be positivist, feminist, symbolic interactionist, Marxist.

Michels, Robert (1876–1936)

German sociologist, renowned for his research into the leadership of left-wing political parties and trade unions, which was influenced strongly by Michels' personal experience in Germany's Social Democratic Party.

Michels formulated the iron law of oligarchy: 'Whoever says organisation says oligarchy'. His arguments were that incumbents always have advantages stemming from their organisational positions that usually enable them to defeat challengers' attempts to replace them; and also by virtue of their control of organisational resources, leaders are usually able to mobilise support for their policies more successfully than is possible for individuals and groups from among the rank-and-file. Michels went on to argue that office holders tended to become more committed to maintaining and strengthening their organisations than pursuing more difficult, risky, radical, social and political objectives. He additionally claimed that leaders were subject to processes of embourgeoisement by virtue of their work experience (as managers/professionals) and their broader middle class lifestyles, and thereby became personally less committed to radical objectives.

See also **Democracy**; **Elites**; **Oligarchy**.

Michels, R. (1962), *Political Parties*, Free Press, New York.

Micro-sociology

See Macro-sociology.

Middle class

This term dates from the Middle Ages when townsfolk were considered to be midway in a social order which had a landed aristocracy at the top and peasants at the base. The term has been retained even though aristocracies have either been abolished or have merged with the wealthiest sections of the middle class.

Sociologists are usually comfortable in describing everyone above the working class as middle class (though some Marxist sociologists prefer to demote lower middle class groups), and middle class is the class label that those concerned are most likely to apply to themselves. However, when analysing the class structure, sociologists unanimously insist that the middle class needs to be sub-divided. Typically (but with some variations depending on theoretical position – Marxist, Weberian or functionalist), the following middle classes are distinguished:

- a very wealthy upper middle class which may alternatively be called a capitalist class or an upper class

M

- a petit bourgeoisie of own-account workers and owners of small businesses
- salaried and self-employed managers and professionals
- a lower middle class of office, sales, laboratory, and some personal service workers.

In the early and mid-twentieth century the middle classes in total were outnumbered by the working classes in industrial societies, and the threat of working class power appears to have been sufficient to unify the middle classes in terms of political proclivities. Today, in the economically advanced countries, the middle classes are the majority, and it is divisions among them – economic, social, cultural and political – that interest sociologists.

> See also **Capitalism; Class; Service class; Upper class; Working class; Wright, E.O.**

> Roberts, K. (2001), *Class in Modern Britain,* Palgrave, Basingstoke.

Middle range theory

A term coined by the American sociologist, Robert K. Merton (1910–2003). He argued that sociology needed to fill the gap between:

- empirical studies, and
- grand theories of history, social structure and change as offered by Auguste Comte (1788–1857), Emile Durkheim (1858–1917) and Merton's contemporary, Talcott Parsons (1902–1979).

Merton's own work on bureaucracy, on anomie and on other topics illustrates the kind of middle range theory that he had in mind, but questions remain:

- Can testable propositions be derived that will prove or disprove the grand theories?
- Will building upwards from empirical studies produce knowledge that resembles the grand theories?
- Is this kind of hierarchy the way in which sociological knowledge should be constructed?

> See also **Grand theory; Merton, R.K.; Theory.**

> Merton, R.K. (1949), *Social Theory and Social Structure,* Free Press, Glencoe, Ill.

Migration

Geographical movement which may be internal or external to a country, and permanent or temporary (though visitors and tourists are not classified as migrants). Emigrants are moving out and immigrants are moving in.

Migration has occurred throughout human history, ever since the species came out of Africa, but at different times different sections of humanity have migrated for different reasons. Nowadays sociologists distinguish 'push' factors (war, violence whether actual or threatened, persecution, famine, hardship) and 'pull' factors (freedom, higher standard of living, opportunity to lead a better life). Often mixtures of push and pull factors operate simultaneously.

During the colonial era European colonists settled all over the world. They created some immigrant countries like the United States where the indigenous people became minorities in their homelands. Since 1945 west European countries have become net immigration societies due to rising numbers of economic immigrants, sometimes from former colonies, from eastern Europe since 1989, and also from most other parts of the world. Migration has become more common simply because it has become much easier (and cheaper relative to incomes) for people to move than at any time in history. Net immigration countries become more ethnically plural. Net emigration countries tend to become more mono-ethnic.

Sociologists have studied how immigrant groups become acculturated in the societies where they settle, how immigrants and hosts may gradually accommodate to and accept each other, which may lead eventually to integration or assimilation. However, progression through these stages is not automatic. Pendulum migrants return home. Every wave of migration tends to generate a counter-wave. Some settlers retain their original cultures and identities, in which case they become part of diasporas. There may be conflict between hosts and settlers. Hostility on the part of hosts may have a genuine basis (competition for jobs and housing) or it may arise from racist beliefs or xenophobia. As an outcome of these processes, immigrant groups may become long-term disadvantaged, marginalised and even excluded, in the societies where they settle.

> See also **Accommodation; Acculturation; Assimilation; Diaspora; Indigenous group; Refugees; Social integration.**

Castles, S. and Miller, M.J. (2003), *The Age of Migration,* Palgrave Macmillan, Basingstoke.

Cohen, R. (1997), *Global Diasporas: An Introduction*, UCL Press, London.

Mill, James (1773–1836)

See Utilitarianism.

Mill, John Stuart (1806–1873)

See Utilitarianism.

Mills, Charles Wright (1916–1962)

A maverick, polemical American sociologist who was harshly critical of both US society and mainstream US sociology in the 1950s. Mills wrote in the 1940s and 1950s but one strongly suspects that if he were writing today little would be changed.

M

Mills' best-known book, *The Sociological Imagination*, lambasted abstracted empiricism (fact gathering for its own sake) on the one side, and 'grand theory' (as produced by Talcott Parsons, 1902–1979, for example) on the other. He believed that a mission of sociology was to convert private troubles into public issues. Unemployment and poverty could be tragedies for individuals and their families, but sociology could show that these problems were shared by very many people and had their sources in the overall organisation of society rather than individuals' inadequacies. This book made Mills probably the most popular American sociologist among sociology students in Europe from the time when it was first published up to the present day. It advocates the kind of sociology that most sociologists would like to produce, but few achieve.

In other major books Mills deplored the demise of an older, more independent US middle class and its replacement by a new middle class of 'cheerful robots' working for large organisations. In *The Power Elite* he purported to show that allegedly democratic America was really run by a small elite composed of the heads of big businesses, political bosses and the military top brass.

See also **Elites; Empiricism; Grand theory**.

Mills, C.W. (1951), *White Collar: The American Middle Classes*, Oxford University Press, New York.

Mills, C.W. (1956), *The Power Elite,* Simon and Schuster, New York.

Mills, C.W. (1959), *The Sociological Imagination*, Oxford University Press, New York.

Mind–body dualism

See Dualism.

Mobilisation

The collective arousal then organisation of a group who become active participants in public life. An everyday use of the term refers to the mobilisation of armies (the opposite is demobilisation), but in sociology the term is used more widely.

Mobilisation can be among residents in a particular place, people with a common aim (opposing abortion or road building, for example), an occupational group or profession, or a social class. Mobilisation can be short term or enduring as with political parties and some religious movements.

Sociology is interested in what triggers mobilisation when people share an interest or concern, how mobilisation is accomplished, which sections of a population are most likely to mobilise (class, age, gender and ethnic differences), the extent to which older forms of mobilisation are being replaced by new forms using the Internet, mobile phone and email, whether there is a general trend towards demobilisation in contemporary societies, and if so how this might be counteracted.

See also **Active citizen; Capital; Communitarianism; Social movements.**

Mode

See Measures of central tendency.

Mode of production

See Marx, K.

Models

A model is a representation of something else. A model may be different in scale or materials, or the model may be pictorial, diagrammatic or mathematical.

In sociology models are initially built with words (concepts) and may alternatively be called theories or ideal types, like Max Weber's (1864–1920) ideal type/model of bureaucracy. Sociological models invariably simplify the real world, and so are always ideal typical.

Nowadays, when sociological work is described as modelling the outcome is invariably a statistical model, most likely a causal model, through which the effects of a change in any part of the model can be traced. For example, the process of educational attainment can be modelled show-ing how family class makes a difference at successive educational junctures (transition into secondary school, whether to continue or leave full-time education when able to do so, progressing into higher education). The over-all effects of family background thereby become huge. The model can demonstrate how a slight narrowing of initial class inequalities would make a substantial long-term difference to class inequalities in educational attainments.

See also **Ideal type.**

M

Modern/Modernity/Modernisation

In sociology modern contrasts with traditional. The modern era (modernity) in Europe is regarded as commencing when the Middle Ages ended. This was well before the first European countries to do so experienced industri-alisation and urbanisation. Sociologists who write about modern society and modernity (rather than industrial society) are signalling their view that industrialisation and urbanisation were developments that occurred as part of a longer-term process of modernisation. Modernisation theory examines this longer-term process.

Exactly how and why modernity began is a matter of debate. Was the religious reformation the catalyst, or the renaissance, the enlightenment, the expansion of trade, or some technological innovation? However, all who use the term modernity agree that a defining characteristics of the age has been confidence that reason and science bring progress, improvement in the human condition. The birth and development of sociology are seen as parts of the broader modernisation process.

Modernisation theory has been opposed by Marxism. Modernisation is viewed as a gradually unfolding process from a starting point. Talcott Parsons' (1902–1979) theory about progressive structural and functional differentiation is an example of a modernisation theory. Marxists reject this thinking. They see the development of capitalism as having required revolutionary change, as will a future transformation into a socialist/communist age.

A current debate among modernisation theorists is whether modernity is/was uniform, or whether there are, or can be, alternative modernities – western, Islamic and Asian, for example.

Another debate is about whether the modern era is now ending and we are entering postmodern times, indicated by a loss of confidence in science and reason.

See also **Enlightenment; Industrialisation; Postmodern; Traditional societies.**

Monetarism

This is an economic doctrine, powerfully advocated by the American economist Milton Friedman (1912–2006), which argues that an economy can be controlled by government, and is best controlled primarily through control of the supply of money.

Since the end of the Fordist era, monetarism has been a linchpin in many governments' neo-liberal economic and social policies. The supply of money in an economy can be controlled by central bank policies (the amount of money in circulation), interest rates, control of lending, and levels of state spending and borrowing. The primary goal in controlling the money supply is to control monetary inflation. Levels of employment and the rate of economic growth are left to market forces which, monetarists argue, produce the best of all possible outcomes.

M

Many governments turned to monetarism during or following the 1970s as a result of the apparent inability of Keynesian economic management to overcome 'stagflation' (a combination of high inflation, high unemployment and low economic growth, which seemed impossible in Keynesian theory).

See also **Fordism; Keynes, J.M.; Neo-liberalism; Post-Fordism; Regulation theory; Stagflation.**

Friedman, M. (1981), *Studies in the Quantity and Theory of Money,* University of Chicago Press, Chicago.

Monogamy

See Kinship.

Moral panic

A public reaction that is out of proportion to an event or set of events. The over-reaction is likely to be inflamed by exaggerated media reporting. The classic example is Stanley Cohen's study of mods and rockers in the early 1960s, whose very minor misdemeanours led to public panic and demands for draconian penalties.

> *See also* **Demonisation; Labelling theory.**

> Cohen, S. (1972), *Folk Devils and Moral Panics*, MacGibbon and Kee, London.

Morals

These are rules that prescribe how we ought and ought not to behave.

Ethics is the philosophical study of the moral domain. Sociologists are interested in the rules (their character, sources and effects) that people internalise and/or expect one another to observe.

Perhaps surprisingly, sociologists have been far less likely to investigate people's moral beliefs than their attitudes and their values (in which more specific moral rules may be grounded).

> *See also* **Ethics; Values.**

Multiculturalism

A multicultural society is where two or more cultures co-exist with neither dominating the other. Multiculturalism is a policy with the aim of building a multicultural society.

Multicultural societies were common before the nation state became the normal political unit. Switzerland is a long-standing example with French, German and Italian communities. The main early examples of multiculturalism in modern societies were where different faiths were granted equal status: Catholics and Protestants, the original 'pillars' of Dutch society, for example. India became an officially multicultural society in 1950 (equal status for all Indian and other languages and cultures). Canada became officially multicultural in 1971 (equal status between Anglo and French-Canadians, their languages and cultures). The United States is sometimes treated as an exemplary multicultural society, though this is not a legal, constitutional position, and the United States is also known as a 'melting pot' but one in which a white Anglo-Saxon Protestant (WASP) culture has been dominant. Mono-culturalism is the opposite of multiculturalism and is official policy in France which seeks to assimilate/acculturate all groups into a unified French society.

M

In recent times multiculturalism has been a common (usually implicit) policy in European countries (though not in France) towards immigrant ethnic minorities. In Britain since the 1960s multiculturalism has been the orthodox stance of liberals/progressives. The aim is to allow minorities to retain their own cultures, to celebrate cultural variety, while guaranteeing all groups equal treatment in public life (in education, employment and politics, for example). It is hoped that multiculturalism will lead to inter-culturalism – all groups learning from each other. However, there are two serious criticisms of multiculturalism.

First, it can be argued that strong societies, certainly strong nation states, need to be bound by a common culture. A multicultural society is said to be a weak society. Will citizens be prepared to fight for a multicultural country? Will they be willing to pay taxes to provide welfare services for all groups? A condition for keeping Switzerland together has been neutrality in foreign affairs. British multiculturalists reply that their own country is a long-standing example, containing English, Scottish and Welsh populations to which new ethnic groups and their cultures can easily be added. Critics wonder whether the adding will be easy in the absence of a shared history (real or imagined). In any case, multiculturalists admit that all groups need to accept certain basic 'British values', including tolerance. So what happens when a group is intolerant and does not accept the premises of multiculturalism? The policy may work when all the relevant cultures are European (as in Switzerland, and in Canada if the original inhabitants are not included) but can it cope with mixtures of western and other cultures, and Christian and Islamic cultures?

Second, it is claimed that multiculturalism is incompatible with equal opportunities. If multiculturalism means permitting education in different languages and the multilingual production of official documents, will the policy encourage segregation? This was the fear of Trevor Phillips, then chair of the UK Commission for Racial Equality, when he denounced multiculturalism in 2004. If all schools are not to follow a unitary national curriculum, and if the same criteria are to be applied impartially when filling university places and jobs, cultural differences seem certain to lead to unequal outcomes. Some people regard having children educated in their own community's language and culture as a human right, but exercising this right may deny them the right to equal opportunities in the wider society.

What works best may well depend on the particular cultures and countries that are involved. What works for French-Canadians in Quebec and for Russians in post-1991 Kazakhstan may not lead to the same outcomes for Moroccans in the Netherlands.

See also **Discrimination; Ethnic; Migration; Nation.**

Kelly, P. (ed.) (2002), *Multiculturalism Reconsidered: Culture and Equality and its Critics*, Polity Press, Cambridge.

Multinational corporations

See Trans-national corporations.

Multiple deprivation/disadvantages

See Deprivation; Social exclusion.

Multivariate analysis

Univariate analysis inspects differences within a population on a single variable such as social class. Bivariate analysis examines the relationship between two variables such as social class and education. Multivariate analysis handles three or more variables simultaneously – class, gender, ethnicity and education, for example.

There are various statistical procedures for multivariate analysis. Which procedure is appropriate depends on the character of the data and the purpose of the analysis. In sociology it is common to use multiple regression to examine the relative importance of several independent variables in predicting a single dependent variable: for example, gender, class and ethnicity as predictors of educational attainment. The output from the analysis will indicate the proportions of the variance in the dependent variable that are accounted for by each of the independent variables.

Two points should always be borne in mind:

* All kinds of analysis are limited by the data that is initially fed in. The exclusion or poor measurement of an important causal variable will therefore lead to false results.
* Correlations and all other statistical associations are not necessarily causal relationships.

The implication of the above is that all analysis needs to begin and end with a sound theory.

See also **Correlation; Regression.**

Murray, Charles (1943–)

Consistently controversial American political scientist and social policy analyst, renowned for his views on the formation of an underclass, and on the role and distribution of IQ (measured intelligence) in US society.

Losing Ground (1984), Murray's first major book, documented the formation of a (largely black) underclass in America's inner-cities. While some black Americans' socio-economic ascent had been assisted by race equality legislation and affirmative action policies and programmes, others had actually been losing ground in terms of risks of poverty and unemployment. Among several contributing explanations, Murray singled out over-generous welfare. His diagnosis has been broadly accepted by successive federal administrations in the United States, and is the intellectual foundation of Workfare policies (making the able-bodied unemployed earn their state benefits).

Following brief visits to Britain at the end of the 1980s and in the early

1990s, Murray claimed to detect the formation of a (mainly white) British underclass, for the same reasons as applied in the United States.

The Bell Curve is a review of the relevant evidence which finds that the best predictor of success in the United States, far more important than parental socio-economic status, is IQ (which was already well known). However, the book also draws attention to differences in the mean IQ scores of different ethnic groups in the United States, and claims that these different mean scores are the best available explanation of the different socio-economic attainments of blacks, whites and Jews. *The Bell Curve* does not take sides over whether IQ is a product of nature or nurture, but simply argues that it has important consequences. Another of the book's controversial arguments is that the powerful role played by IQ in social placement will lead to increased polarisation between the highly intelligent and their opposites.

See also **IQ; Normal distribution; Underclass; Wilson, W.J.; Workfare**.

Herrnstein, R.J. and Murray, C. (1994), *The Bell Curve: Intelligence and Class Structure in American Life,* Simon and Schuster, New York.

Murray, C. (1984), *Losing Ground: American Social Policy, 1950–1980*, Basic Books, New York.

Murray, C. (1990), *The Emerging British Underclass*, Institute of Economic Affairs, London.

Myth

The character and significance of myths have been debated at length in social anthropology, where myths have been defined as sacred tales about origins – of a society, a group or a social practice. Myths (unlike magic, witchcraft and sorcery) are typically part of a society's religion.

The major debates about myths have been identical to those surrounding magic. Are myths functional? Are myths absent from or far less important in the modern world than in simpler societies? Have they now been pushed into the realms of fiction and entertainment? Are myths irrational and incompatible with a scientific outlook?

See also **Barthes, R.; Levi-Strauss, C.; Magic**.

M

Nation

An ethnic group or purported race that has achieved or aspires to statehood and, in the process, claims a specific territory as its homeland. Nationalism refers to doctrines that seek to strengthen a nation by making it more cohesive and able to withstand external forces.

In modern times the nation state has been regarded as the normal unit of sovereign government: hence the title of the United Nations. In pre-modern times most people's sentimental attachments were to a village, tribe or ethnic group rather than whoever ruled the territory that they inhabited. Modern states need to do more than their pre-modern counterparts, which means that they need to be more cohesive. Also, in modern times people have become more active politically. The creation of nation states is believed to be an outcome of these modern realities.

Nations without states usually aspire to statehood, as is currently the case with (some) Scots and, it appears, majorities of Kurds and the population of Kosovo. However, multinational/ethnic states can be viable. The United Kingdom contains the English, Scots and Welsh (and more contentiously the British and Irish in Northern Ireland). Switzerland contains French, German and Italian communities. The population of the United States has multi-national origins. In principle it is possible to imagine a purely civic state composed of all who occupy a particular territory and express allegiance to a single political unit, but any state will be vulnerable without its citizens' sentimental (national) attachment. So citizens of the United States become Americans, citizens of the United Kingdom can be British as well as English, Welsh and Scottish, and citizens of Switzerland can be Swiss as well as French, German or Italian. However, there are plenty of examples of states that have broken up as a result of their component nations' aspirations for self-government – the Soviet Union, Yugoslavia and Czechoslovakia, for example.

Nations and nationalism have been neglected in sociology. This has been due to tacit assumptions from the birth of the discipline that nations would be progressively eroded by internal divisions, especially class divisions, and by the forces that we now describe as globalisation. In the event, nationalism was among the main forces that changed the world during the twentieth century. It was at the heart of the two world wars and many other conflicts. It was the ideology, borrowed from their colonial rulers, with which subject peoples formed independence movements. Nationalism continues to form and destroy political entities and shows no signs of exhaustion.

See also **Ethnic; Patriotism; Race; State.**

Gellner, E. (1983), *Nations and Nationalism,* Blackwell, Oxford.

Smith, A.D. (1986), *The Ethnic Origins of Nations*, Blackwell, Oxford.

Nation state

See Nation.

Nationalisation

The transfer of economic assets from private into public ownership. Privatisation is the reverse process. In Britain the 1945 Labour government nationalised a series of major industries, including steel, coal, gas, electricity, water, railways and air transport.

Communists have believed that all economic assets should be publicly owned to prevent exploitation and to eliminate the inefficiencies of markets. Social democrats have favoured mixed economies with public ownership restricted to strategic industries, firms and services on which the rest of the economy, or the public's health, well-being and security depend. Neo-liberals argue that nationalisation should be a last resort, used only when strategic sectors would otherwise collapse. On grounds of efficiency and consumer choice, they argue that even publicly funded services such as health and education should whenever possible be provided by private profit-seeking businesses that compete for government contracts. For these reasons Britain's Conservative governments in the 1980s reversed the earlier nationalisations and began some new privatisations.

It is usually accepted, even by neo-liberals, that certain operations must remain state owned: the military (though it possible to hire mercenary armies), the police (though there are private security firms), and courts and penal institutions (though there are private prisons).

See also **Communism; Neo-liberalism; Privatisation; Socialism.**

N

Nationalism

See Nation.

Natural attitude

A concept coined by Alfred Schutz (1899–1959), the originator of social phenomenology. A natural attitude takes for granted the existence of an external world and features of that world. Everyday common sense and a scientific outlook are both examples of a natural attitude.

Schutz argued that the task of sociology was to discover how people operate under the natural attitude, that is, whatever they take for granted, which differs from society to society, and may also differ from group to group within a society.

See also **Phenomenology; Schutz, A.**

NEET

An UK acronym for young people who are not in employment, education or training (who when originally discovered were described as the Status Zero group). In Britain in 1988 most 16 and 17-year-olds lost their entitlement to unemployment benefits and therefore the young unemployed disappeared from official registers. They were subsequently rediscovered, and since 1997 an aim of governments has been to reduce the size of the NEET group.

Note that the label defines the problem not as straightforward unemployment, but that in the absence of being able to obtain jobs the young people fail to enrol in education or training.

See also **Unemployment.**

Neighbourhood

A residential area: neighbours live next door or not much further away.

Sociology has paid considerable attention to the social character of neighbourhoods, especially whether or not they are communities. A theme of sociology in the second half of the twentieth century was the decline of neighbourhood communities. This was believed to be a result of privatised lifestyles encouraged by television, the design of new residential areas, the motor car which enabled people to travel for work, to shop and for leisure, and geographical mobility.

See also **Community; Privatism; Urbanism.**

Goldthorpe, J.H., Lockwood, D., Bechhofer, F. and Platt, J. (1969), *The Affluent Worker in the Class Structure,* Cambridge University Press, Cambridge.

Young, M. and Willmott, P. (1957), *Family and Kinship in East London,* Routledge, London.

N

Neo-Fordism

See Post-Fordism.

Neo-liberalism

This is a loosely knit set of ideas which embrace and update classical, nineteenth-century laissez-faire (free market) economics and political liberalism.

Present-day neo-liberals believe in free markets, the right of individuals to own property, to use their property and to dispose of it freely, and argue that this is a precondition for individual liberty. They are in favour of global free trade, low taxes and minimal government, and usually defend the rights of individuals against the state. In recent decades neo-liberals have opposed employment regulation (legal minimum rates of pay, maximum hours of work, equal treatment irrespective of gender etc.), plus restrictions on businesses on environmental grounds.

Clearly, individuals and governments are able to pick and choose from this package, but analysts detect a clear worldwide trend since the 1970s towards governments adopting neo-liberal policies, which have generally been supported by international institutions such as the World Bank, the International Monetary Fund and the World Trade Organization. Global opposition to neo-liberal policies has been expressed in protests organised by the Anti-Globalization Movement.

See also **Monetarism; Post-Fordism; Privatisation.**

Hayek, F.A. (1944), *The Road to Serfdom*, University of Chicago Press, Chicago.

Network

The connections between roles or people. A network differs from a group or organisation; these have members or employees, and a boundary between insiders and outsiders. A network may be relatively closed, but its edges are more likely to be fuzzy. Networks may have a centre, or they may be multi-centred, or there may be no centre.

Originally the networks that sociologists studied were kinship and friendship networks. However, the advent of the Internet has switched attention to the development of network societies, said to be created as a result of the ease with which organisational, local and national boundaries can be permeated.

See also **Castells, M.; Node.**

Bott, E. (1957), *Family and Social Network*, Tavistock, London.

Castells, M. (1996), *The Rise of the Network Society,* Blackwell, Oxford.

Network economy/Network society

See Information economy/Information society; Network.

New Labour

The brand name adopted by the Labour Party under the leadership of Tony Blair before the 1997 general election.

The purpose of the rebranding was to distance the party from earlier (Old) Labour Party policies, specifically the commitment to public ownership and higher taxes on the better-off to finance social services (mainly for the benefit of the less well-off). New Labour also dropped the term 'class' from its vocabulary: it no longer wanted to be regarded as the party of the working class. New Labour's policies have been described as 'Third Way', outside the old spectrum of right and left.

The rebranding worked insofar as Labour won the 1997 election and remained in office for over ten years.

See also **Third Way.**

Nietzsche, Friedrich (1844–1900)

A German philosopher who was critical, harshly critical, of nineteenth-century European civilisation, and especially of the value that was being placed upon reason.

Nietzsche believed that there were two sides to human nature: first a Dionysian, instinctive, impulsive side; and secondly an Apollonian side that was controlled and disciplined. He believed that in the Europe of his time the Apollonian side had gained the upper hand and that this was due to one false god, religion, having been replaced by another false god, reason. Nietzsche saw this imbalance creating a society of mediocrity, of timid, unadventurous individuals. He compared the heroes of his time (businessmen and scientists) with the more inspiring figures of the past. Nietzsche's view was that the Dionysian side of human nature needed to be released. He was critical of how belief in the power of reason made people unwilling even to admit that humans had powerful instincts, including a will to power. He believed in individualism, competition and elitism, and that the exceptional individual, the superman, should be admired and encouraged.

Until recently Nietzsche was ignored in British and US sociology. The German Nazi Party claimed to be an heir to Nietzsche's philosophy, which may have been unfair to Nietzsche and certainly did not win him new friends in the post-war world. It was different in continental Europe, where Nietzsche was regarded an as important intellectual in the nineteenth and early twentieth centuries. Max Weber took account of Nietzsche's thinking. Recently, largely via the work of Michel Foucault (1926–1984), Nietzsche has re-emerged globally from sociological obscurity.

See also **Foucault, M.; Rationality.**

Nietzsche, F. (1967), *The Birth of Tragedy*, Random House, New York.

N

Node

Derived from the Latin word that means knot. In botany a node is the point on a stem where a bud forms which may grow into a leaf, flower or a secondary stem. In computing and telecommunications a node is any terminal in a network that is able to receive, create and transmit messages. This is the meaning that has been imported into sociology, usually as part of network theory.

Nodes can be identified within organisations, in networks of financial and other business corporations, and in online communities. In networks, nodes are terminals where the volume of messages received, created and transmitted peaks. Nodes are formed differently, and are likely to be less stable than, for example, the role of the chief executive in a business or secretary of a club.

See also **Network; Information society.**

Nomethetic

See Ideographic.

Non-parametric statistics

See Parametric statistics.

Non-response

See Response rates; Surveys.

Norm

A rule or looser shared expectation, backed by positive or negative sanctions, that governs human behaviour. A norm may not be statistically typical, but the usual effect of sanctions is that rules are followed and very likely internalised. Behaviour which complies with rules and expectations is called 'normative'.

Normal distribution

So-called because it is the most common distribution of things that can be measured including height, weight and student numbers at different universities. Alternatively called the bell-curve because the normal distribution has a large number of cases clustered around the mean, and diminishing numbers as both extreme points are approached. The reasons why this is the normal distribution remain unclear except that it is the expected distribution when an outcome can be affected by many causes.

The normal distribution is important in sociology (and elsewhere) because many statistical tests operate on the assumption of a normal distribution of cases.

Normalisation

The process whereby a pattern of behaviour becomes not just statistically normal but also accepted as normal and then may be expected within a group. An example of normalisation is the spread of recreational drug use among young people in Britain and other western countries since the 1960s.

Another, older meaning of normalisation is a statistical procedure whereby a set of values in a data set is manipulated to approximate to a normal distribution.

Parker, H., Williams, L. and Aldridge, J. (2002), 'The normalization of "sensible" recreational drug use: further evidence from the north-west England longitudinal study', *Sociology*, 36, 941–64.

Nuclear family

See Extended family; Family.

N

Objectivity

Free of all bias. This kind of knowledge is a conventional goal in all sciences, but present-day sociologists acknowledge that it is very difficult, if not impossible, to achieve.

Claiming objective knowledge is possible only for a 'realist' who believes, first, that mind-free knowledge of an external world is possible, and second, that the researcher's chosen methods of investigation contain no subjective distortions. In sociology purportedly objective research is most likely to use standardised (impersonal) methods of gathering quantifiable data (such as structured questionnaires).

Today few sociologists claim that their research is totally objective. They will admit that there is inevitably a subjective input to the design or selection of research instruments, and the definition of problems to be investigated. However, this does not mean that all knowledge is equally relative to the mind-set of a particular investigator or group of investigators. Full objectivity may never be achieved, but it can be approached by:

- triangulation, the use of a variety of research methods, seeing an object from different angles, and/or,
- propositions surviving all attempted refutations.

See also **Popper, K.R.; Relativism; Triangulation; Value freedom/neutrality.**

Observation

A method of gathering evidence where the investigator directly senses (sees but usually will also hear) whatever is being researched. Knowledge derived from observation is called 'empirical'.

Direct observation may be regarded as the best possible way of learning about people's behaviour, but observation is (labour) expensive, it is difficult (for practical reasons) to observe large populations, people may not want to be observed (in their living rooms as well as in their bedrooms), there is liable to be an observer effect, and it is impossible to observe mental states. These are the reasons why it is more common for sociological research to use quasi-empirical methods such as interviews and questionnaires (allowing people to report their own behaviour, social relationships and mental states).

Observation may be structured. An observer of a classroom or a work group may record on a grid who interacts with whom, and process the data to discover who initiates most interactions and who receives most attention.

The other kind of observation used in sociology is participant observation. A participant may become a researcher, or a researcher may become a participant in a group that is being studied. The observation may be overt (the subjects are told what the researcher is doing) or covert (which raises ethical issues). Participant observation was pioneered by social anthropologists. Once an investigator has been accepted as a participant, observer effects should be eliminated. This enables investigators to observe and listen to undistorted 'natural' behaviour and speech. The outcome is ideally a rich, 'thick' description of a group, situation or event. Participant observation is approved of by most sociologists but practised by far fewer. It is extremely time-expensive. It may take weeks or months for an observer to become an accepted participant. And the observer must make time to write down as fully as possible everything seen and heard as soon as possible after a period of observation.

See also **Empirical; Participant observation; Thick description.**

Occupation

Literally how we are occupied: which in modern societies is ordinarily taken to mean how we earn our livings. The jobs that people do belong to larger families of occupations, each requiring particular skills, knowledge, training and qualifications. Careers are likely to be built within occupations. These are the bases on which workers are most likely to become organised in trade unions and professional associations.

Occupations are most people's main link between the macro (public) sphere and micro private life. It is through our occupations that we make our main contributions to the wider society and are rewarded with pay and other benefits. Knowledge of their occupations allows us to 'place' other people. This indicates that occupations confer social identities. The getting acquainted question, 'What do you do?' is ordinarily understood as meaning, 'What occupation?' Occupations confer social identities and, most likely, personal identities also. We do not just 'do' but also 'are' teachers, motor mechanics, plumbers and so on. Occupational cultures are formed around particular kinds of work. Practitioners identify and take pride in their skills and the importance of their work. This applies even in officially non-skilled occupations such as care assistant. The social and psychological roles of occupations explain why long-term unemployment is likely to inflict serious social and psychological as well as financial damage.

'What is your occupation?' is a standard 'background' question in social surveys (along with age and sex). It is through their occupations that individuals and households are placed in sociology's social class schemes. So in order to locate respondents accurately, 'occupation' is usually a series of questions – occupational title followed by questions about qualifications and training, and management responsibilities (if any).

See also **Career; Class; Employment; Profession; Work.**

O

Oligarchy

Rule of the many by a few.

Sociology's interest in oligarchy remains focused on the claim of Robert Michels (1876–1936), the German sociologist, that all organisations, even those with democratic constitutions such as trade unions and socialist political parties, tend to become oligarchies. If true, the implication us that, at best, democratic political systems can offer voters only a choice between rival oligarchies.

See also **Democracy; Michels, R.; Politics.**

Michels, R. (1962), *Political Parties*, Free Press, New York.

Ontology

A branch of philosophy that seeks to establish the nature of the most fundamental things that exist, about which we can know, and from which other things that we know are built or developed.

Sociologists do their own ontology (rather than leave the job to philosophers). There are different views (ontologies) in sociology about the most fundamental things that are studied, such as social facts, actors or discourses. Ontology is not a separate field within sociology but exists within sociological or social theory.

Metaphysics is a branch of philosophy which seeks the most fundamental things in the entire world, that is, including all the things that are treated as fundamental in other sciences and disciplines (including sociology).

See also **Axiom; Epistemology; Metaphysics; Meta-theory; Problematic.**

Operational definitions, operationalisation

A crucial process in all research, especially in quantitative research. Concepts such as alienation, anomie, intelligence, education and social class must be defined in ways that can be measured. Education may be operationalised as years of schooling, or type of school attended, or highest qualification gained. Social class is usually operationalised as occupation.

It is easy for readers, and even for researchers themselves, to forget that operationalisation invariably compromises concepts to some extent, and maybe to an extent where the measurements have to be regarded as invalid.

See also **Objectivity.**

Organic solidarity

See Durkheim, E.

O

Organisation man

A term coined by the American sociologist and journalist William H. Whyte (1917–1999) in a scathing critique of how large business corporations entered and dominated the personalities and private lives of their (typically male) white-collar employees.

Organisation man is expected to be totally loyal to his employer. In return for an organisational career he is expected to accept repeated relocations (and promotions) to different towns and cities according to the organisation's requirements. He is expected to have appropriate friends (if any) and a suitable wife (who will be involved in business entertaining). Thus organisation man and his family will move from suburb to suburb, forming few genuine friendships. His personality is conformist, and his lifestyle is work-centred and otherwise privatised. Whyte believed that organisation men were replacing an older, more individualistic and competitive US middle class.

See also **Middle class; Mills, C.W.**

Whyte, W.H. (1956), *The Organization Man,* Penguin, Harmondsworth.

Organisations

Max Weber's (1864–1920) ideal type of bureaucracy is still the most common starting point for sociological work on formal organisations. Ever since Weber, organisation and bureaucracy have tended to be treated as synonymous in sociology, though Weber himself regarded bureaucracy as just a modern, legal-rational type of organisation. Organisations/bureaucracies can be government departments, businesses, charities, hospitals, universities, trade unions, political parties and so on. Insofar as these are all large organisations, they tend to be run in similar ways with a division of labour and rules that cover everything including authority relationships and the criteria governing appointments and promotions. Sociology has been a major contributor to the multi-disciplinary field of organisation studies, which has always been linked closely to management studies.

Following Weber, sociology's initial focus was on organisational structure. Typologies of organisations were developed comparing the mechanistic (rigid) with the organic (looser), for example. Managers were interested in establishing the organisation design that would be most effective: rigid or loose, flat or long? The initial answer from sociology was that, 'It depends', but on what? Suggestions included the stability of an organisation's environment and tasks, and the technology being used. Then contingency theory took over, arguing that what was best depended on many different things and that there was always ample scope for organisational choice.

A second area of interest for sociology has been organisational cultures. From the 1960s onwards the success of Japanese businesses, which were believed to benefit from strong corporate cultures, stimulated interest in this topic. An organisation's culture will develop with its history (real or

O

imagined). It can be built on myths, heroes, and tasks and skills that the work requires (which are likely to generate a specialist language), the organisation's mission in the wider world (again, real or imagined), and may be further fostered by corporate communications and company rituals.

Very early on it was discovered that informal relationships and processes existed within formal organisations. No bureaucracies operated 'just like clockwork'. It was found that different groups of employees tended to have their own particular purposes, and that the informal could either assist or frustrate the overall operations of an organisation. The human relations movement sought to align the informal with the formal.

Since the 1970s the entire field of organisation studies has needed to adapt to new times – post-Fordist, post-industrial and postmodern. Organisations have been seeking flexibility. New technology is said to mean that 'small is beautiful'. Large businesses have been sub-dividing themselves into numerous profit centres. New technology has weakened organisations' borders, and enables new social movements to be created using the Internet and mobile phone. The McDonald's restaurant chain has been offered as a business that typifies the new age. The question for sociology today is whether its older organisation theories have become obsolete, or whether they can be revised for the twenty-first century.

See also **Bureaucracy; Human relations; Information society; Network; Post-Fordism; Weber, M.**

Clegg, S. (1990), *Modern Organizations: Organization Studies in the Postmodern World*, Sage, London.

Du Gay, P. (2000), *In Praise of Bureaucracy: Weber, Organization, Ethics*, Sage, London.

Other(s), othering

O

A term imported into sociology from the writings of the French existential philosopher and author, Simone de Beauvoir (1908–1986). She argued that women had been subjected to 'othering' by men and were the second sex because their characteristics had been defined by another group, men, and from that group's standpoint.

Subsequently sociologists had applied the 'other' concept in understanding how various groups are identified: homosexuals, colonised people, ethnic minorities and excluded groups, for example. Othering distances the labellers from the labelled, and portrays the 'other' differently from the ways the group would otherwise have identified itself.

See also **Smith, D.E.; Standpoint theory.**

Beauvoir, S. de (1972, 1997), *The Second Sex,* Vintage, London.

Over-determination

This term was invented by the French Marxist philosopher Louis Althusser (1918–1990) to indicate that an event has multiple causes. Althusser used the term in debates within Marxism against those who wanted to reduce everything to the economic. Althusser insisted that major historical changes were not economically pre-determined but occurred through the operation and interplay of economic contradictions and political and ideological forces.

See also **Althusser, L.; Hall, S.**

O

P p

Panel study

A longitudinal study where the same panel (usually a sample from a larger population) is studied at repeated intervals. The aim is to plot changes over time at the aggregate and individual levels. Information about panel members' social circumstances and attitudes is usually collected. Thus it becomes possible to examine, for example, whether the experience of unemployment has any effect on work attitudes. This would be impossible with successive cross-sectional studies of different samples. Examples of panel studies include birth cohort studies and the British Household Panel Survey.

The drawbacks of panel studies are attrition – loss of panel members, and hence the panel becoming increasingly unrepresentative – and the danger of a research effect (the research itself making the panel different from the rest of the population). Exceptional measures are usually taken to maintain contact with, and to retain the loyalty of, panel members, while not overloading the panel with requests for information.

See also **Birth cohort studies; British Household Panel Survey; Longitudinal study.**

Panopticon metaphor

The original panopticon was a prison design (it was never built to the specification) by the English utilitarian philosopher Jeremy Bentham (1748–1821). Bentham's rational prison architecture would have enabled prisoners to be kept under constant surveillance from a central hub overlooking radiating 'spokes', each housing dozens of cells on several storeys.

The panopticon concept was adopted by the French sociologist Michel Foucault (1926–1984) in arguing that in modern societies people's lives were under increasing surveillance. Foucault was responding to the roles of professions such as medicine, psychiatry and social work. Subsequently the panopticon metaphor has been further extended to include electronic surveillance (of Internet sites, emails and telephone conversations) and the spread of CCTV cameras.

See also **Foucault, M.; Surveillance; Utilitarianism.**

Paradigm

The term used by the American historian of science, Thomas Kuhn (1922–1996), to refer to the problems to be addressed, and the methods of investigation to be used, that are accepted (for periods of time) by the members of scientific communities. What Kuhn called a paradigm, Marxists might call a problematic, others axioms or domain assumptions.

Kuhn believed that scientific knowledge developed with relatively long periods of normal science, conducted within accepted paradigms, punctuated by scientific revolutions, during which new paradigms were introduced and became the basis for further periods of normal science. Sociology appears to have always been different in its uninterrupted competition between paradigms.

See also **Axiom; Kuhn, T.S.; Ontology; Problematic.**

Parametric statistics

These are statistics where the values follow a mathematically modelled pattern, usually the normal (bell-curve) distribution where cases cluster around the mean. Statistics where the values follow no such pattern are non-parametric.

Different statistical procedures such as tests of significance are applied to different kinds of parametric statistics, and other, generally less powerful procedures, can be performed with non-parametric statistics.

See also **Normal distribution.**

Pareto, Wilfredo (1848–1923)

French-born, Italian engineer, turned economist then sociologist, who applied the principles of mechanical systems to economic and social life, and became a sociologist in order to explain 'non-logical action' (which covers most of what people do) which economics (studying rational action) was unable to handle. Pareto was treated as a major figure by Talcott Parsons (1902–1979), but is rarely mentioned in present-day sociology.

However, in economics students are still introduced to the 'Pareto principle', which states that a welfare measure is justified if at least one person is made better off and no one is left worse off. 'Pareto optimality' is said to exist when welfare cannot be improved for one individual without leaving someone else worse off.

Pareto's sociology starts from the view that there are basic human sentiments, some of which are expressed in logical (economic) action. Others, the 'residues', govern the rest of our behaviour. Pareto identified a number of types of residues, including a disposition to combine and a tendency for aggregates to persist. In Pareto's view, lay people develop theories ('derivations' in Pareto's conceptual scheme) to justify their actions. The job of sociology is to identify the underlying residues, the true sources of people's conduct.

Pareto was an elite theorist. He believed that elite rule was inevitable due

P

to 'the unequal distribution of capacities'. 'Elites were said to be composed of superior people, and circulation was necessary in order for the most able to rise and take command. Within elites, Pareto distinguished factions whose behaviour was governed by different residues. 'Lions' were suited to maintaining the status quo (behaviour governed by the residue for the persistence of aggregates), while 'foxes' were innovative and adaptive (governed by the residue for combinations).

See also **Elites**.

Pareto, W. (1973), *The Mind and Society: A Treatise on General Sociology*, Dover, New York.

Parsons, Talcott (1902–1979)

Parsons was a hugely influential, giant figure, in mid-twentieth-century American sociology. His aim was to create a single coherent theoretical framework for the practice and development of sociology. He introduced American sociology to European social theory, and created both structural-functionalism and the 'voluntaristic' view of social action.

The concept of system was pivotal in Parsons' work. He identified a cultural system, a social system, a personality system and a biological system, all inter-dependent on each other and on the physical environment. The cultural system was treated as the repository of values and norms, which were internalised into personality systems through socialisation, with the result that voluntaristic action was compatible with the maintenance of order in the social system.

Parsons divided social systems into four sub-systems, each addressing a functional requirement of the larger social system:

- Adaptation: a sub-system which adapted social life to its physical environment (principally the economy).
- Goal attainment: the sub-system that set goals (primarily political processes).
- Integration: this coordinated the sub-systems (law and other institutions).
- Pattern maintenance (alternatively called latency): developed and maintained appropriate individual motivations (principally the family).

Each sub-system could be further sub-divided (endlessly) using the same AGIP formula until reaching the level of specific roles and actors.

Parsons also identified a set of pattern variables – basic choices which individuals had to make when acting voluntaristically. One choice was between particularism (acting according to the specificities of a person or situation) and universalism (applying universal principles). The appropriate choices were defined in the cultural system and incorporated into personalities.

Completing his framework, Parsons argued that all systems had a tendency towards equilibrium, but this was never achieved, and the outcome was always further differentiation. Thus over time societies became increasingly complex.

P

During his lifetime and ever since, Parsons' work has been subjected to biting criticisms:

- Too abstract, too distant from a recognisable reality. Parsons occasionally ventured 'down to earth' to write about the family, the sick role and schooling, for example, but such work never used his full conceptual scheme.
- An over-socialised concept of man (despite Parsons' insistence that action was voluntaristic), leaving too little scope for human agency.
- Ignores Marx, and ignores all systemic conflicts.

Parsons became unfashionable in the 1970s when his ideas were eclipsed by theories that were then gaining converts, namely Marxism and symbolic interactionism. However, interest in Parsons' work survives for two reasons.

There are functional requisites for any ongoing social order, and specific practices and institutions can be analysed to identify the functions that they perform (if any), or whether they are dysfunctional or functionally neutral.

Non-Marxist sociology has yet to develop an alternative equally comprehensive framework for its enquiries.

> *See also* **Functionalism; Merton, R.K.; Pattern variables; Social system; Voluntaristic action.**

> Parsons, T. (1937), *The Structure of Social Action*, Free Press, New York.

> Parsons, T. (1951), *The Social System,* Routledge, London.

> Parsons, T. (1966), *Societies: Evolutionary and Comparative Perspectives*, Prentice-Hall, Engelwood Cliffs, N.J.

Participant observation

A research method where the investigator becomes a participant in the group or culture that is being studied.

> *See also* **Anthropology; Ethnography; Observation.**

Particularism

See Universalism.

Paternalism

A government or any other group or organisation that is run by a male head as if he were a benevolent father. Other members are treated as if they were children. Examples include master–slave/servant, and colonial ruler–subject relations. Some employers are said to run their businesses in a paternal manner.

> *See also* **Patriarchy.**

Path dependence

A theory of social change, an alternative to sweeping uni-linear theories of evolution and development. Path dependence theory accepts that 'history matters' and that there is a tendency for trends and institutions to be self-perpetuating. An example is a bandwagon effect in public opinion. Another is that neighbourhoods with a particular type of resident tend to attract others of the same type. However, this does not always happen, and path dependency analysis seeks critical junctures when events fix a group's or a society's future path. Examples include a history as a colony locking some countries in longer-term dependency relationships. Another is the long-term implications of some former communist countries opting for rapid privatisation of assets which created super-rich capitalist classes.

See also **Colonialism; Dependency theory; Evolution; Social change.**

Stark, D. and Bruszt, L. (1998), *Postsocialist Pathways: Transforming Politics and Property in East Central Europe*, Cambridge University Press, Cambridge.

Patriarchy

Originally meant rule by a father, but in present-day sociology the term is used more broadly to mean rule of women by men. Patriarchy may exist in families, businesses and governments, or throughout an entire society. All known societies have contained some patriarchal practices. In fact some feminists argue that patriarchy has been a main, if not the main, organising principle in all societies up to now. The questions (all hotly debated) that then arise are:

- How can patriarchy be explained? Is it because men are physically stronger? Is it a consequence of women being the child-bearers and nurturers while men have been able to be hunters and soldiers?
- How might patriarchy today be challenged and replaced?

See also **Feminism; Gender.**

Walby, S. (1990), *Theorising Patriarchy*, Blackwell, Oxford.

Patrimonialism

A type of traditional rule identified by Max Weber (1864–1920). A patrimonial royal household rules by force and bureaucracy, unrestrained by law or custom. Armed forces are led and key administrative positions are staffed not by land-owning aristocrats but mercenaries, slaves or conscripts.

Weber's main example of patrimonial rule was the traditional Chinese Empire. He regarded this kind of political system as inherently unstable (compared with feudalism) because it was always vulnerable to court intrigue, palace revolts and challenges by powerful subjects.

See also **Authority; Weber, M.**

Patriotism

A patriot exhibits strong and emotive support towards a homeland, usually a nation state.

Patriotism is akin to nationalism, but nationalism is basically a doctrine, an ideology, whereas patriotism is a quality of individuals. Patriots express pride in their country and its achievements, desire to preserve its character, identify with other members of the nation, and put the interests of the country ahead of personal and group interests. Patriots are liable to regard with suspicion any persons who put religion, class or any other loyalties ahead of the interests of the homeland.

Patriotic feelings can be aroused by displaying the flag and singing the anthem.

A product of sociology's neglect of nationalism is that the word 'patriotism' does not appear in most of the main sociology textbooks currently in use.

See also **Nation.**

Pattern variables

These are part of the conceptual framework that Talcott Parsons (1902–1979) created for sociology. The pattern variables identify mutually exclusive alternative orientations to action that can be applied in any situation:

- Particularism versus universalism: treating an object (a person, an event, a situation) as unique or as an example of a general class.
- Affectivity versus affective neutrality: emotional involvement or distance.
- Quality versus performance: valuing an object for its own qualities or for its utility.
- Diffuseness versus specificity: relating to all or just one aspect of an object.

The idea is that particular combinations of these variables will characterise, and will be useful in distinguishing and comparing, particular actors, roles, sub-systems, and entire social systems and cultures: for example, exactly how a family differs from an army, and how industrial societies differ from peasant societies.

See also **Parsons, T.**

Peasants

Live(d) in the countryside; engage(d) in agriculture, subsistence agriculture, producing largely for their own needs; the peasant family household is/was a unit of both production and consumption. Peasants were/are found in traditional societies. When agriculture becomes part of a capitalist, market economy, peasants are either driven from the land, or they become independent or tenant farmers or farm labourers.

There were/are various peasant strata, ranging from rich peasants to land-less peasants. Those with land held it by custom or legal entitlement. Serfs were peasants who held land on condition of paying a landowner (lord) in cash, kind or service (work on the owner's land), and who were unable to sell their land or, in some cases, move from it.

See also **Serfs; Traditional societies.**

Wolf, E.R. (1966), *Peasants*, Prentice-Hall, New Jersey.

Peer group

Peers are social equals. They may be peers in terms of age, sex, ethnicity, occupation or other attributes. A peer group is any group of peers, but the term is most often applied to young people's peer groups. This is because peer groups are known to play especially important roles in the life stage between childhood and adulthood, after which individuals (usually heterosexual couples) settle in their own family households.

See also **Youth; Youth culture.**

Penology

The study of policing, legal and court procedures, and the treatment of convicted offenders.

Sociologists study police behaviour, the legal professions, courtrooms as social systems, and the character and outcomes of different ways of dealing with convicted offenders in the community and in custody. 'Unintended conse-quences' are prominent in all this work: the likelihood of experiences with the police and courts convincing offenders that they are victims of injustice, and the likelihood of punishment, especially custody, increasing risks of re-offending.

However, from Emile Durkheim (1858–1917) onwards, sociologists have realised that one role, and a major role, of any justice system is to make the wider public feel that justice has been done.

See also **Criminology; Labelling theory; Law.**

P

Performative

A word used by philosophers to refer to a speech act.

Performativity

A concept used by the French social theorist Jean-Francois Lyotard (1924–1998) in his analysis of a postmodern condition. Lyotard argued that knowledge, including scientific knowledge, is no longer judged by truth standards, but according to its performativity, that is, its ability to deliver results, usually commercial benefits.

See also **Lyotard, J-F.**

Personality

A psychological concept that has been incorporated into sociology, though nowadays sociologists are more likely to approach individuals using the concepts of self and identity.

A personality is normally composed of stable, integrated and coherent traits (characteristics) of a person, which can distinguish that person from others. Psychologists normally measure personality characteristics using questionnaires, though alternatively projection tests or psychoanalysis may be employed. Commonly recognised personality types are the introvert and the extravert, and the authoritarian personality. Personality traits enable a person's behaviour in any situation to be predicted and explained. Attitudes are more specific, and predict and explain behaviour in particular types of situations, and reactions to particular types of events and to particular groups of other people.

Sociologists are interested in personality types insofar as personality characteristics can help to explain behaviour, and equally insofar as particular kinds of societies, social milieux and particular kinds of socialisation produce characteristic personalities. Some sociologists – Herbert Marcuse (1898–1979) for example – have incorporated psychoanalytic propositions into their work. The pattern variables identified by Talcott Parsons (1902–1979) are simultaneously features of particular cultures and of the personalities of individuals.

> See also **Attitudes; Authoritarian personality; Freud, S.; Identity; Marcuse, H.; Parsons, T.; Pattern variables; Self.**

Personnel management

See Human resource management.

Phenomenology

Phenomena are things as perceived by our senses. Phenomenological philosophy, founded by Edmund Husserl (1859–1938), insists that all knowledge is composed of phenomena, that is, what we perceive, and that there is no way in which we can directly apprehend what (if anything) is 'out there'. The implications of this for sociology were explored by one of Husserl's students, Alfred Schutz (1899–1959). Ethnomethodology is the branch of sociology that operates on the basis of a phenomenological view of social reality.

Phenomenology argues that the starting point for all enquiries must be a systematic investigation of consciousness, that is, the processes whereby knowledge is constituted in our minds. Identifying these processes is said to require 'bracketing out' all inputs into consciousness from the outside world. This is called the 'phenomenological reduction'. The aim is to lay bare the basic processes of knowledge constitution.

The implications for sociology (and all the human sciences) are anti-positivist and anti-empiricist. Phenomenologists reject the idea that people are like puppets whose actions can be determined by external social forces. They insist that people are actively involved in creating the social worlds in which they live. Schutz argued that the central problem for sociology had to be how people reach shared understandings about what is happening in the world around. His answer was that people create 'typifications' from their streams of experience, and that inter-subjectively they develop an agreed 'natural attitude', a view of how things are.

Peter Berger and Thomas Luckmann (1967) built on these ideas to explain how 'reality' is a social construction which takes on an objective character only as a result of inter-subjective agreement.

These ideas can be applied to sociology itself and, indeed, to any discipline. Schutz stressed the similarities between everyday common sense and scientific knowledge. A scientific attitude is said to be just one version of the 'natural attitude', entertaining more doubt than everyday common sense, but always keeping doubt within limits. So in sociology, or physics, what is taken to be objectively true retains this appearance only as long as inter-subjective agreement is maintained throughout the scholarly community.

See also **Ethnomethodology; Garfinkel, H.; Husserl, E.; Schutz, A.**

Berger, P. and Luckmann, T. (1967), *The Social Construction of Reality*, Allen Lane, London.

Schutz, A. (1972), *The Phenomenology of the Social World*, Heinemann, London.

Pilot study

A test run, prior to the main fieldwork in an investigation.

Pilot studies are conducted routinely prior to interview and self-completion questionnaire surveys. Interviewers are debriefed. Respondents will also be debriefed if the research instrument is a self-completion questionnaire. The aim is to test whether questions are understood, whether they are in the best order, and whether they allow respondents to record their real experiences and views. High levels of non-response to a question usually mean that the item should be changed or dropped.

See also **Interviews; Questionnaires.**

Pluralism

A plural society contains more than one culture (ethnic, religion, language, for example).

However, the term normally refers to politics. Here, first, pluralism is the opposite of totalitarianism. Pluralism means that power is diffused – within government between legislature, executive and courts, and between government, businesses, trade unions and voluntary associations. Second, pluralism means that two or more political parties compete for power.

See also **Democracy; Multiculturalism; Pressure groups; Totalitarianism.**

Polarisation

The process when a population or group splits towards both extreme points. Polarisation may be in terms of opinions (towards both agreeing and disagreeing strongly), or away from centre political parties and towards more support for extremist parties. Polarisation may also be in terms of conditions: the distribution of wealth and income, educational attainment or housing.

Polarisation is different from a widening of inequalities. The gap (range) between the extremes may widen, while units become more closely clustered around the centre.

Polarisation is an unusual trend. It is more common, for example, for all incomes to rise, albeit to different extents, or for political opinion to drift generally rightwards or leftwards. However, a recent example of polarisation in Britain has been towards a growth in the total paid workloads of households with at least one member in employment (due to more women joining the paid workforce) and a simultaneous growth in the number of households with no one in employment (due mainly to the increased numbers in the retired age groups).

Political economy

A discipline that existed in the eighteenth and nineteenth centuries, after which it was replaced by the economics that we know today. Political economy was about the conditions (primarily political conditions) that were conducive to wealth creation. Adam Smith (1723–1790) is probably the best known (today) of the political economists.

Modern economics has separated the economy from politics, and is more mathematical than the earlier discipline.

See also **Smith, A.**

P

Politicisation

The process whereby an issue ceases to be a purely private concern, is debated in the public sphere, then becomes a matter for politicians to address.

Politicisation is also the process whereby a population or group becomes politically active by expressing views in the public sphere (maybe by writing to newspapers), and begins to take political actions which pressure politicians to take up the concerns (writing to elected representatives, attending meetings, signing petitions, taking part in marches and demonstrations etc).

See also **Habermas, J.; Mobilisation; Social movements.**

Politics

The process of gaining and retaining power. Businesses, voluntary associations, universities and all other social groups have a political dimension. However, politics (unqualified) means gaining and retaining control of a government.

Political sociology is concerned with how non-democratic regimes gain the consent or acquiescence of the governed, and how they can be toppled. The Italian diplomat and political theorist Niccolo Machiavelli (1469–1527) offered advice to princes on how to stay in power. He advised that they should be strong and amoral. Ever since then, these features of politics have been dubbed Machiavellian.

The sociology of modern democratic political systems has focused on political parties (how they are organised and how they mobilise support) and elections (the implications of single-member constituencies, and winner-takes-all voting versus systems of proportional representation, and how parties campaign). The orthodox view in sociology has been that, in multi-party systems, successful parties must compete for and win the centre ground, which ensures that the programme of whoever wins will be at least tolerable for most of its opponents, who in time will have their turn in power, thus maintaining support for the system. However, in recent times sociologists have noted a series of challenges to this classical model of democratic party politics.

Politicians have become less dependent on member-based political parties as the mass media (especially television) have enabled them to communicate directly with voters. Politicians may also claim state funding or attract large donations from wealthy sponsors, thus further reducing their dependence on mass memberships.

Economic trends and changes in the shape of the class structures in economically advanced societies have weakened the working classes and the organisations that have represented them, mainly trade unions and socialist political parties. Political party contests have consequently shifted from battles between left and right to contests between the centre and more extreme right, or new radical movements have appeared, some based on environmental issues and others on nationalist appeals.

Globalisation in its various forms has simultaneously reduced the independence of national governments, and led to the creation of new trans-national social movements such as the Anti-Globalization Movement, and also terrorist groups such as Al-Qaeda.

New social movements are not organised in the same manner as older political parties, but may exist largely in cyberspace with activists linked through websites and email.

See also **Government; Michels, R.; Power; Social movements.**

Dahl, R.A. (1998), *On Democracy*, Yale University Press, New Haven, Conn.

Lipset, S.M. (1960), *Political Man: The Social Bases of Politics*, Doubleday, New York.

Polyandry

See Kinship.

Polygamy

See Kinship.

Polygyny

See Kinship.

Popper, Karl Raimund (1902–1994)

Austrian-born philosopher of science; based at the London School of Economics from 1945; renowned for his advocacy of openness in science and society, and for his critique of historicism.

Popper overhauled notions of what had made the natural sciences so successful in expanding knowledge. He argued that this was the result of all scientific propositions being falsifiable. Popper argued that there were no special scientific procedures for inducing hypotheses; these were always mere conjectures. He claimed that science progressed because members of scientific communities attempted to falsify each other's claims, so only robust hypotheses were left unscathed, and laws and theories had to be modified and improved constantly. He believed that claims that were not falsifiable (closed systems of thought) should be excluded from the field of science. Popper's leading examples of closed systems were Marxism and Freudianism (psychoanalysis). If the working class revolted, this proved that Marx was right; if the working class was acquiescent, Marxism had an explanation – false consciousness.

In *The Poverty of Historicism* Popper argued that all historical trends were just that, simply trends, and should not be mistaken for laws and used to predict the future. In Popper's view, genuine scientific propositions were less extravagant, always of the 'if–then' variety.

Popper believed that closed systems of thought stymied science and were dangerous for society in that they encouraged totalitarianism and the crushing of all dissent. One of Popper's devotees is George Soros (1930–), briefly a student at the London School of Economics in the 1960s, who became a multi-billionaire international financier, and founded the Central European University and the Open Society Institute which, following the end of communism, have supported the creation of open societies throughout eastern Europe and the former Soviet Union.

See also **Positivism; Science.**

Popper, K.R. (1945), *The Open Society and its Enemies*, Routledge, London.

Popper, K.R. (1957), *The Poverty of Historicism*, Routledge, London.

P

Popper, K.R. (1963), *Conjectures and Refutations: The Growth of Scientific Knowledge,* Routledge, London.

Populism

Named after the Populist Party which was formed in the United States in 1892 and appealed primarily to small farmers. Subsequently the term has been applied to any leader or movement that:

- expresses disillusionment with existing parties, leaders and policies
- appeals directly to 'the people', and aims to return power to 'the people', rather than working within existing organisations.

Successful populist movements usually develop into more conventional political parties. Examples include the fascist movements in European countries in the inter-war years, and the Scottish National Party prior to its success in elections.

See also **Charisma; Fascism; Mobilisation; Nietzsche, F.; Social movements.**

Positional goods, services, consumption

These are goods and services whose value depends on others not having them. Examples include fashion clothing, the latest model car (or registration plate) and educational qualifications.

It is argued that as standards of living rise, the positional element in personal consumption increases in importance. An outcome is said to be that economic growth yields diminishing returns in individual well-being. The effects are likened to a crowd where everyone stands on tip-toe and no one sees further.

However, positional consumption is not new. The conspicuous consumption of the US upper class at the end of the nineteenth and early twentieth centuries, which was condemned by Thornstein Veblen (1857–1929), is a classic example.

See also **Quality of life; Standard of living; Well-being.**

Hirsch, F. (1977), *The Social Limits to Growth*, Routledge, London.

Veblen, T. (1899, 1953), *The Theory of the Leisure Class*, Mentor, New York.

P

Positive discrimination

Alternatively called affirmative action or reverse discrimination; refers to discrimination in favour of a group (usually women or an ethnic group) in order to compensate for earlier or concurrent disadvantages. Positive discrimination may be regarded as justified when a group would not be an equal competitor in a procedurally impartial contest (for admission to university or for a job, for example).

In Britain positive discrimination is illegal, but it was permitted in the United States (in favour of non-white Americans) under the 1964 Civil Rights Act. However, in the United States the implementation of this Act proved controversial. While positive discrimination may appear fair at a group level, it can be experienced as acutely unfair by individuals who fail to gain university places or jobs despite superior qualifications to individuals who are successful, and the latter may suffer from the perception that they owe their positions to their group membership rather than to individual merit. Positive discrimination may prove acceptable to all groups only as a short-term measure while historical injustices are rectified. By the 1990s it had become rare to encounter positive discrimination in the United States.

See also **Discrimination.**

Positivism

Positivism is a doctrine formulated by Auguste Comte (1798–1857), who also coined the word 'sociology'. Comte believed that scientific knowledge was the only true knowledge and that sociology should therefore emulate the methods of the natural sciences.

Comte held an empiricist view of science. He believed that scientists worked with evidence obtained by observation, and that sociology should proceed similarly. This evidence would reveal patterns of co-existence and succession among social phenomena from which laws, comparable to the laws of natural science, would be derived. Observations were to be explained by showing that one instance was an example of a more general regularity (a law). Thus scientific knowledge about the social world would replace speculation, tradition, religious authority, custom and common sense. Comte expected the development of a scientific body of sociological knowledge to permit social interventions that would transform and improve society just as the natural sciences had transformed manufacturing and transportation, and tamed nature.

The development of sociology (and other human sciences) as positive disciplines was an orthodox aspiration up until the mid-twentieth century. Emile Durkheim (1858–1917) was a positivist and his study of *Suicide* (1897) has remained a classical example of positivist methodology.

The positivist doctrine was refined by the Vienna Circle of logical positivists in the 1920s and 1930s. They proclaimed the 'verification principle': propositions had to be validated by sensory experience. They departed from Comte in insisting on a clear separation between statements of fact and judgements of value, arguing that 'is' and 'ought' statements could never be derived from one another. They also recognised that some propositions could be proved by pure logic (for example, 4 is greater than 2) and required no empirical verification.

Positivism began to encounter serious criticism from within the social sciences in the mid-twentieth century. Critics queried whether the natural sciences really did proceed in the manner that positivists claimed (Kuhn, 1962; Popper, 1963). They also questioned whether natural science methods were really appropriate when the subjects (humans) possessed consciousness and could act intentionally (Winch, 1958). Positivism retained some defenders (Nagel, 1961) but few sociologists have continued to apply the label to themselves. Indeed, in recent decades 'positivist' has been a term of abuse. Despite this, much (probably most) sociological research proceeds as if the investigators were positivists. There has been huge investment in developing standardised measurements and quantitative methods. Investigators measure aspects such as people's incomes, education, voting intentions or crime rates, and demonstrate relationships between variables which are treated as explanations. On the basis of such evidence sociologists (as Comte envisaged) offer advice to policy makers (and anyone else who cares to listen) on how to reduce crime, boost educational attainments and so on.

See also **Kuhn, T.S.; Objectivity; Popper, K.R.; Science.**

Durkheim, E. (1897/1963), *Suicide: A Study in Sociology*, Routledge, London.

Kuhn, R. (1962), *The Structure of Scientific Revolutions,* Chicago University Press, Chicago.

Nagel, E. (1961), *The Structure of Science: Problems in the Logic of Scientific Explanation,* Routledge, London.

Popper, K.R. (1963), *Conjectures and Refutations: The Growth of Scientific Knowledge,* Routledge, London.

Winch, P. (1958, 1990), *The Idea of a Social Science and its Relation to Philosophy,* Routledge, London.

Post-colonial theory

This centre-stages the histories, situations and experiences of colonised people.

Conventional sociology is criticised for its Eurocentrism, for uncritically incorporating ideological assumptions that are taken for granted (as simply facts) in the powerful west, thereby helping to naturalise the current world order (make it appear inevitable). Other cultures and societies are regarded as less developed, backward and inferior, and colonised people are thereby at least partly dehumanised – their histories, experiences and worldviews are obliterated.

Post-colonial theory is claimed as an emancipatory body of theory (along with critical theory, feminism, queer theory and subaltern sociology). It aims to undermine the orthodox Eurocentric view of how things are, to give voice to the wretched of the earth (Frantz Fanon's (1925–1961) expression), and thereby equip the oppressed with a tool-kit (a set of alternative discourses) with which to struggle for emancipation.

Edward Said (1935–2003) was a leading exponent of post-colonial theory. He has argued that western images of the orient (like 'darkest Africa') have reflected specifically western interests and ideology. The orient that the west has constructed is said to be an 'imagined other' – variously exotic, backward, cruel, intriguing. Constructing these others is said to have been essential for the west to construct then maintain its view of itself, its role in the world and its place in history.

Post-colonial sociology relativises the western point of view, gives voice to the world's subordinated people, and thereby presents alternative views of history, the current world order and possible futures.

See also **Development; Emancipatory sociology; Other.**

Fanon, F. (1967,1990), *The Wretched of the Earth,* Penguin, Harmondsworth.

Said, E.W. (1978, 1995), *Orientalism,* Penguin, Harmondsworth.

Post-Fordism

Post-Fordism is said to have replaced Fordism as the dominant economic and political regime during or since the 1970s. Post-Fordism is charac- terised by its relative flexibility and its capacity to respond to challenges and opportunities presented by globalisation and new technologies.

It is claimed that by the 1970s Fordism was encountering unsolvable internal problems, namely: trade union power disrupting production, perpetuating inefficient work practices, and forcing high wage rises and squeezing profits; and the unsustainable costs of state welfare. The hallmark of post-Fordism is said to be its flexibility. Its main features are:

- Functional flexibility: the ability to introduce rapid changes in an organisation's shape, workforce skills and machinery so as to respond to changes in technology and conditions in local and international markets.
- Numerical flexibility: usually achieved by the division of workforces into functionally flexible cores of skilled employees, and numerical flexibility among lower-skilled peripheries of non-standard employees (part time, temporary and fixed term).
- Smaller, downsized, de-layered enterprises.
- Niche marketing.
- Customers choosing individualised lifestyles by purchasing customised mixtures of products.
- Neo-liberal macro-economic management.
- Scaled-down welfare states and lower taxes.

A major debate in sociology is about exactly how much has changed since the Fordist era. Has there been a complete change of strategy in industry or are the changes better described as neo-Fordist with some new approaches being incorporated within established Fordist methods?

See also **Dual labour market; Fordism; Globalisation; Individualisation; Information technology; Neo-liberalism; Regulation theory.**

Piore, M. and Sabel, C. (1984), *The Second Industrial Divide,* Basic Books, New York.

Wood, S. (1989), *The Transformation of Work? Skills, Flexibility and the Labour Process,* Unwin Hyman, London.

Post-industrialism

This term, obviously enough, is applied to societies that are alleged to have moved beyond the industrial stage. The older industrial societies are believed to have made this transition during the second half of the twentieth century.

A decline in employment in manufacturing, sometimes described as de-industrialisation, is the main indicator of the transition to post-industrialism. In the most advanced economies, service sectors now employ over three-quarters of the workforces. We should note here that the decline in manufacturing employment may or may not be an outcome of a decline in manufacturing output. The main causes of the decline in manufacturing employment are various combinations (in different countries) of:

- the transfer of manufacturing to lower wage cost countries
- technological change in manufacturing which replaces humans with machines
- a growth in demand for services such as education, healthcare and banking as societies become more prosperous.

These developments do not usually reduce the total volume of employment, but they change the character of jobs. Manual employment declines, and non-manual employment increases. This trend requires or is accompanied by an expansion of tertiary (higher) education. There are said to be sufficient social and political consequences to justify likening this transition to the earlier birth of industrial society. It is necessary to emphasise that the above trends are entirely consistent with the preservation of a low-skilled, low-paid and under-employed working class.

One set of debates in sociology is about exactly how post-industrialisation is related to the shift from Fordist to post-Fordist modes of business organisation. Are the two necessarily related, or did they just happen to occur at roughly the same time? Likewise the trends in social thought and social life that are described as postmodern.

Critics of the post-industrial concept point out that there has been considerable employment in service sectors throughout the industrial age. Manufacturing firms have always required services from security and cleaning businesses, banks and other institutions. Does another step during a long-term expansion of service sectors require a change of label for the economy and society? In any case, it is pointed out that western economies remain, and former communist societies have become, capitalist, and the basic features of capitalism remain unchanged.

See also **Capitalism**; **Industrialisation**; **Post-Fordism**; **Postmodern**.

Bell, D. (1974), *The Coming of Post-Industrial Society*, Basic Books, New York.

Postmodern

In sociology this term and its derivatives (postmodernism, postmodernity, and postmodern as an adjective) indicate that society itself, or social thought, or both (probably in reciprocal cause–effect chain reactions) have moved beyond a modern stage.

Postmodern thought abandons belief in science, reason and progress, regards objective truth as a chimera, an illusion, and rejects all 'grand narratives' (big theories that purport to explain everything). It insists that there will always be a plurality of plausible viewpoints. The abandonment of the modernist project (often called the enlightenment project) is regarded as a response to its manifest failure. Where are the laws of society? Where, when and how can be results of science be declared unequivocally as progress? Simultaneously or alternatively, postmodern thought is explained as a response to a new postmodern condition.

The postmodern condition (of society) is usually described in terms of a combination of the following:

- Social structures and groups become weaker.
- Social classes fragment.
- Family roles are negotiated rather than given.
- New social movements are more fluid and less formally organised than modern political parties, trade unions and professions.
- Consumer roles replace producer roles as sources of identity and meaning.
- Culture plays a stronger role in social life, largely due to the growth of the mass media.
- Distinctions between the real and the fictional break down: media images and characters are treated as real happenings and real persons.
- Former high, popular and middle-brow cultures become less distinct.

Sociologists have to decide, and as yet they are collectively undecided, first, about whether the above trends in the social condition, insofar as they have occurred, signify as clear a break with modernity as the earlier shift from traditional to industrial, urban, modern society. Second, must we abandon the 'modernist project'? In practice most sociology remains implicitly if not explicitly modern. Third, if the modernist project is abandoned, where does this leave sociology? Must sociology as known up to now be abandoned? Or can there be a postmodern sociology?

See also **Baudrillard, J.; Derrida, J.; Jameson, F.; Lyotard, J-F.; Post-industrialism.**

Featherstone, M. (ed.) (1988), *Postmodernism: Theory Culture and Society*, Vol. 5, Nos 2 & 3, Sage, London.

Harvey, D. (1989), *The Condition of Post Modernity*, Blackwell, Oxford.

Post-structuralism

This (Paris-based) movement developed from (rather than in direct opposition to) structuralism. Post-structuralists agree with structuralists that language is the bedrock of the social, but while structuralists use language to access underlying structures (such as Levi-Strauss's binaries), post-structuralists insist that it is simply impossible to delve behind language to an underlying reality.

Post-structuralists argue that, on the one hand, languages (all languages) are prisons, vehicles for social control, yet at the same time all languages are potentially unruly, capable of creating ambiguities, contradictions and instability. Within any language there are always many possible ways of seeing things. Hence it is futile to search for one true account (a so-called 'grand narrative').

Post-structuralists are therefore critical of all scientific aspirations and academic conventions (which are treated as mere conventions – agreed rules, ways of using language and thereby of seeing things). They are critical of what they call 'the enlightenment project' – bringing people to freedom through the use of reason.

See also **Barthes, R.; Derrida, J.; Structuralism.**

Harland, R. (1987), *Superstructuralism,* Methuen, London.

Poverty

Originally meant lacking the resources to meet subsistence needs, but today the term is applied to a much wider range of conditions, and its value has diminished proportionately.

- *Subsistence poverty*: lacking what is necessary to maintain a healthy life may be divided into mild and severe levels, and also into primary and secondary poverty.
  - *Primary poverty*: where there is an absolute insufficiency of resources.
  - *Secondary poverty*: where households can meet their subsistence needs only if they spend nothing on anything that is not absolutely necessary.

  Subsistence definitions of poverty are considered most appropriate for, and are most often used in, poorer countries. Sometimes 'rule of thumb' measurements are used such as $1 per capita per day.
- *Relative poverty*. These definitions are generally applied in richer countries where there is little, if any, subsistence poverty. Relative poverty can be assessed in objective or subjective ways.
  - *Objective relative poverty* exists when people are unable to afford (as opposed to choosing not to purchase) items that are considered essential in a normal, decent standard life in their particular countries or socio-demographic groups. Such items might include a television set, an annual holiday, and being able to buy birthday and Christmas presents for close family members. What is required to live decently may be determined by asking representative samples in surveys. Alternatively or in addition, researchers can identify purchases that are (almost) universal at average and higher income levels, but where there are sharp drop-offs at lower incomes. Again, 'rule of thumb' measurements are sometimes

used: beneath 50 per cent, or 60 per cent, or 70 per cent of the median income moderated for household size and composition.
- *Subjective poverty*, when people feel that they are poor, impoverished. These feelings turn out to be related only weakly to objective measurements of poverty because most people assess the adequacy of their own living standards using as points of reference whatever is normal in their own countries, towns, villages or neighbourhoods.

A dilemma in using all relative definitions of poverty is that the condition becomes impossible to eradicate unless all inequalities are abolished.
- *Dimensions of poverty*. These measurements break down poverty into different dimensions – income, education, health and maybe other dimensions also. A multi-dimensional approach is used in the Human Development Indices calculated by the United Nations Development Programme. An objection (or a problem) is that the choice of dimensions can be arbitrary: sometimes gender equity and democracy are included.

The diminishing value of the poverty concept is indicated by the extent to which, in richer countries, it has now been replaced by 'social exclusion'.

See also **Booth, C.J.; Culture of poverty; Cycle of deprivation; Poverty trap; Quality of life; Relative deprivation; Rowntree, B.S.; Social exclusion; Standard of living; Well-being.**

Lister, R. (2004), *Poverty,* Polity, Cambridge.

Poverty trap

This describes the situation where people are unable to escape from poverty due to the interplay between their labour market situations and the tax and state benefit systems.

The trap is usually created by means-tested benefits: for example, when low wages, unemployment benefit or pensions are topped-up to a minimum income level. People can then find that if they move from unemployment into a (low-paid) job, or to a slightly higher-paid job, the withdrawal of means-tested benefits that is triggered, coupled with any tax on their additional earnings, almost cancels out the additions to their incomes. People who are caught in this poverty trap usually experience higher total 'withdrawal rates' than the tax rates on the very highest incomes.

The easiest solution to the poverty trap is to make all welfare benefits universal (not means-tested), but this conflicts with a desire to target support towards the most needy.

See also **Esping-Andersen, G.; Poverty.**

Power

Sociologists are agreed that power is among their discipline's primary concepts, and also that power is difficult to define precisely because it can take so many different forms. The all-encompassing definition is the ability to change how things are, or not to change things when a person or group could effect change.

One kind of power, featured in the work of Max Weber (1864–1920), is the ability to prevail despite the resistance or unwillingness of others. This may be achieved via the control of resources (often money) or the ability to directly command other people. This power may be legitimate, accepted as rightly exercised by those who are commanded (in which case the power becomes authority), or the power may be coercive, imposed ultimately by the use or threat of physical force or restraint. Power can also be subtle, operating through influence or through ideological domination (a condition called hegemony), or it may take the form of leaving things the way they are even if others would prefer change.

There is another kind of power that Talcott Parsons (1902–1979) highlighted, which is created and mobilised consensually to achieve agreed objectives, as when a club appoints officers to act on the group's behalf, and when citizens empower a government. This kind of power is ubiquitous, present in all situations. That said, the state is the ultimate source of all kinds of power insofar as it monopolises the right to use force, or to authorise others to use force, within its territory.

Note that both kinds of power, resisted and consensual, are not finite but can be eroded or expanded, and in the latter case the capabilities of those concerned are enhanced.

See also **Authority; Government; Hegemony; State.**

Lukes, S. (1974), *Power: A Radical View*, Macmillan, London.

Praxis

A Marxist term for theoretically informed action that is capable of changing the world. The test of an idea is said to be not whether it conforms to existing evidence but whether it can be put into practice. Praxis is thus regarded as superior to idle philosophical speculation on the one hand, and naïve action on the other.

See also **Gramsci, A.; Marx, K.**

Preference theory

Catherine Hakim claims that the main change that affected women's lives during the twentieth century was that they were given more choices, and that the outcome is that they choose different lifestyles that accord with their different preferences. These lifestyles are home centred, work centred and adaptive.

Critics (mostly other female sociologists) accuse Hakim of neglecting the constraints under which women's preferences are formed.

See also **Feminism; Gender.**

Hakim, C. (2004), *Key Issues in Women's Work: Female Diversity and the Polarisation of Women's Employment*, Glasshouse, London.

Prejudice

A pre-judgement of something, someone or a group, which is held in spite of the absence of supportive evidence, or even in defiance of contrary evidence. A prejudice may be 'for' or 'against'. In either case its explanation has to be in terms of characteristics of the judges rather than whoever or whatever is judged.

A prejudice (against foreigners, for example) may be functional for an in-group. It may be psychologically beneficial for an individual to be able to blame others. A person or group may be generally prejudiced, or a prejudice may be specifically towards a person, group or practice.

Prejudice may lead to discrimination, but not necessarily, because discrimination may be inhibited by the law. Discrimination may be the result of prejudice, but not necessarily, because discrimination can have other causes.

See also **Authoritarian personality; Discrimination; Racism; Xenophobia.**

Pressure groups

Unlike political parties, pressure groups do not seek to become a government. They operate by exerting pressure on other political actors. They may do this:

- Through political parties: in Britain the trade unions have sought influence through the Labour Party: in fact the trade unions were the main creators of the Labour Party in 1900. Business has sought influence primarily through its links with the Conservative Party.
- Via the civil service: in exchange for information that is useful to government departments, pressure groups may be able to exert influence. An example is the relationship that has existed between the National Farmers Union and whichever UK government department has been responsible for agriculture.
- By shaping public opinion, as attempted by the Campaign for Nuclear Disarmament.

Needless to say, a pressure group may simultaneously use all three avenues. At some point a pressure group may decide to become a political party. This has happened to the Greens in European politics. Movements have to decide whether they will be more effective exerting pressure from the sidelines, or seeking a share of political power.

The existence of a large number of diverse pressure groups is often regarded as a key indicator that a political system is genuinely plural and democratic.

See also **Democracy; Mobilisation; Pluralism; Social movements.**

P

Prestige

This refers to whether a person, group or institution is admired, respected and looked up to, or disdained and looked down upon.

Max Weber (1864–1920) argued that status groups were formed on the basis of the prestige, or degrees of honour, that were attached to their styles of life. Ever since then debate has raged in sociology about whether prestige (or status) is a distinct dimension of social stratification, or whether prestige is dependent on other inequalities (of income, wealth and power, for example), in which case occupational prestige may properly be used as an indicator of an individual's or group's position in the general social hierarchy.

See also **Status**.

Chan, T.W. and Goldthorpe, J.H. (2004), 'Is there a status order in contempo-rary British society? Evidence from the occupational structure of friendship', *European Sociological Review,* 20, 383–401.

Primary socialisation

See Socialisation.

Primitive societies

This term is rarely used today. In the nineteenth century social anthropol-ogists applied the term to what were then believed to be the earliest forms of human society. This was at a time when evolutionary theory was domi-nant, and societies were believed to progress from simple to forever more complex and highly differentiated forms. It was then believed that primi-tive societies would reveal the most elementary forms of family life, reli-gion and so on. In practice, social anthropologists discovered that so-called primitive societies had extremely complex cultures and family systems.

Nowadays some societies may be described as pre-literate, but under-developed or developing (economically) and traditional have become the preferred terms.

See also **Anthropology; Traditional societies**.

P

Private sphere

A division between public and private life is a feature of modern societies. The public sphere is the location of political and economic life. The private sphere comprises family and home life. These spheres are governed by different norms. In the public sphere actors are expected to be rational and unemotional, and to bracket-out private relationships and interests. In private people are not just allowed but are expected to be expressive, sentimental, relaxed, able to 'let themselves go'.

This division between the public and the private has received considerable attention from sociologists of gender since, in the past, the public sphere was dominated by adult males thereby confining women and children to the private sphere. This division of labour has been the bedrock of male masculinity and female femininity. However, since the rise of second wave feminism women have become much more prominent in the public sphere while, to a lesser extent, men have become more involved in private domestic affairs, including child-rearing.

Privatisation

The transfer of assets from public ownership into private ownership.

During the 1980s and 1990s the UK's Conservative governments headed by Margaret Thatcher and then John Major privatised a series of major industries. These included oil, gas, electricity, water, coal, telephones, the railways and air transport. This rolling-back of the public sector marked the end of a post-war political consensus, one of whose features was agreement on a 'mixed economy'. A new period of consensus politics began in the 1990s when the Labour Party abandoned its historical commitment to public ownership and actually continued (albeit at a more moderate pace) the policy of privatisation.

See also **Nationalisation.**

Privatism

Lifestyles that are home and family centred.

A trend towards privatised lifestyles, alongside a decline in neighbourliness and in work-based occupational communities, was noted in the 1950s and 1960s. Television, the design of new housing developments (high rise or with houses separated by gardens and fences), the motor car and above all rising standards of living, which made nuclear families more self-sufficient, were held responsible.

Subsequently it has been claimed that extreme privatism is more likely to be the result of constraints – low incomes and unsocial work schedules – than the lifestyle choice of those concerned.

See also **Affluent workers; Community; Neighbourhood.**

Devine, F. (1992), *Affluent Workers Revisited? Privatism and the Working Class*, Edinburgh University Press, Edinburgh.

Goldthorpe, J.H., Lockwood, D., Bechhofer, F. and Platt, J. (1969), *The Affluent Worker in the Class Structure*, Cambridge University Press, Cambridge.

Probability

All statements about people's behaviour are in terms of probabilities. The possible range is from zero (nobody does it) to 100 per cent (everyone does it). However, the situation is usually between these extremes. Middle class young people are more likely to attend university than working class young people, but some working class young people attend while not every middle class young person does so. Cuts in welfare payments to the unemployed will not lead to them all seeking and finding jobs, but the probability of them doing so within a given time frame is most likely to rise.

Certainty is rare because most patterns of behaviour have multiple causes which include the actors' beliefs, knowledge, preferences and choices.

See also **Normal distribution.**

Problematic

A term first used by the French structural Marxist Louis Althusser (1918–1990), for whom *the* problematic was the preferred (Marxist) way of examining an issue. Subsequently in sociology the term has been used more broadly:

- as a noun to identify a 'definition of a problem' from any theoretical position
- as an adjective, to indicate that the definition of a problem offered elsewhere is contestable rather than the only possible definition.

See also **Althusser, L.; Axiom; Paradigm.**

Profane

Everything that is not sacred (set apart and revered).

See also **Sacred; Religion.**

Professions

A type of occupation, characterised by the existence of a professional association, which:

- supervises and validates practitioners' education and training
- qualifies practitioners
- restricts full membership to the qualified
- imposes standards of professional practice, and polices the profession with the ultimate sanction of disqualification and loss of membership.

A profession may be protected by law (as is the medical profession in most modern societies), but most professions (including the accountancy and engineering professions in Britain) do not enjoy this protection. Professionalisation is a strategy open to any occupational group. Its success depends upon:

- convincing customers (most likely to be called clients) that only members of the profession are able to properly judge and regulate each other's work

- clients regarding it important that they obtain high-quality service.

Occupations differ in the degree to which they have professionalised. There are more semi-professions and aspirant professions than fully fledged professions such as medicine and law. The full professions have highly educated members, and the occupations are prestigious.

Professions are similar to trade unions in that each seeks to protect and enhance its members' interests, but their strategies are different.

- Trade unions seek inclusiveness, to recruit all members of an occupational group, whereas professions seek exclusiveness, to distinguish the qualified from 'quacks'.
- Trade unions bargain with employers whereas professions try to boost demand for their services and what clients are prepared to pay by extolling the quality of their services.

Some occupational associations combine trade union and professional features, but this marriage is never conflict-free.

See also **Management; Occupation; Trade unions**.

MacDonald, K.M. (1995), *The Sociology of the Professions*, Sage, London.

Profiling

In sociology a profile is simply a list of the typical characteristics of a group (gender, age, class, occupational) that distinguish the group concerned from other groups. A profile is a stereotype, albeit one based on evidence.

However, the type of profiling that has captured public attention in recent years is offender profiling. From a profile of the persons known to commit a particular type of crime (typical biological, psychological and social characteristics), and from known characteristics of an offender (scene of crime descriptions and other evidence) it is possible to construct a fuller profile of the person who the police are seeking.

Progress

Progress is change for the better, towards an even better future.

Present-day sociologists are fascinated by the idea of progress because throughout the nineteenth century, during sociology's birth, it was taken as self-evident that European societies were progressing and that sociology was part of this progressive movement. The idea came from the enlightenment philosophers. Reason was to improve the world, to liberate humanity. Technological developments, urbanisation and industrialisation were viewed as progressive changes, evidence of the power of reason and its handmaiden, science. Social research into poverty, life in cities, ill-health and crime proceeded with a conviction that better understanding would lead to social improvement.

During the twentieth century this confidence was lost amid wars,

P

genocides, and suspicions that the quality of life was stagnant despite continuous economic growth. Sociologists started to study just social change. They started to ask, 'Better for whom?' Towards the end of the century postmodern social theorists began to claim that the 'enlightenment project' was manifestly exhausted.

However, all this applies only in the west. People in underdeveloped and post-communist countries (sociologists included) persist in the belief that modernisation (equated with becoming more like the west) means progress.

See also **Development; Enlightenment; Evolution; Positivism; Social change.**

Nisbet, R. (1980), *History of the Idea of Progress*, Heinemann, London.

Proletariat, proletarianisation

Terms used by Karl Marx (1818–1883). He used proletariat to describe the class (otherwise known as the working class) that sold its labour power to employers.

Proletarianisation is a process envisaged by Marx. Intermediate groups (between the bourgeoisie and proletariat) such as self-employed craft workers and professionals, were to be ground down and absorbed into the proletariat. This has not happened in the way that Marx envisaged. However, Harry Braverman (1920–1976) resurrected the thesis in the 1970s by claiming that a progressive degradation of labour was underway, with conception (management) being gradually separated from execution (following instructions) in the workplace.

See also **Braverman, H.; Class; Labour process theory; Marx, K.; Working class.**

Property

Created when a society recognises rights of ownership. The owner may be an individual, the state, a business, a charity or any other organisation. Property is anything to which rights of ownership are attached: land, houses, cars, clothing, television sets, cash in bank accounts, assets in pension and insurance funds, stocks and shares, persons (slaves). There is intellectual property: ownership of literary work, musical compositions and recordings, and computer software.

The rights that accompany ownership are variable, depending on what is recognised and authorised by a particular society. There may be restrictions on the right to sell (and to whom), and on use (how and where we can use our motor vehicles, for example).

Private property rights are a condition for a capitalist economy. According to some political philosophers, private property is also a prerequisite for individual liberty.

See also **Capitalism; Capitalist; Upper class.**

Protestant ethic

This was discovered or invented by Max Weber (1864–1920) and was said to have been a crucial catalyst in the development of capitalism.

Weber constructed an ideal type Protestant ethic, said to be a product of two Protestant doctrines: predestination and the vocation or calling. Protestants could not earn salvation by their own deeds or from the church, but they believed that success in one's calling was a sign of grace. Weber claimed this produced a distinctive ethic: perpetual anxiety, relieved by unremitting work, a worldly asceticism, and an inability to ease up, to relax and consume. So paradoxically (because Protestantism did not condone the pursuit of wealth), via what Weber termed an 'elective affinity', Protestantism triggered the spread of capitalism.

Weber was not proposing Protestant Christianity as the sole or even main cause of capitalism. His claim was simply that amid other favourable circumstances, the Protestant ethic had acted as crucial trigger. Weber realised full well that the pursuit of wealth through industry and commerce preceded Protestantism: what he believed needed to be explained was how and why this way of organising economic life had spread so rapidly at a particular time and had then become dominant. Also, once capitalism was established, Weber did not believe that a Protestant ethic remained necessary to support the system.

In support of his thesis, Weber produced evidence of capitalism developing earlier and faster in Protestant as opposed to Catholic parts of Europe, and that in all regions the early capitalists were more likely to be Protestant than Catholic.

See also **Ideal type; Industrialisation; Modern; Rationalisation; Weber, M.**

Weber, M. (1905, 1930), *The Protestant Ethic and the Spirit of Capitalism*, Allen and Unwin, London.

Psephology

The study of elections, voting behaviour and voters' intentions, and forecasting election results.

Psychoanalysis

See Freud, S.

Public intellectuals

See Intellectuals.

P

Public opinion

In practice public opinion consists of the opinions that are expressed by respondents in surveys of representative samples of a population.

Opinion polling was pioneered by George Gallup (1910–1984), an American social researcher, who believed that making public opinion common knowledge would make governments more accountable. Opinion polls are now very widely used not only by sociologists but also by newspapers (as a basis for stories), political parties and market researchers.

Sociologists are agreed that a degree of scepticism is always in order towards opinion poll results. The opinions that people express may be stable and firmly held or thought up on the spur of the moment, and the views that people can express always depend on the particular questions that they are asked.

Nevertheless, public opinion, as revealed by opinion polls, has become part of the social reality that present-day sociology investigates. The situation was different before we knew (or thought we knew), for example, what most people thought about a particular government policy. We no longer have to gauge opinion by the numbers who are protesting on the streets or writing to newspapers (or Members of Parliament). The opinions of a 'silent majority' can be taken into account.

Public sociology

See Intellectuals.

Public sphere

See Habermas, J.; Private sphere.

Pure relationship

A concept invented by Anthony Giddens (1938–). The pure relationship is a sociological ideal type which is also said to be an ideal that people pursue in present-day societies.

In pure relationships couples become couples and remain couples only for as long as they choose to do so. There is a tacit agreement that they will remain in the relationship if, and only if, they derive sufficient personal benefits by doing so. Tradition, other external rules, other people's expectations and economic need play no part. Pure relationships are held together by pure love, which is based on emotional intimacy, which generates trust, and if this chain breaks, so does a pure relationship

See also **Divorce; Family**.

Giddens, A. (1993), *The Transformation of Intimacy: Love, Sexuality and Eroticism in Modern Societies*, Polity Press, Cambridge.

Purposive sampling

This type of sample is selected on theoretical grounds, because the cases selected will be especially interesting and informative for the purposes of a particular study.

Research into the effects of the privatisation of companies on managers and workers might start with a purposive sample of recently privatised firms. An investigation into the effects of family reconstitution (following the divorce or separation of the parents) might seek a purposive sample of young people known to have undergone this experience.

Purposive samples are used when a representative sample of a larger population would be wasteful, given that the cases in which the researcher is interested would be a small proportion of the total.

See also **Sampling.**

Putnam, Robert (1941–)

An American political scientist, famous for his claim that there has been a decline in social bonds and trust, thus weakening US democracy.

Putnam has shown that since the 1960s in the United States there has been a decline in the membership of most types of voluntary associations. So, for example, people may still go bowling, but they tend to do so in pairs or small groups rather than playing in teams and leagues. Putnam proceeds to show that where social capital (indicated by associational memberships) is low, people are less interested in and less knowledgeable about politics, and have less confidence in their politicians and governments, than where social capital is high.

Politicians in all countries may find these ideas attractive insofar as they suggest that, if voters are not politically aware and active, the 'fault' lies in society rather than in politics.

One query is whether Putnam's analysis has any relevance outside North America. Another query or criticism, this time from within the United States, is that Putnam necessarily draws his evidence from memberships of older associations (those that existed in the 1960s and before) and ignores new associations and relationships that are now formed through the Internet.

See also **Bourdieu, P.; Capital.**

Putnam, R. (2000), *Bowling Alone: The Collapse and Renewal of American Community*, Simon and Schuster, New York.

P

Qualitative analysis, qualitative research

Any work that is not primarily numerical. There is no clear distinction. Primarily qualitative research may include some counting. Quantitative and qualitative methods are not mutually exclusive. They can be combined in the same project. Neither rests on a specific view of the nature of sociology's subject matter. Qualitative work is compatible with all sociological epistemologies, including positivism.

Examples of qualitative research are:

- unstructured interviews, where the interviewer has flexibility over what questions to ask
- open-ended questions, where a respondent writes in or an interviewer writes down each answer
- participant and other kinds of unstructured observation.

Qualitative methods are particularly effective for generating new insights, concepts and hypotheses, and identifying processes that account for how variables are related to one another (social class and educational attainment, for example).

Note that the success of such methods depends considerably on the skill of the researcher. There is bound to be (in fact there is intended to be) a researcher effect, and such effects cannot usually be measured and allowed for because it is rarely possible to repeat a qualitative investigation. Also, much of the quality in qualitative research is lost unless the same investigator collects, analyses and writes up the evidence. If a researcher dies or quits midway through, most of the value of the research already undertaken is lost.

See also **Interviews; Observation; Quantitative analysis; Questionnaires.**

Quality of life

Interest in the quality of life dates from the 1950s when, in western countries, poverty had declined dramatically and an age of mass affluence was dawning, yet crime rates were rising as were cases of mental illness, and in some countries industry was becoming more strike-prone. Hence the desire to measure the quality as well as the standard of living.

There are now two main approaches. One equates quality of life with personal well-being and uses measures of personal life satisfaction and happiness.

The other approach uses alternative or additional measures. The best known is the United Nations Development Programme's Human Development Index, which was developed in 1990 by the Indian economist Amartya Sen (1933–). This uses life expectancy at birth, the literacy rate, rates of enrolment in education and the standard of living. A different index, a Measure of Domestic Progress, has been developed by the London-based New Economics Foundation. This starts with gross domestic product (GDP), the standard measure of economic output, then adds or subtracts points according to trends in crime, the environment and inequality.

A problem with all such measurements is that they clearly involve subjective judgements about what to include in the indexes and how to weight the different factors. None have yet won the same status and influence with politicians and the public as economics' standard measure of gross domestic product (GDP) or medicine's mortality rate.

See also **Standard of living; Well-being.**

Offner, A. (ed.) (1996), *In Pursuit of the Quality of Life,* Oxford University Press, Oxford.

http://hdr.undp.org

www.neweconomics.org

Quango

Stands for 'quasi-autonomous non-governmental organisation'. These are formally independent civil society organisations, which are wholly or partly government-funded, and may actually be created by a government in order to 'hive off' what would otherwise be state functions. Examples in the UK include hospital trusts, the Bank of England, the BBC, city academies (in England) and many others.

The advantages claimed of governing through quangos are savings on state administration costs, the use of managers who are more responsive to 'grassroots' than state employees, and limiting politicians' responsibilities within boundaries inside which they can realistically be held responsible.

The problems (critics say) are that the independence of the voluntary sector is undermined, it becomes difficult to attract genuine volunteers after state funding becomes available, potential informed critics of state policy are muzzled, and a spurious consensus of support for government policies can be created.

See also **Civil society; Government; Voluntary associations.**

Quantitative analysis, quantitative research

Converts sociology's subject matter into numbers, then analyses the numbers.

Examples of quantitative methods are:

- Fully structured questionnaires and interview schedules: where answers are recorded by ticking a box.
- Observation: where the observer ticks a grid to record, for example, who interacts with whom at a particular time.
- Converting non-numerical evidence into numbers: for example, in the content analysis of texts where an investigator counts how often a particular word, phrase, theme or frame appears.
- Using numerical evidence to produce frequencies, cross-tabulations, maybe correlations and regressions, cluster and factor analysis.

There are major strengths in quantitative methods:

- It is possible to study large numbers of cases, which can be samples that represent even larger populations.
- Hypotheses can be formally tested.
- The research can be repeated by a second investigator; on both occasions the findings should be free of hidden researcher effects.
- It is possible to check (through comparisons) for interviewer and coder biases.

The cost of relying entirely on quantitative methods is that the strengths of qualitative research are foregone.

See also **Interviews; Observation; Qualitative analysis; Questionnaires.**

Queer theory

This seeks to normalise and gain equal recognition, treatment and status for alternatives to heterosexuality.

Until recently (maybe still) to call someone 'queer' was an insult. Queer sociology is part of the movement wherein gays, bisexuals and lesbians proclaim their queerness with pride. Queer theory is explicitly social constructionist and post-structural. Its core premise is that there are no natural sexual identities, that they are all socially constructed. This approach to sexuality has been inspired by the work of Michel Foucault (1926–1984) whose historical research revealed that until the nineteenth century homosexuality was an act, not a type of person. It became a label for a type of person as part of a modernising/scientific/medical mania for classifying. The categories (types of people) subsequently became the foundation for the aspirant science of sexology and were assimilated into sociology which thereby became prejudiced in favour of heterosexuality. Other forms of sexuality were regarded as abnormal, deviant.

Queer sociology brings alternative views (the views of those labelled as queer) to the fore. It is claimed that there is a queer view of everything, not just sexual practices but also of war, neighbourhoods and class for example. It seeks to uncouple masculinity from men and femininity from women, to show that it is possible to be a masculine woman and a feminine man. Gender and sexual roles are all said to be social constructs – roles that can be performed by anyone, of either sex. Queer sociology privileges no type of sexual conduct or preference as more natural than another.

Queer sociology is similar to feminist, post-colonial and subaltern sociologies in seeking to disrupt orthodox views and, in the process, to emancipate the hitherto oppressed.

See also **Gay and lesbian movements; Heteronormativity; Sexuality.**

Foucault, M. (1980), *The History of Sexuality*, Random House, New York

Smith, D. (1990), *The Conceptual Practices of Power: A Feminist Sociology of Knowledge,* Northeastern University Press, Boston.

Questionnaires

A list of questions which are read and answered by a respondent. The instrument may be administered by an interviewer, but in this case it is probably called an interview schedule.

Respondent completed questionnaires may be:

- Hand delivered and collected.
- Mailed through the post (with a pre-paid envelope for the reply).
- Online, triggered by an email inviting the recipient to 'click' to a site where the questionnaire appears. This method is being used increasingly as the proportion of households that are online rises. It is not only low cost. Another advantage is that respondents can be tracked electronically to the appropriate follow-up question depending on their answers to an initial question. This is more difficult with paper questionnaires: complicated tracking confuses respondents, which leads to non-response.

Questions may be fully structured (answered by ticking boxes), or open-ended (where the respondent writes in the answer). On self-completion questionnaires, open-ended questions are usually kept to a minimum: respondents often fail to answer, and what they write may be difficult to read, let alone interpret.

The advantages of self-completion questionnaires are the low cost (compared with using interviewers), and that interviewer effects are not possible.

The drawbacks are that response rates can be extremely low, the instrument must be kept short (otherwise respondents will give up), and researchers are limited to asking simple questions that can be answered by box-ticking.

See also **Interviews; Response rates; Surveys.**

Quota sampling

See Sampling.

Rr

Race, racism

The term race is associated with now discredited theories, but the persistence outside science of racist thinking and behaviour keeps the topic alive in sociology.

Until the Second World War it was widely believed among scientists and in public opinion that humans were divided into different races, usually identified by skin colour and facial features, and that different races had distinctive biologically rooted psychological, social and cultural characteristics. These theories were used to justify the different treatment of members of different races.

Since 1945 this thinking has been abandoned by science – it has been shown to have no basis in genetics. Also, after 1945 there was worldwide revulsion at the Holocaust to which the older theories had led, or had helped to justify. When they have continued to use the term 'race', sociologists have often placed it in inverted commas in order to distance themselves from the older thinking. Nowadays most sociologists prefer to describe the field of study as ethnic groups and ethnic relations.

Racism is the term now used to describe the beliefs and behaviour of people who still subscribe to the old thinking, and to others who continue to behave as if the older theories were true. Racism is far from dead. South Africa's apartheid regime which lasted until the 1990s was based on racial theories. Most present-day European countries have political parties which seek to defend the natives (in Europe) and their culture from immigrants of different 'races'. Racism is one (there are others) plausible explanation of the persistence of differences in the treatment accorded to, and different outcomes (in the allocation of university places, higher level jobs and seats in parliaments, for example) of different 'racial' groups.

Another task of sociology is to explain the appeal of racist thinking. The currently leading view is that racial theories developed alongside imperialism – the acquisition of colonies, and in some places the enslavement of the colonised people – because the theories conveniently justified the subjugation of the colonised people.

Perhaps paradoxically, as part of the drive to monitor and thereby enforce equal opportunities, new quasi-racial categories (such as Black British, Indian, etc.) have been invented and are used in the Census, and more widely to categorise applicants for university places and employment in public and private sector organisations.

See also **Authoritarian personality; Discrimination; Ethnic; Holocaust; Prejudice**.

Banton, M. (1997), *Ethnic and Racial Consciousness*, 2nd edition, Longman, Harlow.

Mason, D. (2000), *Race and Ethnicity in Modern Britain*, Oxford University Press, Oxford.

Random sampling

See Sampling.

Range

See Measures of dispersion.

Rational choice theory

This is less of a theory than a method of enquiry and explanation, based on the view that actors select courses of action that will give them the best returns, given what they value. Rational action approaches may be favoured by sociologists who support methodological individualism. Their model is economics, which is seen as enjoying remarkable success using a model of the utility-maximising actor.

However, in sociology rational choice theory has serious limitations. First, much behaviour does not involve choosing but simply following customs or group norms. Second, the rational choices that people make will depend on their knowledge of alternative courses of action and the likely outcomes, and whatever they happen to value. This means that, in itself, assuming that people behave rationally explains very little.

See also **Methodological individualism**.

Goldthorpe, J.H. (1998), 'Rational choice theory for sociology', *British Journal of Sociology*, 49, 167–92.

R

Rationalisation

In sociology this term has two meanings.

According to the first (and closest to the everyday meaning), as in the work of Wilfredo Pareto (1848–1923), a rationalisation is a spurious reason given to justify an action after the event.

The second meaning, from Max Weber (1864–1920), is the process that has underpinned the modernisation of life in the western world. Modernisation, according to Weber, has been driven by the spread of a particular kind of means–ends, calculating rational action, which has led to a general rationalisation of, and consequently disenchantment with, life in general.

See also **Pareto, W.; Weber, M.**

Rationality

This is a term whose many applications threaten to strip it of any useful meaning. Users have to define exactly what they mean by rational.

Something can be called rational if it is said or done on reasonable grounds, but this statement is tautological (true by definition), and leaves open the question of is reasonable. Sociologists usually claim to be rational, meaning that their arguments follow logically from one another and any evidence, but they can still disagree on whose interpretation of a body of evidence is correct and therefore reasonable.

Sociologists may, and if they are rational choice theorists they will, operate on the assumption that the people who they study behave rationally, and therefore that their behaviour will be susceptible to rational explanation. But again, this raises the question of what is rational. Are some people and actions irrational? Are some entire cultures and societies irrational? Or is this label applied only when the labeller has not grasped the rational thought processes of the people concerned?

Rationalism is the philosophical doctrine which claims that reason is the sole basis for objective knowledge. When formulated in the seventeenth and eighteenth centuries, this doctrine contrasted knowledge based on reason with claims to knowledge based on divine revelation, but who is to say that it is irrational to trust revelation that is believed to be divine?

Max Weber (1864–1920) gave rational a more limited (and therefore probably more useful) meaning for sociology. He distinguished rational action from action that was affectual (governed by emotions) and action that was traditional (governed by custom). Rational action, according to Weber, is action selected to achieve an ultimate value or a lesser end. In other words, rational behaviour is calculative behaviour geared to achieving a desired outcome. However, whether all such behaviour will satisfy philosophical tests of rationality is a different matter.

See also **Methodological individualism; Rational choice theory; Weber, M.**

Realism

Realists believe that there is a real universe that exists outside our senses, about which it is possible to obtain mind-free knowledge. This is the standard 'default' position of sociologists. We are nearly all realists. We believe that the societies about which we write exist outside our imaginations. The opposing view is taken by relativists.

It is difficult, maybe impossible, to prove the realist position. Its adopted test is 'practical adequacy': the accounts that are produced on the basis of

R

realist assumptions enable us to understand, explain and predict the events that we perceive.

Present-day sociologists who seek to justify their realist stance usually describe themselves as critical realists.

See also **Critical realism; Relativism.**

Bhasker, R. (1975, 1997), *A Realist Theory of Science*, Verso, London.

Reciprocity

This is believed to be a universal social norm, a necessary condition for orderly social life. Reciprocity means that if you do something for me, I will do something of equal value for you in return. Thus gift giving, although manifestly voluntary, in reality becomes obligatory. The norm of reciprocity is said to be the base from which trust and social capital are created.

See also **Capital; Exchange theory; Trust.**

Mauss, M. (1925, 1954), *The Gift,* Free Press, New York.

Reductionism

Reducing means treating diverse phenomena as examples of a more limited number of cases, or treating a large number of cause–effect relationships as examples of a limited number of underlying laws. Marxism can be said to reduce much else to social class. Weberians can be said to reduce much else to rationalisation. This may or may not be appropriate. Reducing *per se* is not right or wrong.

The term reductionism is also applied to reducing the propositions of one science to those of another: biology to chemistry, chemistry to physics and so on. From sociology such reductions are usually into biology (in explaining gender differences, for example) or psychology (explaining social mobility rates in terms of individual differences, probably differences in mental ability (IQ), is an example). Sociology's classical anti-reductionist is Emile Durkheim (1858–1917) who insisted that social facts be treated as things in themselves and explained in terms of other social facts.

The case for sociology depends on there being some non-reducible social facts (to use Durkheim's expression). However, reducing is not always and necessarily wrong. Sociology's propositions have to be compatible with the propositions of psychology, biology, chemistry and physics, and in some instances what initially appear to be social facts may well be best explained by psychological or biological reduction.

See also **Holism; Individualism.**

Reference group

This term began to be used around the same time, in the 1940s, by several social psychologists in the United States. The concept's invention is disputed, but its value was instantly apparent. A reference group is the group to which an actor refers when assessing his or her own position, attitudes or whatever. This may or may not be a group to which the actor belongs.

Whether a person feels well paid or badly paid will depend partly on the reference group that is used – all teachers, or just teachers in higher education, or just in a particular university and of a particular seniority. In assessing whether their own occupational group (or any other membership group) is treated well or badly, people will refer to other occupational groups. This means that whether people feel deprived or well rewarded will depend not only on their absolute circumstances but also on their reference groups. So in explaining feelings of injustice we have to explain, among other things, how and why particular reference groups are selected.

See also **Justice**; **Poverty**; **Relative deprivation**.

Reflexivity

This is a very high profile concept in present-day sociology. It refers to the ability of human actors to reflect upon themselves (their hopes, goals and plans as well as their behaviour and their circumstances), and to modify their hopes, plans and behaviour accordingly. To be reflexive is fundamentally different from simply reflecting external forces in a stimulus–response fashion.

Sociologists who adopt a symbolic interactionist perspective argue that humans' distinctive reflexive capabilities make positivist (cause–effect, law-like) explanations wholly inappropriate in sociology. However, it is possible to counter-argue that reflexive processes can be built in, as factors, in positivist explanations and/or that reflexivity cannot overcome the constraints of circumstances and that sociology should focus on these structural limits.

Some sociologists argue that the role of reflexivity in social life has been enlarged in societies that have moved beyond the original modern age, as former social structures and divisions (by social class and gender, for example) have weakened, and as old norms and prescriptions have dissolved or become irrelevant, and people are therefore obliged to act reflexively.

The reflexive actors can be sociologists themselves. Social constructionists and critical sociologists/critical theorists may appeal to reflexivity as a means whereby sociologists can gain a superior, more objective view than the lay actors they study. All sociological analysis requires sociologists to step back from society and, in this sense, to view reality from outside. If sociologists take another step back and reflect upon their own positions, acknowledge their partiality and the tacit assumptions that they have been making, it is said that their view will then be superior, more objective, than everyday socially constructed knowledge. Needless to say, it is possible to counter-argue that any step back, and however many are taken, merely

R

gives the observer another socially constructed perspective, and that reflexivity offers no escape from the social constructionists' dilemma.

> *See also* **Beck, U.; Biographisation; Critical sociology/critical theory; Giddens, A.; Individualisation; Positivism; Social construction; Symbolic interactionism.**

Refugees

Defined by the United Nations as persons who are outside and who are unable or unwilling to return to their countries of nationality due to a well-founded fear of being persecuted for reasons of religion, race, nationality, membership of a particular social group or political opinions, plus persons who have fled war or violence in their own countries.

A person seeking to be recognised as a refugee is an asylum seeker.

Refugees are among a larger category of displaced persons, most of whom remain within the same national borders.

In 2006 it was estimated that worldwide there were over 324 million displaced persons including 28 million refugees, the lowest number since 1980.

Around 80 per cent of refugees are women and children.

> *See also* **Migration.**

Regression, regression analysis

A statistical measure of association, similar to correlation, except that with regression the aim is not to establish the strength of an association between two variables but to measure how much of the variance in a dependent factor can be explained by an independent factor. For example, to what extent can differences in educational attainment be explained in terms of differences in children's social class backgrounds?

In a multiple regression, the effects of several independent variables are distinguished, compared and combined: the contributions of family class, gender, ethnic group, school and teacher characteristics in explaining educational outcomes, for example.

> *See also* **Correlation.**

R

Regulation theory

A loosely knit body of Marxist theory, produced originally in France in the 1970s. Regulation theory seeks to remedy perceived weaknesses in Marxist thought, and to update Marxist theory to address late twentieth and twenty-first century capitalism.

Regulationists coined the term post-Fordism and thereby distinguished two stages in the development of capitalism, Fordism and post-Fordism. During each stage regulationists argue that the state is required to regulate its society according to the requirements for the profitable conduct of business (the regime of accumulation). Under Fordism this meant maintaining full employment and developing strong welfare states which would support the levels of consumption required to absorb the mass production of Fordist firms. Post-Fordism is seen variously as a response to crises that were developing within Fordism, new technology and globalisation. These new conditions are said to require flexible labour markets that permit the filling of low-wage, precarious jobs. State welfare has to be cut back, and there needs to be a reorganisation of consumption.

Governments are pressured into regulating their societies by their need for investment in order to maintain employment and protect standards of living.

See also **Dual labour market; Fordism; Neo-liberalism; Post-Fordism; Trans-national corporations**.

Aglietta, M. (1979), *A Theory of Capitalist Regulation: The US Experience*, New Left Books, London.

Gordon, D.M., Edwards, R. and Reich, M. (1982), *Segmented Work, Divided Workers: The Historical Transformation of Labour in the United States*, Cambridge University Press, Cambridge.

Reification

Treating an abstract idea as if it were a thing with the power to act consequentially.

The term originates in Marxism, where it refers to workers' failure to grasp the exploitative social relations of production that create and price different objects. This is said to lead to fetishism.

In the rest of sociology the term reification is applied (invariably in criticism) to those who allegedly reify concepts such as society, social class, structure and ethnic group. The accused are likely to reply that their reifications are justified, and that the entities can rightly be treated as things which act causally. The issue, therefore, is always whether a particular instance of alleged reification is justified or improper.

See also **Commodity fetishism**.

R

Relationships of production

See Marx, K.

Relative deprivation

A Second World War study of the US soldier first discovered that feelings of deprivation depend not only on a person's or group's absolute condition, but also on the comparison or reference group against which their circumstances are assessed by those concerned. This is the explanation of why there is only a weak relationship between objective standards of living and feeling impoverished. People who are well off objectively may well feel unjustly deprived, while people who are objectively poor may insist that they are not badly off.

See also **Deprivation; Poverty; Reference group.**

Runciman, W.G. (1966), *Relative Deprivation and Social Justice,* Routledge, London.

Stouffer, S., Suchman, E.A., DeVinney, L.C., Star, S.A. and Williams, R.M. Jr (1949), *The American Soldier, Vol. 1, Adjustment During Army Life,* Princeton University Press, Princeton, N.J.

Relativism

This doctrine asserts that nothing can be shown to be objectively true; that all truth claims are valid only in relation to criteria which happen to be accepted within a particular culture or by a particular group, including scientific communities. In other words, what appears to be true always depends on the mind of the judge.

Following the arguments of logical positivism, sociologists are likely to accept the relativist case in respect of value judgements, but what about statements of fact? Relativists claim that scientific standards are simply the particular tests that happen to be currently accepted by scientists. They argue that all bodies of knowledge rest on axioms or domain assumptions that are simply taken as given.

A response is to point out that the relativist argument is applicable to the relativist doctrine itself. Even if they cannot disprove the relativist case, virtually all sociologists proceed as if their arguments (based on reason and evidence) can be shown objectively to be true or false.

Their main opponents today are postmodernists who believe that confidence in any grand narratives can no longer be sustained. They have joined forces with a body of opinion which cites the German philosopher Friedrich Nietzsche (1844–1900) as inspiration, and which objects on moral and political grounds to yielding to science a monopoly claim to truth. The Austrian-born philosopher of science, Paul Feyerabend (1924–1994) was the main twentieth-century exponent of this ethically and politically based relativism.

See also **Critical realism; Nietzsche, F.; Objectivity; Rationality; Realism.**

Feyerabend, P. (1987), *Farewell to Reason,* Verso, London.

R

Reliability

An instrument (such as a questionnaire) is said to be reliable if it gives the same results when the same individuals are measured on more than one occasion. Measurements that are unreliable cannot be valid, but reliability does not guarantee validity.

See also **Validity.**

Religion

Sociology does not have an agreed, coherent definition of religion, or even a set of definitions with common elements. Religion has been defined variously as beliefs and associated practices that are:

- supernatural
- spiritual
- sacred (set apart, inspiring awe)
- truths that cannot be questioned
- answering questions to which science, observation and pure reason have no answers: for example, 'Why are we here?'

Two unresolved problems with all definitions of religion are:

- Each definition may fit some religions neatly, but not others (Buddhists do not believe in a supernatural being).
- Religious features can be found in other systems of beliefs and practices. For example, some lay people regard the pronouncements of scientists as beyond challenge; in nationalist and other political movements there may be core beliefs that members are not allowed to question; charismatic leaders (in religious and other movements) may inspire awe.

A solution to these problems is for sociology to study religions without any presumption of common features or any clear distinction between religious and other beliefs and practices.

See also **Church; Profane; Sacred; Sect.**

Aldridge, A. (2000), *Religion in the Contemporary World: A Sociological Introduction*, Polity, Cambridge.

Renaissance

The name given to the rebirth of art, literature and learning that began in Florence (Italy) in the fourteenth century then spread throughout the rest of Europe. During the renaissance the works of ancient scholars such as Aristotle and Plato were rediscovered. Famous 'renaissance men' include Leonardo da Vinci (1452–1519) and Michelangelo (1475–1564).

Replication

A repeat of an earlier project or experiment, usually undertaken to check the reliability and validity of the earlier findings, or to record change.

Replication studies have been quite rare in sociology. One of the most famous is the pair of studies of Middletown (actually Muncie in Indiana) conducted by Robert and Helen Lynd in the 1920s and 1930s. Their initial study explained how, over the previous generation, Muncie had changed from a farming community into a factory town. They returned to 'Middletown' in 1935 at the height of the Great Depression and found, to their surprise, that the basic social structure remained intact.

Lynd, R.S. and Lynd, H.M. (1929), *Middletown: A Study in Contemporary American Culture,* Harcourt, Brace and Co, New York.

Lynd, R.S and Lynd, H.M. (1937), *Middletown in Transition: A Study in Cultural Conflicts,* Harcourt, Brace and Co, New York.

Representative sampling

See Sampling.

Repressive state apparatus

See Ideological state apparatus.

Repressive tolerance

See Marcuse, H.

Reproduction

In sociology this term is less likely to refer to biological reproduction than to how social roles, institutions and structures are perpetuated over time while a population is continuously replaced by births, deaths and migration. The main answer, of course, is socialisation, but in practice the major issue addressed in reproduction theory and research is how class inequalities, structures and cultures are perpetuated in societies which claim to have open class systems, and where opportunities are said to be open to all.

Reproduction theories explain, first, that there is a tendency, even in nominally open class systems, for people to remain close to the levels into which they are born. They then explain how there is also a tendency for children to be educated depending on their social class origins. Parents with economic assets may purchase privileged education. Otherwise the cultural capital which children acquire at home may lead to those with advantaged backgrounds being identified at school as bright and educable. When mobility occurs, this is likely to be accomplished through education, by the end of which children's skills, aspirations and expectations may well have been aligned to their most likely future class positions. In countries such as the United States where overall young people become grossly over-ambitious relative to the opportunities that await them, they can be given a belief that those with the most talent and who make the most effort succeed eventually; thus all continue to strive for success, which means that those who do succeed are admired and emulated rather than resented.

A secondary meaning of reproduction in sociology concerns how labour

R

power is reproduced from day to day. The answers lie in the family and leisure where labour power is re-created.

> See also **Capital; Social mobility; Sponsored (and contest) mobility.**

> Bourdieu, P. and Passeron, J.D. (1977), *Reproduction in Education, Culture and Society,* Sage, London.

> Bowles, S. and Gintis, H. (1976), *Schooling in Capitalist America,* Routledge, London.

> Willis, P. (1977), *Learning to Labour*, Saxon House, Farnborough.

Research methods

The most important methods used by any successful sociological researcher are undoubtedly reading, thereby becoming and remaining highly knowledgeable about a topic, and thinking about which theories to use, hypotheses to interrogate, and how to interpret evidence.

In practice, courses and texts on research methods are about how to gather then process original evidence, or how to gain access and conduct a secondary analysis of existing evidence. Which method or methods to use must always depend on the problem being addressed, the resources available, and the investigator's competencies and preferences.

Sociology has just three ways of gathering original evidence:

- Observation: looking (and listening).
- Asking questions via interviews, or printed or electronic questionnaires. Doing this is called conducting a survey, probably of a sample, probably intended to be representative of a society's population or a section thereof.
- Inspecting material, typically documents, created by actors in the normal course of their lives.

All three ways of gathering evidence may be structured or unstructured. If structured, the evidence will be quantitative or quantifiable. If unstructured the evidence will be qualitative, sometimes described as soft. Quantitative evidence, whether original or already existing, will be analysed using statistical techniques. There are other, equally systematic, techniques that can be applied to qualitative evidence.

> See also, among many others, **Content analysis; Ethnography; Interviews; Longitudinal study; Panel study; Participant observation; Qualitative analysis; Quantitative analysis; Questionnaires; Sampling; Surveys.**

Response rates

All surveys have response and non-response rates from potential respondents who are approached. The response rate in a survey is never 100 per cent. This is always a problem when a sample is intended to represent a larger population, or when the intention is to survey all members of a particular group. Non-response can make the achieved response unrepresentative.

Non-response is normally much lower in interviewer surveys than with mailed or electronically distributed questionnaires. Sometimes the response to mail-outs and emails is well under 10 per cent. Response rates can be improved by having a survey endorsed by an organisation that is known to and trusted by the respondents. Even so, the response to a mail-out is unlikely to exceed 50 per cent. Further measures to reduce non-response such as second mail-outs, telephone calls to non-respondents, and having an interviewer call, will always boost a response rate. These measures are sure to be used in panel studies, especially in very longitudinal panel studies, where it is important to prevent loss from the original panel. With several call-backs an interviewer survey should be able to achieve a response in excess of 80 per cent. A further advantage of using human interviewers is that it becomes possible to separate different reasons for non-response: died, moved away, never in, refused.

There are ways of reducing the likelihood of non-response seriously biasing the results of a survey. If anything is known about a sample prior to conducting a survey (age, sex, and/or educational backgrounds of the sample overall), it is possible to check whether non-respondents differ from respondents. If so, the achieved sample can be weighted to correct for non-response. However, this procedure assumes, for example, that young, well-educated males who fail to respond would have given similar answers to the respondent members of their socio-demographic group. Researchers can check whether late respondents (after two reminders, for example) differ from earlier respondents in any way. If not, this may warrant treating those who never respond as similar to the achieved sample. All that researchers can do is to minimise (they can never eliminate) the possibility of bias.

See also **Surveys.**

Restricted code

See Bernstein, B.

Reverse discrimination

See Positive discrimination.

Revolutions

In political science 'revolution' has a precise meaning. A revolution involves the seizure of state power by violent means (rather than as a result of votes in elections), leading to sweeping changes in a society. The classic examples are the French Revolution (1789–1799) and the Bolshevik Revolution in Russia in 1917. Usually the usurpers are from 'below', but there can be revolutions from 'above'; the Meiji Restoration in Japan in 1868 is usually cited. When usurpers seize power violently but do not implement sweeping changes, this is called a coup d'etat. If no violence is involved, then whether subsequent changes are sweeping or minor, it is called 'regime change'. On these criteria, the 'colour revolutions' between 2003 and 2005 in Georgia, Ukraine and Kyrgyzstan were not true revolutions.

Outside political science, in both sociology and the wider society, the meaning of 'revolution' is less precise. Sweeping changes in an economy or society, whether instigated politically or otherwise, may be called revolutions. The best-known case is the industrial revolution. Breakthroughs in science associated with Copernicus, Einstein and others are called scientific revolutions.

See also **Social change; Social transformation.**

Rights

Some people believe that humans have natural rights. Some believe that rights are God-given. Sociology treats rights as social inventions. Rights are claimed, they may be contested, then granted or rejected. Some claim the 'right to choose'. Others claim the unborn child's 'right to life'.

For rights to be effective they need to be granted and protected by a government. Rights of citizenship – to the protection of the law, freedom of expression, to political representation and welfare rights – may be granted in a constitution or by legislation.

Rights are now conferred by international bodies. In 1948 the United Nations adopted the Universal Declaration of Human Rights. The Council of Europe has a Convention on Human Rights, and has established the European Court of Human Rights. However, the rights conferred by these international bodies become effective only when they are endorsed and enforced by national governments. In 2002 the United Nations created an International Criminal Court to try war crimes, but countries have to join before this court gains jurisdiction over their citizens.

See also **Citizenship.**

Freeden, M. (1991), *Rights*, Open University Press, Milton Keynes.

Kingdom, E. (1991), *What's Wong with Rights? Problems for a Feminist Politics of Law,* Edinburgh University Press, Edinburgh.

R

Risk society

See Beck, U.

Rites of passage

Rituals and ceremonies that may accompany status transitions during the life course. Examples include marriage ceremonies, engagement parties, coming of age parties and retirement parties. These events give public recognition to the changes in status and identity that are involved.

See also **Life course/life cycle; Rituals.**

Van Gennep, A. (1909, 1960), *The Rites of Passage,* University of Chicago Press, Chicago.

Rituals

Regularly repeated patterns of action that have shared meanings. Rituals express meanings, and are not intended to have other results.

Church services are rituals. Many current rituals have religious origins: present giving at Christmas, marriage ceremonies, the annual state opening of the UK Parliament. However, rituals can be entirely profane: hand-shaking or cheek-kissing on greeting someone.

There is always some shared meaning in rituals, but it is possible for someone to participate without sharing the meaning or even knowing the supposedly shared meaning. The de-traditionalisation of contemporary life has stripped many rituals of their original meanings. Hence, in everyday language, to act ritualistically means just 'going through the motions'.

See also **Magic.**

Bocock, R. (1974), *Ritual in Industrial Society: A Sociological Analysis of Ritualism*, Allen and Unwin, London.

Ritzer, George (1940–)

Prolific American sociologist who has authored numerous monographs and texts on social theory, but is best known for the term 'McDonaldization'. *The McDonaldization of Society* (first edition 1993) is among the most popular sociological monographs that have ever been published.

Ritzer claims that the process of rationalisation (first noted by Max Weber, 1864–1920) is currently being extended from manufacturing and large government and private sector bureaucracies into consumer services, where it affects our lives as consumers as well as our lives at work. The fast food chain McDonald's is chosen as a leading example. The key principles of McDonaldization are said to be efficiency, calculability, uniformity and control through automation. These principles, pioneered successfully by McDonald's, are seen as being adopted by other restaurant chains, and also by pubs, numerous retailing chains, plus banks, healthcare, education, sport stadiums and events among others.

Ritzer shares Max Weber's pessimism. He is critical of the trend (McDonaldization) which is believed to be making life bland and boring. Yet he argues that we will continue to purchase McDonaldized services because we know what we will be offered: risk is eliminated from consumption.

See also **Consumption; Rationalisation; Weber, M.**

R

Ritzer, G. (1993), *The McDonaldization of Society*, Pine Forge Press, Thousand Oaks, Calif.

Role, role theory

The patterns of behaviour and expectations associated with a position.

Role is a key concept in micro-sociology. It is used by sociologists of all theoretical persuasions. Its value lies in its numerous derivatives and the distinctions that it facilitates:

- Roles can be pre-scripted, as in a play, but actors can develop and interpret their roles.
- Roles may be specific to a situation (most occupational roles) or diffuse, carried through all domains of life, like the roles of man and woman.
- Roles may be ascribed or achieved.
- Actors may identify with, or they may distance their real selves from, the roles that they play.
- A role set is the relationships with other roles with which the actor in a focal role becomes involved.
- Members of a role set may have different expectations about how a focal role should be played, thus placing the actor in a situation of role strain.
- It may be impossible for a role player to meet everyone's expectations, thus creating a situation of role overload.
- The same individual may play roles where the collective expectations clash with each other, thus creating a situation of role conflict.

See also **Actor; Goffman, E.**

Banton, M. (1968), *Roles: An Introduction to the Study of Social Relations*, Tavistock, London.

Jackson, J.A. (ed.) (1972), *Role*, Cambridge University Press, Cambridge.

R

Routinisation

One of many terms gifted to sociology by Max Weber (1864–1920). Something can be described as routinised when the conditions that brought it into existence become unnecessary for its persistence.

Weber wrote about the routinisation of charisma. The legacy would be lost if the death of a charismatic religious or political leader was not accompanied by the routinisation of the charisma into an office (religious or party leader) and set of religious practices or political policies. The 'spirit of capitalism' had been routinised by Weber's lifetime insofar as it no longer needed the support of Protestant theology. Routinisation involves a loss of enchantment. Practices and leadership become bureaucratised or just customary.

See also **Charisma; Disenchantment; Weber, M.**

Rowntree, Benjamin Seebohm (1871–1954)

Seebohm Rowntree (as he was known) was from the York family that owned the chocolate factory of which he was a director and chairman from 1923–1941, but is best remembered as a philanthropist, reformer and pioneer of social research, especially in his studies of poverty that were conducted in York in 1899, 1936 and 1950.

The initial (1899) poverty survey yielded results similar to those from Charles Booth's concurrent studies in London. Roughly a third of the York working class was in poverty, and the causes were usually beyond the individuals' own control. Along with Booth's evidence, Rowntree's findings and advocacy were important in the development of state welfare provisions in Britain (old age pensions, unemployment insurance, child benefits and municipal housing).

Rowntree's original poverty survey was remarkable for its thoroughness. His researchers attempted to contact every working class household (those without servants) in York. In defining a poverty line Rowntree consulted the results of experiments in prisons into the minimum food intake necessary to maintain normal bodily functioning. He also consulted workhouse diet sheets to discover the cheapest ways of providing life's necessities. Rowntree distinguished between primary poverty (absolute insufficiency of income) and secondary poverty (where households could provide themselves with all necessities only if they spent nothing on 'luxuries'). He also identified the cycle of poverty wherein families sank into then rose out of poverty. The vulnerable life stages were during child-rearing and old age.

Rowntree's second poverty survey in York in 1936 found that the condition of the working class had improved only modestly, but in 1950 he found that poverty had all but disappeared due to full employment, higher wages and a stronger welfare state.

Seebohm Rowntree's father, Joseph Rowntree, created what is now known as the Joseph Rowntree Foundation, the UK's major charitable organisation which funds policy-relevant social research.

See also **Booth, C.J.; Poverty; Welfare state.**

Rowntree, B.S. (1901), *Poverty: A Study in Town Life*, Longman, London.

R

Ruling class

Originally a Marxist term; alternatively called a dominant class. A ruling class, in the Marxist sense, combines economic, political and ideological/cultural power. However, the dominant/ruling class thesis is not supported solely by Marxists. The Italian elite theorists developed non-Marxist versions.

Claims that there is a dominant or ruling class need to show that:

- There is a high level of integration between elites. The evidence may be close connections between the personnel – family connections or similar education for instance – and many movements between top positions in politics, the civil service and business.

- Far greater similarity in circumstances, outlooks and lifestyles between different elite groups than between any of the elites and the people.

Some would say that present-day Britain and the United States are among the many countries where both tests are passed comfortably.

See also **Capitalist; Class; Elites; Upper class.**

Rural

To do with the countryside and agriculture.

Nineteenth and early twentieth-century sociologists constructed an ideal type of the rural way of life which contrasted with the urban lifestyles that were developing around them. The ideal type rural community was composed of small towns and villages. Family life was central. There was a strong sense of community. Life was governed by custom and people knew their proper places in the social order.

It is now recognised that this ideal type tended to overlook rural hardship, feuds between families, and hostilities between peasantry and gentry. Similarly, ideal types of urbanism neglected the continuing importance of the family and the ability of communities to develop and thrive within cities.

Today, most of what was once distinctively rural has disappeared in the economically advanced countries. Villages have become home places for commuters. The more distant countryside has become a playground for tourists, day-trippers and second-home owners. Farms and other enterprises are run as if they were urban businesses. In other words, the urban way of life has now spread into the countryside.

See also **Toennies, F.; Urban.**

Newby, H. (1980), *Green and Pleasant Land? Social Change in Rural England*, Penguin, Harmondsworth.

R

Sacred

Things which are set apart from the profane world, which are revered and inspire awe. Emile Durkheim (1858–1917) treated sacredness as *the* definitive feature of religion. Other sociologists treat it as *a possible* feature.

See also **Durkheim, E.; Profane; Religion.**

Salient

Whatever is most noticed, the focus of people's attention. Something that is salient is not necessarily important in any other sense.

Sampling

A sample is drawn from and is intended to represent a larger population. There are two main ways of seeking representativeness:

- Random sampling, where each member of a population stands an equal chance of being selected. This may be achieved by using random numbers to select names from a comprehensive list. Alternatively (though less technically perfect) every nth name might be selected.
- Quota sampling, where the proportions of a population who are male and female, in different age groups and so on, are already known, and the sample is drawn so that each group is represented proportionately to its presence in the population.

Both methods have supporters and critics. Quota samples are less likely to be truly representative because people who are readily available (at home or on the streets) stand the best chance of being sampled. Random sampling needs an accurate list of all members of a population (which may not be easily obtained), and there is always a non-response rate.

There are simple random and quota samples. Alternatively, samples may be:

- Stratified: with members of different groups sampled separately (pupils at different kinds of schools, for example). A variable sampling fraction may be used in such samples so as to ensure adequate numbers from minority groups (such as ethnic minorities). The results can then be weighted during analysis to restore representativeness.

- Multi-stage: when a national sample is achieved by initially sampling parliamentary constituencies, then wards, then individuals. This enables fieldwork to be clustered, thereby reducing costs.

The accuracy of a sample depends on its size, not the proportion of a population that is sampled. Samples of 1000–1500 are generally considered adequate to represent the population of Great Britain, though larger sizes are required if the results need to be treated as representative of some sub-groups, such as the over-70s.

See also **Convenience sampling; Purposive sampling; Response rates; Snowball sampling.**

Sanction

Any means by which conformity to approved social standards is enforced. Sanctions may be positive or negative (pay rise or dismissal), and may be informal (praise or verbal abuse) or formal (such as the punishments imposed by courts of law).

See also **Social control.**

Sassen, Saskia (1949–)

American sociologist, but born in the Netherlands and also educated in Brazil, France and Italy. Sassen has written extensively on globalisation and migration, with a focus on the effects on urban life, and is best known for the term 'global city'.

Global cities are the main command posts in the global economy. They are the places where trans-national corporations have their headquarters, and where businesses offering banking, marketing, technological and other services to global firms are based. These are the 'nodes' where global production, marketing and banking are coordinated, and where the key coordinators can work in personal contact with one another.

Major global cities (New York, London and Tokyo according to Sassen) are at the peak of a hierarchy in which true global cities are followed by world regional and sub-regional centres.

In global cities the richest businesses and the richest people in the world, and also some of the poorest, live and work (and if the poor work they are likely to be cleaners or have similar status in the richest businesses and in the richest people's homes) in close proximity, yet they are segregated for most of the time by the privatisation and control of space.

See also **Gated communities; Globalisation; Migration; Node; Urbanism.**

Sassen, S. (1991), *The Global City: New York, London, Tokyo*, Princeton University Press, Princeton, N.J.

S

Saussure, Ferdinand de (1857–1913)

Saussure, a Swiss linguist, is generally recognised as the founder of modern linguistics. He gave the name semiology (sometimes abbreviated to semiotics) to his approach to the study of language.

Before Saussure, symbols (words) were understood to stand for (to represent) particular things or events. The things and events gave meaning to, and in this sense preceded, the words. So 'chair' stood for a particular arrangement of materials. 'Sit' represented a particular bodily posture. Once we had created or learnt these building blocks, we could understand that a chair was for sitting, and so on. Languages were believed to be built upwards from these elementary foundations. So after we had established or learnt what 'ball' and 'point' stood for, we became able to identify a ball-point pen. Pre-Saussure, this was supposed to be how languages were learnt and how they developed over time.

Saussure disagreed. He argued that the meaning of any unit (a word or a set of words) arose from its relationship with other units. Languages had to be treated as, and had to be learnt as, total systems that pre-existed all particular acts of speech. It was therefore possible, using language, to know about, say, an aeroplane, before such a machine had even been built. Likewise it is only after we know (through language) that a chair is for sitting that we become able to recognise the chair as an object and sitting as a particular bodily posture.

What has this to do with sociology? It is not uncommon for ideas which arise in one discipline to be imported into another, and Saussure's thinking was imported into the social sciences by, among others, the French social anthropologist Claude Levi-Strauss (1908–). Thus Saussurian linguistics became the foundation for structuralism (not to be confused with structural-functionalism), which became influential in sociology in the 1960s and 1970s. The linking idea is that, according to structuralists, particular social forms and practices are rooted in an underlying structure (either language itself or something akin to language).

See also **Language**; **Levi-Strauss**; **Linguistics**; **Semiotics**; **Structuralism**.

Harris, R. (1987), *Reading Saussure: A Commentary on the* Cours de Linguistique Generale, Duckworth, London.

Saussure, F. de (1983), *Course in General Linguistics*, Duckworth, London.

S

Scapegoat

An innocent party (a person or a group) who is blamed for someone else's troubles. Scapegoating is a way of deflecting blame and responsibility. It may be functional for the scapegoaters. The Jews were scapegoats in Nazi Germany. Ethnic minorities in all societies are liable to become scapegoats for unemployment, housing shortages, crime and other problems.

There is evidence that certain personality types and cultures are particularly prone to scapegoating.

See also **Authoritarian personality; Prejudice.**

Scarman Report

The report of the official, government ordered inquiry into the rioting in Brixton (London) during 10–12 April 1981.

The rioting had begun when the actions of police who were attending to an injured black youth were misunderstood. The police were attacked with stones, bricks, iron bars and petrol bombs. The rioting extended over three days. Over 300 people were injured, 83 premises were damaged, as were 23 police and other vehicles, and there was widespread looting. Later in 1981 there were similar disorders in Liverpool, Manchester and other cities, which were also considered by the Scarman inquiry.

The report argued that a predisposition to violent protest existed before the incident that sparked the rioting. It noted the disadvantaged situation of the black population in Brixton in terms of housing, educational attainment, and especially the high level of youth unemployment. However, the main predisposing condition was said to be a loss of confidence and trust in the police and their methods of policing. The report concluded that the rioting was spontaneous rather than planned, but had to be understood as a response to the perceived harassment of black young males by the police.

The Scarman Report rejected charges of institutional racism, but acknowledged that there had been individual acts of racial discrimination against a background of general racial disadvantage that had to be addressed. The report recommended the recruitment of more ethnic minority police officers, changes in police training and a greater emphasis on community policing.

See also **Discrimination; Macpherson Report; Race.**

Scarman, Lord (1981), *The Brixton Disorders, 10–12 April, 1981,* Cmnd 8427, HMSO, London.

S

Schutz, Alfred (1899–1959)

Schutz was the major figure in the foundation of phenomenological sociology. He was an Austrian-born philosopher and sociologist who moved to New York in 1935 and worked as a banker while continuing his academic work before taking an academic post in 1952.

Schutz was a critic of Max Weber, who had claimed to take account of actors' meanings but did this inadequately (in Schutz's view). Schutz worked out the implications of Husserl's phenomenological philosophy for sociology. He argued that the basic subject matter for sociology was the 'natural attitude', that is, whatever is ordinarily just taken for granted among members of a society. This meant somehow uncovering the typifications (concepts) with which ordinary actors construct common-sense knowledge and organise their daily tasks.

This agenda was taken up and applied by ethnomethodologists.

See also **Ethnomethodology; Natural attitude; Phenomenology.**

Schutz, A. (1972), *The Phenomenology of the Social World*, Heinemann, London.

Science

Originally science meant simply 'knowledge'. Then during the renaissance, from the fourteenth century onwards, science became a particular kind of knowledge, that which was recorded systematically. At that time science was alternatively known as natural philosophy, the study of natural things (including living things). It was not until the nineteenth century that the term science was restricted to the study of non-human natural things. Towards the end of the nineteenth century the term began to be applied specifically to the methods that scientists used. Thereafter attempts were made to identify *the* scientific method. Science was defined in terms of systematic observation, developing theories, conducting experiments, testing hypotheses and establishing laws.

At this point the question arose as to whether these methods could be applied in sociology and other human sciences. Here, there have always been juxtaposed points of view. Some argue that humans are different from all other objects, and that knowledge about the social must therefore be developed differently, and will be different in kind, from the knowledge of the natural sciences.

Sociologists have been at the forefront in trying to establish the methods that scientists actually use, and have shown that there neither is nor ever has been a single scientific method for the social sciences to adopt. Hence, nowadays, sociologists are far more relaxed than in the early and mid-twentieth century about whether their discipline is or can become a real science.

See also **Kuhn, T.; Popper, K.R.; Positivism.**

S

Scientific management

Alternatively called Taylorism after its American originator, Frederick Winslow Taylor (1856–1915). From his experience managing a steel plant Taylor developed a scientific approach to management that he believed would lead to gains in efficiency, higher profits and wages, and an era of prosperity and industrial harmony.

The basic principles of Taylor's scientific management were:

- Managers were to regain control over production instead of leaving it to workers and foremen to decide how to tackle their various tasks.
- Develop the division of labour; break down production into simple tasks. This would make it possible for employers to hire relatively

cheap unskilled workers, who could be trained quickly, and through specialisation they should quickly become reliable and efficient.

- Use time and motion study to discover 'the one best way' to perform each task.
- Incentivise workers through payment by results (piecework).

Taylor believed that scientific management could be introduced consensually because it would be seen by all concerned to be scientific and therefore the best way, because paying workers according to their output would be perceived as fair, and workers would benefit from increases in output; thus industrial relations would become conflict-free.

Henry Ford was one of the first to apply scientific management when between 1908 and 1914 he set the production of Ford motor cars on moving assembly lines.

The major criticism of scientific management has always been that it dehumanises workers and therefore leads to workforce opposition.

In sociology the main (and continuing) controversy has been about the extent to which Taylorist principles are still applied in practice, even though the labels (Taylorism and scientific management) are rarely used today.

See also **Braverman, H.; Fordism; Human relations; Human resource management; Industrial relations; Labour process theory.**

Taylor, F.W. (1964), *Scientific Management,* Harper, New York.

Scottish enlightenment

See Enlightenment.

Secondary analysis

The analysis of existing data, usually a quantitative (statistical) data set, though qualitative material such as interview transcripts may also be subjected to secondary analysis.

The aim may be to check the conclusions drawn in a previous, primary analysis, or more typically to trawl existing data before embarking on fresh research.

Secondary socialisation

See Socialisation.

Sect

A breakaway movement from a church which claims to be the bearer of the true faith.

Sects are most likely formed by charismatic leaders but are relatively egalitarian, with less distinction and distance between priests and laity than in churches. Sects are always radical in their religious outlooks (they have broken from the mainstream), and they are also typically radical in their socio-political messages. They tend to appeal to disadvantaged sections of a population.

Sects are dynamic; they seek converts actively. However, if successful, then over time they are likely to develop into denominations (mid-way in character between a church and a sect).

Cults are extreme sects, usually smaller, with esoteric beliefs and practices. They are so extreme that they set themselves outside (and will be disowned by) the mainstream religions from which their members are drawn.

See also **Charisma; Church; Religion.**

Wilson, B. (1970), *Religious Sects,* Weidenfield and Nicolson, London.

Secularisation

A process in which religious beliefs and practices lose influence and significance.

A conventional view in sociology used to be that secularisation was an inevitable part of modernisation: that religion would inevitably yield to science and reason, and that this was indicated by falling church memberships and attendances, the diminishing role of religion in education, the separation of church and state (civil rights ceasing to be dependent on accepting an official faith), and religion, insofar as it survived, becoming a matter of personal choice.

However, it has now become evident that religious beliefs remain far more widespread than religious practice. Moreover, in at least one important modern society, the United States, church attendance remains high. Religion has continued to play a central role in change movements (in communist Poland and in the case of radical Catholicism in Latin America, for example). Since 9/11, and alongside the continuing wars and liberation struggles in the Middle East, and talk of a 'clash of civilisations', sociologists have acknowledged that religion still needs to be taken into account.

The secularisation thesis survives in sociology only in a more limited form: describing and explaining a past trend in Europe, a trend which will not necessarily continue indefinitely, and which may or may not prove universal as the rest of the world becomes modern.

See also **Clash of civilisations; Religion.**

Martin, D. (1978), *A General Theory of Secularisation*, Blackwell, Oxford.

Segmentation

Social anthropologists (and Emile Durkheim, 1858–1917) recognised a group of segmented societies. These societies were composed of several segments (such as clans) which existed in parallel, each largely independent except for limited and regulated links such as through marriages and mutual assistance in warfare. Some segmented societies were stateless, but were still treated as societies because, apart from the limited links, they shared a common culture. Such segments are not strata. They exist in parallel.

In modern societies the term segment has been used mainly in analysing labour markets. They are said to become segmented through different firms building their own core workforces who acquire firm-specific skills and know-how, then compete for jobs and promotion in internal labour markets. A firm may provide a variety of benefits for its core employees in addition to wages or salaries: healthcare, housing and recreation, for example, thus making the firm into a mini-society for its employees. However, in the sociology of labour markets, interest in segmentation has been a response to how this behaviour creates a workforce-wide schism between primary groups of workers (members of the core workforces of firms who obtain the benefits associated with internal labour markets) and other workers who become locked out in secondary labour markets, thus, overall, creating a dual labour market.

Workforces may be segmented, but firms themselves are interdependent as suppliers and customers. Unless the term segmentation is restricted to parallel, largely independent units, segmentation becomes indistinguishable from the division of labour. Knowledge and thereby students and teachers are segmented into different disciplines. Workers are segmented into different occupational groups. The reality, of course, is that many employees do spend their working lives within what, for them, become more or less self-contained occupational groups.

The merit of the segmentation concept for present-day sociology lies in drawing attention to the horizontal dimension of the division of labour, thereby correcting what might otherwise be an over-emphasis on the vertical (stratification) dimension.

See also **Dual labour market.**

Segregation

S

This means keeping apart different sections of a population for one, more or all of employment, marriage, housing, education and leisure. The groups that are kept apart may be races/ethnic groups, the sexes, age groups or social strata (classes, estates, castes etc).

Segregation may be required by law or custom. It may be consensual; separate toilets for men and women. In Islamic countries the sexes may be segregated in all public places, and private contact may be restricted to the family. Prisoners are segregated into prisons. Within prisons some inmates are segregated for their own protection (child murderers and paedophiles, for example). Children are segregated from adults for education and in many sports. Persons with contagious diseases are segregated in isolation wards and hospitals. Races or ethnic groups may be segregated, as under apartheid in South Africa until the 1990s, and in the southern states of the United States until the 1950s. Indian castes have lived apart, especially the outcastes or untouchables. Some instances of segregation have clearly not been consensual but have been imposed by one of the parties. Some have been and still are fiercely contested within all groups. Should there be separate swimming sessions for men and women?

Sometimes, indeed very often, segregation is an outcome of general processes of social stratification: the separation of different classes into different neighbourhoods, their children into different schools, and different leisure milieux for all ages. The sexes remain largely segregated in mainly male and mainly female occupations. Here segregation is a matter of degree, which can be measured. Preventing or limiting segregation may require special measures such as zoning children into different schools so as to create balanced social intakes in each, and requiring builders to construct mixed (in price) residential developments.

Segregation is not always contrary to the wishes of any of the parties, and it is an issue on which there is often a difference between what people regard as desirable in principle (racially integrated schools, for example), and how they behave when (they feel quite properly) pursuing their own private interests (maybe sending their children to the best school or the nearest school, for example).

There could be benefits if sociologists agreed a more precise meaning for segregation: maybe segregation when it is required, and separation when it is just an outcome.

Self

In sociology our selves are the objects of our thoughts: the desires, beliefs and feelings of which we are aware. Psychoanalysts do, and other psychologists may, recognise a deeper unconscious self that is capable of driving our behaviour. Certain types of psychotherapy aim to bring the unconscious into consciousness where it can be controlled. However, unless sociology is being combined with psychoanalysis, the only self that is taken into account is the self in our thoughts.

The self is a core concept in symbolic interactionism. The self is said to be created during social interaction, through our ability to recognise how others see us. These processes are believed to make humans different from other species.

The self can have derivatives: a desired self (how I would like to be), and a presented self (how I try to appear to others).

A claim in contemporary sociology is that unstable postmodern conditions make it more difficult than formerly to develop and maintain a stable and coherent self-concept. It is said that we develop several compartmentalised selves that are activated in different situations (when I am at home, and when I am at work), or that we are denied any solid sense of who we are.

See also **Identity; Mead, G.H.; Symbolic interactionism.**

Self-actualisation

A concept that will forever be associated with the American psychologist Abraham Harold Maslow (1908–1970). He postulated a hierarchy of human needs. Once one level of need was met it ceased to be a motivator, and the next level was activated. The Maslow hierarchy is:

- physiological
- security
- social (love, belonging, esteem and status)
- self-actualisation, when a person becomes everything that he or she can be.

This theory has enjoyed prolonged influence in organisation and management thought. Once lower-level needs have been met, it is argued that employers need to motivate their staff by addressing higher-level social and self-actualisation needs.

See also **Human relations.**

Maslow, A.H. (1954), *Motivation and Personality,* Harper, New York.

Self-fulfilling prophecy

One of many concepts introduced into sociology by Robert Merton (1910–2003), the American sociologist. The self-fulfilling prophecy illustrates how the human sciences can become part of their own subject matter.

An authoritative prediction of the collapse of a share price can lead to investors selling, which brings the share price down. Another example is the bandwagon effect of opinion polls where voters join what appears to be a winning side. However, the self-fulfilling prophecy has an opposite, the self-destroying prophecy. Confidence that their party will win may induce its supporters to stay at home instead of voting, leading to the party's defeat. Both effects are very exceptional rather than the rule.

The medical equivalent is the placebo effect where a patient's confidence that a drug will work is sufficient to improve the patient's condition.

S

Semantics

A branch of linguistics, the study of language, which addresses how meanings are produced and recognised in words and combinations of words.

Outside the discipline of semantics itself, statements are described (and typically dismissed) as semantic if the point being made is about the appropriateness or inappropriateness of the use of words, phrases or sentences rather than the substance of an argument.

See also **Language.**

Semiology

See semiotics.

Semiotics

Named by the Swiss linguist, Ferdinand de Saussure (1857–1913); alternatively known as semiology. It is the study of signs or symbols (these terms also are used interchangeably). The Frenchman Roland Barthes (1915–1980) has been the main exponent of semiotics.

Semiotics studies the relationships between signifiers (words, sounds, images) and signified (what the signifier stands for). Semiotics is the core discipline in cultural studies, and is used extensively in media studies. It explores the meanings of advertisements, TV programmes, foodstuffs, types of clothing and so on.

Sociology's standard complaint about semiotics is that its practitioners postulate meanings, but are less energetic in establishing what the producers of signifiers intend to mean, and what the signifiers mean to the normal receivers.

See also **Barthes, R.; Hall, S.; Saussure, F. de.**

Barthes, R. (1967), *Elements of Semiology,* Cape, London.

Barthes, R. (1972), *Mythologies,* Cape, London.

Sennett, Richard (1943–)

An American sociologist, who writes about the personal consequences of employment in different kinds of occupations, usually highlighting the downside.

In 1973 Sennett co-authored *The Hidden Injuries of Class*, a critique of the damage inflicted on individuals' self-concepts by being poorly qualified, poorly paid, and holding low status jobs in the United States. Subsequently, in *The Corrosion of Character*, Sennett has examined how under 'the new capitalism' things have become worse for employees at all levels. Skilled production workers have become computer button pushers, no long able to feel in control of production processes or even their own jobs. Highly qualified and well-paid professionals are required to be flexible, adaptable, mobile and willing to take risks for the sake of their careers. Loyalty, commitment, trust and all long-term goals are said to be undermined. Sennett argues that the bonds that once held people together, and which kept their characters intact, are being corroded.

Critics say maybe, but ask whether upcoming cohorts for whom the new capitalism is simply normal, who have no experience of different times, will be affected in the same ways as their elders.

See also **Career; Neo-liberalism; Occupation; Technology.**

S

Sennett, R. (1998), *The Corrosion of Character: The Personal Consequences of Work in the New Capitalism*, Norton, London.

Sennett, R. and Cobb, J. (1973), *The Hidden Injuries of Class*, Vintage Books, New York.

Serfs

Unfree peasants who were tied to their land by law or custom, and who had obligations to the landowners, their lords. These obligations were usually to provide labour, goods (produce) or money.

Serfdom had disappeared from most of western Europe by the end of the fifteenth century, but lasted much longer in central and eastern Europe. In Russia serfdom was formally abolished in 1861, and in Tibet there were serfs until 1959.

See also **Peasants; Traditional societies.**

Backman, C.R. (2003), *The Worlds of Medieval Europe*, Oxford University Press, Oxford.

Service class

This term was first used by the Austrian socialist politician Karl Renner (1870–1950), but has been adopted in worldwide sociology through its use by the Oxford sociologist John H. Goldthorpe (1935–). The service class is composed of managers and professional employees in government and private industry. Their jobs are distinctive on account of their trust relationships with their employers. They have exceptional autonomy at work, and they are better rewarded than any other employees in terms of pay and other benefits. In exchange they are expected to be loyal (like servants, hence service class). Alternative terms are salariat and (upper) middle class.

The term service class has become well known through its use in the Goldthorpe class scheme, which is now used by sociologists throughout the world. A version has been adopted as the official UK class scheme, and a slightly different version as the official European Union class scheme.

See also **Class; Goldthorpe, J.H.; Management; Middle class; Profession.**

Goldthorpe, J.H., Llewellyn, C. and Payne, C. (1980, 1987), *Social Mobility and Class Structure in Britain,* Clarendon Press, Oxford.

S

Service industries

A service is anything that you cannot drop on your foot. Manufacturing industries produce goods – such as motor cars or television sets. Services are intangible: banking, architecture, law, health, education, security, cleaning, entertainment and the like.

In the economically advanced societies employment in manufacturing has been declining for several decades. Consumption of manufactured goods continues to rise, but some of the jobs have been transferred to lower-wage-cost countries, and others have been replaced by technology. Employment in service sectors has expanded. By the beginning of the twenty-first century around 80 per cent of all UK jobs were in services. Hence the advanced economies are sometimes called service-based economies as an alternative to post-industrial.

Services can be exported (financial services, designs of anything and intellectual property rights can all be sold to overseas customers). However, many services, especially consumer services, have to be produced and delivered in the consumer's presence (retailing, restaurant meals, live entertainment etc.). Overall, jobs in services are less mobile than manufacturing jobs.

There are lots of low-level service sector jobs (in retail, hotels, cleaning firms etc.), but overall the proportion of high-level jobs is greater in service sectors than in manufacturing. Banks, legal, education and health services, and government administration all have high proportions of employment in the management and professional grades. Hence the shift in employment towards service sectors drives another shift – towards an increasingly middle class workforce.

See also **Creative industries; Cultural industries; Post-industrial.**

Sex

In sociology the term 'sex' refers to the biological differences between males and females. 'Gender' is used to refer to masculine and feminine characteristics that are cultural and acquired through socialisation.

See also **Gender.**

Sexism

Treating people differently depending on their biological sex. This is now illegal in Britain and in many other countries in education and employment, and in the provision of many services, but people are still, and are allowed to be, sexist in inter-personal relationships outside their work roles.

Sexuality

This refers to feelings and orientations. People can be sexually hetero, gay, lesbian or bi. There is an unresolved debate about whether sexual preferences are inborn or learnt.

See also **Queer theory.**

Weeks, J. (2003), *Sexuality,* Routledge, London.

Sick role

A concept introduced into sociology by Talcott Parsons (1902–1979). Aside from any physical or mental condition, the concept draws attention to how there is a sick role that people need to play in order to be recognised as sick. This involves:

- seeking professional help
- following doctor's orders
- wanting to return to normal as soon as possible.

A person who is recognised as sick will be:

- not blamed
- not expected to look after himself or herself
- relieved of normal responsibilities.

The value of distinguishing the sick role from any underlying condition is that we are able to recognise that:

- People who could qualify may try to avoid being categorised as sick; they may prefer to carry on as normal.
- People may try to qualify for the sick role because they regard it as preferable to other positions in which they might be cast – unemployed or criminal, for example.

See also **Body; Health**.

Parsons, T. (1951), *The Social System,* Routledge, London.

Sign

Anything that stands for something else. Semiotics/semiology is the discipline that studies signs. In semiotics a sign is a signifier plus whatever is signified.

Sociologists have to be interested in signs because most relationships between people are conducted through signs. The most common way of signalling is through words. Hence, if sociology can grasp how signs, and in particular how languages, work, this should be a major step towards understanding the constitution of social life.

See also **Semiotics**.

Significance tests

Statistical tests that are applied to test whether differences between two groups within a sample (men and women, for example) will apply throughout the population from which the sample has been drawn. In other words, can we be confident that the differences are not due to sampling error?

All tests of significance give results at different confidence levels. They tell us that we can be 90 per cent, 95 per cent or 99 per cent (but never 100 per cent) certain that a difference in a sample is not due to sampling error. The higher the confidence level required, the wider must be the difference between groups within the sample to be deemed a significant difference.

There are many tests of statistical significance. Their appropriateness depends on the character of the data (parametric or non-parametric, for example). The chi-square is one of the simplest and probably the most widely used test of significance in sociology.

Significant others

A key concept in George Herbert Mead's (1863–1931) theory of the mind. Significant others are other people whose views matter to us: it makes a difference to us whether or not we have their approval.

A person's first significant others will usually be parents, then maybe other relatives and siblings, teachers, friends, and later on work colleagues and employers. Mead believed that the views of all significant others become merged in a generalised other and internalised in a subject's mind. This, according to Mead, enables us to see ourselves as others see us, and to anticipate their reactions to how we might behave in the future. Mead argued that this is how the 'self', our self awareness, is created. Thus, according to Mead's theory, the self is not pre-social but is actually a social product.

See also **Identity; Mead, G.H.; Self; Symbolic interactionism.**

Simmel, Georg (1858–1918)

A German sociologist who was regarded as a maverick in his own lifetime since his work consisted mainly of short essays on a wide variety of topics. However, a consequence has been that Simmel has been influential in many areas of sociology – including symbolic interactionism, functionalism, reference group theory, role theory, conflict theory, theories about modernity and postmodernity – but most of all in urban sociology via his influence on the Chicago School.

It is now acknowledged that the impression of Simmel as a lightweight maverick was always misleading. He believed that it was impossible to study any society as a totality. Rather, he believed that the character of the whole was best grasped through a detailed study of particular parts. Simmel also believed that it was possible in sociology to separate the study of form from content, and he is regarded as a founder of formal sociology. Examples of forms include dyads, triads, patronage relationships, encounters with strangers, and large organisations (bureaucracies). Simmel believed that the detailed study of an example could lead to conclusions that applied to all similar forms.

Sociology has never been convinced that form and content can be usefully separated, and Simmel has never been accorded the status of 'founding

S

father' such as his contemporaries, Emile Durkheim (1858–1917) and Max Weber (1864–1920). However, Simmel's influence has been extensive, and nowadays he is likely to be cited in most specialised branches of sociology.

See also **Chicago School; Formal sociology.**

Frisby, D. (1984), *Georg Simmel*, Tavistock, London.

Simmel, G. (1903, 1950), 'The metropolis and mental life', in K. Wolff (ed.), *The Sociology of Georg Simmel,* Free Press, New York.

Simulacra

A term coined by the French postmodern theorist Jean Baudrillard (1929–2007). A simulacrum is a representation of a representation, an image of an image, a media story about an earlier media story, for example. Baudrillard believed that the postmodern world was saturated with such media representations; so much so that simulacra constituted the real world in which people were living, a condition that Baudrillard described as hyper-reality.

See also **Baudrillard, J.; Hyper-reality.**

Situationalism

Situational ethics teach that the choice of which ethical principle to observe must depend on the situation: the end will justify the means (choice).

Situationists was the name adopted by a revolutionary artistic/political group which was formed in France in 1957, then spread to other countries.

In sociology situationalism is a methodological doctrine very similar to methodological individualism. It insists that behaviour must be analysed and explained in terms of the goals and motivations of actors in a specific situation.

See also **Methodological individualism.**

S

Slavery

A form of stratification where the slaves are the property of another group. Slaves may be the property of persons, or the property of a group such as the state. Slaves are not paid for their labour. Thus slavery is a form of unfree labour, like serfdom, but serfs had more rights than slaves.

Slavery has been practised throughout history. People have become slaves through conquest or as a punishment for crimes, and have been sold into slavery by their families, sometimes by themselves (usually only under extreme conditions, such as to pay off heavy debts). Slavery is now illegal in nearly all countries, but it is estimated that there are still around 27 million slaves worldwide. There is a debate about whether the decline of slavery in modern times has been due to its inhumanity or inefficiency.

There have been very different kinds of slavery: according to whether manumission (freeing slaves) was possible and how common; and the extent to which the treatment of slaves was regulated by custom, law and religion. In some societies owners had affectionate, paternal relationships with their slaves. Sometimes slaves performed important administrative and judicial functions. The slavery that was practised on the colonial plantations of the Caribbean and North America was an extreme form of slavery where slaves had zero rights. They were the owners' personal property and could be bought and sold (which is called chattel slavery), or even killed on the whim of an owner.

See also **Serfs; Stratification.**

Turley, D. (2000), *Slavery,* Blackwell, Oxford.

Walvin, J. (2006), *Atlas of Slavery*, Pearson Longman, Harlow.

Smith, Adam (1723–1790)

A leading member of the Scottish enlightenment who wrote on a variety of topics but is world famous for his treatise on *The Wealth of Nations*, which is generally regarded as the foundation text in classical economics Smith believed that the common good was best achieved through:

- the division of labour, which permitted specialisation
- the pursuit of self-interest
- the 'invisible hand' of the free market.

He was fully aware of the possible negative outcomes of extreme forms of the division of labour (stupid and ignorant workers) but was unable to recommend corrective measures that would not jeopardise the common good. Unlike later free market economists, Smith was not opposed to the state playing an active role in social affairs – to promote education and to alleviate poverty, for example.

See also **Division of labour; Enlightenment; Neo-liberalism.**

Smith, A. (1776, 1976), *An Inquiry into the Nature and Causes of the Wealth of Nations*, Clarendon Press, Oxford.

S

Smith, Dorothy Edith (1926–)

British-born, Canadian sociologist, based in Toronto since 1977; famous for developing standpoint theory and institutional ethnography.

Smith's pioneering work began with a realisation that the intellectual and cultural worlds in which she and other women were participating had been put together from men's standpoints. Smith responded by working on a sociology *for* women, starting from the standpoint of a housewife and mother in her everyday world.

This led to the development of institutional ethnography, a method of inquiry that allows people to explore the social relations that structure their everyday lives. Institutional ethnography is now used in all areas of sociology.

Subsequently Smith extended the boundaries of standpoint theory to include race and class as well as gender.

See also **Androcentrism; Standpoint theory.**

Smith, D.E. (1988), *The Everyday World as Problematic: A Feminist Sociology*, Open University Press, Milton Keynes.

Smith, D.E. (1990), *The Conceptual Practices of Power: A Feminist Sociology of Knowledge,* Northeastern University Press, Boston.

Snowball sampling

When an initial respondent helps a researcher contact others.

This method of sampling may be used when there is no sampling frame from which a representative sample can be drawn, or when the researcher cannot access such a sampling frame. Persons recently released from prison, or attending sessions to treat alcoholism, will usually be willing to assist a trusted researcher to make contact with others in the same categories. This can be a very efficient way of building a sample of persons with a highly specific (and quite rare in the general population) type of experience.

See also **Sampling.**

Social anthropology

See Anthropology.

Social capital

See Capital.

S

Social change

Change has occurred whenever a current condition differs from a preceding state. Clearly, there are different kinds of change:

- biographical, during a person's life course
- cyclical, as in the daily round and annual cycle of events
- the flux that is normal in some societies, as in market economies where some businesses are constantly being created while others are disappearing
- societal change, which alters normal biographies, cycles, and what is and is not in flux.

The latter type of change has always been a central issue in sociology. The discipline was born in the nineteenth century in efforts to understand the new social orders that were coming into existence in Europe, and to identify the drivers of change. After the Second World War western sociology examined changes associated with the spread of mass affluence and the advent of welfare states. Later in the twentieth century the discipline addressed post-Fordism, post-industrialism and a postmodern condition.

Until the mid-twentieth century many sociologists sought a general all-encompassing theory of change. They debated whether change was evolutionary (comparable to the evolution of animal species), whether it was making societies better integrated and better adapted to their environments, whether change was revolutionary, with societies lurching from one unstable state to another; and whether new ideas were the cause or outcomes of material changes.

Nowadays most sociologists have abandoned the quest for a general theory of change and examine particular changes or sets of changes: for example, the transformation of former communist countries, the development of underdeveloped societies, and all the new conditions prefixed with 'post'.

> *See also* **Development; Evolution; Modern; Revolution; Social transformation.**

Social closure

A term introduced into sociology by Max Weber (1864–1920); it refers to how a group may control and restrict entry, and confine access to resources to insiders. This may be regarded as an important way, if not the only or the most important way, in which the boundaries between social strata are created and maintained.

Entry to a group may be solely by birth, as in the Indian caste system. Entry may also be controlled by prohibiting or discouraging inter-marriage. In modern societies important examples of exclusion are by occupational groups (professional associations and trade unions) that restrict entry to those with the right education, training and qualifications. Social clubs, golf clubs and suchlike may restrict entry according to gender, skin colour and occupation. Note, however, that in Britain and many other modern societies, exclusion from most formal groups and occupations on grounds of gender, race, religion, age and disability is now unlawful.

The opposite process to closure is usurpation whereby a lower status group seeks access to resources and positions that other groups monopolise. Closure and usurpation are perpetual processes that are continuously both maintaining to some extent, and at the same time changing, the boundaries between social strata. The same group may simultaneously be seeking to usurp those above and close itself to those below. However, the bottom strata have no one to exclude and may be comprehensively excluded, as with the outcastes/untouchables in India.

S

262 Key Concepts in Sociology

See also **Caste; Class; Stratification; Social exclusion.**

Parkin, F. (1974), 'Strategies of social closure in class formation', in F. Parkin (ed.), *The Social Analysis of Class Structure*, Tavistock, London, 1–18.

Social construction

The opposite of essentialism. In sociology constructionists believe that things such as gender and crime are constructed through human beliefs and actions. Crime is treated as a label that is applied to, rather than the essence of, any particular acts. Biology may make us male or female, but according to constructionists we learn to act as, and we have collectively created what it means to be, masculine and feminine.

The extreme constructionist position maintains that the whole of society is a social construct, which takes on the appearance of being 'out there', a naturally occurring entity, and is able to confront us as an external force, only while people keep believing and acting in ways that sustain the 'reality'.

See also **Essence; Labelling theory; Structuration.**

Berger, P.L. and Luckmann, T. (1967), *The Social Construction of Reality*, Allen Lane, London.

Social control

The mechanisms whereby the members of a society are induced to abide by social norms.

* Norms may be internalised during socialisation.
* They are also enforced by sanctions, positive and negative, formal and informal.

Note that under certain circumstances the application of social control may be counterproductive and may actually amplify deviance.

See also **Deviance; Labelling theory; Sanction; Socialisation.**

S

Social Darwinism

This applies Charles Darwin's (1809–1892) theory about the evolution of species by natural selection to social practices and societies.

Arguably, the true Social Darwinists have been Herbert Spencer (1820–1903) who coined the phrase 'the survival of the fittest', functionalists who argue that the evolution of societies over time, and specifically the trend towards greater social differentiation (division of labour), can be explained in terms of the more advanced societies being better adapted to their environments, and laissez-faire economists who approve of free competitive markets and oppose state interventions that prop up weaker 'social organisms'.

In practice, however, the term Social Darwinism is applied to theories that link the strength of societies to genetic characteristics of their populations (races), and to the eugenics movement that advocates strengthening populations and societies by encouraging the fittest to breed and discouraging (or preventing) the weak.

Nowadays the term Social Darwinism is nearly always applied pejoratively, in criticism.

See also **Eugenics; Evolution; Socio-biology; Spencer, H.**

Dickens, P. (2000), *Social Darwinism: Linking Evolutionary Thought and Social Theory*, Open University Press, Buckingham.

Social exclusion

Excluded groups are outside mainstream society. They may be excluded by the wider society, by themselves or by a mixture of the two. People can be excluded from any combination, and by the implications of the term they are typically excluded from some combination of wealth, income, employment, education, political representation, and social and emotional support. This condition used to be called multiple deprivation or multiple disadvantage. It has long been recognised in sociology that any one form of deprivation is liable to trigger others.

The term 'social exclusion' was first used in the European Union (as it is now known) in the 1980s, when unemployment had become a serious problem in several member states, and when immigration was rising. There was concern about the formation of groups that were not just unemployed and not just poor but more generally apart from mainstream society. Britain had its own race relations problem and debates, and in Britain the spread of unemployment in the 1970s and 1980s had been accompanied by a debate about an emergent underclass. During the 1990s the latter term was displaced from political discourse, and by the time that it won the 1997 General Election New Labour had adopted social exclusion as its preferred label for the disadvantaged groups and forms of disadvantage that it intended to address.

Social exclusion has subsequently become part of sociology's vocabulary, but some sociologists have strong reservations. There are dangers of misleading reification – inventing a word then assuming that it corresponds to a real social formation.

Exclusion suggests that the groups concerned are comprehensively outside mainstream society. Sociologists do not dispute that disadvantages tend to cluster and trigger one another, but exactly how closely are all disadvantages locked together? The unemployed and the poor are not necessarily deprived of social and emotional support. Their families and neighbours are often extremely supportive. In terms of political attitudes and partisanship, they differ little from the employed working class.

Exclusion suggests that the condition is long term. In practice there is considerable mobility (even if this is mostly 'churning') between unemployment and poverty on the one hand, and low-paid jobs on the other.

S

Sociologists are also mindful that over time the term 'social exclusion' has been incorporated into different political discourses. Ruth Levitas distinguishes three:

- RED: a redistribution discourse, proposing that more resources, especially money, be channelled to the poor.
- SID: a social integration discourse, which emphasises the need to integrate the excluded, primarily by getting them into jobs.
- MUD: a moral underclass discourse, which attributes exclusion to the excluded's own moral deficits.

Sociologists need to remember that the concept of social exclusion has political rather than social science origins, and to be sceptical about whether it really adds value to a vocabulary that already included poverty, unemployment, multiple deprivation and social class.

See also **Deprivation; Poverty; Unemployment; Underclass.**

Levitas, R. (1998), *The Inclusive Society? Social Exclusion and New Labour*, Macmillan, Basingstoke.

Social facts

See Durkheim, E.

Social inclusion

See Social exclusion.

Social integration

A term with several meanings which need to be distinguished even though the processes are likely to be inter-related. The British sociologist David Lockwood originally made the basic distinction between:

- Social integration: the integration of the individual into society, which can be achieved via socialisation and other social controls.
- System integration: between the parts of a social system, which according to Emile Durkheim (1858–1917) could be achieved by shared values (mechanical solidarity) or the division of labour (organic solidarity).

Often the word integration is used entirely appropriately in both senses simultaneously: when referring to the integration of immigrant groups into a host society, for example.

See also **Cohesion; Solidarity.**

Lockwood, D. (1964), 'Social integration and system integration', in
   Z. Zollschan and W. Hirsch (eds), *Explorations in Social Change,* Routledge,
   London.

Social institution

A settled pattern of behaviour and the associated culture that performs a specific role or function in the wider society. A social institution will usually contain a large number of inter-related roles, primary groups, and possibly larger organisations. Examples include educational institutions, political institutions, and the institution of the family.

See also **Institutionalisation.**

Social interaction(ism)

See Symbolic interactionism.

Social justice

See Justice.

Social mobility

This refers to movements up and down the social class structure. Studying social mobility requires individuals to be placed within a class scheme (usually on the basis of occupation). Thereafter their positions at different points in time can be compared. Provided the same class scheme is used, it is possible to compare mobility in different societies and within the same society at different historical points in time.

There are several ways in which we can compare mobility rates (the volume of upward and downward movements), and mobility paths and processes (how mobility is accomplished):

- *Intra- and inter-generational mobility*: Intra-generational mobility is between different points in the same person's life. A main finding here is that in middle class jobs people are far more likely to experience career-long upward mobility than are people in working class jobs. Mobility researchers have paid rather more attention to inter-generational mobility which is generally regarded as the best indicator of the openness of a society's class structure, and openness is typically equated with fairness and societal efficiency since open societies allow talent to triumph whatever its origins.
- *Absolute and relative mobility:* Absolute rates of mobility are the proportions of people from different origins who reach different destinations, and the proportions at particular destinations who started out in different class positions. The main findings from studies of absolute rates of mobility are that short-range movements are more common than long-range mobility, and that upward mobility has become more common in the economically advanced societies as the number of lower-level occupations has contracted and the number of higher-level

S

occupations has expanded. In contrast, rates of relative mobility (the relative chances of people from different origins reaching particular destinations) have varied little over time or between modern societies. There is unresolved controversy over how to explain this constancy: bio-psychological processes (inheritance of ability) or socio-cultural processes?

- *Objective and subjective mobility:* The main finding here is that subjectively people are far more likely to acknowledge upward than downward movements. 'Skidding' may be concealed by regarding one's current position as temporary, and by the fact that standards of education, living and most other things have risen over time, so people who slip down the occupational class structure may not experience any absolute decline (vis-à-vis their parents) in any other aspects of their experiences of life.

See also **Achievement; Class; Sponsored mobility; Stratification.**

Erikson, B. and Goldthorpe, J.H. (1992), *The Constant Flux: A Study of Class Mobility in Industrial Societies*, Clarendon Press, Oxford.

Social movements

There may be an organisation or organisations within or even at the head, but a social movement is more than an organisation. Social movements exist outside regular political channels, they are certainly not political parties, but they are emphatically political, seeking to bring about or resist change. There may be members of associated organisations, but a movement will always have a much larger number of supporters. Social movements are movements of the people. They are products of civil society. Their activities are likely to include meetings, rallies, marches and petitions. They both express and try to shape public opinion.

The term social movement was first used by the French philosopher, Comte Henri de Saint-Simon (1760–1825). The best-known movement of his time was the movement among the people of Paris which created the French Revolution (1789–1799). The nineteenth century saw the birth of labour movements in Europe, from which trade unions and associated political parties developed. There were temperance movements and the suffragettes. More recent social movements include anti-nuclear campaigns, the civil rights movement in the United States, second-wave feminism, gay rights, Solidarity in Poland and the environmentalists. Broader globalising forces have made it possible for global social movements (like the Anti-Globalization Movement) to be more effective than in the past.

Social movements were not unknown before modern times. There were peasant movements in Europe. However, urban conditions and mass education facilitate the development of movements of the people. These movements are so varied that a definitive typology is impossible. Generalising is hazardous. They challenge sociology's standard vocabulary of structures, institutions, parties and organisations.

See also **Castells, M.; Civil society; Politics; Pressure groups; Voluntary associations**.

Staggenborg, S. (2008), *Social Movements*, Oxford University Press, Oxford.

Social policy

Social policies are all government policies that affect the lives of the members of society. This can mean all government policies. Foreign and defence policy, and economic policy are normally excluded, but not altogether since tax and budgetary policies, for example, have social consequences. The core social policies are social security, health, education, housing and personal social services. Labour market and industrial relations services, training for employment, policing and the justice system are sometimes added.

Social policy exists as a separate academic discipline (formerly called social administration), and also within sociology where it is approached from, and hosts debates between, all the discipline's theoretical perspectives.

See also **Welfare state**.

Baldock, J., Manning, N. and Vickerstaff, S. (2007), *Social Policy*, Oxford University Press, Oxford.

Hill, M.J. (2000), *Understanding Social Policy*, Blackwell, Oxford.

www.social-policy.com

Social security

Cash welfare payments by the state. In the United States this term refers specifically to the state pension. In the UK it refers to all state cash benefits, means-tested or available to all who otherwise qualify for retirement pensions, disability and jobseekers allowances, child benefits and the like.

See also **Poverty trap; Welfare state**.

Social services

In Britain this term has a narrow and a broad meaning. The narrow meaning is the services provided by local authority social services departments in which social workers are the key profession. The broad meaning is all services delivered by social policies.

In the early and mid-twentieth century the social services (in the broad meaning, collectively known as the welfare state) were expanding. An aim was to guarantee security 'from the cradle to the grave'. In the decades immediately following the Second World War, many commentators expected the social services to continue to grow – to become wider (to include the arts, sport and other forms of leisure provision, for example), and to become stronger (better funded). Spending on social services was described as the 'social wage' through which the entire population enjoyed some of the benefits of economic growth.

Since the 1970s, in most countries, neo-liberal economic policies have become ascendant. Spending on social services has been restrained. Neo-liberals argue that as populations become richer, state-provided services become less necessary, and more people prefer to provide for themselves. There has also been a trend towards contracting out some services to voluntary and commercial organisations. It is claimed that competition between service providers can deliver better value for money and wider choice for 'consumers'.

See also **Beveridge, W.H.; Social policy; Social work; Welfare state.**

Social structure

This term metaphorically likens societies to buildings where the parts fit together and support one another. Take any part away, and the entire structure will be weakened and may collapse unless the part is replaced by a similar element. The term structure emphasises the stable, enduring features of societies.

The structure analogy allows foundations to be identified, and a façade (outward appearance) to be different from the core materials. Thus structure is likely to be a favoured concept for sociologists (like Marxists) who wish to distinguish base from superstructure, and ideology from what lies behind.

Social surveys

See Surveys.

Social system

Use of this term likens societies to other systems. For some sociologists – for example Talcott Parsons (1902–1979) and Niklas Luhmann (1927–1998) – this is the preferred analogy. For most sociologists, 'system' is just one of several analogies, each of which has a value for particular purposes.

Systems have interconnected parts. Change in any one part has repercussions throughout the whole. Emphasising the systemic properties of societies encourages sociologists to search throughout the remainder of the social system in seeking the sources and effects of any specific change. This is an alternative to treating societies as bundles of discrete social facts (factors), which can be drawn out of their contexts for analysis.

Motor car engines prove that systems may be, but are not necessarily, self-regulating with homeostatic mechanisms maintaining them in equilibrium under all circumstances.

See also **Luhmann, N.; Parsons, T.**

Social transformation

This term does not have a precise, generally accepted meaning. However, in practice the term 'transformation' is applied to changes where:

- The change cannot be described as evolution or development (where the momentum is from a society's or group's previous condition).
- The criteria for describing changes as a 'revolution' are not met (violent seizure of state power, followed by sweeping changes in politics and beyond, in political science).
- The outcome of the changes is not known in advance, as in a 'transition'.

Transformations are thorough changes. The most sweeping changes are described as revolutions, such as the industrial revolution, though technically it would probably be preferable to describe such events as transformations. Transformations are not necessarily instigated by political change. Usually there is a crucial intervention by a transformative agent. This may be a change of management in an organisation. It may be a popular social movement such as feminism. It may be an outside investor in a developing country, such as the World Bank. It may comprise diffuse global changes which transform a local community.

The transformations of the ex-communist countries are probably misleadingly referred to as 'transitions'.

See also **Development; Evolution; Revolution; Social change; Transition.**

Social work

The professional work of the personal social services. Social work deals mainly with clients with special problems which require personalised intervention: the physically and mentally ill, senior citizens, children and families that are 'at risk', and delinquents and criminals. Nearly all social work clients are poor. Most present multiple problems.

Social work was originally pioneered by voluntary associations then, during the twentieth century, it was largely taken over by the welfare state and professionalised. Sociology has always been part of the training of professional social workers, who are mostly employed either by the public sector or by voluntary associations.

There is a perpetual debate about whether social workers' responsibilities are primarily to their clients or to their employer – ultimately, nearly always the state.

See also **Social services; Welfare state.**

Jones, C. and Novak, T. (1999), *Poverty, Welfare and the Disciplinary State*, Routledge, London.

Thompson, N. (2000), *Understanding Social Work: Preparing for Practice*, Macmillan, Basingstoke.

S

Socialisation

The influence of society on the development of the person, whereby society actually becomes part of the individual, who internalises the knowledge and beliefs, and builds a personality, enabling him or her to become a full member of society. In explaining exactly how socialisation occurs, most sociologists draw heavily on the ideas of either George Hebert Mead (1863–1931) or Sigmund Freud (1856–1939).

Primary socialisation is the initial socialisation of a child, usually within a family. Secondary socialisation is all that follows at school, in peer groups and at work. Socialisation continues throughout the life course, but later stages have to build on the foundations laid early on.

Sociologists today recognise the possibility of self-socialisation, said to have become common as a result of the biographisation of life courses in (post) modern societies, with individuals selecting milieux that will enable them to develop their selves into the persons that they wish to become.

See also **Biographisation; Bourdieu, P.; Freud, S.; Mead, G.H.**

Lee, N. (2001), *Childhood and Society: Growing Up in an Age of Uncertainty*, Open University Press, Maidenhead.

Socialism

A political ideology that was developed in the nineteenth century, mainly in Britain and France, which envisaged the economy being owned and run in the interests of all the people, and the entire society guaranteeing the welfare of all its members.

There was never agreement on how this might be achieved. Many writers contributed to socialist thought: Karl Marx (1818–1883) and Friedrich Engels (1820–1895), but also Comte Henri de Saint-Simon (1760–1825) in France, Robert Owen (1771–1858) in Britain, and many others. It was argued by some that social ownership and control, and the provision of welfare, should be by the state, but there were advocates for local governments, and workers' and consumers' cooperatives.

By the beginning of the twentieth century there was a clear division between socialists who believed that progress to socialism would require a revolution (probably violent) and those who believed in a democratic road (democratic socialists). Related to this division of opinion, there was another slightly different division between those who believed that building a socialist society would need the state and a socialist party to take total control, and those who argued that progress could be gradual, evolutionary, by reform (Fabians in Britain), and that private businesses and the market could continue to operate under regulations which ensured that private enterprise served the common good (a social market economy, or social democracy).

By the end of the twentieth century the communist alternative had all but disappeared throughout the world, and social democracy had 'no enemy to the left'. Its achievements were then under attack from a globally ascendant neo-liberalism.

See also **Communism; Engels, F.; Marx, K.**

Newman, M. (2005), *Socialism: A Very Short Introduction*, Oxford University Press, Oxford.

Societies

The largest units that sociology studies. There is no agreed, authoritative definition, but sociologists will (probably) all agree that a society:

- contains all the institutions and processes that are necessary to be self-perpetuating
- has a common culture
- occupies a bounded territory
- has a population who feel that they constitute a distinct entity.

In practice, the societies that sociologists write about are (nearly) always states. Any lesser unit would not fulfil the self-perpetuating test. States do not exist in isolation. There have always been interdependencies (and wars). However, these links have not necessarily required societies to shed any vital functions (for self-perpetuation).

That said, it can be argued that in the twenty-first century, globalisation and the growth of trans-national organisations (economic, cultural and political) have made borders crumble, and that in the future sociology may have to operate in a world without societies (as known up to now).

See also **Globalisation; Information economy/Information society.**

Urry, J. (2000), *Sociology Beyond Societies: Mobilities for the Twenty-First Century*, Routledge, London.

Socio-biology

Seeks to explain human behaviour patterns in terms of their evolutionary advantages, the fittest traits being those that survive processes of natural selection. Unlike Social Darwinism, socio-biology seeks to explain traits that are common throughout humanity. Also unlike Social Darwinism, socio-biology has plenty of current high-profile supporters with impressive academic credentials (in biology).

Sociologists are virtually unanimous in resisting the claims of socio-biology. Sociology has an inbuilt preference for socio-cultural explanations, and seeks theories that explain differences as well as what is common throughout humanity.

See also **Ethology; Social Darwinism.**

Alcock, J. (2001), *The Triumph of Sociobiology*, Oxford University Press, Oxford.

S

Dawkins, R.I. (1989), *The Selfish Gene*, Oxford University Press, Oxford.

Wilson, E.O. (1975), *Sociobiology: The New Synthesis*, Harvard University Press, Cambridge, Mass.

Socio-economic groups

The UK Registrar General (now the Office for National Statistics) used to group the population into six social classes, and also into 17 socio-economic groups; some sociologists collapsed these into six socio-economic classes, and preferred to use these groupings rather than the Registrar General's six-class scheme. Since 1998 the six-class scheme has been replaced as the UK official classification by a version of the Goldthorpe class scheme, and the practice of collapsing the socio-economic groups has become redundant.

Sociologists may still refer to socio-economic groups rather than classes if they wish to avoid implying that the groups possess features (social, cultural and political) that are associated with social classes.

See also **Class; Stratification.**

Socio-legal studies

Studies the operation of legal institutions (mainly courts) and the roles of specialist personnel (solicitors, barristers, legal advice centres etc.).

See also **Law.**

Banakar, R. and Travers, M. (eds) (2005), *Theory and Method in Socio-Legal Research,* Hart, Oxford.

Socio-linguistics

Studies the relationships between languages on the one hand, and cultures, social patterns and behaviour on the other.

Knowing the language is a basic requirement in order to be a competent member of any society. Social anthropologists have always considered it necessary to learn the languages of the people they have studied. Languages can tell us a great deal about how users perceive and evaluate their environments and each other.

Sociologists study variations in linguistic practices between societies and within societies where they are interested in the significance of dialects, accents and the different rules of language that are observed in different ethnic groups, by males and females, and in different social classes.

See also **Bernstein, B.; Language; Linguistics.**

S

Sociometry

A technique for studying social relationships in small groups and networks that was invented by the American social psychologist Jacob Moreno (1890–1974). Members are given questionnaires and are asked to rank each other in terms of attractiveness or whom they would choose as friends. The results are plotted on a sociogram which reveals stars, cliques and isolates.

See also **Group; Network.**

Moreno, J.L. (1934, 1953), *Who Shall Survive?* Beacon House, New York.

Solidarity

Emile Durkheim (1858–1917) wrote about mechanical solidarity and organic solidarity, but subsequent sociologists have tended to use 'solidarity' only when referring to Durkheim's mechanical type of integration. Solidarity was believed to exist (but only remnants now survive) in working class neighbourhood communities and industrial workplaces where members recognised common unifying interests, shared goals and values, experienced a sense of belonging, and were prepared to act as one body, solidaristically, in support of one another.

There are alternative ways in which social integration and cohesion can be achieved and maintained.

See also **Cohesion; Integration.**

Solipsism

A solipsist doubts everything. The name is from an ancient Greek philosophy which maintained that we can know nothing except what is in our own minds. The main representative of solipsism in modern philosophy is the Frenchman René Descartes (1596–1650).

See also **Phenomenology.**

Sovereignty

A sovereign was originally a monarch or ruler who exercised unrestricted power within a territory. Nowadays it is states that are said to be sovereign. In practice, the powers of modern states are restricted, usually by law (a constitution) and by international agreements, and claims to literal sovereignty can survive only by arguing that states are restricted merely because, and insofar as, they allow themselves to be restricted.

See also **Government.**

S

Spencer, Herbert (1820–1903)

Britain's sole representative (in the second rank) among the 'founding fathers' of sociology, who began working life as a railway engineer and draughtsman, moved into journalism, and subsequently became an independent scholar. He is remembered as a founder of Social Darwinism, and as the originator of the 'organic analogy'.

Spencer believed that the struggle for survival, 'the survival of the fittest' (Spencer's phrase), was the engine of evolution. As such he was a founder of Social Darwinism. He believed in free markets and a minimal state lest government slow down or warp the evolutionary process.

Spencer also believed that the evolutionary principle was applicable in all fields, and could therefore unify the sciences. During evolution he believed that all phenomena became increasingly complex and internally differentiated and, as a result, better adapted to their environments. Societies, he believed, developed in much the same way as biological organisms, and could indeed be likened to biological organisms.

Although never lauded in Britain, during his lifetime Spencer was something of an international celebrity, especially in the United States and Japan.

See also **Evolution; Functionalism; Social Darwinism.**

Peel, J.D.Y. (1971), *Herbert Spencer: The Evolution of a Sociologist*, Heinemann, London.

Sponsored (and contest) mobility

These terms were coined by the American sociologist Ralph Turner (1919–), in comparing education in Britain and the United States. The contrast is not in terms of the volume of mobility (where there is little difference between Britain and the United States) but in how mobility is organised, how it is legitimised, and how all this is related to broader class relationships.

British education was characterised by Turner as a regime of sponsored mobility. Turner was writing in the era of the 11-plus examination and when Britain had a small, elitist higher education system (only 5 per cent of young people went to university). Turner likened ascent into higher-level occupations in Britain to admission to an exclusive club, with future members being selected by representatives of the existing members at a young age, then having their progress sponsored. They were given the schooling that would enable them to gain the qualifications that success required. Other young people were excluded. This kind of regime was said to encourage the fortunate ones to think of themselves as superior persons. Those who were not selected learnt that they were not suited to higher-level positions. All this was legitimised by a popular belief that talent was in short supply and that the well-being of the society depended on nurturing an exceptional minority.

Turner argued that US education with its comprehensive high schools and open college system regulated a regime of contest mobility. In a contest system the identification of winners is left until the latest possible moment. Competitors are allowed to use different tactics. Ability is an acceptable substitute for family support. Effort is an acceptable substitute for raw ability. At the end of the contest those who have made the best use of their assets are ahead. The winners are seen as deserving through having triumphed in an open and fair contest. Others admire the winners. Contest mobility is said to match popular sentiments in a society where it is believed that everyone should be encouraged to develop their talents to the fullest possible extent.

Sponsored and contest mobility, as described by Turner, are ideal types. He realised that there were features of sponsorship in US education and features of a contest in the British system. However, as ideal types the concepts can be used more widely in inter-country comparisons, and to identify trends over time, which globally appear to be away from sponsorship and towards contest mobility.

See also **Social mobility.**

Turner, R.H. (1960), 'Sponsored and contest mobility in the school system', *American Sociological Review*, 25, 855–67.

SPSS

Statistical Package for the Social Sciences, the computer software that is most often used in the analysis of social science data sets. It will perform all the calculations and tests that are commonly used in sociology.

Stagflation

A term coined in the 1970s to refer to a combination of events and trends that looked improbable in Keynesian and classical economic theory. Stagflation is a combination of economic stagnation, and therefore rising or high unemployment, alongside rising or high rates of wage and price increases.

Events in the 1960s and 1970s demonstrated that the combination could occur as a result of external shocks, like steep increases in the global prices of key commodities such as oil, or of trade union power forcing pay rises (leading to price rises) despite high unemployment which should normally (in market economic theory) have held wages down.

See also **Keynes, J.M.; Monetarism.**

Stalinism

Named after Joseph Stalin (1879–1953), who emerged from the power struggle which followed Lenin's death in 1924 as the undisputed leader of the Soviet Union from 1928 until his death in 1953. Stalin gave communism many of what, ever since, have been regarded as its defining features:

S

- firm central economic planning
- five-year plans
- the collectivisation of agriculture
- the use of physical terror as state policy
- purges of party officials
- bogus show trials
- labour camps
- executions of actual and alleged opponents
- forced famines
- the 'cult of personality'.

Many features of Stalinism survived his denunciation by his successors as Soviet leaders in 1956, and endured until the end of the Soviet Union in 1991.

In the eyes of Soviet and ex-Soviet citizens, Stalin is also remembered as the leader who led his country to victory in the Great Patriotic War (known as the Second World War in the west). A statue of Stalin still stands in his home town of Gori (Georgia), where the Stalin museum is now the main tourist attraction.

Standard deviation

See Measures of dispersion.

Standard of living

The material well-being of a population. This is usually calculated by dividing total economic output (gross domestic product, GDP) by the size of a population.

Standards of living in different countries can be compared by converting each national currency into a common currency (the US$ is normally used). Trends over time in countries can be calculated, taking price inflation into account. These calculations can be made for specific sections of any population – the retired or students, for example – among whom living standards and trends may differ widely from the national average.

There are two serious objections to the conventional way of measuring living standards:

- All production is never included. Unofficial (hidden) economic activity can never be measured accurately. Nor can the value of self-provisioning (food production for own consumption, for instance). Housework and informal childcare are invariably ignored.
- Material welfare is easily equated with well-being, which is completely unjustified in the world's richer countries.

See also **Quality of life; Poverty; Well-being.**

Standpoint theory

Claims that no objective, detached, neutral location is available, and that all sociology can achieve is to produce accounts of the world from different standpoints.

Standpoint theory arose within the second-wave feminist movement. It arose out of critiques of the idea that the neglect of women and gender in conventional sociology could be rectified by adding women and gender to the mainstream/malestream. The malestream was said to be fundamentally unable to represent the experiences of women who, therefore, needed to develop a separate sociology consistent with their standpoint.

This view has been, and remains, controversial even among feminist sociologists. Needless to say, the same reasoning can be applied by or to any group – gays, lesbians, colonial people, the working class, the disabled – that considers itself, or is considered by others, to be unrepresented or unfairly represented in mainstream sociology. Standpoint theory is anti-objectivist; it is fundamentally relativist. It adopts the view that all knowledge is socially determined. Members of all social categories are said to occupy privileged positions in respect of, and only in respect of, understanding the experiences of that category, be the category women, men, the middle class, the working class or whoever.

It is sometimes argued (though this argument is at odds with the basic premises of standpoint theory) that subordinate groups occupy especially privileged positions. Karl Marx (1818–1883) believed, and Gyorgy Lukacs (1885–1971) built on the idea, that the proletariat, as a result of its daily experiences at work, would inevitably, in time, come to understand the true character of capitalism and how the system could be replaced (to the proletariat's advantage). Similarly, some feminists argue that women are uniquely equipped to understand patriarchy given their remorseless experiences on the receiving end.

Standpoint sociology encounters major criticisms. One concerns exactly whose standpoint any speaker/writer can claim to represent. Can anyone claim to represent the experiences of all women? Likewise all colonised/disabled/gay people? Does standpoint theory lead into alleys in which no one can claim to be speaking for anyone except himself or herself?

In any case, sociologists (including feminist sociologists) are not all prepared to abandon the 'modernist' project of seeking objective knowledge. Standpoint sociology dismisses the possibility of an external validation of any account. We are left in the postmodernist predicament of confronting each other with how things look from our particular standpoints, lacking any means to persuade each other to see things in our preferred ways.

See also **Objectivity; Relativism; Smith, D.E.**

Smith, D.E. (1990), *The Conceptual Practices of Power: A Feminist Sociology of Knowledge*, Northeastern University Press, Boston.

State

A state comprises the institutions that govern a territory. A modern state will usually possess a legislature, a civil service, a judicial system, police and armed forces. A state will always claim a monopoly over legitimate violence within its territory.

In pre-modern times, state power (and therefore states themselves) were often diffused between magnates who mobilised their own armies and created other state institutions such as laws and courts. Modern states have concentrated state functions in a central authority.

Modern states usually represent (at least symbolically) a titular nationality – hence the expression 'nation state'.

The geographical borders of states can shift, as can the internal borders between a state and the surrounding society. This happens through nationalisations and privatisations, the extension or rolling back of state welfare, and governments implementing or ceasing to implement policies through civil society organisations, which may thereby become quangos.

See also **Government; Quango**.

Mann, M. (1988), *States, War and Capitalism: Studies in Political Sociology*, Blackwell, Oxford.

Status

This word is sometimes used to refer to any position or role, but in sociology it is also used in a more limited way to refer to a position in a social hierarchy where people are ranked by esteem or prestige (usually seen to be conferred by either their occupations or their overall lifestyles).

There is an unresolved debate among sociologists about whether status rankings simply reflect other inequalities, class inequalities in particular, or whether, as Max Weber (1864–1920) argued, status is a separate dimension of stratification which interacts with but is not reducible to any other kind of inequality.

In recent years some sociologists have argued that status rankings have become more important (relative to class divisions) as a result of the growth of consumption, and hence people's ability to establish lifestyles and to create identities for themselves according to what, where and how they consume (their houses, cars, holidays etc.). Market researchers who wish to identify sections of the population that are likely to buy particular products have begun adding lifestyle variables to long-standing predictors (age, gender and social class). Postal code areas are identified according to the typical lifestyles of the residents, who are able to use the Internet to discover the groups to which they (and other people) belong simply from knowing their addresses. Moreover, the lifestyle groups in which we are placed by market researchers increasingly govern who tries to sell what to us, and our credit ratings.

See also **Class; Geodemographics; Stratification; Weber, M.**

Burrows, R. and Gane, N. (2006), 'Geodemographics, software and class', *Sociology*, 40, 793–812.

Chan, T.W. and Goldthorpe, J.H. (2004), 'Is there a status order in contemporary British society? Evidence from the occupational structure of friendship', *European Sociological Review*, 20, 383–401.

Stereotype

A generalised view of a group that governs how individuals from that group are viewed and treated. People may hold stereotyped views about men and women, specific ethnic groups, religious groups, persons from particular educational backgrounds or in specific occupations.

Stereotyping has unsavoury connotations, but it is actually a pervasive feature of social life, which would become incredibly complicated if we did not make any assumptions about others from a limited knowledge about them. Employers stereotype when they judge job applicants as probably suitable or unsuitable on the basis of educational qualifications and/or work experience. Market researchers stereotype when they decide from knowledge of past purchases that members of a particular social group are the most likely purchasers of a further product.

Stereotypes can be criticised as inaccurate, or because they are used too inflexibly, and may be experienced as simply unfair and objectionable because, for example, the ascriptive criteria that are used (sex, ethnicity, age) clash with achievement values.

Stigma

An old term which Erving Goffman (1922–1982) introduced into sociology. A stigma is any attribute (physical, psychological or social), which is likely to disqualify a person from full social acceptance in a particular milieu. Examples of potential stigma are severe physical disfigurement, a criminal record and a history of mental illness. A stigmatised identity is a spoiled identity. Stigma may be very difficult to conceal, and if hidden those concerned have to live with, and to manage, potentially discreditable identities.

Sociologists are interested in stigma because they can assist in identifying the boundaries of what is considered normal and acceptable, and because large sections of the population (maybe all of us) have to manage potentially discreditable biographies.

See also **Goffman, E.; Identity; Role; Self.**

Goffman, E. (1964), *Stigma: Notes on the Management of Identity,* Penguin, Harmondsworth.

S

Strain theories

The name given to a group of theories that attempt to explain deviance. Most of these theories incorporate the concept of anomie.

Strain, in these theories, is not something that individuals necessarily experience; rather it is a feature of the social system. The strain identified is usually between socially approved goals and the means to their attainment that are available to different sections of the population. The individuals concerned may or may not experience tension and frustration because an outcome of structural strain has very likely been the formation of a subculture which replaces normally approved goals or means, or a combination of the two.

Strain is also identified in role theory. It exists in a role set when an actor confronts conflicting expectations, or expectations which, in total, the actor is simply unable to meet. Strain can also be created when different roles (parent and worker, for example) make contradictory demands on an actor.

In all these circumstances, some kind of deviance becomes structurally inevitable irrespective of whether the individuals concerned experience strain.

See also **Anomie; Merton, R.K.; Role.**

Strata

See Stratification.

Stratification

This is sociology's general term referring to socially structured inequalities. The term makes a geological analogy: it suggests that societies can be likened to geological formations of layer upon layer of different minerals.

There are different types of stratification that have existed and sometimes coexisted in different societies. Some societies have been divided into estates, some into castes, and in some there have been masters and slaves. However, the main strata recognised in modern societies are:

- Classes: with an economic foundation.
- Status groups: defined by the prestige attached to their occupations or lifestyles.
- Elites: groups situated at the pinnacle of organisations and institutions.

Societies may be, and usually are, also stratified by gender, ethnicity/race, according to sexuality, and into groups with different abilities and disabilities. However, there is a point where it is necessary to decide whether we are dealing not with inequalities but simply differences, and whether the differences or inequalities simply reflect individual characteristics as opposed to being generated by social processes.

A major debate in sociology has always been about how different strata are created, how advantaged groups maintain their positions, and how and why they are sometimes dislodged. Here the main protagonists have been functionalist and conflict theorists.

See also **Caste; Class; Conflict theory; Elites; Estates; Functionalism; Reproduction; Slavery; Social closure; Status.**

Stratified samples

See Sampling.

Stress

This has become a commonly reported condition to which various physical and psychological ailments are attributed. Reported stress can be measured, but there is not, and probably cannot be, any objective measurement, and stressors have proved elusive.

Which is more stressful, a heavy workload or no work? One person's stressful situation can be relaxing to another and invigorating to someone else. Social support is said to buffer or relieve stress, but this is impossible to prove in the absence of reliable known stressors and an objective measurement of stress. Reported stress seems most likely to arise from the interaction between a person's character (physical and psychological) and that person's total environment.

Few sociologists attempt to investigate stress: strain is the discipline's preferred concept.

See also **Anomie; Strain theories.**

Zuzanek, J. (2004), 'Work, leisure, time-pressure and stress', in J.T. Haworth and A.J. Veal (eds), *Work and Leisure,* Routledge, London, 123–44.

Zuzanek, J. and Mannell, R. (1998), 'Life cycle squeeze, time pressure, daily stress, and leisure participation: a Canadian perspective, *Leisure and Society,* 21, 513–44.

S

Strikes

The temporary, collective withdrawal of labour by a workforce. The aim is usually to pressure an employer to concede a pay claim or other improvements in terms and conditions of employment; sometimes to oppose redundancies or other changes in terms and conditions proposed by an employer; occasionally in support of workers in another firm or industry who are in dispute (which is called secondary industrial action); occasionally to pressure a government in support of a political objective (as when workers went on strike at the Gdansk shipyard in Poland in 1980, and created Solidarity, which challenged and eventually brought about the collapse of communism in east-central Europe).

Over time strikes have receded in frequency and significance in the economically advanced countries. This has been during, and has been largely due to, the transition from industrialism to post-industrialism. Strikes are most likely to occur when workers share, and are aware of sharing, common interests and grievances, and when managements and employers are regarded as 'the other side'. Taking strike action was once regarded as evidence of at least an embryonic working class consciousness. Effective strikes depended on workforce solidarity, united action. Strike-breakers were known as 'scabs' or 'blacklegs'.

The proportion of all employment that is in industries which were formerly strike-prone (docks and motor manufacturing, for example), has declined. Workforces and electorates (in which manual workers are now a minority) have accepted legal restraints on employees' 'right to strike'. Globalisation has placed employees' jobs at risk if employers concede demands that make enterprises uncompetitive. Simultaneously, legislation on minimum pay has transferred the grievances of lower-paid workers out of the industrial and into the political arena.

Workers have become more likely to pursue improvements in their terms and conditions by negotiating 'the labour process'; addressing issues such as training and job grading. That said, strikes are still a powerful weapon, but usually with high risks to the strikers as well as their employers.

See also **Human resource management; Industrial relations; Trade unions.**

Hyman, R. (1972, 1984), *Strikes,* Fontana, Glasgow.

Lane, T. and Roberts, K. (1971), *Strike at Pilkingtons*, Fontana, London.

Silver, B.J. (2003), *Forces of Labor: Workers' Movements and Globalization Since 1870,* Cambridge University Press, New York.

Structural differentiation

See Division of labour.

Structural-functionalism

See Functionalism.

Structuralism

A France-based intellectual movement which insists that the task of the social and cultural sciences is to identify stable, underlying structures on which the immediately observable (and relatively unstable and variable) rests.

Marxism, insofar as it claims that all else arises from a sub-structure of class relationships, can be regarded as a structuralist theory. At the time when structuralism was fashionable, Louis Althusser (1918–1990) was its main Marxist exponent in France. However, the French structuralists were inspired mainly by Saussurian linguistics. Claude Levi-Strauss (1908–) became structuralism's best-known and leading exponent. He sought to identify universal ways of thinking, always expressed through language, which he believed were rooted in basic human nature (the constitution of the human brain).

Structuralism enjoyed a brief period of popularity in the 1960s and 1970s before encountering a formidable post-structuralist critique.

See also **Althusser, L.; Critical realism; Levi-Strauss, C.; Post-structuralism.**

Hawkes, T. (2003), *Structuralism and Semiotics*, Routledge, London.

Structuration

The concept was coined by Anthony Giddens (1938–), the British sociologist. It is an attempt to overcome the opposition in sociology between explanations in terms of social structure (society creates man) and explanations in terms of human agency (man creates society).

Giddens contends that structure and agency are not really in opposition, that each is embedded in the other. Structures are said to be outcomes of behaviour, and are maintained only as a result of actors behaving in ways that are meaningful to them. However, we act in regular and fairly predictable ways because our knowledge is socially structured. So action presumes structure, and structure presumes agency. Structuration is a process, indicating that what we call structures have some fluidity and are susceptible to change.

Whether Giddens really has solved any key problems in sociology remains a matter of debate. There had been earlier efforts to reconcile structure and agency: Talcott Parsons' (1902–1979) 'voluntaristic' theory of action, and Peter Berger and Thomas Luckmann's account of the social construction of reality. Critics argue that Giddens simply restates the problem, and that inventing the term structuration does not of itself generate any testable hypotheses about the relative strengths of structure and agency, or the conditions on which their relative strengths depend.

See also **Agency; Giddens, A.; Symbolic interaction; Voluntaristic action.**

Berger, P. and Luckmann, T. (1967), *The Social Construction of Reality*, Allen Lane, London.

Giddens, A. (1979), *Central Problems in Social Theory,* Macmillan, London.

S

Subaltern studies

Subaltern sociology seeks to recover and use the experiences and knowledge of groups who occupy privileged positions (for seeing all sides), but where a normal condition for occupying these positions is that they remain voiceless.

Subalterns were officers below the rank of captain in European colonial armies. In Britain's Indian army, subaltern positions could be occupied by Indians while higher ranks were exclusively European. Subalterns were required to follow orders and to convey commands to other ranks. They occupied a unique position from which they could know about, and had to know about, the experiences and feelings of both officers and men. However, the subaltern's private thoughts, whatever these were, had to remain hidden from all parties. Subalterns had invisible power. They could covertly foment unrest among the ranks. They could subvert their superiors' intentions by following instructions rigidly to the letter (taking things to extremes) even when they could see that this was subverting the aims. A condition, always, was public silence.

Subaltern sociology is an emancipatory sociology, akin in many ways to post-colonial sociology. The term subaltern studies was first used by Marxism-influenced Indian historians who wanted to challenge the western imperialist historical story. However, the term has been adopted more widely – in other disciplines (including sociology) and in studies of other subordinate people. Subaltern sociology is similar to but simultaneously critical of other attempts to give voice to the oppressed.

Critics query whether it is possible to represent the positions, feelings and outlooks of diverse bodies of allegedly oppressed people, be they women, gays or the colonised. The views of those who speak out are likely to be heard and recorded, but do they speak for, have they ever spoken for, larger numbers of 'silent voices'? Gayatry Spivak (1942–), an Indian-American, has discussed the problem of gaining access to the minds of people whose subordinate conditions have been designed to prevent them from even developing, let alone publicly proclaiming, alternative discourses. She offers the case of Hindu widows in India who have practised suttee – self-immolation on their husbands' funeral pyres. None have been able to explain after the event how and why they submitted to this practice.

See also **Colonialism.**

Spivak, G. (1988), 'Can the subaltern speak?' in C. Nelson and L. Grossberg (eds), *Marxism and the Interpretation of Culture*, Macmillan, Basingstoke.

S

Subculture

The culture of any specific group (an age group, occupational group, neighbourhood or religious group, or gays, for example) which is constructed from elements of a wider culture of which it is therefore a sub.

The concept has been most used in studying youth subcultures, but a central issue has always been to identify the wider cultures of which specific youth cultures are subs. Is it specifically consumer culture nowadays? Are some youth cultures better described as counter-cultures rather than subcultures? Functionalist sociologists have regarded mainstream youth cultures as subs of a general societal culture, thus enabling youth cultures to accomplish continuing socialisation. Marxist sociologists have preferred to interpret youth cultures as subs of particular class cultures – middle class and working class. In practice, most youth cultures appear to combine mixtures of elements.

The subculture concept has also been used extensively in the study of deviance. In deviant subcultures behaviour which is regarded as deviant (and criminal) in the wider society is both normal statistically and regarded as perfectly normal. An example is the recreational use of soft drugs by young people. Petty thieving in certain subcultures is another example. The question then becomes how to account for the genesis of deviant subcultures, which is addressed by various theories of deviance.

See also **Counter-culture; Deviance; Youth culture.**

Brake, M. (1980), *The Sociology of Youth Culture and Youth Subcultures*, Routledge, London.

Suburb

See Urbanism.

Superstructure (and base)

See Marx, K.

Surplus value

A Marxist concept: it is the difference between the value produced by a person's labour and what the worker is paid by the employer. The difference, the surplus value, is appropriated as profit by the capitalist employer.

See also Marx, K.

Surveillance

The monitoring of a population's activities, usually the activities of citizens by the state, but also of employees by employers, and citizens by non-state organisations.

The French sociologist Michel Foucault (1926–1984) is the original source of the view that surveillance has increased in modern societies. Foucault based his arguments on the surveillance accomplished by professions, especially medicine and social work. Subsequently the surveillance concept has become even more prominent in sociology on account of the heightened capacity for surveillance created by new technologies:

- The possibility of eavesdropping on email and telephone communications, and Internet use. In the UK around a quarter of a million intercepts are authorised every year, 1000 every day.

S

- The spread of CCTV.
- Market research organisations that draw together data on households' characteristics, their consumer behaviour and credit profiles.
- The quantity of data on citizens that is stored by government departments in computer files which are susceptible to theft and hacking.
- Tracking citizens' movements via scannable bars on passports (one part of the 'war on terror').
- Proposals to introduce identity cards in the UK, on or through which various bundles of information about individuals may be shared and accessed.

Earlier sociologists saw the modern city as a milieu in which individuals could be anonymous, and commented on individuals' ability to compartmentalise their lives. Some present-day sociologists believe that we are now in age where privacy is increasingly endangered.

See also **Foucault, M.; Panopticon metaphor.**

Coleman, R. (2004), *Reclaiming the Streets: Surveillance, Social Control and the City*, Willan, Cullompton.

Surveys

This is the kind of research with which sociology is most closely associated. Ever since sampling theory was developed in the early decades of the twentieth century, and researchers realised that a relatively small sample could allow conclusions to be drawn about a much larger population, the survey has been sociology's favoured method of data collection.

Surveys are not necessarily, but in practice they are almost always, sample surveys. Samples may be selected randomly or by quota. Respondents may be interviewed face to face or by telephone. Alternatively, questionnaires can be sent out by mail, or placed on the World Wide Web, while a sample is invited by email to 'click' to the site and answer the questions. The information gathered is most likely to be quantitative or quantifiable, but qualitative evidence (answers to open-ended questions) may also be collected. These different kinds of evidence will then be analysed using different methods.

Thanks to surveys, in nearly every country there is now a wealth of information about people's circumstances, behaviour and attitudes. Future historians will know far more about ourselves than we have been able to discover about our own ancestors.

See also **Interviews; Qualitative analysis; Quantitative analysis; Questionnaires; Sampling.**

Marsh, C. (1982), *The Survey Method*, Allen and Unwin, London.

Symbol

See sign.

Symbolic interactionism

This term was coined by Herbert Blumer (1900–1987). The core contentions are that societies are constituted of interacting individuals and that we mostly interact symbolically rather than physically or otherwise mechanistically. Hence the proper subject matter of sociology is symbolic interaction.

Symbolic interactionism notes that we behave towards and attempt to influence the behaviour of others using symbols – such as words, gestures, dress. In selecting symbols we attempt to convey meanings which will be interpreted (accurately, we usually hope) by the receivers. In a similar way we interpret the symbolic behaviour of others. We all act towards events, situations and people on the basis of what they mean to us. Symbolic interactionists study how people convey and interpret meanings in their own and other people's bodies, words, biographies and situations. We act not on the basis of how things really are (whatever this may mean) but according to how we perceive them. Following George Herbert Mead (1863–1931), symbolic interactionists treat our 'selves', our conceptions of who we are, as a product of our interactions with others. A symbolic interactionist claim is that both our selves and societies are always emergent. We constantly 'negotiate' with others about what each of us means, and how to construe and respond to a given situation. Sometimes there is consensus, sometimes there is conflict, sometimes there is simply a difference in points of view. The key point, according to symbolic interactionists, is that society is not solid but is always unstable, in a process of becoming.

In the 1960s symbolic interactionism provided the first serious challenge to positivism in sociology. Symbolic interactionists insist that humans' ability to communicate symbolically makes them different from other animals, and that human behaviour needs to be interpreted rather than explained in terms of hard and fast laws of cause and effect. Rather than conducting large-scale surveys and measuring variables, symbolic interactionists have preferred participant observation and other qualitative methods. In the 1960s the symbolic interactionist approach in sociology clashed head-on with functionalist perspectives. Symbolic interactionism had supportive sister movements – ethnomethodology and Erving Goffman's (1922–1982) dramaturgical work – but among these symbolic interactionism was the senior, the most widely supported, partner.

The big criticism to which symbolic interactionism has always been vulnerable is that it fails to address big issues concerning politics, the economy and the associated inequalities. Symbolic interactionists reply that their intention is not to exclude such big issues but that the macro-picture needs to be built upwards starting from the study of small-scale interactions. In practice this building up has never been accomplished. So by the 1970s the coexistence of two sociologies was being noted. One sociology saw individuals' actions as the product of larger social structures. The other treated structures as the always unstable and emergent outcomes of the actions/interactions of individual agents.

In the 1960s symbolic interactionism rapidly became more than just a theory. It inspired a series of new sociologies – of crime, education, organisations and more. This was largely through an immediate spin-off, namely, labelling theory. Symbolic interactionists argue that crime is not a property of acts themselves but a label applied by particular labellers. Similarly, criminal and deviant are labels. So who is doing the labelling and what are the consequences of being labelled? The same questions could be asked about under-achievers at school, hospital patients who are labelled as sick and other groups. The premises of symbolic interactionism require investigators to 'appreciate' (to somehow get inside the minds) of their subjects. On account of the investigators' predilection for studying drug users, convicted offenders and other low-status groups, the movement gave sociology a reputation for habitually being on the side of the underdog. In principle there was no reason why appreciative studies should not have been undertaken of white elites in South Africa in the apartheid era, but this was not the investigators' choice. Many were willing to be identified with 'the other side'. Another shibboleth of positivism that was under attack in the 1960s was value neutrality. Many sociologists decided that this was neither possible nor desirable and were upfront in parading their own values, politics and sympathies.

See also **Blumer, H.; Ethnography; Hermeneutics; Labelling theory: Mead, G.H.; Participant observation.**

Blumer, H. (1969), *Symbolic Interactionism: A Perspective on Method*, Prentice Hall, Engelwood Cliffs.

Rock, P. (1979), *The Making of Symbolic Interactionism*, Macmillan, London.

Symmetrical family

A new type of nuclear family that Michael Young (1915–2002) and Peter Willmott identified as emergent in Britain in the 1960s and early 1970s, initially among the middle classes. Husbands and wives both held paid jobs. Housework and childcare were shared between the partners.

Subsequent investigations have all indicated that family roles remain far less symmetrical than Young and Willmott envisaged.

See also **Dual-career family; Family; Young, M.**

Young, M. and Willmott, P. (1973), *The Symmetrical Family*, Routledge, London.

S

Taboo

Anything that is absolutely forbidden; infringement is totally unacceptable. Incest and sex between an adult and a child are examples.

Tautology

Something that is necessarily true as a result of the definitions of the terms that are used. Tautological propositions cannot be falsified. If classes are defined as groups standing in common relationships to the means of production, then persons who sell their labour power are necessarily a class.

The appearance of tautologies in sociology often indicates an attempt to settle by appropriate definitions matters which should really be settled on the basis of evidence.

Taxonomy

An alternative term for a typology.

See Typology.

Taylor, Frederick Winslow (1856–1915)

See Scientific management.

Taylorism

See Scientific management.

Technocracy

Rule by technical experts.

This theory had a brief wave of popularity between the 1940s and 1960s. It was believed that dependence on technical experts would lead to control of businesses and government passing into the hands of a new class of technocrats. This was among the processes allegedly leading to a convergence between all industrial societies (capitalist and socialist).

Today the consensus in sociology is that technical experts are part of a 'service class' rather than the ultimate rulers.

See also **Convergence thesis; Managerial revolution; Information economy/Information society; Service class; Upper class.**

Ellul, J. (1965), *The Technological Society*, Cape, London.

Galbraith, J.K. (1967), *The New Industrial State*, Penguin, Harmondsworth.

Touraine, A. (1971), *The Post-Industrial Society,* Random House, New York.

Technological determinism

This treats technology as the independent variable that causes other things. The most common expressions have been the claim that industrialism was the result of scientific and technological discoveries such as steam power, and treating technology as the determinant of organisational structure and work processes.

Nowadays there are few, if any, technological determinists in sociology. The counter-arguments are that, first, the kinds of scientific and technological knowledge that are developed, and second, the uses to which such knowledge is put, are dependent on the prevailing economic, political and social arrangements.

See also **Alienation; Information economy/Information society; Labour process theory; Organisations.**

Blauner, R. (1964), *Alienation and Freedom*, University of Chicago Press, Chicago.

Woodward, J. (1965), *Industrial Organization: Theory and Practice,* Oxford University Press, London.

Technology

Machines, equipment and implements which, allied to appropriate techniques, are used to produce goods, services and experiences.

Teleology

An explanation in terms of an outcome or effect.

In the natural sciences explanations are almost always in terms of antecedent or concurrent causes. In the human sciences teleological explanations are generally considered acceptable if they are in terms of individuals' or groups' purposes, and sometimes (far more controversially) the functions performed for a larger social body.

T

Telework

Work that is done remotely, when the worker is linked to a workplace by telephone or, nowadays more typical, email and the Internet. Telework may be done at home, but not necessarily – it can be done anywhere. Homework may be, but is not necessarily telework.

Telework is expected to become more common basically because it has become possible to organise many tasks in this way. There are said to be benefits to the employer (saves on office space) and employee (saves travel time and costs, and can work flexible hours). In practice, however, the number of 100 per cent teleworkers remains small. It appears that people (managements and workers) need regular face-to-face interaction in order to establish and maintain trust relations. Also, teleworkers often feel deprived of the socio-psychological benefits of workplace interaction, and feel at risk of being treated as second-class employees (overlooked for promotion etc.).

See also **Domestic labour.**

Texts

In sociology a text can be a written document or anything else that can be analysed as if it were a written document (TV programmes and films, for example). The key criterion is that a text has an existence beyond its author and the context of its creation. Texts are therefore believed to have different properties and (potentially) different and wider implications than mere speech.

See also **Content analysis.**

Thatcherism

The policies associated with Margaret Thatcher, who was UK prime minister from 1979–1990.

Margaret Thatcher is the sole British politician whose name has become an ism. Her governments broke a former post-war political consensus, and her policies led to radical changes in most aspects of life in Britain. The key Thatcher policies were:

- Monetarism: treating the money supply as the key economic indicator, and making control of the money supply, so as to control price inflation (rather than holding down unemployment), the principal aim of economic policy.
- Free market, neo-liberal economic policies: the privatisation of nationalised industries; opening markets, including financial markets, to international competition; disempowering (some) professions; and curbing the power of trade unions.
- Rolling back the welfare state: transferring council houses into owner-occupation; tying state welfare payments to the rate of price

increases rather than the (usually higher) rate of wage rises – work had to be made to pay.

- Boosting the rewards for success via lower taxes on high incomes.

Margaret Thatcher was also (in)famous for her tough stances vis-à-vis immigration and law and order, and her willingness to stand up for Britain's interests (as she perceived them) in Europe, and her anti-communism. Although she was the UK's first female prime minister, Thatcher was a self-declared non-feminist.

See also **Monetarism; Neo-liberalism; Privatisation.**

Evans, E.J. (2004), *Thatcher and Thatcherism*, Routledge, London.

Theory

This term is very widely used (possibly over-used) in sociology, and can refer to any statement that is not a straightforward description of what can be observed. A theory may be:

- An explanatory statement, which identifies a cause.
- Definitions of concepts and their relationships to one another; a classifying scheme; a typology.
- Claims about the character of entire societies, usually modern societies. This is the kind of theory that is associated with sociology's founding fathers. Their successors have engaged in debates about the new kinds of industrial societies that were being created after 1945 with the spread of affluence and strengthened welfare states, and the differences (were they lessening?) between different kinds of industrial societies (capitalist and communist); and current debates about the character of post-industrial or postmodern societies.
- The philosophy of the social sciences (sometimes called social theory to distinguish it from the above types of sociological theory): the kinds of true knowledge about the social that are possible; ontological claims about the fundamental nature of social reality – is it a structure, a system, symbolic interaction, social facts, or something else?

The major theories in sociology (such as Marxism, functionalism, symbolic interactionism) embrace all the above meanings of theory.

Cuff, E.C, Sharrock, W.W. and Francis, D.W. (2006), *Perspectives in Sociology*, fifth edition, Routledge, London.

Thick description

A likely goal of extended qualitative fieldwork, which includes participant observation and unstructured interviews. A thick description is a highly detailed account of a situation or event, which contains evidence about the participants' actions, thoughts and feelings.

Third Way

See Giddens, A.

Third world

A redundant term, except for historical purposes. The first world was the capitalist west. The second world was communist. The third world was the rest. These other countries were being beckoned towards the capitalist and communist roads, but it was possible that they would independently choose entirely different futures.

The old second world has now disappeared, and the globe is now conceptualised in alternative ways, sometimes as comprising advanced, intermediate and developing or poorer countries, and sometimes into civilisations (western, Islamic, Asian etc.).

See also **Development.**

Thomas, William Isaac (1863–1947)

'If men define situations as real they are real in their consequences.'

Thomas is best known in present-day sociology for the above quotation which is from a paper that he presented at the 1927 meeting of the American Sociological Society and which subsequently appeared in its (somewhat obscure) proceedings. However, Thomas was a prominent member of the Chicago School and was interested primarily in life histories, and how social histories are reflected in the biographies of individuals. His really major work (with Florian Znaniecki) was a study of Polish peasants who migrated into the United States.

See also: **Chicago School; Mead, G.H.**

Thomas, W.I. (1927), 'The behavior pattern and the situation', *Publications of the American Sociological Society: Papers and Proceedings,* 22nd Annual Meeting, Vol. 22, Nos 1–13.

Thomas, W.I. and Znaniecki, F. (1918/1920), *The Polish Peasant in Europe and America,* Dover, New York.

Time

Time is among the major ways in which we organise our lives. Most things have proper times or best times, and need enough time. The importance of social relationships to those involved may be judged by how much time they spend together. Who waits for whom and for how long, is a good guide to the relative class positions, status and authority of those concerned. Hence sociology must be interested in how time is organised, by whom, and the implications for everyone. Sociology has probably erred by tending to take time for granted, as simply given.

Time does have natural, given properties. The day and the year are not social constructs. However, this does not apply to the ways in which, around these givens, we organise working days, weeks, years and lives. All domains of life have their own 'social times'; work organisations, families, religions, leisure activities. How most of these social times arose is now lost in history. Once established they have become resilient, deeply embedded in human cultures and individuals' minds.

However, industrialisation and urbanisation required major changes in the organisation of social times. In modern societies people work by the clock as opposed to the requirements of nature. Activities are coordinated by the minute, and by fractions of a second in the case of some electronic operations. During industrialisation workforces had to be disciplined to accept the new time regime. This has subsequently been modified, but never subjected to a thorough overhaul. Rather, since the nineteenth century workdays have generally become shorter, while weekends and holidays have lengthened.

In recent decades a further phase of modernisation, the transition to post-industrialism, has involved the destandardisation of much that had formerly become standard. Work has been dispersed into evenings and weekends. Increased rates of employment among women have created higher total paid workloads in work-rich households. This is the context of current debates about mounting time pressure, the so-called time crunch. Are some people basically short of time? Or is the problem a clash of working time and family time schedules? What about leisure? It seems to have become more difficult for members of teams and clubs to coordinate their schedules so that they are all available at the same time once or twice a week. So teams and clubs may become pools from which those who are available participate on given occasions. Individual exercise (in gyms, parks or streets) enables people to participate at their own convenience. Are there costs in social capital?

Some forecast that time will become a major political issue during the twenty-first century.

Adam, B. (1995), *Timewatch: The Social Analysis of Time*, Polity, Cambridge.

Zerubavel, E. (1981), *Hidden Rhythms*, University of Chicago Press, Chicago.

Time budgets, time diaries

Surveys in which samples are persuaded to keep diaries recording their activities at successive intervals (usually every 15 or 30 minutes). They may also be asked to state where they were, and who else was present. Specific uses of time (such as ironing clothes) are aggregated into broader categories (usually housework, childcare, paid work, travel, personal maintenance, and a residue which is described as leisure time).

The evidence from these studies, which in Britain have been conducted occasionally since the 1960s, makes it possible to chart historical trends in time use (are we working less?), to compare time use in different countries, and by different sections of the populations within countries (age groups, men and women, social classes).

These diaries offer reasonably accurate accounts of the amounts of time that are spent on activities that are done regularly and frequently, and which account for substantial amounts of time (such as paid work and watching television) but are less sensitive to activities that are done occasionally (such as going on holiday or playing cricket) which would probably not occur at all on the days for which diaries were completed by most respondents.

> Gershuny, J. (2000), *Changing Times: Work and Leisure in Postindustrial Society*, Oxford University Press, Oxford.

Time series

A set of standardised measurements at equally spaced intervals, such as annual birth rates, death rates and crime rates.

Time–space distanciation

A rather clumsy phrase that is used to describe how space has been compressed by improvements in transport and electronic communications. It is now possible to be in touch instantaneously by email or telephone with someone on the opposite side of the world. Electronic communication takes no time at all, and air travel enables us to reach in hours destinations which two centuries ago would have involved a journey of a week or more. In this sense, time, like space, is compressed.

> *See also* **Information economy/information society**.

Tocqueville, Alexis de (1805–1859)

A French aristocrat and Member of the Chamber of Deputies who visited the United States in 1831–2, officially to examine the prison system, but subsequently produced acclaimed books which compared the history and politics of the United States, France and Britain.

De Tocqueville believed that there was an inevitable tension between the principles of liberty and equality (two clarion calls of the French Revolution, along with fraternity), and that democracy was liable to produce authoritarian governments which ruled fragmented masses, or a tyranny of the majority over minorities. In the United States, be argued, these dangers had been avoided because the colonies had gained experience of self-government prior to independence from Britain, the decentralised political system left space that could be filled by voluntary associations and within which minorities could organise, and religious pluralism led to higher levels of participation (good for building a strong civil society) than in France. Moreover, he found that the United States was pervaded by a culture of individualism.

T

De Tocqueville also believed that there was inevitable tension between Europe's traditional status hierarchies on the one hand, and, on the other, trade, the market and money. This meant that old regimes could not last. He concluded that Britain had avoided revolution because its traditional hierarchies had been more open and fluid than was the case under the *ancien regime* in France.

See also **Democracy**.

Tocqueville, A. de (1835 and 1840, 1968), *Democracy in America*, Collins, Glasgow.

Tocqueville, A. de (1856, 1955), *The Old Regime and the French Revolution*, Doubleday, New York.

Toennies, Ferdinand (1855–1936)

A German sociologist who based his work around the distinction between *Gemeinschaft* and *Gesellschaft* (translated as community and association).

Toennies' concepts were intended to specify exactly how the European societies of his day were being transformed. In traditional *Gemeinschaft* societies life had been governed by natural will (*Wesenwille*) which expressed instincts, habits and convictions. Social relationships were organic, real, emotional and cooperative. People were typically immobile, positions were ascribed, and family and church played major roles in people's lives. Toennies (like many others of his time) regretted what was being lost. In *Gesellschaft* societies life was relatively artificial, governed by rational will (*Kurwille*), social relationships were contractual and impersonal, individualism ruled, and life was competitive.

Toennies' contrasts between the old and the new were similar to juxtapositions proposed by his contemporaries: Durkheim's distinction between mechanical and organic solidarity, and Weber's thesis about rationalisation.

See also **Association; Community; Urbanism**.

Toennies, F. (1887, 1955), *Community and Association*, Routledge, London.

T

Total institution

A term coined by the American sociologist Erving Goffman (1922–1982). Total institutions are actually total organisations in which inmates spend all their time, possibly for their entire lives, in isolation from the wider society to which the organisation belongs. Hospitals, prisons, boarding schools and closed monasteries are examples.

A total institution has extraordinary power over its inmates. Those entering may be subjected to rituals which mortify their existing identities. As inmates they will then acquire new social and personal identities. They are likely to become institutionalised, that is, dependent on the organisation and unable to cope with living in the wider society.

See also **Goffman, E**.

Totalitarianism

A total state, which controls all spheres of life – businesses, trade unions, professions, the media, sport, the arts and all others. State control may extend into the family and other parts of otherwise private life.

Totalitarianism is best used as a sociological ideal type to which specific regimes approximate to various extents. The term was coined in the twentieth century and was first applied to fascist regimes, then extended to communist states. Their power was believed to be more total than that of earlier authoritarian governments on account of their use of bureaucracy and multiple surveillance techniques.

See also **Communism; Democracy; Fascism; Pluralism.**

Roberts, D.D. (2006), *The Totalitarian Experiment in Twentieth Century Europe*, Routledge, London.

Tormey, S. (1995), *Making Sense of Tyranny: Interpretations of Totalitarianism*, Manchester University Press, Manchester.

Totemism

Emile Durkheim (1858–1917) believed that totemism was the most elementary, fundamental, form of religious life. It is certainly a widespread form. A totem is an object, animal or plant which is endowed with human qualities, treated as representing a group, a people, regarded as sacred, and worshipped accordingly.

How to explain totemism remains a topic of hot debate, especially among social anthropologists.

See also **Durkheim, E.; Religion.**

Trade cycle

See Keynes, J.M.

Trade union consciousness

This term was coined by Vladimir Lenin (1870–1924), the leader of the victorious Russian Bolsheviks. Lenin argued that if left to their own devices, workers would develop only a stunted form of class consciousness. This would be economistic and reformist, concerned about increases in wages, reduced working time, marginal improvements in conditions of work and so on. Lenin believed that a vanguard political party was needed to lead the working class to full revolutionary class consciousness.

See also **Lukacs, G.; Marxism.**

T

Trade unions

Combinations (their original name) of employees. A trade union aims to replace individual bargaining with collective bargaining over pay, hours of work and other terms and conditions of employment. Trade unions may also have wider political objectives which are pursued through support of a political party, The strike (and the threat of strike action) have always been trade unions' main weapons.

Initially trade unions had to struggle for the legal right to organise, and then for recognition by employers. Over time they were accepted in most industries and by most large companies, and collective bargaining was regarded as a means of enabling disputes to be settled peacefully. It has never been possible to establish and gain agreement over whether trade unions have been able to raise the share of economic output taken by labour.

Various kinds of trade unions have been identified. They can be based on skilled trades (the source of the name, *trade* unions), or they may seek to recruit all grades of employees in a particular industry, or they may be general unions, but these distinctions have never been clear cut (except in theory) and have become increasingly blurred over time due to union mergers.

There is agreement that the economic restructuring associated with post-industrialism has changed the character of trade union movements. In many countries, including Britain, trade union membership has declined, due mainly to the decline of employment in industries that had been densely unionised. Trade unionism used to be associated with the manual working class, but today in Britain managers and professional grade staff are the employees who are most likely to be in trade unions. Membership is generally much higher in the public sector than in the private sector.

An issue currently confronting trade unions in all countries is how to address the globalisation of the market economy and the growth of trans-national corporations. Internationalism has always been a trade union aspiration. It is now recognised that internationalisation is becoming a requirement if trade unions are to remain effective.

See also **Industrial relations; Professions; Strikes.**

Jackson, M.P. (1982), *Trade Unions*, Longman, London.

Traditional societies

In sociology traditions are not treated as having existed only in the past, though most (but not all) pre-modern societies are regarded as traditional. Something is said to be traditional if it is based on and legitimised by tradition, by custom. There can be traditional forms of family life, agriculture and government, for example. Needless to say, there are many different kinds of traditions and traditional societies – feudal and tribal, for example.

Max Weber (1864–1920) argued that in modern societies life was governed by a different kind of rational outlook, but even so, some traditions survive in all modern societies. Britain still has a monarchy. In modern societies traditions are sometimes revived, even invented, possibly as tourist attractions, and possibly in efforts to create or strengthen national or ethnic identities.

See also **Authority.**

Transexuals

See Transgender.

Transformation

See Social transformation.

Transgender

An umbrella term for a variety of conditions and groups. Note that there is a war over words among the signified about the correct terms to apply to different groups and conditions.

That said, transvestism is cross-dressing; men dressing as women and women as men. This may be an accepted ritual, as in Christmas pantomime and drag entertainment. Alternatively, cross-dressing may be covert. Those involved may or may not be gay, lesbian or bisexual.

Transexuality is crossing to the other sex from the one assigned at birth (usually on the basis of biology). Nowadays sex surgery may be involved. Thus persons who were formerly gay or lesbian become heterosexuals.

How to explain these cases is hotly debated. Sociologists are interested primarily for any light that may be shed on how gender and sexual identities are constructed and acquired.

See also **Gender; Sexuality.**

Ekins, R. and King, D. (2006), *The Transgender Phenomenon*, Sage, London.

http://transexual.org

Transition

A type of change: from a start point to a known destination. The change may be by an individual or group (such as the transition of young people from school to work), or by a society (from communism to capitalism, for example).

The term is probably over-used. Its use is justified only when:

- just one destination is possible, or
- the destination is the goal of all the relevant actors, and they have the capability to achieve this goal.

Using the transition concept is always liable to overlook the role of the agency of those allegedly in transition, and others who are able to intervene. The adulthoods towards which young people head may be transformed adulthoods as a result of the young people's experiences during childhood and youth. Post-communist countries have in fact become different kinds of democracies and market economies.

Transition is just one of many possible kinds of change, and there are enough concepts available to distinguish between these many different types.

> *See also* **Development; Evolution; Revolution; Social change; Social transformation.**

Trans-national corporations

These are key players in the global market economy. Trans-national corporations have bases in particular countries, but operate in many others as well. Trans-nationals are products of the expansion of capitalism. They have helped to drive, and simultaneously they are strengthened by, globalisation.

The original multinationals (the term that was then used) were the big oil companies and motor vehicle manufacturers. Trans-nationals now operate in all business sectors – soft drinks, alcohol, fast food, banking, advertising and so on.

Trans-nationals are necessarily of interest to sociology on account of their sheer power. Their budgets exceed the value of the national economies of many smaller countries. All countries want the trans-nationals to invest, to create jobs and boost the local economies. The companies can drive hard bargains. They can decide to 'make' or at least 'take' their profits wherever taxes are lowest. Their top executives do likewise. Countries can chose either low taxes or no tax receipts from the trans-nationals. The companies are able, in effect, to buy the services of local politicians. They can produce where labour is cheapest and sell wherever prices are highest.

Some well-known trans-nationals such as Coca Cola are basically just brand names. They do not produce any raw materials. They do not manufacture. They do not transport their products or retail the goods. Everything is outsourced. The brand names rule.

The growth of trans-national companies raises hugely important questions. How can they be controlled? In what sense can countries be truly democratic when their economic fates depend on making themselves hospitable to trans-nationals?

> *See also* **Capitalist; Globalisation; Upper class.**

> Klein, N. (2000), *No Logo: Taking Aim at the Brand Bullies*, Flamingo, London.

> Sklair, L. (2002), *Globalization: Capitalism and its Alternatives*, Oxford University Press, Oxford.

Transvestites

See Transgender.

Triangulation

Examining a subject from two or more angles. The basic principles are from geometry. Photographing a building from two angles enables a viewer of the photographs to work out the shape of the entire object. In sociological research the equivalent is to use two or more research methods (maybe observation and interviews, or quantitative and qualitative) and two or more investigators. The end result should be a more valid description of the subject than would arise from repeated use of the same method.

See also **Research methods.**

Trust

Social relationships where the parties feel that they can rely upon each other for particular kinds of assistance, which may be financial, emotional support, information, assistance in finding a job or other help. Trust is a key component of social capital. Sociologists are interested in trust because:

- It is regarded as a condition for orderly social life.
- There is a debate about whether, in our present time, trust (and social capital) are declining.
- Trust relationships can create included and excluded groups.

See also **Bourdieu, P.; Capital; Putnam, R.**

Typology

Any scheme containing two or more categories into which specific cases can be placed.

Sociologists use typologies constantly. Societies are classified into traditional and modern, industrial and post-industrial. Groups are classified as primary and secondary. Workers are placed into types of social classes (such as working class and middle class).

Typologies may be constructed ad hoc, on the basis that they appear useful for arranging the evidence from an investigation. However, enduring typologies tend to have the following characteristics:

- The criteria for distinguishing types are explicit.
- The criteria are selected because they are believed to have (and evidence tends to confirm that they do have) significant implications and consequences.
- All possible cases can be placed.

T

Unconscious

See Freud, S.

Underclass

A class that is separate from and beneath the employed working class.

In sociology, debates about the possible emergence of an underclass in Britain began in the 1970s amid rising levels of unemployment. During the 1980s the underclass debate spread into politics and the media where two versions of the underclass thesis were created:

- a left version which blamed unemployment and harsh government welfare policies which prevented the poorest from leading normal, decent lives
- a right version which blamed 'workshy scroungers' and an over-generous welfare state.

Meanwhile, sociologists were disputing whether an underclass really existed. There were certainly long-term unemployed and very poor people in Britain. However, these households were not set apart socially because they lived in neighbourhoods and their children attended schools alongside children from employed families. Also, it was shown that most of the unemployed – the vast majority – were keen to work, and were typically working class in their political proclivities. Moreover, the split between the employed and the unemployed was blurred by people who were in and out of work.

During the 1990s the term underclass was set aside in favour of its European equivalent, excluded groups, which are currently surrounded by the same controversies as the underclass in the 1980s – left and right versions, and whether there really are any truly excluded strata.

> *See also* **Murray, C.; Poverty; Social exclusion; Unemployment; Working class.**
>
> MacDonald, R. (ed.) (1997), *Youth, the Underclass and Social Exclusion*, Routledge, London.

Underdevelopment

See Development.

Unemployment

In Britain there are two ways of measuring unemployment. First, the 'claimant count' of the number of people receiving state benefits due to their unemployment. Second, there is the method recommended by the International Labour Office which is used for making international comparisons This is based on Labour Force Surveys and counts people as unemployed if they are not working, are looking for work, and are willing to start immediately if offered a suitable job. This gives a consistently higher figure than the claimant count. A point to note is that unemployment is different from non-employment: the economically inactive (retired, students, long-term incapacitated) are not unemployed on either definition.

Economists distinguish several types of unemployment: frictional (when people are between jobs), cyclical (due to economic recession) and structural (when there is a mismatch between characteristics of the unemployed and the available jobs – the unemployed may lack appropriate skills or live in the wrong places). It has been suggested that we now face a fourth, a new type of unemployment, the result of jobless growth.

In terms of the experiences of the unemployed, a rather different set of distinctions than the above is probably more relevant:

- One-off, transitional, during job changing, or straight after leaving school or college.
- Recurrent, when people are in and out of work. This condition is sometimes called sub-employment or under-employment.
- Long-term.

The effects of long-term unemployment on those concerned have been investigated since the 1930s, and there appears to have been no significant change over time. The unemployed suffer a number of deprivations:

- Reduced income.
- A deficit in 'categories of experience' that are vital for psychological well-being. Having something to do, and social contact, are examples of such basic categories.
- Time structure.
- Status and self-identity.

Researchers have noted how, when unemployment becomes long-term, those concerned tend to go through an initial optimistic stage, which gives way to frustration, which eventually becomes resignation and apathy.

See also **Social Exclusion; Underclass**.

Forrester, V. (1999), *The Economic Horror*, Polity, Cambridge.

Jahoda, M. (1982), *Employment and Unemployment: A Social-Psychological Analysis,* Cambridge University Press, Cambridge.

U

Unintended consequences

'The unexpected always happens.' Unintended consequences have not been newly discovered by sociology, but in sociology these outcomes are considered extremely important, and are treated as 'the rule' rather than the exception.

Examples of unintended consequences include cases where public alarm amplifies crime; Max Weber's (1864–1920) arguments about a Protestant ethic accidentally assisting the take-off of capitalism; and people seeking upward mobility generating economic growth but leaving no one any further ahead.

Functionalist sociologists distinguish manifest and latent functions. The latter may be explained in terms of a 'hidden hand' that guides our conduct.

Action theorists recognise that identifying people's intentions is just the first stage in sociological explanation. The outcomes of behaviour may be very different from the actor's intentions. Indeed, everyone pursuing their own purposes may lead to outcomes that no one intended or desired, to which all parties then react, thus repeating the cycle *ad infinitum*.

Universalism

This means applying the same rule to all, or in all situations, when selecting applicants for university entry or for jobs, for example. Particularism is the opposite of universalism. This means 'treating each case on its individual merits' which may allow people from given families, schools, a sex or ethnic group to be favoured.

Universalism and particularism are one set of Talcott Parson's (1902–1979) pattern variables, but the terms are now used in sociology outside the remainder of the Parsonian theoretical scheme.

See also **Parsons, T.; Pattern variables.**

Unobtrusive measurements

Research methods which leave the subjects unaware that they are being investigated. The advantage of unobtrusiveness is that observer/experimenter effects (called Hawthorne effects in sociology) are avoided.

Unobtrusive measures may be:

- Covert: observation (participant or non-participant), using one-way mirrors, or tape-recording without disclosure of the recording (or at least the purpose of it) to the subjects.
- Indirect: via documents and other 'debris'.

All unobtrusive measurements, especially covert methods, raise ethical issues.

See also **Hawthorne effect; Research methods.**

Upper class

Sociologists are agreed that there is an upper class in present-day Britain and in all other capitalist societies, though this class does not feature in the discipline's class schemes. The reasons for this absence are the tiny size of the upper class (a core of only around 25,000 individuals in Britain), and that the questions about occupations that are used to classify the rest of the population fail to identify the upper class.

The pre-industrial upper class comprised the landowning aristocracy, headed by the monarch and titled nobles, and represented politically in the House of Lords. During the nineteenth century this upper class fused with the grand bourgeoisie (wealthy industrialists). The latter bought land and stately homes. The aristocracy invested in business. Both groups sent their sons to elite independent schools (paradoxically known as public schools).

The core of the present-day upper class comprises immensely wealthy individuals. Their life chances depend on how they deploy their wealth rather than the sale of labour power. This class is powerful (a result of its wealth) and is now international. Wealthy individuals are most likely to be based in particular countries but their wealth goes wherever in the world it will be safest, least taxed and command the highest returns. Members of the upper class have privileged access to the political elite. They have a very distinctive lifestyle through which they are linked to the traditional aristocracy and modern celebrities, and thereby are able to share the status of these groups.

See also **Capitalist; Class.**

Scott, J. (1982), *The Upper Class: Property and Privilege in Britain*, Macmillan, London.

Urbanism

Towns and cities are urban. Villages and the countryside are rural. Urbanisation is the shift of population from countryside to urban areas. Urbanism refers to the ways of life of urban dwellers. The importance of the concept of urbanism in sociology hinges on whether:

- there is a distinctive urban way of life, or ways of life, and
- whether any distinctive features are products of the characteristics of urban settlements themselves.

In the nineteenth and early twentieth centuries European and North American sociologists believed that they had identified such an urban way of life. This was during the era when urbanisation was at its peak in Europe and North America. At that time there were some glaring differences between village and city life, and these differences seemed most easily explained in terms of characteristics of the settlements themselves. In urban areas more people from more diverse backgrounds were packed together more densely than in rural settlements. In urban areas, residents

U

interacted with more people, but more of the people with whom they interacted were strangers, and social relationships tended to be more superficial than in rural areas. The German sociologist Ferdinand Toennies (1855–1936) juxtaposed *Gemeinschaft* and *Gesellschaft* (community and association). These words convey what were perceived as the most glaring rural–urban differences.

Whether the urban–rural contrast remains useful in economically advanced twenty-first-century societies is debatable. By the first half of the twentieth century 'urban villages' were being discovered within cities. Thus the community study became the staple way of investigating urban ways of life, and the urban–rural contrast seemed less glaring than had been suggested. Also, investigators revealed many different urban ways of life, and the ways of life in particular urban districts seemed to owe far more to characteristics of the inhabitants (their class and age composition, for example) than the districts themselves. Rural areas themselves have changed. Today villages are often populated partly by commuters and second-home owners. People who work in the countryside own televisions and motor cars, and rural businesses are run in much the same way as urban businesses. Urbanism has spread beyond geographically urban areas.

New words have been invented as cities have grown. A suburb is a residential district some distance from a city centre. Suburbanisation was made possible by the creation of mechanical public transport systems (buses, trains and trams). As suburbs were built, the 'inner city' became a particular type of urban district. Some inner-city districts became 'zones of transition' as businesses seeking central locations jostled residents for space. Residents who were able to do so uprooted to the suburbs, leaving 'zones of transition' to immigrants and other disadvantaged groups. However, in more recent times manufacturing and retail businesses have been uprooting to greenfield sites, and the middle classes, or sections of the middle classes, mainly students, young singles and childless couples, have moved back into the city centres and 'gentrified' these districts. This has provided further evidence of how it is characteristics of the residents rather than the physical properties and locations of settlements that determine the ways of life of the inhabitants. Television which keeps people 'in', and the motor car which enables them to 'go out' in private and travel further afield for services, have made people's lifestyles less dependent on exactly where they happen to live.

A conurbation is created when former separate urban areas fuse together, typically as a result of a large city swallowing smaller towns. The term metropolis was coined over 100 years ago to describe especially large and important cities. Megopolis was then proposed for the largest metropolises. Global cities contain concentrations of head offices and top executives of global businesses

See also **Chicago School; Conurbation; Gated communities; Gentrification; Wirth, L.**

Usurpation

See Social closure.

Utilitarianism

An English philosophical doctrine associated with Jeremy Bentham (1748–1832), James Mill (1773–1836) and the latter's son John Stuart Mill (1806–1873). The word 'utilitarianism' was coined by John Stuart Mill. However, Bentham is the source of its famous summary with the phrase that the greatest good is always that which brings 'the greatest happiness for the greatest number'.

The utilitarians were energetic in their advocacy of social reform (through applying utilitarian principles). Nowadays, the lasting reforms with which they are most closely associated, namely, the modern prison and the lunatic asylum, look less inspiring than the philosophy.

See also **Panopticon metaphor.**

Utopia

A term invented by Thomas More (1478–1535). Utopia is an ideal, perfect future state; an island in Thomas More's book. Today the term may be used to ridicule ideas as impractical, but a characteristic of humans is their ability to imagine alternative states, and ideas sometimes play a part in changing the world.

In sociology, debates about utopian thought usually start with Karl Mannheim's (1893–1947) claim that utopias (religious or secular) usually appeal to the disadvantaged who hope to change the world. Mannheim contrasted utopias with ideologies – ideas that justify the status quo and usually appeal to groups with vested interests in resisting change.

In recent times it has been argued that in our present post-industrial age, visions of the future are more likely to be dystopian than utopian: we worry about nuclear or ecological calamity and are bereft of visions of a better society.

See also **Progress.**

Frankel, B. (1987), *The Post-Industrial Utopians*, University of Wisconsin Press, Wisconsin.

Mannheim, K. (1929, 1936), *Ideology and Utopia*, Routledge, London.

U

Validity

A measurement is valid if it measures what it purports to measure. Invalidity is just one of several reasons why the information collected by researchers may be untrue. Others include the representativeness of samples.

Measurements may be invalid for different reasons:

- Questions are answered untruthfully.
- Lapses of memory by respondents.
- Unreliable questions, to which the same individuals give different answers on different occasions. Unreliable questions are always invalid, whereas reliability is not a guarantee of validity.
- Questions do not probe sufficiently (the sport participation rate will be higher if respondents are presented with a list of separate sports rather than just asked a single question).

Note that there are alternative ways of measuring the level of unemployment which produce very different estimates of the true level.

See also **Reliability; Sampling; Unemployment.**

Value freedom/neutrality

Can value judgements be derived from sociological research? No, sociology can resolve only disputes about facts.

Can sociological research itself be value free? No, our values must influence our choices of subjects to study, and the interpretations of evidence that we consider. In any case, objectivity (value freedom) is itself a value, and even if sociologists themselves try to be uncommitted, their work can still be shaped by the values of sponsors, and any effects can be shaped by the values of users.

Can sociology reach conclusions that are valid independently of anyone's values? Most sociologists will say 'Yes'.

Max Weber (1864–1920) began what became a heated debate about value freedom in sociology which, as suggested above, can be drawn to an agreed set of conclusions by separating the several issues that are involved.

See also **Weber, M.**

Values

Value has different meanings which are not easily separated from one another.

The value that we place on marketed goods and services can be measured by price. We also value our health, families and so on, but can these values be measured by price? Different people and different cultures may place different values on various things, but evaluations are part and parcel of life in all societies, so sociology clearly needs to pay attention to people's values.

Talcott Parsons' (1902–1979) functionalist scheme assumes both of the above, and treats social integration as depending ultimately on shared values. Critics have argued that social integration can be secured in other ways (power and interdependence). They also point out that people can interpret values and moral rules in different ways depending on the actor and the situation.

Since 1981 a programme of research has explored the values of the populations in a total of 85 different countries. These World Values Surveys have revealed some clear differences between western, Islamic, Asian and other groups of countries. The surveys also suggest that a global shift is taking place as countries first modernise and industrialise, then subsequently as they become post-industrial and postmodern. Initially there is decline in respect for traditions and religion, and more emphasis on economic betterment. Then there is a subsequent shift towards stressing the importance of quality of life issues – democracy, equality between the sexes and environmental matters.

Values are also ethical principles, examined by philosophers and promoted by moral entrepreneurs (religious and secular). These values tell us what is good and what is bad, and how we ought to behave. General values (truthfulness, the sanctity of human life) can be said to validate specific moral rules. In survey research, like the World Values Surveys, people's underlying values may be inferred from their answers to lists of attitude questions. Are the values that are inferred on this basis the same kinds of values that philosophers discuss, or the basis of the evaluations (maybe indicated by price) that people make in their everyday lives?

See also **Consensus; Morals; Pattern variables.**

Halman, L., Inglehart, R., Diez-Medrano, J., Luijkx, R., Moreno, A. and Basanez, M. (2007), *Changing Values and Beliefs in 85 Countries*, Brill, Leiden.

V

Variables

Things such as age, gender and social class which are not constant but vary from person to person and group to group are variables. The variations may be continuous, as with age and income, and these variations are measured on interval scales. Other variations are discrete (gender and social class, for example) and are measured on nominal or ordinal scales. Which type of scale is created has implications for the kinds of statistical analysis that can be undertaken.

'Variable sociology' has critics. It is accused (by symbolic interactionists, for example) of being inappropriately positivist, and misrepresenting the subject matter by splitting people and their cultures into separate variables.

See also **Blumer, H.**

Variance

See Measures of dispersion.

Verstehen

A German word that was introduced into sociology by Max Weber (1864–1920). *Verstehen* is a method for gaining access to other people's meanings and intentions. Weber believed that this was a necessary prelude to or part of causal explanation.

Verstehen is similar to understanding and empathising, but implies a more scientific process than lay people use in their everyday lives. A debate continues in sociology about whether *Verstehen* can really be qualitatively different from the imagining and introspection that are part of everyday life, and the sense in which this can be part of or a prelude to causal analysis and explanation.

See also **Empathy; Hermeneutics; Interpretive sociology; Weber, M.**

Victimology

The study of the victims of crime; a growth subject during the last 30 years.

The study of victims has produced more accurate estimates than were previously available about the true levels of different types of crime, and the social distribution of risks of vcitimisation. It has also:

- shown how the experience of being a victim of different kinds of crime varies by age, gender and social class
- produced a better understanding of the fear of crime
- facilitated better counselling and support for victims
- led to demands for victims' experiences and perspectives to be taken into account during the sentencing of offenders.

Victimology has also highlighted the roles of victims in the causation of various kinds of crime, ranging from leaving car and house doors unlocked to rape.

See also **British Crime Survey; Criminology.**

Walklate, S. (ed.) (2007), *Handbook of Victims and Victimology*, Willan, Cullompton, Devon.

Virtual reality

This is any computer-simulated environment. People participate in vision and often in sound also; tactile sensations are likely to be added, but smell and taste are unlikely to follow.

Sociologists are interested in virtual reality because people are spending more time using computers and 'online', that is, on the Internet. The impact of virtual reality on human societies is potentially momentous.

Will virtual realities replace real life as known up to now, with more and more 'anoraks' unwilling to leave their fantasy worlds?

Or, as currently seems more likely, will virtual realities add another dimension to conventional real world activities, relationships and interests?

See also **Cyberspace; Digitisation; Information economy/Information society**.

Woolgar, S. (ed.) (2002), *Virtual Society? Technology, Cyberbole, Reality*, Oxford University Press, Oxford.

Visual sociology

Most sociology exists as words. Information is gathered in interviews and questionnaires. Observations are written up as fieldnotes. Findings are presented in books, articles and lectures. Visual sociology adds another dimension.

There is a visual dimension to social life. Our experiences are, at least in part, of the buildings, mountains or whatever we can see. Visual sociology seeks to capture this dimension by recording the visual dimension that accompanies most speech communication and is part of human relationships, and which is inevitably debased when reduced to mere words.

www.visualsociology.org

www.visualsociology.org.uk

Vocabularies of motive

A phrase coined by C. Wright Mills (1916–1962). Vocabularies of motive are accounts which are acceptable (in given situations) as explanations and maybe justifications of actions. Whether an account will be accepted in either of these senses depends on the situation. For example, a young male may offer different accounts of his delinquent acts in court and when talking to friends.

Vocabularies of motive may be used as rationalisations (when actors wish to conceal their real reasons, and to justify to themselves or others having behaved in a particular way). However, as these vocabularies are learnt during socialisation as members of our societies, they are just as likely to be causes of our behaviour. Either way, becoming a competent member of a society requires learning its accepted vocabulary of motives.

V

See also **Rationalisation**.

Mills, C.W. (1940), 'Situated action and vocabularies of motive', *American Sociological Review*, 5, 904–93.

Voluntaristic action

The term 'voluntaristic' was coined by Talcott Parsons (1902–1979), and plots a mid-course between determinist and voluntary explanations of action.

A voluntaristic concept of action rejects the idea that people respond to their environments mechanistically, and that the socialisation of humans is akin to training other species to give involuntary responses to stimuli. Simultaneously, a voluntaristic concept rejects explanations in terms of free will, individuals acting purely on the basis of instincts, or their own purposes, choices and decisions. Action is regarded as retaining voluntary elements which operate within structural constraints, which may be internalised during socialisation. External constraints are treated as influencing action without eliminating choice.

The voluntaristic view has become the orthodox concept of social action in sociology. It is incorporated within symbolic interactionism, structuration theory, humanistic Marxism and elsewhere. However, whatever terms are used, the problem remains of assessing the relative weights of structure and agency in the explanation of all particular actions.

See also **Agency; Parsons, T.; Structuration**.

Voluntary associations

Alternatively called the third sector, non-governmental organisations (NGOs) or not-for-profit/non-profit organisations. These associations exist in civil society, in the space between the state and market on the one side, and families, kin, friends, neighbours and the rest of private life on the other. The 'voluntary' label indicates that the associations are not commanded into existence by governments, and membership is voluntary.

V

Voluntary associations may be charities, promote a sport, art or hobby, or campaign for a particular cause. Churches, trade unions, professional associations and political parties are sometimes included within definitions of the voluntary sector. Active voluntary associations with members from all sections of a population are taken to indicate that civil society is flourishing, and this is often regarded as a precondition for multi-party democracy to function properly.

See also **Active citizen; Civil society; Quango**.

Weber, Max (1864–1920)

A German scholar whose work ranged over several fields which, during his lifetime, were separating into different academic disciplines – sociology, law, politics and economics. Weber is claimed as a founding father by present-day sociology on account of his major contributions on a large number of topics that remain key issues in sociology today – about the subject's philosophical and scientific status, and the features that characterise western civilisation.

Weber argued that the social sciences were necessarily different from the natural sciences. He was definitely not a positivist. He rejected the notion that scientific laws govern human conduct. In Weber's view, behaviour had to be 'understood'. It could then be explained in terms of the meaningful actions of those concerned under specific historical conditions, not by referring to general laws. So Weber did not produce a general theory of society and history: he did not believe that such a theory was possible.

Weber was a methodological individualist (though he did not use this term). He did not believe that states, the economy or the family could actually do things. Explanations had to be meaningful at the level of individual actors. In constructing such explanations Weber argued that it was necessary to use ideal types (of Protestant, capitalist, charismatic leader etc.). Ideal types are logically pure simplifications of tendencies in orientations to action and actual conduct, and his supporters claim that Weber demonstrated their value in making real people's real behaviour comprehensible.

Another of Weber's well-defined positions was that the social sciences should be guided by the ideal of value freedom. This was despite the fact that individual social scientists would have values that influenced their choice of subject matter, interpretations of their evidence and so on. Value freedom was to be guaranteed by making individual scientists' claims subject to scrutiny and criticism by a scientific community which would distil truth which was independent of anyone's values.

In all the above ways Weber made important contributions to debates about the character of sociology as a discipline, and he is equally important in sociology for his ideas about the character of modern societies. In Weber's view, rationalisation was the master trend that underpinned the development of modern western civilisation. Weber distinguished several types of social action: affectual (governed by emotion), traditional (governed by custom), and rational within which action could be rational in relation to an ultimate value or in relation to a less exalted end, but in either case 'means' were selected in a calculating manner, as the best way of achieving a result.

Rationalisation was said to give rise to a particular kind of social organisation, bureaucracy, in which tasks were divided into offices, which were linked in a rational manner, each office was governed by clear rules, and officials were appointed strictly on the basis of their suitability. So a huge bureaucracy could then ruthlessly pursue its given objective (whatever this might be). Weber believed that bureaucratic (legal-rational) authority had replaced traditional authority under which leaders were recognised according to custom (and obeyed for similar reasons), and charismatic authority where leaders inspired followers by force of their personal qualities. In the modern age, charisma was said to be subject to routinisation (identified through rational procedures). This, in Weber's view, was leading to progressive disenchantment. There was a gloomy pathos in Weber's writing. People were believed to be surrendering their freedom, and excitement was being squeezed from life by an 'iron cage' of bureaucracy. Weber believed that a planned socialist economy would take rationalisation to a further extreme rather than deliver liberation.

Weber claimed to have identified the spark that had ignited the process of rationalisation in the west. This was Protestant religion with its values of individualism, hard work and self-reliance. Protestantism was not treated as 'the' cause of capitalism or any other features of the modern world, but was seen as a necessary catalyst amid other propitious conditions. Weber's work included studies of major world religions – Confucianism, Hinduism and Judaism. He believed that it was only within the occidental (Judaic-Christian) religions that a movement such as Protestantism could arise and that the consequent rationalisation of life could occur spontaneously. In other civilisations he believed that this simply could not happen, though this did not preclude any of the other civilisations adopting capitalism, bureaucratic administration and the like once the relevant models had been developed elsewhere.

Weber's relationship to Marx and Marxism has never been clear. One view is that Weber was engaged in a perpetual debate, seeking to rebut Marx. Another view is that Weber's targets were the Marxists of his own time, especially Germany's Social Democrats, and that Weber regarded his own work as adding to and amending rather than rebutting the work of Marx himself.

Weber's concept of class was somewhat different from that of Marx. Weber treated classes as products of markets (rather than formed through relationships of production). However, Weber agreed with Marx that a major class division was between those who bought and those who sold labour, though Weber went on to argue that there were class divisions among workers according to the types of labour that they could offer (their skills and qualifications). Weber also distinguished status groups (defined by the degrees of honour attached to their lifestyles). Class and status divisions were regarded as interdependent, but in Weber's view neither was reducible to the other. Weber went on to argue that political parties and other movements that sought power could mobilise support from specific classes or status groups, or a combination of the two, but that for politicians power could be an end in itself.

See also **Bureaucracy; Disenchantment; Hermeneutics; Ideal type; Methodological individualism; Protestant ethic; Rationality; Ritzer, G.**

Gerth, H.H. and Mills, C.W. (eds) (1946), *From Max Weber: Essays in Sociology*, Oxford University Press, New York.

Weber, M. (1905, 1930), *The Protestant Ethic and the Spirit of Capitalism*, Allen and Unwin, London.

Welfare state

A term used since the 1940s to refer to a state that guarantees the welfare of all citizens. Welfare is generally taken to include income maintenance (during sickness, long-term disability, unemployment and retirement, and child benefits), a minimum wage, education and healthcare. Housing, transport and some recreational services may also be included.

The foundations of the first welfare state were laid in Germany by Bismarck in the 1880s. The beginnings of a modern welfare state in Britain date from the national insurance schemes for healthcare, unemployment and retirement pensions introduced by the Liberal governments of 1906–14. Britain's welfare state was consolidated after the Second World War when the Labour government (1945–51) implemented the recommendations in the Beveridge Report (1942).

Welfare states have been stronger and more comprehensive in Northern Europe than in most other countries, However, an alternative way of interpreting the evidence is to recognise several different welfare regimes.

Since the 1970s in Britain and some other countries the welfare state has become weaker. In Britain, state benefit rates have fallen further and further behind other incomes. The role of social housing has been reduced. Private finance has become more important in higher education.

A current debate is about whether strong welfare states remain necessary to maintain social solidarity and cohesion, or whether such provisions may have been necessary and desirable during a particular stage in economic development, but have become less necessary and maybe undesirable as people have become better able to provide for themselves.

See also **Beveridge Report; Esping-Andersen, G.; Poverty; Social exclusion; Social policy; Social services; Socialism.**

Esping-Andersen, G. (1990), *The Three Worlds of Welfare Capitalism*, Princeton University Press, New Jersey.

W

Well-being

A concept that is being promoted by the positive psychology movement. Instead of preoccupation with negatives (the incidence of physical and mental illnesses), positive psychology seeks to understand how to raise people up the rungs of positive well-being. Levels of well-being are normally assessed by attitude scales measuring happiness and/or life satisfaction. Interest in well-being has spread alongside awareness that once people have been lifted out of poverty, further improvements in living standards do not leave them happier or more satisfied with their lives.

The relevant research has been successful in identifying happiness/life satisfaction promoters – good health, being married, having a good marriage, having supportive friends, work that is intrinsically satisfying and socially valued, and leisure activities that are pursued seriously and that involve working in groups. Exactly how to use this knowledge is unclear, and there is some dispute about the wisdom of making people more content with their current environments (economic, political, social, cultural and natural).

See also **Consumption; Positional goods; Quality of life; Standard of living.**

Haworth, J. and Hart, G. (eds) (2007), *Well-Being: Individual, Community and Social Perspectives,* Palgrave Macmillan, Basingstoke.

Layard, R. (2003), *Happiness: Lessons from a New Science*, Allen Lane, London.

Offner, A. (ed.) (1996), *In Pursuit of the Quality of Life,* Oxford University Press, Oxford.

White-collar crime

Illegal acts, typically committed by white-collar employees, including captains of industry, which are not regarded as real, serious crime by public opinion, where rates of detection are low, and detection rarely leads to criminal proceedings. Edwin Sutherland (1883–1950), the American sociologist, coined this term in an attempt to counter-balance what he regarded as criminology's unwarranted concentration on working class crime.

Sutherland's category of white-collar crime included what would now be called corporate crime (copyright infringements, false advertising, breaches of health and safety laws, for example). Nowadays the term white-collar crime refers to the offences of middle class employees such as pilfering from work and fiddling expenses.

See also **Crime; Criminology.**

Sutherland, D.E. (1945), 'Is "white-collar crime" crime?' *American Sociological Review*, 10, 132–9.

Wilson, William Julius (1935–)

American sociologist, selected by *Time* magazine in 1996 as one of the United States's 25 most influential people; famous for his books on poverty, unemployment, race and the underclass in the United States.

Wilson has argued that in the United States the significance of race is waning and that class has become more important in determining the life chances of all ethnic groups. However, he also argues that while many blacks have experienced socio-economic ascent, others in the inner cities have been left behind and constitute an underclass. Wilson argues that the underclass's unemployment, and the instability of the families and high rates of crime are due to the flight of industrial jobs from the inner cities, and that, contrary to other accounts, generous welfare plays no part in these processes.

See also **Murray, C.; Race; Underclass.**

Wilson, W.J. (1987), *The Truly Disadvantaged: The Inner-City, The Underclass and Public Policy*, University of Chicago Press, Chicago.

Wirth, Louis (1897–1952)

German-born, but migrated to and settled in America where he became a leading member of the Chicago School. He is the author of the classic essay, 'Urbanism as a way of life' that has remained a standard on student reading lists and in edited collections that deal with the rural–urban contrast.

See also **Chicago School; Urbanism.**

Wirth, L. (1938), 'Urbanism as a way of life', *American Journal of Sociology*, 44, 1–24.

Wittgenstein, Ludwig (1889–1951)

Austria-born, but was based at Cambridge University (UK) for most of his career as a philosopher; regarded within his discipline as among the greatest, if not the greatest, twentieth century philosopher.

Since Wittgenstein grappled with fundamental philosophical questions such as what it is possible for us to know, his work must be relevant in sociology (and all other disciplines). However:

W

- Philosophers are agreed that Wittgenstein is difficult to understand.
- He produced two philosophies, one after the First World War and the other after the Second World War in which he repudiated his earlier work.
- Wittgenstein complained repeatedly that he was misunderstood by other philosophers including his original mentor at Cambridge, Bertrand Russell.
- Wittgenstein is credited with saying that anyone who really understood his philosophy realised that what he had written was nonsense.

That said, one of Wittgenstein's ultimate positions was that language could operate successfully only within its normal contexts and for its normal tasks, that many philosophical problems arose from extracting language from its normal contexts, and that once this was appreciated the philosophical problems disappeared.

The importance that Wittgenstein attached to language led to him being cited in support of the linguistic turn (paying greater attention to language) in the social sciences from the 1950s onwards. His insistence that language can be properly understood only in its normal contexts led to him being cited in support of phenomenological and ethnomethodological methods and in opposition to positivist approaches in sociology.

Grayling, A.C. (2001), *Wittengenstein: A Very Short Introduction*, Oxford University Press, Oxford.

Work

A broader concept than employment. Work is any activity undertaken in order to create value, whether for the benefit of the worker personally or someone else. So housework, childcare, do-it-yourself, good deeds, and volunteering for charities, churches, sports and arts clubs, trade unions and political parties, all count as work.

Sociologists are interested in why so much, but not all work, has become paid work within an employment relationship, and why paid work and other types of work tend to be done by different groups, like men and women respectively. Capitalism has converted an ever wider range of goods and services into commodities that employees are paid to produce or provide, but communism did likewise, actually to an even greater extent with its ideology-inspired attempts to collectivise food preparation and childcare. Employment enables work organisations to develop a division of labour and to use technologies that increase the productivity of employees (thereby raising general standards of living), and it also enables employees to purchase a wider range of goods and services with their money wages or salaries than they would be able to obtain through other kinds of work.

The question then becomes why employment has not eliminated all other kinds of work. At this point we recognise that work can perform non-economic functions – strengthening a family or some other social group, job satisfaction, and gaining the appreciation and gratitude of others.

W

See also **Division of labour; Employment.**

Pahl, R.E. (ed.) (1988), *On Work: Historical, Comparative and Theoretical Approaches*, Polity, Cambridge.

Work ethic

Max Weber (1864–1920) claimed that a Protestant ethic originally made work a moral imperative for believers. Whether or not Weber was right about this, by the nineteenth century a work ethic had been routinised in countries that were then industrialising. This ethic decrees that people (men, at any rate) have a moral duty to work to support themselves and their families. Since work is felt to be a duty, it is only through work that they can gain self-respect and the respect of others.

Actually there is scant evidence that most workers were ever motivated primarily by a sense of moral duty. A work ethic may have been preached by churches and endorsed by employers and in schools, but most workers appear to have complied for financial reasons, pragmatically, because this was the only way in which they could secure livelihoods. Some people liked their jobs, some enjoyed the company of workmates, and some appreciated the status that their occupations conferred, but all this was possible without believing that work was a moral duty.

Some writers argue that since the mid-twentieth century the work ethic has weakened and has been replaced by a leisure, fun or consumption ethic. These claims probably exaggerate the strength of a work ethic in the past. In any case, work has not receded from its position at the centre of workers' lives in the sense of structuring their time – the day, the week, the annual calendar and the life course – or in conferring social status and social and self-identities.

See also **Protestant ethic; Weber, M.**

Clayre, A. (1974), *Work and Play*, Weidenfeld and Nicolson, London.

Workfare

The popular term for packages of welfare measures that require participants to work for their benefits. The 'work' may be education, training or work experience, subsidised employment or on special community/public works programmes.

Workfare measures began to be introduced in parts of the United States in the 1980s, then spread across the country. Alongside other reforms, these measures have been intended to end welfare as formerly known. By the end of the 1990s, in most parts of the United States single mothers were limited to 60 months on welfare during their lifetimes. For two-parent families the time limit was 24 months. Single parents were required to be available for work for at least 30 hours per week.

W

Workfare policies have now spread to many other countries including Canada, Australia, and (in a mild form) the UK under post-1997 Labour governments' New Deal Welfare to Work programmes.

In the United States supporters of workfare point to steep declines in the number of welfare claimants (usually by around a third). Critics point out that many who leave welfare disappear without entering employment, that the progression rate from workfare into stable, unsubsidised employment is low, that the measures replace some regular public sector jobs and employees, and that the total costs of the training, education, work programmes, job subsidies and wage supplements typically exceed the original costs of welfare payments.

See also **Churning**; **Murray, C.**; **Poverty trap**; **Welfare state**.

Peck, J. (2001), *Workfare States*, Guilford Press, London.

Working class

This term is used by sociologists and also by (some) workers to describe their own class positions. The groups described as working class by sociologists are broadly the same groups of workers who apply the label to themselves. Exactly how sociologists define the working class depends on the broader theories of class to which they subscribe. For functionalists the working class is composed of workers whose occupations are towards the bottom end of the skill, prestige and pay hierarchies. For Marxists the working class comprises employees who sell their labour power pure and simple. Nowadays Marxist sociologists exclude employees who are paid a premium for performing (management) functions of capital, or on account of their higher-level skills and qualifications. Weberians define the working class in terms of its pure contractual employment relationship: there is little trust on either side, just an exchange of labour, measured by the hour or unit of output, for money.

Until the mid-twentieth century the working classes comprised the majority of the working populations in industrial countries, and it was possible to envisage working class power (mobilised in trade unions and working class political parties) forcing revolutionary changes that would radically upgrade the positions of workers. At that time a major issue for sociology was why the revolution was not happening.

Subsequently in the advanced industrial (post-industrial) countries, the working classes have shrunk in size (they no longer amount to the majority of all workers). The issue for sociology today is exactly what is happening to the working class in these 'new times'. The working class jobs that remain in the advanced economies tend to be in service sectors rather than manufacturing or extractive industries. Workers are employed in smaller establishments than in the past. They are less likely to be organised in trade unions. Much lower-level employment is being 'Brazilianised' or exported. Workers are at greater risk of unemployment and descent into an underclass or excluded strata.

See also **Brazilianisation**; **Class**; **Dual labour market**; **Post-Fordism**; **Post-industrialism**; **Social exclusion**; **Underclass**.

Beck, U. (2000), *The Brave New World of Work*, Cambridge University Press, Cambridge.

Gorz, A. (1982), *Farewell to the Working Class*, Pluto, London.

World system, World system theory

World system theory is the theory of the American sociologist, Immanuel Wallerstein (1930–). It is not a general theory about world societies but specifically about the world capitalist system which has developed since the fifteenth century. Wallerstein's theory predates globalisation becoming an everyday part of sociology's vocabulary.

Wallerstein contends that the organisation of capitalism is basically global, not national, and that since the fifteenth century the capitalist system has been dividing the world into core and peripheral countries. The former are economically and politically dominant. Peripheral countries supply raw materials, plus various forms of unfree and otherwise cheap labour. Governments in peripheral countries are typically weak, unable to resist the world system. Wallerstein contends that the operation of the world economic system keeps core and peripheral countries locked in these positions. The theory incorporates some smaller theories such as dependency theory.

See also **Capitalism; Dependency theory; Globalisation**.

Wallerstein, I. (1979), *The Capitalist World-Economy*, Cambridge University Press, Cambridge.

World Values Surveys

These surveys commenced in 1981. Up to now there have been four sweeps in which a total of 85 countries have participated, in some cases on successive occasions, thus enabling both change over time and inter-country differences to be investigated.

See also **Values**.

Halman, L., Inglehart, R., Diez-Medrano, J., Luijkx, R., Moreno, A. and Basanez, M. (2007), *Changing Values and Beliefs in 85 Countries*, Brill, Leiden.

World Wide Web

Internets which link computers together were developed, by military and business organisations, and universities, from the 1960s onwards. What we now call *the* Internet is a network of networks, a worldwide series of interconnected Internet systems. This Internet was created (on paper) by Tim Berners-Lee in 1989. He called it the World Wide Web. In 1993 the www was made free to anyone. It enables documents to be accessed from computers in any part of the world. On the www emails can be sent to anyone in the world who has an email address. After 1993 there was an explosion (still ongoing) in the number of sites and documents available on the www (the web). Today, in the economically advanced countries, virtually all businesses, public services and substantial voluntary associations have websites, and most households are online.

The Internet has changed the way in which we communicate with one another, how we shop, and how we obtain the information that we need in our private and professional lives. The potential economic, political, cultural and social implications are enormous. Sociologists today cannot ignore the

W

www. Some governments – China, North Korea, Cuba, Saudi Arabia, Iran and Myanmar (Burma) – restrict Internet use by blocking websites for political or religious reasons. The Scandinavian countries have a voluntary agreement with Internet service providers to block websites at the request of the police (supposed to be solely for preventing child pornography). Other countries make it illegal to download particular items (like child pornography, and also gambling in the United States). However, making these practices illegal does not stop them happening.

On the one hand, the Internet is hailed as a great democratising innovation on account of the amount of information that it makes available to everyone (who has access), and the ease with which this information can be obtained. On the other hand, the Internet is deplored for submerging us in garbage.

See also **Cyberspace; Virtual reality.**

Wright, Erik Olin (1947–)

American sociologist who has developed a neo-Marxist class scheme (which contains some Weberian features) which is suitable for use in international comparative research. The Wright class scheme separates owners from workers; divides the owners into capitalists proper, a petit bourgeoisie with employees, and without employees; then divides workers according to whether they have skill assets (which increase their value to their employers) and whether they exercise any delegated (from their employers) management authority in the workplace. Thus a pure proletariat can be distinguished from groups of workers who occupy contradictory class locations and who may well regard their own interests as closer to those of their employers than to the interests of other groups of workers.

See also **Class.**

Wright, E.O. (2000), *Class Counts: Student Edition*, Cambridge University Press, New York.

W

Xenophobia

A strong dislike, maybe hatred, of foreigners *per se* rather than on any specific ethnic, religious or cultural grounds.

See also **Authoritarian personality; Ethnocentrism; Prejudice; Race, racism.**

Young, Michael; Baron Young of Dartington (1915–2002)

An eminent British sociologist and much more besides. As its young director of research, Michael Young wrote the Labour Party's successful 1945 General Election manifesto. Throughout his life he was a hyper-social activist. He was involved in founding the Consumers Association, the National Consumer Council, the Open University, the University of the Third Age, the School for Social Entrepreneurs, Language Line (a telephone interpreting business) and many more.

Young was most active as a sociologist in the 1950s and 1960s. In 1954 he founded the Institute for Community Studies (now called the Young Foundation), based in Bethnal Green, which launched a series of path-breaking sociological enquiries. The most famous of these led to the book that Young co-authored with Peter Willmott, *Family and Kinship in East London*, which revised Britain's ideas about the quality of life in inner-city slum districts. Also in the 1950s Young wrote *The Rise of the Meritocracy*. He invented the term meritocracy for this book, which was a satirical account of how awful life would be in a society where some people knew that they deserved no more than their very modest achievements, while the successful knew that their rewards were all due to their own efforts and abilities. By the 1950s Young was already disillusioned by the extent to which the Labour Party was replacing the aim of equality of condition with equality of opportunity. Towards the end of his life he was gravely disappointed to hear New Labour politicians treating meritocracy as something to strive for, and citing his own book (which obviously they had never read) in support.

See also **Meritocracy**.

Young, M. (1958), *The Rise of the Meritocracy*, Thames and Hudson, London.

Young, M. and Willmott, P. (1957), *Family and Kinship in East London*, Routledge, London.

Youth

Nowadays sociologists define youth as the life stage between childhood and adulthood. It is now recognised that the chronological ages when youth begins and ends vary between and within societies.

Youth became the term normally used for this life stage after the Second World War, a period of full employment, when teenagers' earnings rose rapidly and the gap between youth and adult earnings closed. Older terms were dropped. These were 'juvenile' (which post-war youth clearly were not) and 'adolescence' which was associated with the biological changes of puberty.

The sociology of youth is concerned with all the status transitions that normally occur during the youth life stage:

- from education to employment
- from being a child in one's parents' household to being a parent and a householder
- from having things bought by a parent or another adult to being an independent consumer
- political enfranchisement
- becoming subject to full adult justice
- becoming eligible for adult welfare entitlements.

The major issues in the present-day sociology of youth are about how the life stage has changed since the immediate post-Second World War decades. There is agreement that:

- The life stage has been prolonged for most young people.
- There is no longer one proper order in which to make all the youth life stage transitions. For example, young people today typically become independent consumers, exit their parents' homes, and may cohabit prior to establishing themselves in full-time employment.
- Biographies have been individualised.

The heated debates are about:

- Whether old predictors of young people's life courses (social class origins and gender) have become weaker, and whether today's youth are able to take personal charge of their own biographies.
- Whether the baby boomers (the cohorts born between the 1940s and 1960s) were a lucky generation, and post-1970s cohorts are scarred generations, or whether this mistakenly judges one era's youth using the standards of earlier times.

See also **Adolescence; Youth culture.**

Furlong, A. and Cartmel, F. (2007), *Young People and Social Change*, Open University Press, Maidenhead.

Youth culture, youth subculture

Youth cultures are the styles constructed from music, dress, places and activities that youth peer groups cultivate or adopt in their leisure time. A new type of youth culture attracted comment (and, indeed, fuelled a moral panic) after the Second World War when affluent young workers had unprecedented amounts of disposable income. The issue for sociology has always been how to interpret these youth cultures.

By the 1960s there were two schools of thought in sociology (both alternatives to psychology-based theories of adolescence). Functionalists said that youth cultures were socialising milieux in which young people acquired skills (relating to peers without adult supervision, and adult gender and sexual roles) that were necessary before they could become part of adult society. Conflict theorists drew attention to how young people and their youth cultures were divided by class and gender. Working class youth cultures were said to draw on the values of a broader working class culture, including a willingness, indeed a desire, to resist all authorities. Writers who wish to stress that youth cultures have adult parents use the prefix 'sub'.

There is agreement that since the 1970s youth cultures have fragmented and no longer map neatly onto any other social divisions. Sociologists are not agreed on the significance of this. However, they all realise that most young people have never aligned themselves with any particular youth cultures, but have insisted that they are just 'normal' or 'ordinary'.

See also **Adolescence; Subculture; Youth.**

Bennett, A. and Kahn-Harris, K. (eds) (2004), *After Subculture: Critical Studies in Contemporary Youth Culture,* Palgrave, Basingstoke.

Hall, S. and Jefferson, T. (eds) (1976), *Resistance Through Rituals*, Hutchinson, London.

Y

Zeitgeist

German word, literally meaning spirit of the age, but now used to refer to the general cultural character of a historical period.

Zero-sum

One party's gains must be at the expense of another party's losses, as in a sport event where only one side can win. If the economy grows, then in principle everyone can be a winner (win-win), whereas if income or mobility chances are redistributed the situation is zero-sum.

See also **Game theory.**

Revision

20 major theorists

Baudrillard, J.
Beck, U.
Blumer, H.
Bourdieu, P.
Castells, M.
Durkheim, E.
Foucault, M.
Garfinkel, H.
Goffman, E.
Habermas, J.
Levi-Strauss, C.
Lyotard, J-F.
Marx, K.
Mead, G.H.
Michels, R.
Parsons, T.
Popper, K.
Ritzer, G.
Schutz, A.
Weber, M.

50 major concepts

Agency
Alienation
Anomie
Authority
Bureaucracy
Capitalism
Citizenship
Class
Community
Culture
Deviance
Elite
Ethnic
Evolution
Family
Fordism
Frankfurt School
Functionalism
Gender

Globalisation
Habitus
Ideal type
Identity
Individualisation
Labelling theory
Legitimacy
Marxism
McDonaldization
Modern
Neo-liberalism
Network
Other
Phenomenology
Positivism
Post-Fordism
Postmodern
Post-structuralism
Race
Rationality
Reflexivity
Reproduction
Role
Self
Semiotics
Social construction
Social exclusion
Social mobility
Socialisation
Symbolic interactionism
Urbanism

Bibliography

Abercrombie, N., Hill, S. and Turner, B.S. (1980), *The Dominant Ideology Thesis*, Allen and Unwin, London.

Ackers, P. and Wilkinson, A. (2003), *Understanding Work and Employment: Industrial Relations in Transition,* Oxford University Press, Oxford.

Adam, B. (1995), *Timewatch: The Social Analysis of Time*, Polity, Cambridge.

Adorno, T., Frenkel-Brunswick, E., Levinson, D. and Sanford, R. (1950, 1991), *The Authoritarian Personality,* Norton, New York.

Aglietta, M. (1979), *A Theory of Capitalist Regulation: The US Experience,* New Left Books, London.

Alcock, J. (2001), *The Triumph of Sociobiology*, Oxford University Press, Oxford.

Aldridge, A. (2000), *Religion in the Contemporary World: A Sociological Introduction,* Polity, Cambridge.

Alexander, J. (ed.) (1985), *Neo-Functionalism*, Sage, London.

Allan, G. (1996), *Kinship and Friendship in Modern Britain*, Oxford University Press, Oxford.

Althusser, L. (1971), *Lenin and Philosophy and Other Essays,* New Left Books, London.

Andreski, S. (ed.) (1974), *The Essential Comte*, Croom Helm, London.

Apter, D.E. (1987), *Rethinking Development: Modernization, Dependency and Postmodern Politics,* Sage, Newbury Park, Calif.

Arblaster, A. (1987), *Democracy*, Open University Press, Milton Keynes.

Backman, C.R. (2003), *The Worlds of Medieval Europe*, Oxford University Press, Oxford.

Baldock, J., Manning, N. and Vickerstaff, S. (2007), *Social Policy*, Oxford University Press, Oxford.

Banakar, R. and Travers, M., (eds) (2002), *An Introduction to Law and Social Theory*, Hart, Oxford.

Banakar, R. and Travers, M., (eds) (2005), *Theory and Method in Socio-Legal Research,* Hart, Oxford.

Banton, M. (1968), *Roles: An Introduction to the Study of Social Relations,* Tavistock, London.

Banton, M. (1997), *Ethnic and Racial Consciousness*, 2nd edition, Longman, Harlow.

Barthes, R. (1967), *Elements of Semiology,* Cape, London.

Barthes, R. (1972), *Mythologies,* Cape, London.

Baudrillard, J. (1988), *Selected Writings*, Polity, Cambridge.

Baudrillard, J. (1998), *The Consumer Society*, Sage, London.

Bauman, Z. (1989), *Modernity and the Holocaust*, Cornell University Press, New York.

Bauman, Z. (2006), *Liquid Times: Living in an Age of Uncertainty*, Polity, Cambridge.

Beauvoir, S. de (1972, 1997), *The Second Sex,* Vintage, London.

Beck, U. (1992), *Risk Society: Towards a New Modernity*, Sage, London.

Beck, U. (2000), *The Brave New World of Work,* Cambridge University Press, Cambridge.

Beck, U., Giddens, A. and Lash, S. (1994), *Reflexive Modernization: Politics, Tradition and Aesthetics in the Modern Social Order,* Polity, Cambridge.

Becker, G.S. (1964, 1993), *Human Capital: A Theoretical and Empirical Analysis with Special Reference to Education*, University of Chicago Press, Chicago.

Becker, H.S., Geer, B., Hughes, E. and Strauss, A. (1961), *Boys in White: Student Culture in Medical School,* University of Chicago Press, Chicago.

Becker, H.S. (1963), *Outsiders: Studies in the Sociology of Deviance*, Free Press, Glencoe, Ill.

Bell, D. (1960), *The End of Ideology*, Collins, New York.

Bell, D. (1974), *The Coming of Post-Industrial Society*, Basic Books, New York.

Benjamin, W. (1999), *The Arcades Project*, Harvard University Press, Cambridge, Mass.

Bennett, A. and Kahn-Harris, K. (eds) (2004), *After Subculture: Critical Studies in Contemporary Youth Culture*, Palgrave, Basingstoke.

Berger, P.L. and Luckmann, T. (1967), *The Social Construction of Reality*, Allen Lane, London.

Berle, A. and Means, G. (1932), *The Modern Corporation and Private Property*, Harcourt Brace, New York.

Bernstein, B. (1971–7), *Class, Codes and Control* (3 vols), Routledge, London.

Beveridge, W. (1942), *Social Insurance and Allied Services,* HMSO, London.

Bhasker, R. (1975, 1997), *A Realist Theory of Science*, Verso, London.

Blau, P.M. (1964), *Exchange and Power in Social Life*, Wiley, New York.

Blauner, R. (1964), *Alienation and Freedom*, University of Chicago Press, Chicago.

Bloch, M. (1961), *Feudalism* (2 vols), Routledge, London.

Blumer, H. (1969), *Symbolic Interactionism: A Perspective on Method*, Prentice Hall, Engelwood Cliffs, N.J.

Bocock, R. (1974), *Ritual in Industrial Society: A Sociological Analysis of Ritualism,* Allen and Unwin, London.

Bott, E. (1957), *Family and Social Network*, Tavistock, London.

Bottomore, T. (1984), *The Frankfurt School*, Tavistock, London.

Bourdieu, P. (1984), *Distinction: A Social Critique of the Judgement of Taste,* Routledge, London.

Bourdieu, P. and Passeron, J.D. (1977), *Reproduction in Education, Culture and Society,* Sage, London.

Bowles, S. and Gintis, H. (1976), *Schooling in Capitalist America,* Routledge, London.

Brake, M. (1980), *The Sociology of Youth Culture and Youth Subcultures,* Routledge, London.

Braverman, H. (1974), *Labour and Monopoly Capital: The Degradation of Work in the Twentieth Century,* Monthly Review Press, New York.

Bulmer, M. (1984), *The Chicago School of Sociology*, University of Chicago Press, Chicago.

Bulmer, M. and, J. Solomos (eds) (1999), *Ethnic and Racial Studies Today*, Routledge, London.

Burawoy, M. (2005), 'For public sociology', *American Sociological Review*, 70, 4–28.

Burnham, J. (1943), *The Managerial Revolution*, Putnam, London.

Burrows, R. and Gane, N. (2006), 'Geodemographics, software and class', *Sociology*, 40, 793–812.

Bury, M. and Gabe, J. (eds) (2004), *The Sociology of Health and Illness: A Reader*, Routledge, London.

Butler, J. (1990), *Gender Trouble: Feminism and the Subversion of Identity*, Routledge, New York.

Butler, R.N. (1975, 2003), *Why Survive? Being Old in America*, Johns Hopkins University Press, Baltimore, Ma.

Castells, M. (1977), *The Urban Question: A Marxist Approach*, Edward Arnold, London.

Castells, M. (1996), *The Rise of the Network Society*, Blackwell, Oxford.

Castles, S. and Miller, M.J. (2003), *The Age of Migration*, Palgrave Macmillan, Basingstoke.

Chan, T.W. and Goldthorpe, J.H. (2004), 'Is there a status order in contemporary British society? Evidence from the occupational structure of friendship', *European Sociological Review*, 20, 383–401.

Chomsky, N. (1957), *Syntactic Structures*, Mouton, The Hague.

Clayre, A. (1974), *Work and Play*, Weidenfeld and Nicolson, London.

Clegg, S. (1990), *Modern Organizations: Organization Studies in the Postmodern World*, Sage, London.

Cohen, R. (1997), *Global Diasporas: An Introduction*, UCL Press, London.

Cohen, S. (1972), *Folk Devils and Moral Panics*, MacGibbon and Kee, London.

Coleman, R. (2004), *Reclaiming the Streets: Surveillance, Social Control and the City*, Willan, Cullompton.

Collins, R. (1979), *The Credential Society*, Academic Press, New York.

Connerton, B. (ed.) (1976), *Critical Sociology*, Penguin, Harmondsworth.

Cooley, C.H. (1909), *Social Organization*, Scribner, New York.

Coser, L. (1956), *The Functions of Social Conflict*, Free Press, New York.

Cox, O.C. (1959), *Caste, Class and Race*, Monthly Review Press, New York.

Crompton, R. (1998), *Class and Stratification: An Introduction to Current Debates*, Polity, Cambridge.

Crouch, C. (1990), *Corporatism and Accountability: Organized Interests in British Public Life*, Clarendon Press, Oxford.

Crozier, M. (1964), *The Bureaucratic Phenomenon*, Tavistock, London.

Cuff, E.C., Sharrock, W.W. and Francis, D.W. (2006), *Perspectives in Sociology*, 5th edition, Routledge, London.

Dahl, R.A. (1998), *On Democracy*, Yale University Press, New Haven, Conn.

Dahrendorf, R. (1959), *Class and Class Conflict in an Industrial Society*, Routledge, London.

Davis, K. and Moore, W.E. (1945), 'Some principles of stratification', *American Sociological Review*, 10, 242–9.

Dawe, A. (1971), 'The two sociologies', in K. Thompson and J. Tunstall (eds), *Sociological Perspectives,* Penguin, Harmondsworth.

Dawkins, R.I. (1989), *The Selfish Gene*, Oxford University Press, Oxford.

Delanty, G. (2003), *Community,* Routledge, London.

Derrida, J. (1978), *Writing and Difference,* Routledge, London.

Derrida, J. (1981), *Positions,* Athlone Press, London.

Devine, F. (1992), *Affluent Workers Revisited? Privatism and the Working Class,* Edinburgh University Press, Edinburgh.

Dickens, P. (2000), *Social Darwinism: Linking Evolutionary Thought and Social Theory,* Open University Press, Buckingham.

Dilthey, W. (edited by H.P. Rickman) (1976), *W. Dilthey, Selected Writings,* Cambridge University Press, Cambridge.

Dore, R. (1976), *The Diploma Disease*, Allen and Unwin, London.

Du Gay, P. (2000), *In Praise of Bureaucracy: Weber, Organization, Ethics*, Sage, London.

Durkheim, E. (1893, 1938), *The Division of Labour in Society*, Free Press, Glencoe, Ill.

Durkheim, E. (1895, 1938), *The Rules of Sociological Method*, Free Press, Glencoe, Ill.

Durkheim, E. (1897,1970), *Suicide: A Study in Sociology*, Routledge, London.

Durkheim, E. (1912, 1956), *The Elementary Forms of Religious Life*, Allen and Unwin, London.

Ekins, R. and King, D. (2006), *The Transgender Phenomenon*, Sage, London.

Elias, N. (1939, 1978), *The Civilizing Process*, Blackwell, Oxford.

Ellul, J. (1965), *The Technological Society*, Cape, London.

Engels, F. (1845,1958), *The Condition of the Working Class in England*, Blackwell, Oxford.

Erikson, B. and Goldthorpe, J.H. (1992), *The Constant Flux: A Study of Class Mobility in Industrial Societies,* Clarendon Press, Oxford.

Esping-Andersen, G. (1990), *The Three Worlds of Welfare Capitalism*, Princeton University Press, New Jersey.

Etzioni, A. (1968), *The Active Society: A Theory of Social and Political Processes*, Free Press, New York.

Evans, E.J. (2004), *Thatcher and Thatcherism*, Routledge, London.

Fanon, F. (1967, 1990), *The Wretched of the Earth*, Penguin, Harmondsworth.

Featherstone, M. (ed.) (1988), *Postmodernism: Theory Culture and Society,* 5, Nos 2 & 3, Sage, London.

Festinger, L., Riecken, H.W. and Schachter, S. (1956), *When Prophecy Fails*, University of Minnesota Press, Minneapolis.

Fevre, R. (1992), *The Sociology of Labour Markets*, Harvester Wheatsheaf, Hemel Hempstead.

Feyerabend, P. (1987), *Farewell to Reason,* Verso, London.

Florida, R.L. (2002), *The Rise of the Creative Class: And How it's Transforming Work, Leisure, Community and Everyday Life,* Basic Books, New York.

Forrester, V. (1999), *The Economic Horror*, Polity, Cambridge.

Foucault, M. (1963, 1973), *The Birth of the Clinic*, Tavistock, London.

Foucault, M. (1975, 1977), *Discipline and Punish: The Birth of the Prison*, Tavistock, London.

Foucault, M. (1976, 1980), *The History of Sexuality*, Random House, New York.

Frank, A.G. (1969), *Capitalism and Underdevelopment in Latin America*, Monthly Review Press, New York.

Frankel, B. (1987), *The Post-Industrial Utopians*, University of Wisconsin Press, Wisconsin.

Fraser, S. (1995), *The Bell Curve Wars: Race, Intelligence and the Future of America*, Basic Books, New York.

Freeden, M. (1991), *Rights*, Open University Press, Milton Keynes.

Freud, S. (1930), *Civilization and its Discontents*, Hogarth Press, London.

Friedan, B. (1965, 1997), *The Feminine Mystique*, Norton, New York.

Friedman, M. (1981), *Studies in the Quantity and Theory of Money*, University of Chicago Press, Chicago.

Frisby, D. (1984), *Georg Simmel*, Tavistock, London.

Fromm, E. (1955), *The Sane Society*, Holt Rinehart, New York.

Fukuyama, F. (1992), *The End of History and the Last Man*, Penguin, London.

Furlong, A. and Cartmel, F. (2007), *Young People and Social Change*, Open University Press, Maidenhead.

Gadamer, H. (1960, 1975), *Truth and Method*, Sheed and Ward, London.

Galbraith, J.K. (1958), *The Affluent Society*, Hamish Hamilton, London.

Galbraith, J.K. (1967), *The New Industrial State*, Penguin, Harmondsworth.

Galton, F. (1869, 1892), *Hereditary Genius*, Macmillan, London.

Gamble, A., Marsh, D. and Tant, T. (1999), *Marxism and Social Science*, Macmillan, Basingstoke.

Garfinkel, H. (1967), *Studies in Ethnomethodology*, Prentice Hall, Engelwood Cliffs, N.J.

Geddes, P. (1915), *Cities in Evolution*, Williams and Norgate, London.

Gellner, E. (1983), *Nations and Nationalism*, Blackwell, Oxford.

Gershuny, J. (2000), *Changing Times: Work and Leisure in Postindustrial Society*, Oxford University Press, Oxford.

Gerth, H.H. and Mills, C.W. (eds) (1946), *From Max Weber: Essays in Sociology*, Oxford University Press, New York.

Gibson, M. (2002), *Born to Crime: Cesare Lombroso and the Origins of Biological Criminology*, Praeger, Westport, Conn.

Giddens, A. (1973, 1981), *The Class Structure of the Advanced Societies*, Hutchinson, London.

Giddens, A. (1979), *Central Problems in Social Theory*, Macmillan, London.

Giddens, A. (1984), *The Constitution of Society*, Polity, Cambridge.

Giddens, A. (1993), *The Transformation of Intimacy: Love, Sexuality and Eroticism in Modern Societies*, Polity, Cambridge.

Giddens, A. (1998, *The Third Way: The Renewal of Social Democracy*, Polity, Cambridge.

Gilleard, C. and Higgs, P. (2005), *Contexts of Ageing: Class, Cohort and Community*, Polity, Cambridge.

Giner, S. (1976), *Mass Society*, Martin Robertson, London.

Glaser, B. and Strauss, A. (1968), *The Discovery of Grounded Theory*, Weidenfeld and Nicolson, London.

Glass, R. (ed.) (1964), *London: Aspects of Change*, MacGibbon and Kee, London.

Goffman, E. (1959), *The Presentation of Self in Everyday Life*, Doubleday Anchor, New York.

Goffman, E. (1961), *Asylums*, Penguin, Harmondsworth.

Goffman, E. (1964), *Stigma: Notes on the Management of Identity*, Penguin, Harmondsworth.

Goffman, E. (1974), *Frame Analysis*, Penguin, Harmondsworth.

Goldthorpe, J.H. (1998), 'Rational choice theory for sociology', *British Journal of Sociology*, 49, 167–92.

Goldthorpe, J.H., Llewellyn, C. and Payne, C. (1980, 1987), *Social Mobility and Class Structure in Britain*, Clarendon Press, Oxford.

Goldthorpe, J.H., Lockwood, D., Bechhofer, F. and Platt, J. (1969), *The Affluent Worker in the Class Structure*, Cambridge University Press, Cambridge.

Gordon, D.M., Edwards, R. and Reich, M. (1982), *Segmented Work, Divided Workers: The Historical Transformation of Labour in the United States*, Cambridge University Press, Cambridge.

Gorz, A. (1982), *Farewell to the Working Class*, Pluto, London.

Gorz, A. (1999), *Reclaiming Work: Beyond the Wage-Based Society*, Polity, Cambridge.

Gould, S.J. (1983), *The Mismeasurement of Man*, Penguin, Harmondsworth.

Gramsci, A. (1971), *Selections from Prison Notebooks*, New Left Books, London.

Grayling, A.C. (2001), *Wittengenstein: A Very Short Introduction*, Oxford University Press, Oxford.

Habermas, J. (1976), *Legitimation Crisis*, Heinemann, London.

Habermas, J. (1984, 1988), *The Theory of Communicative Action* (2 vols), Polity, Cambridge.

Hakim, C. (2004), *Key Issues in Women's Work: Female Diversity and the Polarisation of Women's Employment*, Glasshouse, London.

Hall, G.S. (1904), *Adolescence*, Appleton, New York.

Hall, S. (1992), *Modernity and its Futures*, Polity, Cambridge.

Hall, S., Critcher, C., Jefferson, T., Clarke, J. and Roberts, B. (1978), *Policing the Crisis: Mugging, the State, and Law and Order*, Macmillan, London.

Hall, S. and Jacques, M. (1989), *New Times*, Lawrence and Wishart, London.

Hall, S. and Jefferson, T. (eds) (1976), *Resistance Through Rituals*, Hutchinson, London.

Halman, L., Inglehart, R., Diez-Medrano, J., Luijkx, R., Moreno, A. and Basanez, M. (2007), *Changing Values and Beliefs in 85 Countries*, Brill, Leiden.

Halsey, A.H., Heath, A.F. and Ridge, J.M. (1980), *Origins and Destinations: Family, Class and Education in Modern Britain*, Clarendon Press, Oxford.

Harland, R. (1987), *Superstructuralism,* Methuen, London.

Harris, R. (1987), *Reading Saussure: A Commentary on the* Cours de Linguistique Generale, Duckworth, London.

Harvey, D. (1989), *The Condition of Post Modernity*, Blackwell, Oxford.

Hawkes, T. (2003), *Structuralism and Semiotics*, Routledge, London.

Haworth, J. and Hart, G. (eds) (2007), *Well-Being: Individual, Community and Social Perspectives,* Palgrave Macmillan, Basingstoke.

Hayek, F.A. (1944), *The Road to Serfdom*, University of Chicago Press, Chicago.

Held, D. (1980), *Introduction to Critical Theory*, Hutchinson, London.

Held, D. and McGrew, A. (eds) (2003), *The Global Transformations Reader*, Polity, Cambridge.

Herrnstein, R.J. and Murray, C. (1994), *The Bell Curve: Intelligence and Class Structure in American Life,* Simon and Schuster, New York.

Hesmondhalgh, D. (2007), *The Cultural Industries,* 2nd edition, Sage, London.

Hill, M.J. (2000), *Understanding Social Policy*, Blackwell, Oxford.

Hirsch, F. (1977), *The Social Limits to Growth*, Routledge, London.

Hoggart, R. (1957), *The Uses of Literacy,* Chatto and Windus, London.

Homans, G.C. (1961), *Social Behaviour: Its Elementary Forms*, Harcourt Brace, New York.

Horkheimer, M. (1972), *Critical Theory: Selected Essays*, Herder, New York.

Huntington, S.P. (1996), *The Clash of Civilizations and the Remaking of World Order,* Simon and Schuster, New York.

Husserl, E. (1970), *The Crisis of the European Sciences and Transcendental Phenomenology,* Northwestern University Press, Evanston, Ill.

Hyman, R. (1972, 1984), *Strikes,* Fontana, Glasgow.

Illich, I. (1972), *Deschooling Society*, Calder and Boyars, London.

Illich, I. (1975), *Medical Nemesis*, Calder and Boyars, London.

Jackson, J.A. (ed.) (1972), *Role,* Cambridge University Press, Cambridge.

Jackson, M.P. (1982), *Trade Unions*, Longman, London.

Jahoda, M. (1982), *Employment and Unemployment: A Social-Psychological Analysis,* Cambridge University Press, Cambridge.

Jameson, F. (1991), *Postmodernism, or, The Cultural Logic of Late Capitalism*, Verso, London.

Jones, C. and Novak, T. (1999), *Poverty, Welfare and the Disciplinary State*, Routledge, London.

Joseph, J. (2006), *Marxism and Social Theory,* Palgrave Macmillan, Basingstoke.

Kallis, A.A. (ed.) (2003), *The Fascism Reader,* Routledge, London.

Keddie, N. (ed.) (1973), *Tinker, Tailor … The Myth of Cultural Deprivation,* Penguin, Harmondsworth.

Kelly, P. (ed.) (2002), *Multiculturalism Reconsidered: Culture and Equality and its Critics,* Polity, Cambridge.

Kemp, S. and Squires, J. (eds) (1997), *Feminisms*, Oxford University Press, Oxford.

Kerr, C., Dunlop, J.T., Harbison, F.H. and Myers, C.A. (1962), *Industrialism and Industrial Man,* Heinemann, London.

Keynes, J.M. (1936), *The General Theory of Employment, Interest and Money.* Macmillan, London.

Kingdom, E. (1991), *What's Wong with Rights? Problems for a Feminist Politics of Law,* Edinburgh University Press, Edinburgh.

Klein, N. (2000), *No Logo: Taking Aim at the Brand Bullies*, Flamingo, London.

Kornhauser, W. (1960), *The Politics of Mass Society*, Routledge, London.

Kotarba, J.A. and Johnson, J.M. (2002), *Postmodern Existential Sociology*, Altamira Press, Lanham, Md.

Krippendorf, K. (2004), *Content Analysis: An Introduction to its Methodology*, Sage, Thousand Oaks, Calif.

Kuhn, T. (1962), *The Structure of Scientific Revolutions,* Chicago University Press, Chicago.

Lacan, J. (1989), *Ecrits: A Selection*, Routledge, London.

Lacan, J. (1995), *Lacan's Four Fundamental Concepts of Psychoanalysis*, State University of New York Press, New York.

Laing, R.D. (1971), *The Politics of the Family and Other Essays*, Tavistock, London.

Lane, T. and Roberts, K. (1971), *Strike at Pilkingtons*, Fontana, London.

Lash, S. and Urry, J. (1987), *The End of Organised Capitalism*, Polity, Cambridge.

Layard, R. (2003), *Happiness: Lessons from a New Science*, Allen Lane, London.

Leadbetter, C. (1999), *Living on Thin Air: The New Economy,* Viking, London.

Lechner, A.J. and Boli, J. (eds) (2000), *The Globalization Reader*, Blackwell, Oxford.

Lee, N. (2001), *Childhood and Society: Growing Up in an Age of Uncertainty*, Open University Press, Maidenhead.

Legge, K. (2004), *Human Resource Management: Rhetorics and Realities,* Palgrave Macmillan, Basingstoke.

Levitas, R. (1998), *The Inclusive Society? Social Exclusion and New Labour,* Macmillan, Basingstoke.

Levi-Strauss, C. (1969), *Totemism,* Penguin, Harmondsworth.

Levi-Strauss, C. (1972), *The Savage Mind,* Weidenfeld and Nicolson, London.

Lewis, O. (1961), *The Children of Sanchez,* Random House, New York.

Lipset, S.M. (1960), *Political Man: The Social Bases of Politics*, Doubleday, New York.

Lipset, S.M. and Marks, G. (2000), *It Didn't Happen Here: Why Socialism Failed in the United States,* Norton, New York.

Lister, R. (2004), *Poverty,* Polity, Cambridge.

Lockwood, D. (1964), 'Social integration and system integration', in Z. Zollschan and W. Hirsch (eds), *Explorations in Social Change,* Routledge, London.

Low, S.M. (2003), *Behind the Gates: Life, Security and the Pursuit of Happiness in Fortress America,* Routledge, New York.

Luhmann, N. (1997), *Social Systems*, Stanford University Press, Stanford, Calif.

Lukacs, G. (1923, 1971), *History and Class Consciousness*, Merlin Press, London.

Lukes, S. (1974), *Power: A Radical View*, Macmillan, London.

Lynd, R.S. and Lynd, H.M. (1929), *Middletown: A Study in Contemporary American Culture*, Harcourt, Brace and Co, New York.

Lynd, R.S. and Lynd, H.M. (1937), *Middletown in Transition: A Study in Cultural Conflicts*, Harcourt, Brace and Co, New York.

Lyotard, J-F. (1984), *The Postmodern Condition: A Report on Knowledge*, Manchester University Press, Manchester.

Mac an Ghaill, M. and Haywood, C. (2006), *Gender, Culture and Society: Contemporary Femininities and Masculinities*, Palgrave Macmillan, Basingstoke.

MacDonald, K.M. (1995), *The Sociology of the Professions*, Sage, London.

MacDonald, R. (ed.) (1997), *Youth, the Underclass and Social Exclusion*, Routledge, London.

Macpherson, S.W. (1999), *The Stephen Lawrence Inquiry*, HMSO, London.

Malthus, T.R. (1798, 1986), *An Essay on the Principle of Population*, Pickering, London.

Mann, M. (1988), *States, War and Capitalism: Studies in Political Sociology*, Blackwell, Oxford.

Mannheim, K. (1929, 1936), *Ideology and Utopia*, Routledge, London.

Mannheim, K. (1952), 'The problem of generations', in *Essays on the Sociology of Knowledge*, Routledge, London.

Marcuse, H. (1955, 1991), *Eros and Civilization: A Philosophical Inquiry into Freud*, Beacon Press, Boston, Mass.

Marcuse, H. (1964), *One Dimensional Man: Studies in the Ideology of Advanced Industrial Society*, Routledge, London.

Marsh, C. (1982), *The Survey Method*, Allen and Unwin, London.

Marshall, G., Rose, D., Newby, H. and Vogler, C. (1988), *Social Class in Modern Britain*, Hutchinson, London.

Marshall, T.H. (1963), *Sociology at the Crossroads*, Heinemann, London.

Martin, D. (1978), *A General Theory of Secularisation*, Blackwell, Oxford.

Marx, K. (edited by T.B. Bottomore and M. Rubel) (1979), *Selected Writings on Sociology and Social Philosophy*, Penguin, Harmondsworth.

Marx, K. (edited by D. Sayer) (1989), *Readings from Karl Marx*, Routledge, London.

Marx, K. and Engels, F. (1848, 1985), *The Communist Manifesto*, Penguin, London.

Maslow, A.H. (1954), *Motivation and Personality*, Harper, New York.

Mason, D. (2000), *Race and Ethnicity in Modern Britain*, Oxford University Press, Oxford.

Mauss, M. (1925, 1954), *The Gift*, Free Press, New York.

Mayo, E. (1949), *The Social Problems of an Industrial Civilization*, Routledge, London.

McClellan, D. (1975), *Marx*, Fontana/Collins, London.

McLuhan, M. and Fiore, Q. (1967), *The Medium is the Message*, Penguin, Harmondsworth.

Mead, G.H. (1934), *Mind, Self and Society*, Chicago University Press, Chicago.

Mead, M. (1928, 1961), *Coming of Age in Samoa,* Penguin, Harmondsworth.

Mead, M. (1935, 1963), *Sex and Temperament in Three Primitive Societies,* Morrow, New York.

Merton, R.K. (1949), *Social Theory and Social Structure,* Free Press, Glencoe, Ill.

Merton, R.K. (1957), 'Bureaucratic structure and personality', in R.K. Merton, *Social Theory and Social Structure*, 2nd edition, Free Press, Glencoe, Ill.

Michels, R. (1962), *Political Parties*, Free Press, New York.

Miles, S. (1998), *Consumerism – As a Way of Life,* Sage, London.

Milgram, S. (1974, 2005), *Obedience to Authority: An Experimental View*, Pinter and Martin, London.

Miller, N. (2006), *Out of the Past: Gay and Lesbian History from 1869 to the Present,* Alyson Books, New York.

Mills, C.W. (1940), 'Situated action and vocabularies of motive', *American Sociological Review,* 5, 904–93.

Mills, C.W. (1951), *White Collar: The American Middle Classes*, Oxford University Press, New York.

Mills, C.W. (1956), *The Power Elite,* Simon and Schuster, New York.

Mills, C.W. (1959), *The Sociological Imagination*, Oxford University Press, New York.

Moreno, J. L. (1934, 1953), *Who Shall Survive?* Beacon House, New York.

Mosca, G. (1939), *The Ruling Class*, McGraw-Hill, New York.

Mouzelis, N.P. (1995), *Sociological Theory: What Went Wrong?* Routledge, London.

Murray, C. (1984), *Losing Ground: American Social Policy, 1950–1980*, Basic Books, New York.

Murray, C. (1990), *The Emerging British Underclass*, Institute of Economic Affairs, London.

Nagel, E. (1961), *The Structure of Science: Problems in the Logic of Scientific Explanation,* Routledge, London.

Newby, H. (1980), *Green and Pleasant Land? Social Change in Rural England*, Penguin, Harmondsworth.

Newman, M. (2005), *Socialism: A Very Short Introduction*, Oxford University Press, Oxford.

Nietzsche, F. (1967), *The Birth of Tragedy,* Random House, New York.

Nisbet, R. (1980), *History of the Idea of Progress*, Heinemann, London.

Oakley, A. (1972), *Sex, Gender and Society*, Temple Smith, London.

Offner, A. (ed.) (1996), *In Pursuit of the Quality of Life,* Oxford University Press, Oxford.

Ogburn, W.F. (1964), *On Culture and Social Change: Selected Papers*, Chicago University Press, Chicago.

Pahl, R.E. (ed.) (1988), *On Work: Historical, Comparative and Theoretical Approaches,* Polity, Cambridge.

Pahl, R.E. (2000), *On Friendship*, Polity, Cambridge.

Pareto, W. (1973), *The Mind and Society: A Treatise on General Sociology*, Dover, New York.

Parker, H., Williams, L. and Aldridge, J. (2002), 'The normalization of "sensible" recreational drug use: further evidence from the north-west England longitudinal study', *Sociology*, 36, 941–64.

Parker, M. (2002), *Against Management: Organization in the Age of Managerialism,* Polity, Cambridge.

Parkin, F. (1974), 'Strategies of social closure in class formation', in F. Parkin (ed.), *The Social Analysis of Class Structure*, Tavistock, London, 1–18.

Parsons, T. (1937), *The Structure of Social Action*, Free Press, New York.

Parsons, T. (1951), *The Social System,* Routledge, London.

Parsons, T. (1966), *Societies: Evolutionary and Comparative Perspectives*, Prentice-Hall, Engelwood Cliffs, N.J.

Paxton, R.O. (2005), *The Anatomy of Fascism*, Penguin, London.

Peck, J. (2001), *Workfare States*, Guilford Press, London.

Peel, J.D.Y. (1971), *Herbert Spencer: The Evolution of a Sociologist*, Heinemann, London.

Pilcher, J. (1995), *Age and Generation in Modern Britain*, Oxford University Press, Oxford.

Piore, M.J. and Sabel, C.F. (1984), *The Second Industrial Divide: Possibilities for Prosperity,* Basic Books, New York.

Pipes, R.E. (2002), *Communism: A History of the Intellectual and Political Movement,* Phoenix Press, London.

Popper, K.R. (1945), *The Open Society and its Enemies*, Routledge, London.

Popper, K.R. (1957), *The Poverty of Historicism*, Routledge, London.

Popper, K.R. (1963), *Conjectures and Refutations: The Growth of Scientific Knowledge*, Routledge, London.

Prandy, K. (1990), 'The revised Cambridge Scale of Occupations', *Sociology*, 24, 629–55.

Putnam, R. (2000), *Bowling Alone: The Collapse and Renewal of American Community,* Simon and Schuster, New York.

Rapoport, R. and Rapoport, R.N. (1971), *Dual Career Families,* Penguin, Harmondsworth.

Redfield, R. (1930), *Tepozlan, a Mexican Village: A Study of Folk Life*, Chicago University Press, Chicago.

Reiss, E. (1996), *Marx: A Clear Guide,* Pluto Press, London.

Ritzer, G. (1993), *The McDonaldization of Society*, Pine Forge Press, Thousand Oaks, Calif.

Ritzer, G. (1999), *Enchanting a Disenchanted World: Revolutionizing the Means of Consumption,* Pine Forge Press, Thousand Oaks, Calif.

Roberts, D.D. (2006), *The Totalitarian Experiment in Twentieth Century Europe,* Routledge, London.

Roberts, K. (2001), *Class in Modern Britain*, Palgrave, Basingstoke.

Roberts, K. (2006), *Leisure in Contemporary Society*, 2nd edition, CABI, Wallingford.

Roberts, K., Clark, S.C. and Wallace, C. (1994), 'Flexibility and individualisation: a comparison of transitions into employment in England and Germany', *Sociology*, 28, 31–54.

Robinson, W.S. (1950), 'Ecological correlations and the behaviour of individuals', *American Sociological Review*, 15, 351–7.

Rock, P. (1979), *The Making of Symbolic Interactionism*, Macmillan, London.

Roethlisberger, F. and Dickson, W. (1939), *Management and the Worker*, Harvard University Press, Cambridge, Mass.

Rojek, C. (2001), *Celebrity*, Reaktion Books, London.

Rose, M. (1988), *Industrial Behaviour*, Penguin, Harmondsworth.

Roszak, T. (1970), *The Making of a Counter-Culture*, Faber, London.

Rowntree, B.S. (1901), *Poverty: A Study in Town Life*, Longman, London.

Runciman, W.G. (1966), *Relative Deprivation and Social Justice*, Routledge, London.

Sacks, H. (1992), *Lectures on Conversation* (2 vols), Blackwell, Oxford.

Said, E.W. (1978, 1995), *Orientalism*, Penguin, Harmondswortth.

Sassen, S. (1991), *The Global City: New York, London, Tokyo*, Princeton University Press, Princeton, N.J.

Saussure, F. De (1983), *Course in General Linguistics*, Duckworth, London.

Savage, M. (2000), *Class Analysis and Social Transformation*, Open University Press, Buckingham.

Scarman, Lord (1981), *The Brixton Disorders, 10–12 April, 1981*, Cmnd 8427, HMSO, London.

Scholtz, J.A. (2005), *Globalization: A Critical Introduction*, Palgrave Macmillan, Basingstoke.

Schutz, A. (1972), *The Phenomenology of the Social World*, Heinemann, London.

Scott, J. (1982), *The Upper Class: Property and Privilege in Britain*, Macmillan, London.

Seeman, M. (1959), 'On the meaning of alienation', *American Sociological Review*, 24, 783–91.

Segal, L. (2007), *Slow Motion: Changing Masculinities, Changing Men*, Palgrave Macmillan, Basingstoke.

Selznick, P. (1966), *TVA and the Grassroots*, Harper Torch Books, New York.

Sennett, R. (1998), *The Corrosion of Character: The Personal Consequences of Work in the New Capitalism*, Norton, London.

Sennett, R. and Cobb, J. (1973), *The Hidden Injuries of Class*, Vintage Books, New York.

Sharrock, W. and Anderson, R. (1986), *The Ethnomethodologists*, Tavistock, London.

Shilling, C. (2003), *The Body and Social Theory*, Sage, London.

Silver, B.J. (2003), *Forces of Labor: Workers' Movements and Globalization Since 1870*, Cambridge University Press, New York.

Simey, T.S. and Simey, M.B. (1960), *Charles Booth, Social Scientist*, Oxford University Press, London.

Simmel, G. (1903, 1950), 'The metropolis and mental life', in K. Wolff (ed.), *The Sociology of Georg Simmel*, Free Press, New York.

Singer, P. (1983), *Hegel,* Oxford University Press, Oxford.

Skinner, B.F. (1953), *The Science of Human Behaviour,* Macmillan, New York.

Sklair, L. (2002), *Globalization: Capitalism and its Alternatives*, Oxford University Press, Oxford.

Smelsner, N.J. (2003), 'On comparative analysis, interdisciplinarity and internationalisation in sociology', *International Sociology*, 18, 643–57.

Smith, A. (1776, 1976), *An Inquiry into the Nature and Causes of the Wealth of Nations,* Clarendon Press, Oxford.

Smith, A.D. (1986), *The Ethnic Origins of Nations*, Blackwell, Oxford.

Smith, D.E. (1988), *The Everyday World as Problematic: A Feminist Sociology*, Open University Press, Milton Keynes.

Smith, D.E. (1990), *The Conceptual Practices of Power: A Feminist Sociology of Knowledge,* Northeastern University Press, Boston, Mass.

Song, M. (2003), *Choosing Ethnic Identity,* Polity, Cambridge.

Spence, J.D. (1999), *Mao,* Weidenfeld and Nicolson, London.

Spivak, G. (1988), 'Can the subaltern speak?' in C. Nelson and L. Grossberg (eds), *Marxism and the Interpretation of Culture*, Macmillan, Basingstoke.

Staggenborg, S. (2008), *Social Movements*, Oxford University Press, Oxford.

Stark, D. and Bruszt, L. (1998), *Postsocialist Pathways: Transforming Politics and Property in East Central Europe,* Cambridge University Press, Cambridge.

Stouffer, S., Suchman, E.A., DeVinney, L.C., Star, S.A. and Williams, R.M. Jr (1949), *The American Soldier, Vol 1, Adjustment During Army Life,* Princeton University Press, Princeton, N.J.

Sutherland, D.E. (1945), 'Is "white-collar crime" crime?' *American Sociological Review,* 10, 132–9.

Swingewood, A. (1977), *The Myth of Mass Culture*, Humanities Press International, New Jersey.

Taylor, F.W. (1964), *Scientific Management,* Harper, New York.

Taylor, S. and Field, D. (eds) (2007), *Sociology of Health and Health Care*, Blackwell, Oxford.

Therborn, G. (2004), *Between Sex and Power: Family in the World, 1900–2000,* Routledge, London.

Thomas, W.I. and Znaniecki, F. (1918, 1920), *The Polish Peasant in Europe and America,* Dover, New York.

Thomas, W.R. (1927), 'The behavior pattern and the situation', *Publications of the American Sociological Society: Papers and Proceedings*, 22nd Annual Meeting, Vol 22, 1–13.

Thompson, E.P. (1968), *The Making of the English Working Class*, Penguin, Harmondsworth.

Thompson, K. (1976), *Auguste Comte: The Foundations of Sociology,* Nelson, London.

Thompson, N. (2000), *Understanding Social Work: Preparing for Practice,* Macmillan, Basingstoke.

Tocqueville, A. de (1835 and 1840, 1968), *Democracy in America*, Collins, Glasgow.

Tocqueville, A. de (1856, 1955), *The Old Regime and the French Revolution*, Doubleday, New York.

Toennies, F. (1887, 1955), *Community and Association*, Routledge, London.

Tormey, S. (1995), *Making Sense of Tyranny: Interpretations of Totalitarianism*, Manchester University Press, Manchester.

Touraine, A. (1971), *The Post-Industrial Society*, Random House, New York.

Troeltsch, E. (1912, 1956), *The Social Teachings of the Christian Churches*, Allen and Unwin, London.

Turley, D. (2000), *Slavery*, Blackwell, Oxford.

Turner, R.H. (1960), 'Sponsored and contest mobility in the school system', *American Sociological Review*, 25, 855–67.

Turner, V. (1967), *The Forest of Symbols: Aspects of Ndembu Ritual*, Cornell University Press, Ithaca, N.Y.

Tylor, E.B. (1871, 1958), *Primitive Culture*, Harper, New York.

Urry, J. (1990), *The Tourist Gaze*, Sage, London.

Urry, J. (2000), *Sociology Beyond Societies: Mobilities for the Twenty-First Century*, Routledge, London.

Van Gennep, A. (1909, 1960). *The Rites of Passage*, University of Chicago Press, Chicago.

Veal, A.J. (1993), 'The concept of lifestyle: a review', *Leisure Studies*, 12, 233–52.

Veblen, T. (1899, 1953), *The Theory of the Leisure Class*, Mentor, New York.

Vinken, H. (2007), 'New life course dynamics? Career orientations, work values and future perceptions of Dutch youth', *Young*, 15, 9–30.

Von Neumann, J. and Morgenstern, O. (1944), *Theory of Games and Economic Behaviour*, Princeton University Press, Princeton, N.J.

Walby, S. (1990), *Theorising Patriarchy*, Blackwell, Oxford.

Walklate, S. (ed.) (2007), *Handbook of Victims and Victimology*, Willan, Cullompton, Devon.

Wallerstein, I. (1979), *The Capitalist World-Economy*, Cambridge University Press, Cambridge.

Walvin, J. (2006), *Atlas of Slavery*, Pearson Longman, Harlow.

Watson, T. and Harris, P. (1999), *The Emergent Manager*, Sage, London.

Weber, M. (1905, 1930), *The Protestant Ethic and the Spirit of Capitalism*, Allen and Unwin, London.

Weeks, J. (2003), *Sexuality*, Routledge, London.

Whyte, W.H. (1956), *The Organization Man*, Penguin, Harmondsworth.

Wiener, N. (1949), *Cybernetics: or Control and Communication in Man and Machine*, MIT Press, Cambridge, Mass.

Williams, R. (1963), *Culture and Society, 1780–1950*, Penguin, Harmondsworth.

Willis, P. (1977), *Learning to Labour*, Saxon House, Farnborough.

Wilson, B. (1970), *Religious Sects*, Weidenfield and Nicolson, London.

Wilson, E.O. (1975), *Sociobiology: The New Synthesis*, Harvard University Press, Cambridge, Mass.

Wilson, W.J. (1987), *The Truly Disadvantaged: The Inner-City, The Underclass and Public Policy,* University of Chicago Press, Chicago.

Winch, P. (1958, 1990), *The Idea of a Social Science and its Relation to Philosophy,* Routledge, London.

Wirth, L. (1928), *The Ghetto,* University of Chicago Press, Chicago.

Wirth, L. (1938), 'Urbanism as a way of life', *American Journal of Sociology,* 44, 1–24.

Wolf, E.R. (1966), *Peasants,* Prentice-Hall, New Jersey.

Wollstonecraft, M.A. (1792, 2004), *A Vindication of the Rights of Women,* Penguin, Harmondsworth.

Wood, S. (1989), *The Transformation of Work? Skills, Flexibility and the Labour Process,* Unwin Hyman, London.

Woodward, J. (1965), *Industrial Organization: Theory and Practice,* Oxford University Press, London.

Woolgar, S. (ed.) (2002), *Virtual Society? Technology, Cyberbole, Reality,* Oxford University Press, Oxford.

Wright, E.O. (2000), *Class Counts: Student Edition,* Cambridge University Press, New York.

Young, M. (1958), *The Rise of the Meritocracy,* Thames and Hudson, London.

Young, M. and Willmott, P. (1957), *Family and Kinship in East London,* Routledge, London.

Young, M. and Willmott, P. (1973), *The Symmetrical Family,* Routledge, London.

Zerubavel, E. (1981), *Hidden Rhythms,* University of Chicago Press, Chicago.

Zuzanek, J. (2004), 'Work, leisure, time-pressure and stress', in J.T. Haworth and A.J. Veal (eds), *Work and Leisure,* Routledge, London, 123–44.

Zuzanek, J. and Mannell, R. (1998), 'Life cycle squeeze, time pressure, daily stress, and leisure participation: a Canadian perspective, *Leisure and Society,* 21, 513–44.

Zweig, F. (1961), *The Worker in an Affluent Society,* Heinemann, London.

Index